HEALTH POLICY MAKING

Fundamental Issues in
The United States
Canada
Great Britain
Australia

The Press was established in 1972 with the support of the W. K. Kellogg Foundation as a joint endeavor of the Association of University Programs in Health Administration (Washington, D.C.) and The University of Michigan Program and Bureau of Hospital Administration

HEALTH POLICY MAKING

Fundamental Issues in The United States Canada Great Britain Australia

By Anne Crichton

Health Administration Press
Ann Arbor, Michigan

Library of Congress Cataloging in Publication Data

Main entry under title:

Health policy making.

Bibliography: p.
Includes indexes.
1. Medical policy—Addresses, essays, lectures.
2. Medical policy—Australia—Addresses, essays, lectures. 3. Medical policy—Canada—Addresses, essays, lectures. 4. Medical policy—Great Britain—Addresses, essays, lectures. 5. Medical policy—United States—Addresses, essays, lectures.
I. Crichton, Anne. [DNLM: 1. Health policy. 2. Policy making. 3. Social change. WA541.1 C928h]
RA394.6.H42 362.1'068 80-19194
ISBN 0-914904-44-2

Health Administration Press
The University of Michigan
Ann Arbor, Michigan 48109

For Murray Stratton and other students whom I have taught.

Contents

List of Illustrations xiii
Foreword xv
Acknowledgments xix

PART I: BOUNDARIES

Chapter 1. Introduction 3
Thomas McKeown: "The Determinants of Human Health: Behaviour, Environment, and Therapy" 7
Marc Lalonde: "The Health Field Concept" 17

Chapter 2. What Is Policy? 23
Definitions 23
Boundaries 23
Bounded Rationality 27
Linking Policy Analysis to Decision Making 29
Policy Frameworks 30
Kenneth E. Boulding: "The Boundaries of Social Policy" 32
David G. Gil: "A Systematic Approach to Social Policy Analysis" 45

Chapter 3. Practical Policy Frameworks 56
Academic Frameworks for Analysis 56
The Blind Men and the Elephant 65
Brian Abel-Smith: "The History of Medical Care" 72
Theodore R. Marmor: "Medicare: Social Policy and American Politics" 89
Rudolf Klein: "Policy Problems and Policy Perceptions in the National Health Service" 98

PART II: THE SOCIAL ORDER

Chapter 4. Maintenance and Change 111
Policies as Guidelines for Social Development 111
Social Control 111
Social Change 118
Barbara Ehrenreich and John Ehrenreich: "Health Care and Social Control" 126

PART III. AN OVERVIEW OF POLICIES: SOCIAL GOALS AND THEIR ATTAINMENT

Chapter 5. Resource Development 135
The Protestant Ethic 135
The Open Question: Is Small Beautiful? 137
Doing Better and Feeling Worse 138
Individualism and Collectivism 139
M. Patricia Marchak: "Free Enterprise in (Relatively Moral) Nation States" [I] 142
Aaron Wildavsky: "Doing Better and Feeling Worse: The Political Pathology of Health Policy" 146

Chapter 6. Social Organization 158
Social Reciprocities 158
The Organization of the Task and Manpower System 159
New Occupational Groups 159
Occupational Groups as Interest Intermediary Groups 162
The Ubiquity of Stratification 163
The Negotiated Order 164
Maladjustment of the Task and Manpower System and Allocation of Prerogatives 164
Present Day Recognition of Social Reciprocities 167
Melvin M. Tumin: "Social Stratification: Some Theoretical Problems" 171

	Terence J. Johnson: "Types of Occupational Control"	178
	David R. Maines: "Mesostructure and Social Process"	184
Chapter 7.	Human Rights	189
	Rights and Justice	190
	Time Lags in Achieving Social Change	193
	Methods of Operationalizing Rights	197
	David Donnison: "Social Issues" [I]	203
Chapter 8.	Prerogatives and Rights	211
	Ideologies—Guides to Negotiation?	212
	National Ideologies	214
	Group Ideologies	219
	General Trends in Relating Prerogatives and Rights in Health Care	224
	Clifford Geertz: "Ideology as a Cultural System"	230
	M. Patricia Marchak: "Free Enterprise in (Relatively Moral) Nation States" [II]	240
	David Donnison: "Ideologies and Policies"	242
	David Donnison: "Social Issues" [II]	246
Chapter 9.	Health Policy Making: The Fundamental Issues	251
	Defining Health	252
	Health: End or Means?	253
	Health, Health Care or the Preservation of Life?	254
	The Development of Health Policies	256
	R. H. S. Crossman: "A Politician's View of Health Service Planning"	268

PART IV: POLICIES INTO PRACTICE

Chapter 10.	The General Will	271
	Maintenance and Change	271
	Levels of Legitimacy	271
	Feasibility of Introducing New Policies	275

Service Delivery: Policies into Practice 276
Generating General Support for Changes in Policy 278
Specific Support and Diffuse Support 283
Phoebe Hall, Hilary Land, Roy Parker, and Adrian Webb: "Change, Choice and Conflict in Social Policy: Propositions Emerging from Case Studies on Social Policy" 287

Chapter 11. Science and Policy Making 298
Development of Science Policies 298
Communication of Ideas 302
Some Problems of Applying Science to Social Policy Analysis 304
Dennis Lees and Stella Shaw: "Impairment, Disability and Handicap: Report on a Conference of Research Workers" 308

Chapter 12. Policy, Planning and Administration 312
Policy Research, Planning and Administrative Processes 312
Values and Evidence 315
The Context of Planning 317
James S. Coleman: "Problems of Conceptualization and Measurement in Studying Policy Impacts" 330
Avedis Donabedian: "Evaluating the Quality of Medical Care" 336
Robert R. Alford: "The Political Economy of Health Care: Dynamics Without Change" 339

Chapter 13. Policy Development and Planning by Health Agencies 345
Controlling Standards of Practice 346
Controlling Costs 349
The Contribution of Voluntary Organizations 354
Corporate Policies 355
Hubert L. Laframboise: "Moving a Proposal to a Positive Decision: A Case History of the Invisible Process" 361

Chapter 14. The Use of Paradigms in Policy Analysis 369
Structuring Thinking 369
Knowledge and Its Uses 371
Policy Formulation and Knowledge 376
The Movement of Issues through Political Systems 380
Envoi 382

Bibliography 383
Index 406

List of Illustrations

1-1 World Population 8

1-2 Death Rate 9

3-1 Matrix Showing Approaches to Social Science Investigations 59

3-2 The Teaching of Social Science to Students of Health Care 60

4-1 The Cyclical Development of Social/Health Policies 120

10-1 A Dynamic Response Model of a Political System 272

10-2 Paradigm Showing Stages in the Process of Translating Social Philosophies into Social Services 279

10-3 Stages in Political Policy Development in a Democracy 280

11-1 The Gap Between Those With Scientific Training and the Rest of Society 301

12-1 Stages in Administrative Policy Development 319

14-1 Knowledge and Its Applications 377

Foreword

After teaching Social Policy and Administration in Wales for many years to students who were mainly intending to become social workers or administrators of social service departments, I moved to Canada in order to develop a new program for students intending to become planners, administrators or researchers in the health services. As this program was expected to address the problems of organizing an integrated health care system rather than training administrators in the maintenance of traditional health services, it had to be concerned with preparing students to manage policy change.

Canadian students of health service organization are quite different from British social administration students. The latter tend to be fairly homogeneous in outlook—accepting the western democratic liberal ideology as modified by British Christian socialism—for the left wing radicals seem to have chosen sociology rather than social administration as a subject of study in the sixties, and the scientists to have chosen economics or psychology. The former, the Canadian students of health services planning, are a much more heterogeneous group, coming from backgrounds in health sciences, life sciences, social sciences or commerce; many have clinical experience in the health care system. Their ideological approaches vary from what Alford (1975) has described as "pluralist or market" oriented through the "bureaucratic and planning perspective" to the "institutional or class perspective." Most have had backgrounds in the physical or hard social sciences because all are expected to graduate as Masters of Science and to be able to cope with understanding scientific theory and its application to analysis of health care matters.

Clearly, a modification of the British approach to the teaching of social policy was necessary in this Canadian setting. Whilst it was possible to transfer some British ideas about the coordination of services and about the need to take a broader view than had been current, until then, in most Canadian policy making, it began to be obvious that students entering the health care system faced a whole range of problems which had lain unrecognized by me in Britain whilst teaching students preparing to enter the personal social services.

It is hoped that the contents of this book will be helpful to students of social and health policy, to make them raise questions about their values and about proposed technical solutions.

Policy makers at all levels—politicians, bureaucrats, institutional administrators—are obliged to sort out those issues which they consider to be important and which need to be dealt with. Later in this book, the concept of a "frame of inference" is discussed (Marmor, 1973). Unlike a "frame of reference," which may be defined as a conceptual scheme—"the most general framework of categories in which empirical work makes sense" (Parsons, 1964), "a set of basic assumptions necessary to determine the subject matter to be studied and orientation towards such study" (Gould and Kolb, 1964)—"a frame of inference is an action orientation which sets the boundaries for examination of a problem and its possible resolutions." This book hopes to enlarge the frames of reference and the frames of inference of its readers.

It is beginning to be realized that the organization of health and social services in the liberal western democracies might become more efficient and effective if there were more rational planning in their organization. But what is meant by rational planning? There is no clear answer to this question, for what is rational to one nation, state government or service institution seems irrational to others.

This book attempts to explain what kinds of choices are made in developing or maintaining a policy. It is primarily descriptive of the processes of policy analysis, and it is intended for students, whether in graduate programs at universities or continuing learners presently in employment in health and social services, in the hope that they may be better able to identify what kind of contribution they can make to policy development and by so doing, to enable policy makers to improve their choices. By increasing awareness of these choices, it is hoped that policy analysts or policy makers will become more thoughtful, less responsive to the pressures of the moment, less often taken by surprise.

Some may find the discussion of policy issues too greatly concerned with fundamentals, and not enough with techniques of health program development in a medical care setting; but the decision to take a broad view was made deliberately.

And, whilst the book presents selections from others' works, it is, perhaps, somewhat different from the conventional reader, which usually consists of selections of articles or chapters with editorial comment. This is a cross between a reader and a textbook. The editorial chapters go far beyond commenting on the selections; they attempt to develop an overview approach, and to indicate the importance of topics which could not be included in the selections. Thus, it includes an extensive bibliography and, at the end of each chapter, suggestions for further reading and exploration, for there are many important subjects which could only be given passing mention in this volume but which readers may wish to follow up—subjects such as Social Indicators, the optimal form of organization for a national civil service, alternative approaches to resource allocation, and so on. The readings have had to be limited severely because of the costs of reprinting under copyright provisions.

In general, policy analysts are committed to their national and personal ideologies. This selection of readings is idiosyncratic, it presents my biases. However, an attempt has been made to review different approaches, and to show the validity and limitations of each of them so that students can make up their own minds about where they wish to stand. Since it is assumed that it will be used mainly by English-speaking students in western liberal democracies there is little more than a mention of Marxist ideologies, communist forms of organization or authoritarian regimes.

The readings and references have been selected from a number of different disciplines, although the majority were written by sociologists. They are, at times, beclouded by jargon. Yet, it is important to struggle with Parsons' (1952) style whilst assimilating the content of his influential chapter on the "sick role," or to consider Watkins' (1975) explanation of sociologists' efforts to explore "the social order." Political scientists sometimes seem to be more straightforward in their use of language—Lasswell's (1948) description of practices of elites for maintaining their power position, or Geertz's (1964) analysis of the uses of ideologies are very persuasive. But it is the journalists, the politicians, or the civil servants—such as Klein (1974) (a journalist, now become an academic), Powell (1975) (ex-minister of health for England and Wales), and Laframboise (1973) (a Canadian civil servant)—who say what they have to say succinctly and sharply. The reader is asked to try to read as many as he can, for what they have to say is, like this book, pitched at a number of different levels, presenting some simple and some very involved ideas.

What are regarded as important readings are reprinted after the discussion chapters. Others can readily be found in large libraries because they have become classics (and are often reprinted in other readers). However, much has had to be left out. Other important readings are indicated in the discussion of references in each chapter. At the end of some later chapters, may be found reading lists on special topics.

The text will be found to repeat ideas, but it does so in order to present them in different contexts.

Acknowledgments

An opportunity to stand back and review my own frames of reference and inference was provided by the chance to take a sabbatical year in 1976–77, partly funded by the University of British Columbia and partly by the Josiah Macy, Jr. Foundation of New York. This enabled me to return to Britain for five months to examine developments in the National Health Service, to visit Australia for five months to explore health/health care policy making there, and to read about policy making generally.

The students whom I have taught over the years have helped me to begin to understand what are the fundamental issues. And there are many others whom I would like to thank—academic colleagues and librarians in the four countries concerned, and practising administrators in Great Britain, Canada and Australia—too numerous to name. However, I must express special gratitude to John H. Phillips, who, over the years, has provided logistical support and pointed commentary on the National Health Service; Morton M. Warner, Vancouver; Roger J. Lawson, Southampton; Joyce Warham, Keele; Stephen Duckett and John Lawrence, University of New South Wales and Theodore Marmor, Yale University, for collegial support; Jean Lawrence, Lynn Wilson and Jill Hardwick for help in preparation of the manuscript. In addition, I would like to acknowledge assistance from:

Canadian National Health and Welfare Grants Programs, which, by funding projects NHG 710–21–1, NWG 2559–26–7 and the Community Health Centre Project, enabled me to learn more about Canadian policy making;
the Josiah Macy, Jr. Foundation;
The Canadian College of Health Service Executives for some assistance with typing the manuscript;
and the Department of Health Care and Epidemiology at the University of British Columbia for general support.

Acknowledgments of permissions to reprint are made at the foot of the first page of each of the readings selected.

Anne Crichton
Department of Health Care and Epidemiology
The University of British Columbia

PART I

Boundaries

1 Introduction

This book is addressed to all those who make policy in the health field—politicians, administrators, professionals, businessmen in the health care industry and consumers of health services. The purpose of the book is to increase understanding about the content and processes of decision making which may have implications for peoples' health and the provision of health services.

The view to be taken is a broad one: health policy making in four countries will be considered. Politics may differ in the four western liberal democratic countries of Great Britain, the United States, Canada and Australia, but what will be stressed here are the similarities, the fundamental issues, which have to be decided by all nations. These countries still have much in common because of their shared heritage in English social and political developments up to the late eighteenth century and in continuing close cross-cultural exchanges ever since.

The reason for taking this broad view is related to the definition of health chosen as a foundation for the following discussion, namely, that sponsored by the World Health Organization (WHO) in 1958: "Health is a state of complete physical, mental and social well-being and not merely the absence of disease or disability" (p. 459). This definition sets much wider boundaries than are customarily employed when discussing health policy making. Customarily, national health policies, developed aggressively in the nineteenth century, have been concerned with public sanitation and infection control and with the development and application of the technology of medical care.

It is thought that a better understanding of fundamentals may lead to more effective health policy decision making—better interventions because of better understanding of the context, and therefore more recognition of the potentiality for reaching broad goals and better outcomes.

McKeown (1975) and others have endeavoured to persuade health policy makers that nineteenth century boundaries are no longer very relevant because epidemics are now well controlled. He, and others like Illich (1975), have been critical of the present emphasis upon technical medical care as the best means of attaining and maintaining health. By managing sickness and prolonging life, doctors may be increasing morbidity, no longer promoting health in the WHO sense, but creating new difficulties in coping with disability or disease.

A recent Canadian policy statement, *A New Perspective on the Health of Canadians* (Canada, 1974), has been hailed as a great advance by health policy analysts because it broke through the customary confines of medical technology to discuss the promotion of healthier lifestyles, a wider kind of environmental control than "mains" and "drains," and improvement of preventive attention to high risk populations. (There have been some criticisms that it has expanded the boundaries at the expense of blaming individuals for unhealthy behaviour, but it has been welcomed by many authorities.)

De Miguel (1975) analysed research which had been done on health issues and developed a framework for the study of national health systems and, consequently, health policies. He broke down these research studies into eleven factors in four main areas, as follows:

Individual:	A1	Health Status
	A2	Bio-Medical Factors
	A3	Psychological Factors
Institutions:	B1	Health Services
	B2	Health Organization
	B3	Health Planning
Society:	C1	Socio-Cultural Patterns
	C2	Political Structure
	C3	Economic Development
	C4	Demographic Structure
Larger Systems:	D1	Environment (p. 12).

It will be noted that, as the list proceeds towards what he calls the macro end of the scale, health policies cannot be separated easily from economic and social policies. It becomes a matter of discretion for different nations to decide what is to be called economic policy territory or social policy territory, health policy territory or social welfare territory, or use some other designation, for WHO's definition and De Miguel's equate a policy for health with broad national policies generally.

The book is organized into five parts with subsections. The first part is concerned with boundaries—with the problems of defining and analyzing policy so that policy makers and policy analysts can begin to see where they can make their best contribution to decision making in a wide and ill-defined territory. What theories might help to structure their thinking? What frameworks can they use?

The second part is concerned with the social order—with an examination of the forces of maintenance and change in society. The third part takes Gil's (1970) broad view of social policy (discussed in chapter 2), adds some areas excluded by him, but indicated by De Miguel, and uses the framework as a guide to four content areas with which health policy makers need to be concerned. Gil described them as the basic societal mechanisms—resource development, the allocation of statuses (or the task and manpower system), the distribution of rights, and the extent of linkage between the allocation of statuses and the distribution of rights. This part ends by considering what are the fundamental issues in policy making.

Part IV explores how policies are put into practice. How is the general will ascertained? To what extent can science be applied to policy making? How does planning relate to policy making? Can scientists, policy researchers and policy makers learn to work better together to improve social and health policy making? What are the reasons for their present failures in communication? Why do well-meaning inputs fail to emerge at the end of the policy-making process as well organized outcomes? How does a society deal with bridging the gaps between its policy intentions and its service delivery performance?

The book ends with a discussion of the paradigms which could now be used by policy makers to structure their thinking so that more thoughtful decisions could be made. These paradigms, propositions emerging from the work of some policy analysts, can set up frames of inference for politicians, administrators and consumer groups which may be useful for improving understanding of issues and communication about them.

Discussion of Readings and References

Two readings and one particular reference—the WHO definition of health (WHO 1958) have been chosen to set the scene.

1. Thomas J. McKeown's paper, "The determinants of human health: behaviour, environment and therapy," raises questions about the contribution of medical care to health and well-being.

2. Building on McKeown's work, the Canadian government published a working paper called "A New Perspective on the Health of Canadians" in 1974—a paper promoted by the federal minister of Health and Welfare, the Honourable Marc Lalonde. This paper has elicited a strong response from citizens and from many of those concerned with providing health services. This response would seem to indicate that it has met the need for a restatement in the 1970s of Canadian values regarding health care. It raises questions about the way in which national values can begin to be translated into policies. What part should government play in distributing, regulating, or

redistributing national resources? Should the pursuit of health be left to private enterprise alone, or shared between private enterprise and government? If so, in what ways?

3. The WHO definition of health should be considered carefully. How can such a broad objective be met?

4. The contributions of De Miguel and Gil who raise questions about the use of systems theory as a general framework are considered further in chapter 2.

The Determinants of Human Health: Behaviour, Environment and Therapy

Thomas McKeown

The Improvement in Health and Growth of Population

Although all estimates of world population are subject to a considerable error, the basic facts are not in doubt. During most of his time on earth man has lived as a nomad, dependent for his food on hunting, fishing and food gathering. Under such conditions the earth supported no more than a few people per square mile, and it has been estimated that when cultivation of plants and animals began about 10,000 years ago, the total population was below, and probably well below, 10 million. By 1750, when the modern rise of population had just begun, the number had increased to 750 million; it was 1000 million in 1830, 2000 in 1930, 3000 in 1960 and 4000 in 1975 (Figure 1–1). That is to say it took hundreds of thousands of years for the human population to expand to the first billion; the second was added in 100 years, the third in 30 and the fourth in 15.

The modern rise of population and the associated transformation of health are among the great themes of history, in interest and importance perhaps second only to the origin of life. Both changes have occurred in—to give an outside limit—the past three centuries. They are clearly related phenomena for the rapid growth of population was caused by a substantial decline in mortality. In England and Wales the trend of mortality can be followed from the early nineteenth century (Figure 1–2) and in Sweden,

---

From *Health Care Teaching & Research,* ed. William C. Gibson, (Vancouver, B. C.: U.B.C. Alumni Association and The Faculty of Medicine, U.B.C., pp. 59-63 and 71-77, by permission of W. C. Gibson and the author.

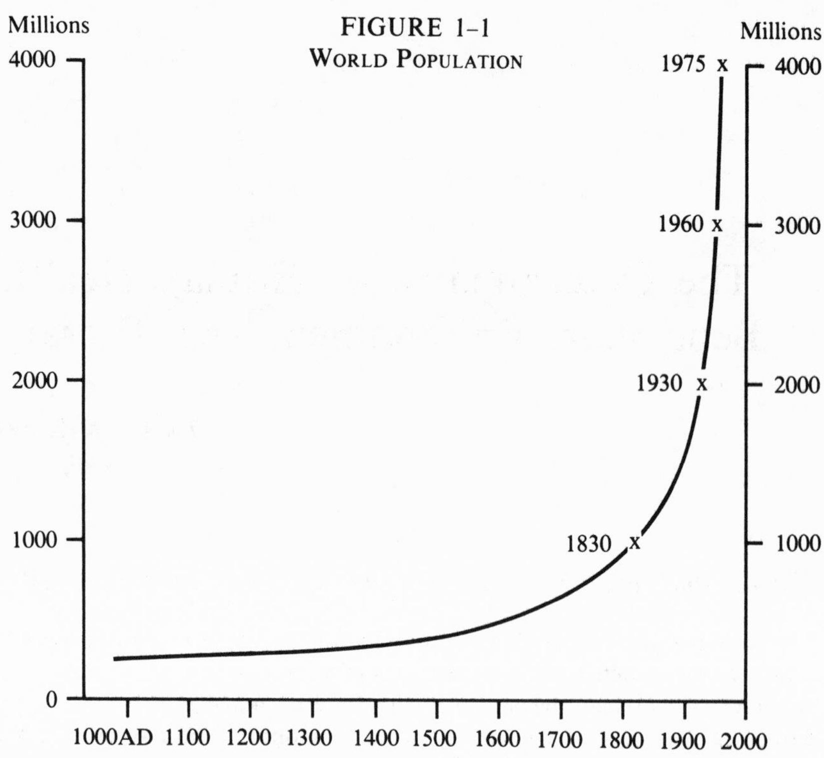

where it was first recorded nationally, it is known from the mid-eighteenth.

Table 1–1 shows the proportion of the reduction of mortality in England and Wales which occurred in three periods: 1700 to the mid-nineteenth century (33%); the second half of the nineteenth century (20%); and the twentieth century (47%). Thus slightly more than half of the improvement took place before 1900. These estimates are based on the assumption that the death rate in 1700 was 30, a little higher than the rate first recorded in Sweden fifty years later (27.4).

The table also shows the proportion of the decline of mortality that was associated with infectious diseases, 92% in 1848-54 to 1901 and 73% in 1901 to 1971. Indeed it is unlikely that there was an appreciable decrease in deaths from non-infective conditions in the second half of the nineteenth century, for most of the apparent reduction (8%) was associated with two classes of deaths—"old age" and "other diseases"—neither of which provides convincing evidence of a decline. (In the first case the diagnosis was clearly unsatisfactory, and in the second the diseases referred to as "other" comprise

FIGURE 1–2
DEATH RATE (Standardized)

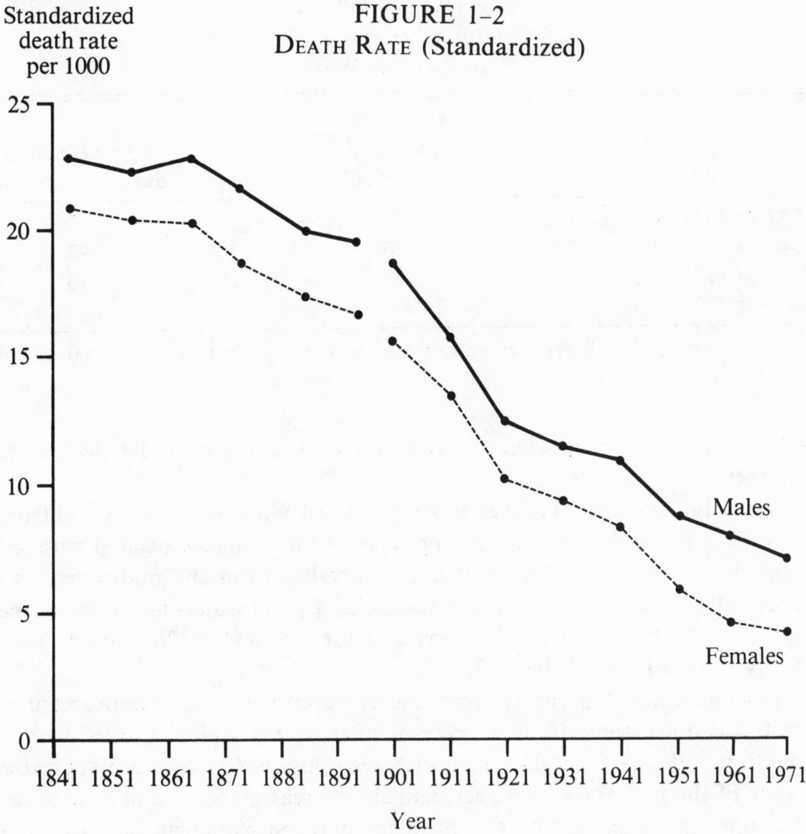

a heterogeneous group of conditions, many of which were also unreliably classified.)

Although national data are not available for the eighteenth and early nineteenth centuries, it seems reasonable to conclude that the reduction of mortality in that period also was mainly in respect of the infections. There are, however, two non-infective causes of death which may have been important, although this cannot be confirmed from national statistics. I refer to infanticide and starvation. Infanticide was practiced on a substantial scale in both ancient and modern times and became uncommon only from about the last quarter of the nineteenth century; and it is probable that death did occur, at times not infrequently, as a result of starvation. I conclude that with these important exceptions, there is no convincing evidence of a decrease of deaths from non-infective conditions before 1900. From then until

TABLE 1–1
REDUCTION OF MORTALITY SINCE 1700:
ENGLAND AND WALES

Period	% of total reduction in each period*	% of reduction due to infections
1700 to 1848–54	33	?
1848–54 to 1901	20	92
1901 to 1971	47	73
1700 to 1971	100	

*The estimates are based on the assumption that the death rate in 1700 was 30.

1971 the latter were associated with about a quarter of the decline of mortality.

Cause of death was registered in England and Wales in 1838, so that from that time it is possible to identify the types of infections associated with the improvement in health. Of the fall of mortality from the mid-nineteenth century, 40% was from airborne diseases, 21% from water- and food-borne diseases, 13% from other infections and the remainder (26%) from non-infective conditions. (Table 1-2)

The conclusion that the modern rise of population and improvement in health was due essentially to a decrease of mortality which resulted from a reduction of deaths from infectious diseases brings us to a central issue in the history of the past three centuries, namely the reasons for the decline of the infections. In broad terms the problem may be stated as follows. It is probable that the predominance of infectious diseases dates from the First Agricultural Revolution when man began to aggregate in populations of substantial size. Why then did the infections decline from about the time of the Industrial Revolution, which led to the aggregation of still larger and more densely packed populations? The answer to this paradox must be sought in the character of micro-organisms, the conditions under which they spread and the response of the human host, inherited or acquired. . . .

[In summary,] the decline of mortality which was responsible for the modern improvement in health and growth of population . . . was due initially to a large increase in food supplies, which changed the relationship between micro-organisms and man, against the parasite and in favour of the host. From the second half of the nineteenth century this advance was supported powerfully by reduction of exposure to infection, which resulted indirectly from the falling prevalence of disease and directly improved hygiene affecting, in the first instance, the quality of water and food. With

TABLE 1–2
REDUCTION OF MORTALITY, 1818–54 TO 1971: ENGLAND AND WALES

	% of reduction	
Conditions attributable to micro-organisms.		
1. Airborne diseases	40	
2. Water- and food-borne diseases	21	
3. Other conditions	13	
Total		74
Conditions not attributable to micro-organisms.		26
All diseases		100

the exception of vaccination against smallpox, the effect of immunization and treatment of disease was restricted to the twentieth century, mainly since 1935, and although now significant, over the whole period since the eighteenth century they have been less important than the other influences.

To complete this brief interpretation of the modern improvement in health, one other influence should be mentioned, namely the limitation of numbers which followed the fall of the birth rate (in England and Wales from about 1870). This was the reason for the decline and eventual disappearance of the practice of infanticide, which from the earliest times had been responsible for the death of a considerable proportion of all infants. It was also the means which ensured that the advance in health which resulted from other influences was not lost, as previous advances in man's health were presumably lost, by rising numbers.

INFLUENCES ON HEALTH TODAY

I have concluded that the influences responsible for the modern improvement in health were mainly behavioural (the change in reproductive practice which led to the decline of infanticide and restricted the growth of population) and environmental (comprising two changes, an improvement in food supplies and removal of hazards from the physical environment); the contribution of immunization and therapy has been recent and, over the whole period, relatively small. But since the character of health problems has changed profoundly, it is necessary to enquire whether the major influences have also been transformed.

Behavioural Influences

If limitation of numbers is no longer so critical in developed countries, internationally it remains an essential requirement for improvement in health. However, the conclusion that behaviour is still predominant now rests on the significance of another class of influences, personal behaviour in relation to smoking, diet, exercise, etc. The evidence linking smoking with carcinoma of the lung, obesity with reduced expectation of life and sedentary living with coronary artery disease, is well known and need not be referred to here. The relation between refined diets and intestinal and other diseases has been discussed more recently, but the evidence, though still mainly circumstantial, is very suggestive.

What is not in doubt is the profound effect of such features of personal behaviour on health; a moderate or heavy smoker would probably live longer by giving up smoking and giving up doctors than by retaining both. Indeed in developed countries the individual's health is now largely in his own hands, for if he is fortunate enough to be born free of congenital disease or disability, and to have an income which meets the costs of essentials, by controlling his behaviour he can do more to preserve his health and extend his life than can be achieved by specific preventive or therapeutic medicine.

There is also little doubt about the reasons why these features of personal behaviour have become so important. Smoking, consumption of refined foods and sedentary living are all profound departures from the conditions under which man evolved. Moreover the changes are very recent: refined foods probably became widely available in the early nineteenth century, sedentary living dates mainly from the introduction of the automobile and smoking on a significant scale has occurred only in recent decades. In time no doubt man could adapt by natural selection to these as to other changes in the environment during his evolution; but adaptation cannot take place quickly and it will not take place at all without extensive and early mortality among the susceptible.

Environmental Influences

Throughout the world deficient food remains a serious problem and even in the wealthiest countries there are sections of the population which are inadequately, to be distinguished from unwisely, fed. Because the deficiency is determined by economic conditions rather than by the individual's personal choice, it is classified here as an environmental rather than a behavioural influence.

The second type of environmental measures referred to above was removal of hazards from the physical environment. Again a distinction should be made between developing countries, where control has only recently begun, and developed countries where a great deal has been achieved during, roughly, the past century. Even so, many well recognized risks associated with atmosphere, housing, traffic, insect vectors, etc., are far from being eliminated, while others inherent in the conditions of contemporary life have not been measured or even, in some cases, identified.

In the light of these conclusions the requirements for health can be stated simply. Those fortunate enough to be born free of significant congenital disease or disability will remain well if three basic needs are met: they must be adequately fed; they must be protected from a wide range of hazards in the physical environment; and they must not depart radically from the pattern of personal behaviour under which man evolved, for example by smoking, over-eating or sedentary living.

Until recently it would have been prudent to restrict this interpretation to early and middle life, and to recognize that the ill-named degenerative diseases, being manifested at late ages, may be less affected or unaffected by natural selection and therefore little influenced by the environment. Whether this reservation is necessary now seems doubtful in the light of recent work on some of the common forms of cancer, which earlier would have been regarded as typical of "intractable" degenerative conditions. There is now evidence that cancer of the bronchus, cancer of the breast and probably cancer of the intestine are due to unfavourable environmental conditions and might be prevented largely by their modification. The same is true of some other diseases of late life, such as coronary artery disease and chronic bronchitis.

The interpretation outlined above suggests that what is true for other living things is also true for man, namely that health depends essentially on control of environmental influences, including those which, by his own behaviour, the individual makes for himself. It is not difficult to see why this should be so. The only diseases and disabilities which are inevitable are those which have been determined irreversibly at fertilization. So defined, they comprise conditions due to abnormal single genes, which are rare; conditions due to chromosome aberrations which are relatively common at conception (about 5% of pregnancies appear to be affected) but uncommon at birth because they are usually eliminated by abortion; and conditions associated with aging and death. The large majority of live births (well over 99%) have not been programmed genetically in such a way that disease is inevitable, at least until they reach late life, and sickness and premature death are determined essentially by environmental influences. Of course response to the environment depends on genetic constitution; nevertheless an individual, however prone, will not acquire tuberculosis unless he encounters the tubercle bacillus, just as, however gifted, he will never become a concert pianist unless as a child he has access to a piano.

It should be noted that these distinctions apply to congenital conditions (those present at birth) as well as to those which arise in postnatal life. Most cases of mental retardation and congenital malformations are not determined irreversibly by disorders of genes and chromosomes, any more than was the high level of infectious diseases which occurred soon after birth. They are attributable to the character of the prenatal environment, and the chief distinction to be made between prenatal and postnatal influences is that whereas the latter are relatively easy to control, at least in so far as they are in the physical environment, implantation and early embryonic development are hazardous processes whose risks are difficult to identify and eliminate. A few congenital abnormalities are due to influences such as thalidomide and rubella which can often be removed; probably many more are associated with chemical and physiological changes during pregnancy which are as yet unrecognized.

The Significance of the Conclusions

The recognition that human health is determined mainly by way of life has profound implications for the public, for governments and for medicine and the related health professions. Some years ago J. B. S. Haldane wrote: "The General Public is rather suddenly beginning to realize that the present age differs from all others as the result of the application of science to human affairs." In relation to health, however, the message has been miscontrued; it has been interpreted to mean that *we are ill and are made well,* whereas it would be nearer the truth to say that *we are well and are made ill.* It is essential that the public should come to understand the distinction, and to realize that the health of the individual is determined essentially by the pattern of life which he adopts. One can only hope that the understanding will come about gradually and quietly, as a return to the classical concept of a thoughtful approach to life and health, rather than through a re-enactment of the strident "Strength through Joy" movement which happily disappeared with the regime that invented it.

Recognition of the requirements for health should also lead to reappraisal of the role of governments. While continuing to take responsibility for personal medical services, they should concern themselves much more with the major behavioural and environmental influences. For example, by prohibiting the misleading image of the smoker projected gratuitously by press and television they can help to create for the adolescent an environment in which it seems less attractive to smoke than—as at present—not to. By judicious use of food subsidies they can ensure not only that the poorest sections of the population are able to buy enough food but also that people have some inducement to choose the foods that are good for them and to avoid those that are harmful. Fortunately the human palate (like the bladder and unlike, I sometimes think, the cerebral cortex) is extremely educable, and with the added incentive of economy many people could quickly come to like tea and coffee without sugar, and to prefer bread made from wholemeal rather than refined flour.

Finally, I must consider briefly the significance for medicine of recognition that the major influences on man's health are behavioural and environmental, rather than the provision of personal medical care. In *The Mirage of Health,* Dubos[1] outlined two ideas concerning health which were rooted in the classical tradition: one, an approach through a rational way of life, symbolized by the Goddess Hygeia; the other, belief in the physician as healer of the sick, associated with the God Asclepius. Both concepts are to be found in Hippocratic writings, and they have survived in medical thought and practice down to the present day. However, since the seventeenth century at least, the Asclepian approach has been predominant. Philosophically it derived support from Descartes' concept of the living organism as a machine which might be taken apart and reassembled if its structure and function were fully understood; practically it seemed to find confirmation in the work of Keppler and Harvey and the success of the physical sciences.

The consequences of this viewpoint are reflected widely in medicine today. Medical education begins with study of the structure and function of the body, continues with the examination of disease processes and ends with clinical instruction on selected sick people. Having regard to the determinants of health, it is as though a training in agriculture ignored limitation of numbers, selective breeding, control of the environment, feeding and care and concentrated on the diagnosis and treatment of sick animals.

The medical services of today are the result of more than a century (three centuries in the case of hospitals) of unplanned development which reflects both the predominant interest in the diagnosis and treatment of acute illness and the relative lack of concern for population measures and the provision of care. Contraceptive advice is only reluctantly accepted as an obligation of health services; whether to use financial subsidies to make food available to everyone and to influence the kinds of foods that are eaten, is considered to be an economic rather than a medical question; and the control of the physical environment and modification of personal behaviour are regarded as subjects of marginal interest which can be relegated to ancillary staff or even removed altogether from medical concern. But perhaps the most serious effect of the mechanistic approach on health services is that it has led to neglect of large classes of patients—the congenitally handicapped, the psychiatric and the geriatric—who require prolonged medical and nursing care but appear to offer little scope for technology and the predominant preoccupations of diagnosis and treatment.

It is against the same background that we should consider the direction of contemporary medical research, epitomized by the enormous investment in hope and resources in "finding a cure for cancer," a disease which a few decades of pragmatic and not particularly intensive epidemiological work have shown to be essentially preventable. We should ask ourselves which approach offers the better prospect of a solution of the problems presented by the common forms of cancer: extension of the traditional lines of laboratory and clinical investigation; or cessation of cigarette smoke (or, second best, removal of the carcinogenic constituents of the smoke), consumption of high-residue foods and identification of those features of reproductive practice which are responsible for the high incidence of breast cancer.

Notes

[1]Dubos, R. *The Mirage of Health* (London: George Allen and Unwin, 1959).

The Health Field Concept

Marc Lalonde

Background

A basic problem in analysing the health field has been the absence of an agreed conceptual framework for sub-dividing it into its principal elements. Without such a framework, it has been difficult to communicate properly or to break up the field into manageable segments which are amenable to analysis and evaluation. It was felt keenly that there was a need to organize the thousands of pieces into an orderly pattern that was both intellectually acceptable and sufficiently simple to permit a quick location, in the pattern, of almost any idea, problem or activity related to health: a sort of map of the health territory.

Such a Health Field Concept[1] was developed during the preparation of this paper and it envisages that the health field can be broken up into four broad elements: HUMAN BIOLOGY, ENVIRONMENT, LIFESTYLE and HEALTH CARE ORGANIZATION. These four elements were identified through an examination of the causes and underlying factors of sickness and death in Canada, and from an assessment of the parts the elements play in affecting the level of health in Canada.

Human Biology

The HUMAN BIOLOGY element includes all those aspects of health, both physical and mental, which are developed within the human body as a

---

From (Canada) *A New Perspective on the Health of Canadians.* (Ottawa: Department of National Health & Welfare, 1974), pp. 31-37, by permission of the Minister of Supply and Services, Canada.

consequence of the basic biology of man and the organic make-up of the individual. This element includes the genetic inheritance of the individual, the processes of maturation and aging, and the many complex internal systems in the body, such as skeletal, nervous, muscular, cardio-vascular, endocrine, digestive and so on. The human body being such a complicated organism, the health implications of human biology are numerous, varied and serious, and the things that can go wrong with it are legion. This element contributes to all kinds of ill health and mortality, including many chronic diseases (such as arthritis, diabetes, atherosclerosis, cancer) and others (genetic disorders, congenital malformation, mental retardation). Health problems originating from human biology are causing untold miseries and costing billions of dollars in treatment services.

Environment

The ENVIRONMENT category includes all those matters related to health which are external to the human body and over which the individual has little or no control. Individuals cannot, by themselves, ensure that foods, drugs, cosmetics, devices, water supply, etc. are safe and uncontaminated; that the health hazards of air, water and noise pollution are controlled; that the spread of communicable diseases is prevented; that effective garbage and sewage disposal is carried out; and that the social environment, including the rapid changes in it, do not have harmful effects on health.

Lifestyle

The LIFESTYLE category, in the Health Field Concept, consists of the aggregation of decisions by individuals which affect their health and over which they more or less have control. . . . Personal decisions and habits that are bad, from a health point of view, create self-imposed risks. When those risks result in illness or death, the victim's lifestyle can be said to have contributed to, or caused, his own illness or death.

Health Care Organization

The fourth category in the Concept is HEALTH CARE ORGANIZATION, which consists of the quantity, quality, arrangement, nature and relationships of people and resources in the provision of health care. It includes medical practice, nursing, hospitals, nursing homes, medical drugs, public and community health care services, ambulances, dental treatment and other health services such as optometry, chiropractics and podiatry. This fourth element is what is generally defined as the health care system.

Until now most of society's efforts to improve health, and the bulk of direct health expenditures, have been focused on the HEALTH CARE ORGANIZA-

TION. Yet, when we identify the present main causes of sickness and death in Canada, we find that they are rooted in the other three elements of the Concept: HUMAN BIOLOGY, ENVIRONMENT and LIFESTYLE. It is apparent, therefore, that vast sums are being spent treating diseases that could have been prevented in the first place. Greater attention to the first three conceptual elements is needed if we are to continue to reduce disability and early death.

Characteristics of the Health Field Concept

The HEALTH FIELD CONCEPT has many characteristics which make it a powerful tool for analysing health problems, determining the health needs of Canadians and choosing the means by which those needs can be met.

One of the evident consequences of the Health Field Concept has been to raise HUMAN BIOLOGY, ENVIRONMENT and LIFESTYLE to a level of categorical importance equal to that of HEALTH CARE ORGANIZATION. This, in itself, is a radical step in view of the clear pre-eminence that HEALTH CARE ORGANIZATION has had in past concepts of the health field.

A second attribute of the Concept is that it is comprehensive. Any health problem can be traced to one, or a combination of the four elements. This comprehensiveness is important because it ensures that all aspects of health will be given due consideration and that all who contribute to health, individually and collectively, patient, physician, scientist and government, are aware of their roles and their influence on the level of health.

A third feature is that the Concept permits a system of analysis by which any question can be examined under the four elements in order to assess their relative significance and interaction. For example, the underlying causes of death from traffic accidents can be found to be due mainly to risks taken by individuals, with lesser importance given to the design of cars and roads, and to the availability of emergency treatment; human biology has little or no significance in this area. In order of importance, therefore, LIFESTYLE, ENVIRONMENT and HEALTH CARE ORGANIZATION contribute to traffic deaths in the proportions of something like 75%, 20% and 5% respectively. This analysis permits program planners to focus their attention on the most important contributing factors. Similar assessments of the relative importance of contributing factors can be made for many other health problems.

A fourth feature of the Concept is that it permits a further sub-division of factors. Again for traffic deaths in the Lifestyle category, the risks taken by individuals can be classed under impaired driving, carelessness, failure to wear seat-belts and speeding. In many ways the Concept thus provides a road map which shows the most direct links between health problems, and their underlying causes, and the relative importance of various contributing factors.

Finally, the Health Field Concept provides a new perspective on health, a perspective which frees creative minds for the recognition and exploration of hitherto neglected fields. The importance on their own health of the behaviour and habits of individual Canadians is an example of the kind of conclusion that is obtainable by using the Health Field Concept as an analytical tool.

One of the main problems in improving the health of Canadians is that the essential power to do so is widely dispersed among individual citizens, governments, health professions and institutions. This fragmentation of responsibility has sometimes led to imbalanced approaches, with each participant in the health field pursuing solutions only within his area of interest. Under the Health Field Concept, the fragments are brought together into a unified whole which permits everyone to see the importance of all factors, including those which are the responsibility of others.

This unified view of the health field may well turn out to be one of the Concept's main contributions to progress in improving the level of health.

Issues Arising from the Use of the Health Field Concept

The Concept was designed with two aims in view: to provide a greater understanding of what contributes to sickness and death, and to facilitate the identification of courses of action that might be taken to improve health.

The Concept is *not* an organizational framework for structuring programs and activities, and for establishing lines of command. The rigid allocation of problems and activities to one or another of the four elements of the Concept would be contrary to reality and would perpetuate the present fragmentary approach to solving health problems. For example, the problem of drug abuse needs attention by researchers in human biology, by behavioural scientists, by those who administer drug laws and by those who provide personal health care. Contributions are needed from all of these and it would be a misuse of the Health Field Concept to exploit it as a basis for capturing all aspects of a problem for one particular unit of organization or interest group.

A second practical problem is the perennial one of federal-provincial jurisdictional boundaries in the health field. Since the Concept was intended to cover the whole health field without regard to jurisdiction, and since there are very real limits on federal powers, the argument could be made that we were looking at matters which had no history of federal concern or authority. The only answer here, of course, is that the right questions must be posed about the health field before a determination can be made of legitimate federal responses.

A third issue, more theoretical, was whether or not it was possible to divide external influences on health between the environment, about which the individual can do little, and lifestyle, in which he can make choices. Particularly cogent were arguments that personal choices were dictated by environmental factors, such as the peer-group pressures to start smoking cigarettes during the teens. Further, it was argued that some bad personal habits were so ingrained as to constitute addictions which, by definition, no longer permitted a choice by a simple act of will. Smoking, alcohol abuse and drug abuse were some of the lifestyle problems referred to in this vein.

The fact that there is some truth in both hypotheses, i.e., that environment affects lifestyle and that some personal habits are addictive, requires a philosophical and moral response rather than a purely intellectual one. This response is, that if we simply give up on individuals whose lifestyles create excessive risks to their health, we will be abandoning a number who could have changed, and will be perpetuating the very environment which influenced them adversely in the first place. In short the deterministic view must be put aside in favour of faith in the power of free will, hobbled as this power may be at times by environment and addiction.

One point on which no quarter can be given is that difficulties in categorizing the contributing factors to a given health problem are no excuse for putting the problem aside; the problem does not disappear because of difficulties in fitting it nicely into a conceptual framework.

Another issue is whether or not the Concept will be used to carry too much of an analytical workload by demanding that it serve both to identify requirements for health and to determine the mechanisms for meeting them. Although the Concept will help bring out the problems and their causes, and even point to the avenues by which they can be solved, it cannot determine the precise steps that are needed to implement programs. Decisions as to programs are affected by so many other considerations that they will require the analysis of many practical factors outside the Concept proper.

The ultimate philosophical issue raised by the Concept is whether, and to what extent, government can get into the business of modifying human behaviour, even if it does so to improve health. The marketing of social change is a new field which applies the marketing techniques of the business world to getting people to change their behaviour, i.e. eating habits, exercise habits, smoking habits, driving habits, etc. It is argued by some that proficiency in social marketing would inevitably lead government into all kinds of undesirable thought control and propaganda. The dangers of governmental proficiency in social marketing are recognized but so are the evident abuses resulting from all other kinds of marketing. If the siren song of coloured television, for example, is creating an indolent and passive use of leisure time, has the government not the duty to counteract its effects by marketing programs aimed at promoting physical recreation? As previously mentioned, in Canada some 76% of the population over age 13 devotes less than one hour a week to participation in sports while 84% of the same population spends four or more hours weekly watching television. This kind of imbalance extends to the amount of money being spent by the private sector on marketing products and services, some of which if abused, contribute to sickness and death. One must inevitably conclude that society, through government, owes it to itself to develop protective marketing techniques to counteract those abuses.

Finally, some have questioned whether an increased emphasis on human biology, environment and lifestyle will not lead to a diminution of attention to the system of personal health care. This issue is raised particularly by those whose activities are centred on the health care organization. On this issue it can be said, first of all, that Canadians would not tolerate a reduction in personal health care and are in fact pushing very hard to make service more accessible and more comprehensive. In response to this demand, several Canadian Provinces have extended insured health care services beyond those whose cost is shared by the Federal Government. These extensions will no doubt continue.

More important, if the incidence of sickness can be reduced by prevention, then the cost of present services will go down, or at least the rate of increase will diminish. This will make money available to extend health insurance to more and more services and to provide needed facilities, such as ambulatory care centres and extended care institutions. To a considerable extent, therefore, the increased availability of health care services to Canadians depends upon the success that can be achieved in preventing illness through measures taken in human biology, environment and lifestyle.

In this section some practical, theoretical and philosophical issues arising out of the Health Field Concept have been sketched out. No doubt other problems, including those of analytical methodology, will be encountered, but as long as the ultimate goal is kept in mind, which is to increase the average number of disability-free days in the lives of Canadians, these difficulties can be overcome.

Notes

[1] Hubert L. Laframboise, "Health Policy. Breaking it Down into More Manageable Segments," *Journal of the Canadian Medical Association,* 3 February 1973.

2 What Is Policy?

Definitions

Dictionary definitions of policy are confusing. *The Concise Oxford Dictionary of Current English* distinguishes between two separate concepts derived from two different Greek roots by way of Old French. The first is from the root *politeia,* or citzenship, the second from *apodeixis,* demonstration or proof. The latter is the meaning used in, for example, insurance policy, which is defined as a document containing contract of assurance, or insurance. The first definition, related to citizenship (the definition with which this book is concerned), is *policy:* "political sagacity; statecraft; prudent conduct; sagacity; craftiness; course of action adopted by government, party, etc. . . ." Other words derived from the same root are *polity:* "condition of civil order; form, process of civil government, organized society, state," *politic:* "(of person) sagacious, prudent; (of actions, etc.) judicious, expedient, scheming, crafty" and *politics:* "science and art of government, political affairs or life; political principles. . . ."

Policy making as discussed in this book is concerned with maintaining and developing the polity—"the condition of civil order, the form and process of civil government, organized society and state," with the adoption of courses of action by political parties, governments and other important social organizations, and finally, with issues in "the science and art of governing."

Boundaries

And if dictionary definitions are confusing, so are the writings of policy analysts. Whilst in general they put forward the idea that the development of a policy is concerned with the adoption or maintenance of a course of action, each analyst takes a different view of what should be included or excluded in his considerations of data relevant to analyzing that course of action. Marshall (1970), for one, said that policy analysts would decide what to examine as a matter of convention or convenience. And when he took a critical look at what was included conventionally in comparative analyses of social security policies, he expressed his dissatisfactions with the conventions bounding that analysis. In his view, the limits were set in such a way that the essence of British social security policy was left unexamined. He then proceeded to argue that an analyst might provide more insights by following the approach which suited his own convenience and was bounded by his special interests rather than by observing any conventions.

Whilst idiosyncratic approaches can be justified in a new discipline, most academics yearn for order, to bring discussions into conventional frameworks so that findings can be related to one another and progress reviewed. Consequently, many policy analysts have been concerned to establish a framework acceptable to others which may be used for advancing academic analyses and measuring empirical progress.

Of course, it is not only academic policy analysts who are interested in frameworks or the establishment of boundaries—limits of concern are important for practical purposes. As some decision makers are accountable for actions taken in their prescribed territories, they feel the need to know what are their frontiers, whilst others prefer to maintain indeterminate mandates, to preserve more of their own discretion to act on matters which seem relevant to them. Bureaucrats usually fall into the first group, entrepreneurs and professionals into the second, so it is in lower levels of bureaucracies that boundary definition is usually most highly developed. Experts may have less power if their mandate is quite clear, thus many professionals prefer to maintain an indeterminacy in their territorial claims (Watkins, 1975). Doern and Aucoin (1971) have described how senior Canadian federal civil servants spend a lot of time struggling for positional authority (or relative power in marginal territories).

For people living in simple solidary societies, social responsibilities are clear. Social exchange patterns are well-established and members of the community know what is expected of them. This is not so in complex mass societies where there are many ambiguities about authority and responsibility. Whilst most people are reasonably clear about their duties to family members and in their daily round of work, they are not so certain nowadays about their more general responsibilities towards others. There was a good deal of soul searching about this in America in the late 1960s. Social workers, doctors and other personal service professionals were accused by those interested in social change of having tunnel vision, seeing only the problems of their individual clients and ignoring where they stood in society. Wars make members of a society more conscious of the strengths and weaknesses of their community as a whole, and the Vietnam War had this effect on the U.S.A. (as earlier it had happened in European communities).

It was in this setting that the two policy analysts Boulding and Gil wrote. A much-quoted article by Boulding, "The Boundaries of Social Policy" (1967), sought to make American social workers more aware of the policy decisions they could hope to influence. Originally written for delivery at a national social workers' conference, this paper must be read in context. By explaining the distinction between economic and social policy, Boulding seems to have been seeking to chart a large but limited territory he considered suitable for social workers to enter. No doubt he hoped to increase their inputs into policy decision making by informing them about its existence and its limits. Boulding thought that social policy was characterized by the absence of market forces; that governments make unilateral transfers in order to distribute socially-owned resources of money, goods and services to meet socially defined needs; and that these policies have integrative purposes for society for, rather than requiring individuals to accept existing economic and other limitations on the range of decisions and actions available to them, they assist them in getting access to services through this transfer of funds. Thus, through this exposition, the social workers were guided towards taking a wider view than that of their individual relationship to clients, agency and even neighbourhood responsibilities—they were being moved towards a national viewpoint. However, Boulding drew the line at expecting their involvement in economic affairs. Questions about resource development in American society were not, in his view, social policy questions.

Boulding's boundaries were too limited for Gil, working in another setting. A new Social Policy Study Program was set up at Brandeis University in the same period, and Gil (1970) produced a document laying out the concerns of an academic centre directed towards analyzing social policy questions. Whereas Boulding seems to have tailored his boundaries to fit his audience, Gil took a broader view. His purpose was to provide a model against which all Americans could measure the strengths and weaknesses of their country's social organization. For Gil, social policy could not exclude economic decision making, for economic decisions have implications for social organization. His boundaries excluded only foreign policy and religion from a proposed framework for analyzing social policy. He said:

> This framework includes in social policies all policies, the primary function of which is to govern the nature of all possible sets of human relationships and to shape the quality of life or well-being, within a given society. The model conceptualizes all such policies as forming a single system, which means that no social policy is operating entirely independent of other social policies which constitute a given society's social policy system. However, while all social policies are conceived to be component parts of a system, the model does not view them as necessarily logically consistent with each other. On the contrary, it states specifically that internal inconsistency is a likely characteristic of social

> policy systems. Such internal inconsistency is, of course, a reflection of the conflicting tendencies which. . . underlie the process of social policy evolution. [pp. 8-9]

Gil proposed that the policy analyst must take the widest possible view, and give consideration to four basic societal mechanisms: "the development of life-sustaining and enhancing resources, the allocation of statuses, roles and prerogatives, the distribution of rights, and the extent of linkage between the allocation of statuses and the distribution of rights. . ." (pp. 10-11). He explained that, "The major operative dimensions or variables of social policy systems appear to be the mechanisms of resource development, status allocation and rights distribution, as well as the quality of interaction between these mechanisms" (p.11).

Many social policy analysts make rights distribution their main focus of attention. By taking this wider view, Gil has incorporated into social policy discussions a number of issues which were concealed or went unchallenged in liberal democratic societies in earlier days. Although the exploitation of labour has been a matter of policy concern since men became conscious of the evils of slavery, it is only recently that the overexploitation of natural resources or of technology has been brought into question. In the 1960s, the wastefulness of affluent societies, the pollution caused by industrial production and the evident exhaustion of the world's resources led some policy makers to propose a retreat from economic growth (Schumacher, 1974) and to point out the dangers of overreaching in technology. Illich (1975), for example, forecast a *Medical Nemesis* of iatrogenic disease if the development of medical technology continued at the same pace as before.

Gil's framework is broader and much more inclusive than the conventional comparative frameworks discussed by Marshall, yet, by excluding foreign policy, he, too, has demonstrated limitations stemming from his ethnocentricity. Living in a powerful self-sufficient country, he felt this area of consideration could be excluded, but his decision seems questionable if we are to regard Gil's model as presenting an internationally viable comparative framework. For those living in colonializing or colonized countries (whether the imperialism is political or economic) such as Britain or Canada, Gil's decision to exclude foreign policy from his proposed all-inclusive national framework cuts out a major influence upon social policy. Citizens of these countries are only too well aware how much their resources for social policy development are dependent upon their own nation's or others' foreign investment decisions and react accordingly.

Equally, religion, far from dealing only with supernatural relationships, as Gil suggested, is a powerful force in defining social relationships in many countries. Glaser (1970) has demonstrated how hospitals differ according to the predominating religious beliefs of a country. Birrell and Murie (1974-5) have shown how, in Northern Ireland, religious prejudices and religious linkages are able to submerge and subvert the welfare state policies which prevail in other parts of the British Isles.

Yet, subject to these criticisms, Gil's framework seems to provide a useful model for academic consideration. What is missing from it is one of four sectors outlined by De Miguel who considered a health system to consist of four subsystems, viz: individuals, institutions, society and the larger system (or environment). This analysis is paralleled by Gil's individuals, social units and society. He excluded the larger environment because he seems to have been responding to the concurrent Social Indicators movement. This movement was led by a group of policy analysts, inspired in part by the questioning of the radicals who had begun to ask why the richest country in the world seemed to be saddled with so many social problems. How was the U.S. succeeding in realizing the American Dream? More than that—how could the strengths and weaknesses of a democratic society be identified and corrected by methods more rational than violent confrontations?

Bounded Rationality

Whilst some policy analysts may be prepared to explore broadly all the territory laid out by Gil, few policy makers can easily manage to do so, for they are constrained by what political scientists have called "bounded rationality," that is, by time and by ability to put together and act upon all the relevant data. As we have seen already, even policy analysts may set their own or choose to work to others' constraints because they find the whole territory so large as to be incomprehensible, or at least unmanageable for practical purposes. De Miguel reviewed all the research into health and health care up to 1974 which might be considered useful for developing policy, but concluded that work done at the micro and macro ends of the range was unlikely to be useful—at the micro end because it dealt with too few variables, at the macro end because there were too many to control.

Nevertheless, both De Miguel and Gil defended the position that we need to begin to understand the health or social system as a whole, even if it is only through descriptive information, because it is important to understand how policy decisions in one part interact with those in another, and how equilibrium is maintained.

Constraints on Decision Making

The academic policy analyst is not usually constrained by time or by those other factors which exert pressure upon the practising policy maker. It is theoretically possible for him to look at and describe the system as a whole if he wishes to do so, but the politician or the administrator is conscious of the pressures to take, defer or avoid decision making at all times.

The complexities of political life are spelt out in Barry's *Political Argument* (1965). He began his discussion of politicians' activities by considering how potential decisions are evaluated or appraised before going on to look at the way in which the "public interest" is maintained through their intervention. Students may find this a helpful exposition.

Lindblom (1965, 1959) has described how he has perceived individuals' short term behaviour at the intuitive level, making day-to-day compromise decisions or "muddling through." Over the long term, if decision makers realize that their muddling incrementalism is not working out well enough, they may choose to make a disjunction—to take a sideways step and introduce a new policy.

Other political scientists have studied policy decision making and, although their interpretations of the processes may differ, they agree with Lindblom that rationality is bounded, that decisions are taken on partial knowledge, often with tradeoffs, to get support for a cause.

Territoriality is involved in much decision making. Politicians become identified with certain areas of interest. Experts in economics, social security, urban and regional planning, race relations, etc. all have their bounded territories, and administrators are appointed to defined areas of jurisdiction.

Tradeoffs and Bargains

Despite the necessity to establish relatively permanent bounded territories, policy makers often find it necessary to make forays across these boundaries. Politicians, forced to move from one territory to another as the party commands, are expected to have some acquaintance with the whole range of the "public interest."

Barry outlined the social decision procedures used in political life: combat, bargaining, discussion on merits, voting, chance, contest and authoritative determination. But in democracies, in the end, tradeoffs are worked out, such as the pairing of opposing party members in the British House of Commons which cancels out negative votes, or, more positively, engagement in bargaining to support one another's causes such as a vote for more resources to go to higher education in return for support of an environmental policy affecting a member's local constituency.

Some causes encourage tradeoffs and others do not. Hospitals are an example of a cause that politicians cannot afford not to support. As Somers (1969) has pointed out, they are symbolic of much more than medical care. She has compared them to mediaeval cathedrals because they are centres of employment, technology and art. In Canada and Australia hospital construction was an important mechanism for redistributing wealth across the country at the end of the Second World War when both countries were on the brink of economic development and many tradeoffs were made around this area of policy development.

LINKING POLICY ANALYSIS TO DECISION MAKING

If decision making is so pragmatic, is it possible, then, to link intellectual policy analysis into the system of tradeoffs? Can those taking the broad view (the philosophical or ideological stance), or the investigative view be helpful to the practical politician or administrator?

The distinction between decision making and decision taking in the management literature may be useful in considering the relationship between the policy analysts, researchers and pragmatic policy makers.

In general, societies prefer to continue with existing policies and small incremental developments unless strong pressures have built up for reform, because pressures for change threaten the social order and established social relationships. It is important, therefore, to understand something about middle-range and long-term trends in social policies. It is there that the analysts can be of the greatest help to the pragmatists. They may be able to indicate when the time has come for individual initiatives to bear results.

In recent years academics have begun to explain social maintenance and social change processes so that we can try to understand how short-term events, middle-range processes and long-term trends are linked together. (See chapter 4.)

More specific to our purpose here is to discuss how in the short-term, using individual initiatives, policy analysts might bring their knowledge to bear on decision taking. Donnison's discussion (1972) of how a standing plan (such as that proposed by Kahn (1969), an American academic) can be translated into action has helped in understanding some of the processes. On the one hand, policy makers' (decision takers') knowledge of the plan may help them to have effective input into incremental decision making because it suggests possible immediate courses of action to them; on the other hand, it provides ideal guidelines indicating when incrementalism may have gone too far and a disjunction may be necessary (see chapter 8).

The lack of a clear statement of middle-range or long-term policy does not mean, however, that there is no ongoing thrust. Christian and Campbell (1974) have explained the kind of situation which exists in many sectors of policy making, particularly in basically conservative countries. Their discussion of Canadian ideologies may be applied to policy making, too:

> There are two kinds of ideology operating in any political community. One is a type of ideology which expresses itself in the actual operating institutions. . . . The full theory will be contained in the actual functioning of the institutions. . . . A second kind of ideology is also present . . ."an abstract principle,

> or a set of related abstract principles, which has been independently premeditated." [P. 5]

This observation by Christian and Campbell suggests that some policies may have evolved within organizations and become structured into the fabric without really being recognized as policies by many, and that other policies may be very consciously worked out and presented to constituents for consideration, adoption and implementation. There is a tendency to ignore these evolving maintenance policies because they are so ill-formulated, to pay attention only to clearly stated change policies.

Policy Frameworks

Although it may not be possible to set one useful boundary for the study of social policy, the desire to set boundaries is clear. Three main groups who have expressed the need for boundaries seem to be identifiable—academic policy analysts, policy researchers (more carefully described in chapter 11) and pragmatic decision makers. The first group, the analysts, needs to take a broad view in order to explain the meaning of policies for a society to those who wish to hear them (or if, like Marshall, they choose a convenient piece of the whole, then they need to set their piece in context). The second group, the researchers, needs to define the variables to be studied and may have to cut off a part of the whole in order to be able to do so. But how often do they see where they fit into the scheme of things—either the whole (taking the long-term view), or the immediate, practical short-term situation? The third group, the decision takers (the pragmatists) are on shifting ground, but they may find it helpful to consider what frameworks may be used to bound rationality, to make it possible to function in their complex world.

In chapter 3 the focus will be on those frameworks which have been found to be of practical use to policy analysts and to policy makers.

Discussion of Readings and References

1. The two readings which follow this chapter are concerned with the problem of defining the limits of policy analysis and making it a useful conceptual tool.

Kenneth Boulding's "The Boundaries of Social Policy" was chosen in order to illustrate one attempt at bounding the definition to coincide with the interests of one particular group—those interested in promoting redistributive social welfare programs.

David Gil's "A Systematic Approach to Social Policy Analysis" was developed for long-term teaching and research purposes. Gil extended the boundaries usually imposed upon social policy analysis because he did not think that the questions being raised by critics of American society in the late sixties could be answered without not only exploring commitment to resource development but also examining the organization of the task and manpower system of the country as well as Americans' attitudes to human rights and the linkages between task allocation and rights. Many policy analysts concentrate on one or other of these four areas (particularly the third, as was demonstrated by Boulding and will be demonstrated again in later chapters). They bound their work by these sectoral considerations, thus limiting their analyses. But many do so in a way differing from Boulding's.

It should be noted that De Miguel's "Framework for the Study of National Health Systems" (outlined in the previous chapter) closely parallels Gil's framework and, although its health orientation narrows its overall scope, its boundaries are larger than Gil's because it is principally concerned with establishing a framework for making international comparisons. Both authors have made the supposition that the societies they are describing can be better understood if considered as total social systems. De Miguel's paper is not reprinted here, but can easily be found. Gil's framework has been used as a guideline for chapters 5-9.

Some students (particularly, those with British backgrounds) have found Peter Townsend's *Sociology and Social Policy* helpful for explaining the less obvious aspects of the health system in that country. Sociologists may also find his definition of policy as process interesting and useful.

2. Some explanations of the way in which political decisions are taken may help to show why boundaries seem to be wanted by policy makers. (No readings are included here, but references should be consulted.) Lindblom's explanations of intuitive adjustment and incrementalism, from *The Intelligence of Democracy: Rational Policy Through Mutual Adjustment* and "The Science of Muddling Through" from the *Public Administration Review,* Spring 1959 pp 79-88, have often been reprinted. These well known discussions of short-term decision making will not be reprinted here, since they appear in a number of political science and planning readers as well as in their original form. Lindblom is concerned with short-term policy making, but others have been anxious to show that not all inputs into policy are of this kind. Donnison, (see chapter 8) building on Lindblom's analysis, has agreed that longer-term planning can be related to and even integrated into short-term decision making. If a standing plan is prepared (as described by Alfred J. Kahn in *Theory and Practice of Social Planning*), then the politicians can use this to guide them when they are required to make short-term decisions or tradeoffs. The plan may also help to show when there is need to stop incrementing and to consider making a "disjunction," that is, making a major shift in direction.

The Boundaries of Social Policy

Kenneth E. Boulding

"Social Policy" is a vague term the boundaries of which are ill defined, but the content of which is rich. In its widest sense it would include all policies directed toward making some change in the structure of society, and since no policy could be excluded from this, social policy would simply be another name for government policy. If the term is to become meaningful, obviously it must become some kind of subset of the larger set of policy in general. Some things must be found to distinguish it and at least mark out roughly where the boundaries lie.

A further difficulty of definition arises here because of the complexity and extreme interrelatedness of all aspects of social life and all subsystems of the larger social system. A rough distinction can be made, for instance, between foreign policy and domestic policy, or between the international system and the domestic system. Yet this distinction becomes harder to maintain all the time. Thus the war in Vietnam is affecting every aspect of American life and every aspect of domestic policy. Likewise this country's agricultural policy—which initially, at any rate, was conceived primarily as domestic—has turned out to have enormous consequences for the international system. Furthermore, there are aspects of foreign policy, such as foreign aid, that are more clearly related to certain principles of social domestic policy than to the international system as such.

One despairs, therefore, of finding any clear definition or clean boundaries. The vagueness of a distinction, however, does not destroy its importance. Almost all the great distinctions of life are vague, and in the intricate many-dimensional spectrum of social life we certainly perceive regions much

---

Reprinted with permission of the National Association of Social Workers, from *Social Work,* vol. 12. no. 1. January, 1967, 3-11, and permission of the author.

as we perceive colors in the continuous spectrum of light. If we are clear, therefore, that what we are looking for is a region rather than a boundary we will save ourselves a good deal of verbal frustration.

A tricky question is whether we want to distinguish social policy from economic policy. They are obviously closely related; if they are regions they are certainly adjacent and overlapping. If there is a distinction, it is simply that of a world of discourse. There are some things about which economists talk and some things they neglect. Perhaps the best definition of economic policy is simply "that about which economists talk." It is a little unsatisfactory to define social policy as that about which economists do not talk, but unfortunately this does reflect a certain reality in the world of discourse. What economists talk about, such as prices, wages, income, unemployment, stabilization, and so on, seems to have a certain unity and coherence that the other aspects of social policy lack. It is a little unkind to say that whereas economists have models, sociologists have hypotheses, but it is not wholly untrue. Consequently social policy is not generally perceived as opposed to economic policy, as something that has clear structure and a relatively simple body of principles. In contrast with economic policy social policy looks like a sticky conglomeration of the ad hoc. It may well be, of course, that this reflects the nature of the system itself and is not, therefore, a criticism of our knowledge about it but a reflection of the realism of our image. However, in the human mind the rage for order is quite strong; the urge for intellectual tidiness can hardly be disobeyed.

Common Threads

Let us then look over the spectrum of various economic and social policies and see if any common thread that unites them can be found. At one end are policies that usually are thought of as economic, such as monetary stabilization, price policy, most aspects of tax policy, fiscal policy, policies directed toward specific industries and segments of the economy, such as agriculture or public utilities, railroads, and the like. Coming a little closer to what might be thought of as social policy would be labor legislation, with the minimum wage clearly economic and policies regulating the growth and structure of labor unions more social. Antitrust policy would seem to be fairly clearly economic; policies directed toward truth in advertising and packaging or the elimination of discriminatory hiring practices would be more social. At the other end of the scale are policies that are much more social than economic, such as those relating to divorce, the treatment of children (including Aid to Families with Dependent Children), relief and rehabilitation, most of the War on Poverty, education, the exercise of religion, and so on.

It may be that part of the difficulty in defining social policy arises from the fact that in American society, at any rate, social policy is still much more laissez-faire than economic policy. By the separation of church and state it is virtually said that there shall be no policy toward religion, although the difficulties involved in prayers in public schools indicate that even the separation of church and state does not relieve us from the necessity of some policy toward religion. Similarly, in regard to education, at the national level until very recently, at any rate, the policy has been to have no policy and to leave education almost wholly to local initiative or even to private enterprise. Another aspect of policy that seems to be clearly social rather than economic is racial policy and civil rights; here the government is attempting to change overt behavior through the introduction of legal sanctions against certain types of behavior involving discriminatory practices. More fundamentally, through the educational system it hopes to change attitudes.

Finally, there is a whole range of policies toward the so-called underprivileged: relief, social security, various forms of aid to those in need, Medicare, and so on. A great deal of this is usually subsumed under the head of income maintenance, although actually the policies go far beyond the maintenance of income in a simple quantitative sense.

Going still further away from the economic we run into policies involving administration of the law, the police, criminal procedures, the protection of citizens. This finally goes beyond the field of social policy into matters of national defense and international relations.

The main question of this paper is whether there is any guiding thread through this maze of policies, agencies, objectives, and organizations that could at least help us organize our thinking about it and perhaps assist us in making evaluations. As long as everything is ad hoc, as long as every case is a special case, it is hard to make any evaluations. Any evaluation implies reducing things that are essentially heterogeneous and disparate to some kind of common denominator or measure. The desire for a simplifying principle, therefore, is not just a matter of intellectual esthetics and the rage for order; it is essential if any attempt is to be made to evaluate this enormous complex as a whole and to develop a critique that may be useful in directing further development. One could say, of course, that the only principle that is necessary is the perception of a political need large enough and vigorous enough to get itself expressed in legislation or adminstrative law. While this principle is no doubt realistic, it is not very helpful. It says, in effect, with Alexander Pope, "Whatever is, is right," and offers little hope of organized criticism or principles of evaluation. It may indeed be so that this will finally be all that we are left with, but it would not be absurd to at least search for some more general principle.

Principles of Economic Policy

In the case of economic policy, the general principles are perhaps easier to perceive and a good deal of thought has gone into expounding them. The economist postulates what might be called the first approximation ideal for the price system, such as, for instance, that the price structure should correspond to the structure of alternative costs. To use a famous example of Adam Smith: if giving up one deer in the forest enables us to catch two beavers, then if the price in the market is not two beavers for one deer some justification for this divergence from the first approximation ideal must be made. Many such justifications are possible, of course. It may be thought that the wearing of beaver hats is unseemly and a sumptuary tax may be imposed to discourage them. It may be believed that the eating of venison is peculiarly favorable to the health and the hunting of deer may therefore be subsidized to encourage the consumption of venison. All agree that vice should be taxed and virtue subsidized, unless taxation legitimizes vice and hence encourages it or subsidization corrupts virtue. Everyone agrees also that when prices established by the market mechanism do not reflect real costs and benefits they should be modified by regulations, prohibitions, taxes, subsidies, and grants.

On the minor detail of what is vice and what is virtue there may be wide disagreement. In actual practice this beautiful general principle does not remove as much argument as one might think. Nevertheless, the existence of the general principle is valuable and it gives the economist a sharp advantage over other social scientists when it comes to the critique of policy. This apparent advantage, however, rests partly on the fact that economists study primarily that segment of the social system that is dominated by exchange, and a system of exchange introduces the possibility of a "measuring rod"—which may be money or any other convenient commodity—by which heterogeneous aggregates of goods may be reduced to a common measure. This advantage is clearly a real one. A good deal of the apparent success of economics in producing welfare propositions rests, however, on a largely unexpressed ethical proposition that may easily be challenged—the principle of what is called the "Paretian optimum," which is that any change is for the better as long as nobody is worse off and at least one person is better off, each in his own estimation. This rests on the ethical assumption of the absence of malevolence. Unfortunately, in political and international life especially, malevolence is a real factor in human behavior and people are frequently willing to damage themselves if an enemy can be damaged more.

In *The Principles of Economic Policy* this writer outlined four major objectives of economic policy, summarized as progress, stability, justice, and freedom.[1] The first two can be combined into one under the heading "stable growth," that is, a rate of growth that over the years averages some optimum rate in the sense that, at least in the estimate of the present generation, a higher rate of growth would not be worth the sacrifices involved. Stable growth means that the fluctuations of the rate of growth would be kept within tolerable limits—again, what is tolerable being rather vague. It can be defined more sharply in terms of keeping unemployment below some unacceptable level. These are fairly clearly economic goals, in the sense that they are reasonably subject to the measuring rod of money and can be measured, for instance, by the over-all growth rate of real income or real product per capita. There will be wide agreement that a zero rate of growth represents failure, a negative rate of growth disastrous failure, that 2 percent is better than 1 percent and 3 percent better than 2 percent, but there might be some hesitation as to whether 8 percent is better than 7 percent.

Even in the evaluation of economic growth, purely economic considerations may need to be modified by something that looks like social policy. Even the economist cannot afford to be wholly indifferent to the distribution of the growing income. Economists have had a good deal to say about this but the upshot of many of their remarks is that we do not know much about it. Almost everybody would agree that a growth pattern that results in a substantial rate of growth of income for 20 percent of the population but stagnation for 80 percent is not only undesirable but likely to be politically unstable, as the experience in Cuba shows. At the other extreme, a society that is so equalitarian that the fruits of progress always slip out of the hands of those who initiated the progress is in danger of inhibiting growth and stagnating, unless it can pull the Communist trick of pretending to be equalitarian and in fact creating enormous inequalities of economic power. In regard to ideal distribution, economics comes up with the excellent principle that the last dollar of income should have the same significance for everybody. Unfortunately, the absence of any interpersonal measures of significance prevents any real application of this principle except through the loose apparatus of the political process by which, for instance, such things as the schedule of a progressive income tax are determined.

Contrast Between Approaches

The contrast between an economic and a social approach to problems can be seen clearly in the case of a minimum standard of living. Virtually all societies, once they attain a certain stage of development, accept some responsibility for the social minimum below which their members should not be allowed to fall. At first this may be established in a loose and unorganized manner through mendicancy, charity, and the extended family, a system so loose that many individuals are likely to fall through the gaps. As the essential organizational skills of a society increase, however, it usually gets to the point at which, as for instance in the Elizabethan Poor Law, society itself takes some ultimate responsibility for the social minimum. As the society gets richer the social minimum tends to rise correspondingly. The purely economic approach to this problem, which has probably never existed although it is now proposed seriously in many quarters, would simply be to establish a minimum income to which every citizen would have a right, whether rich or poor, employed or unemployed, old or young, incapacitated or sturdy. From the very beginning, however, this solution has never seemed acceptable. There has been social discrimination against those who have received subsistence grants, designating them as paupers, and there has been constant fear that grants to relieve the poverty of the poor would lead to the exploitation of the productive by the unproductive. Therefore, the simple economic solution of giving people money has usually been rejected in favor of payments in kind, workhouses, and the administration of relief by social workers. Somehow, lying in the background has been the persistent idea that the recipient of charity should be deserving and that the minimum should be administered in such a way that it does not discourage self-help and self-support. This is a debate that has been carried on for a long time, at least since Speenhamland and Malthus, and we still seem to be a long way from its resolution. The very fact that the argument continues, however, suggests that there are problems of social policy that go beyond simple economic solutions.

If there is one common thread that unites all aspects of social policy and distinguishes them from merely economic policy, it is the thread of what has elsewhere been called the "integrative system." This includes those aspects of social life that are characterized not so much by exchange in which a quid is got for a quo as by unilateral transfers that are justified by some kind of appeal to a status or legitimacy, identity, or community. The institutions with which social policy is especially concerned, such as the school, family, church, or, at the other end, the public assistance office, court, prison, or criminal gang, all reflect degrees of integration and community. By and large it is an objective of social policy to build the identity of a person around some community with which he is associated. It sounds a little cynical to say that the object of this is to make the individual content with rather poor terms of trade and to persuade him to give up a lot and not get very much in return. There may be very good reasons, however, why unfavorable terms of trade at the psychological level are necessary. In the world of physical commodities terms of trade are usually favorable because exchange in this area is so efficient and is almost always a gain to both parties. What one party gives up, the other party receives. The actual cost of the transaction is small in terms of the satisfaction gained by both parties.

As we move into the more subtle exchanges that take place between persons and organizations, what one party gives up is not necessarily what the other party receives. This is seen even in the industrial relationship in the purchase and sale of labor, which is perhaps why the labor market is almost universally regarded as "social" rather than "economic." In the labor bargain, what the worker gives up is the alternative uses of his time; what the employer receives is the product of the work, which is something totally different. The possibility, therefore, of high costs in the exchange relationship is quite great in the sense that something is lost in the transfer. This is seen particularly in the political relationship, in which the terms of trade of the individual with the state are often very bad indeed. The individual gives up a great deal in terms of being taxed, conscripted, killed or injured in wars, and burdened with the guilt of murder and destruction; in return the state seems to give him little, except perhaps a bit of security and a larger identity. It is not surprising, therefore, that we have been urged to ask not what our country can do for us but what we can do for our country. The first question might prove to be too embarrassing.

Perhaps, therefore, we can identify the "grant" or unilateral transfer—whether money, time, satisfaction, energy, or even life itself—as the distinguishing mark of the social just as exchange or bilateral transfer is a mark of the economic. This means also, however, that social policy has to concern itself profoundly with questions of identity and alienation, for alienation destroys the grant system. It is this that destroys the family when one or the other partner feels that the terms of trade are not satisfactory and that he (or she) is giving a lot to the marriage and getting little out of it. It is this that leads to criminality when the individual attempts to take out of society more than he has put in, or refuses to make the grant to society of his time and energy that is necessary if he is to be a fully functioning member. By and large, it is the alienated who create social problems and the integrated who solve them. One would think, therefore, that social policy is that which is centered in those institutions that create integration and discourage alienation. The success of social policy, then, would be measured by the degree to which individuals are persuaded to make unilateral transfers in the interest of some larger group or community.

Even as one states this proposition, however, one begins to qualify it, even to deny it. Without alienation there can be no progress. If everybody is socialized into conformity with what is, nobody dares to have a dream of what might be. It is only the nonconformist who is the entrepreneur, the prophet, the artist, the creator. There are societies that have been too successful in creating integration and conformity, such as classical Chinese civilization, and have therefore tended to stagnate at the very level of perfection they have achieved. It was the disintegrated, disorganized, troubled, chaotic society of Western Europe that was the spearhead of social evolution and that produced the great mutation into science. It cannot therefore be assumed that the more integration, the more conformity, the better. In any social situation there is an optimum degree of integration. Societies that are too little integrated, too disorganized, too much ridden with factions and conflicts are incapable of creating an adequate framework of law and order and that minimum of mutual trust that is necessary for any complex development. Many societies around the world today show how the failure to achieve a sufficient degree of integration checks or even reverses economic development as resources are wasted in internal conflict and mistrust that might be devoted to improving the society's condition. On the other hand, societies are also found that are too homogeneous, in which opposition has been suppressed and in which practically everybody conforms to the prevailing culture or ideology so that each generation simply reproduces itself in the next.

Problem of the Optimum

In many ways the concept of an optimum degree of anything is unsatisfactory because it is hard to put into operation. The trouble with the Aristotelian mean is that nobody knows where it is. Nevertheless, this is a problem that is inescapable in any field of policy or behavior of any kind. We are always trying to live precariously between the too little and the too much and are always in danger of falling into one or the other. This problem is just as important in economic policy as it is in social policy; it cannot even be assumed that higher rates of economic growth are always better. Even here there is a problem of the optimum. A society that forces itself into too high a rate of growth may pay dearly for this in terms of social disorganization, misunderstanding between the generations, and the break-up of its traditional integrative system. Fortunately for the peace of mind of the policy planner there are many dimensions of policy in which society is clearly on one side or the other of the optimum and hence there is not much doubt about the direction in which it should go. If the rate of economic growth is zero it clearly ought to be increased; if the economic fluctuations involve a great depression they should be diminished. If the lack of a sense of community results in widespread destructive strikes, riots, great personal insecurity, and war, clearly the integration of the system is what is desirable. As long as we are far below the optimum we do not have to worry about overshooting it. Certainly, as one looks at the international system one can hardly help being appalled by its cost; it is no exaggeration to say that the failure to achieve world integration may cost the human race its very existence. As we look at domestic policy, we see the high cost of the class structure, the race structure, the structure of discrimination, and here again our society seems to be so far below the optimum level of integration that it hardly seems to be possible to put too much into increasing it.

How to increase it, however, is the tricky question. As a result of a combination of theoretical models and improved information-gathering, in regard to the economy, we have some confidence that we know how to avoid depression, to improve stability, and perhaps even to increase the rate of growth. When it comes down to improving the integrative structure of society we have very little theory of the over-all system and practically no over-all apparatus for collecting, processing, and feeding back information. It is not surprising, therefore, that our efforts in the direction of social policy so often seem to be frustrated. With all the effort put into the police department, criminality seems to increase. With all that is put into work among young people, juvenile delinquency seems to increase. With all that is being put into race relations, there are more race riots. With all that is being put into the poverty program, poverty does not seem to diminish. With all that is being put into the international system, the danger of war constantly mounts. With all that is being put into foreign aid, the problem of economic development of the underdeveloped nations remains totally unsolved. With all that is being put into urban renewal, our cities seem to become increasingly disorganized. With all that is being put into family counseling and psychiatric casework, the number of divorces, disorganized families, and neglected children is increasing rather than diminishing. With all that is being put into education, even in the reduction of illiteracy we are barely holding our own.

The picture here painted is perhaps too depressing; if it is a caricature it is at least a caricature of a grim truth. In these days all who are concerned with human betterment are in danger of getting what might be called "Canute complex"; we stand on the shore of an increasing tide of human misery and disorganization and busy ourselves frantically in sweeping it back, but for all our efforts the tide seems to creep in and in. In economic policy, at least, some of the tide is being turned back; we no longer feel the sense of despair about unemployment, for instance, that was felt in the thirties when the creeping tide of unemployment seemed to threaten society as a whole. When we come to the more subtle things, however—criminality, delinquency, the self-perpetuating poverty subcultures, family disorganization, neighborhood decay, mental ill health and political paranoia—we feel helpless. We sweep the waves back here and there but the tide constantly engulfs us. We must learn the same lesson here that we have learned in economics, that the sources of a system are often very far from its results. Unemployment is related mainly to tax policy, not to labor policy. Similarly, it may well be that criminality, delinquency, social disorganization, divorce, race hatred, and war are related to elements in the total social information system that have not yet been identified.

THE KNOWLEDGE STRUCTURE

One thing is clear: we must look upon the total dynamic process of society as essentially a process in human learning. Even economic development is essentially a learning process. It is not merely a mechanical process of investment in piling up old knowledge; it involves learning of new skills, development of new ambitions, the widespread diffusion of new values, and often a complete reorientation both of muscles and of minds. It is even clearer that the development of social integration is a learning process. We have to be taught to love just as we have to be taught to hate. Practically nothing in human life comes naturally. It is from vague and formless biological drives and the extraordinary learning potential of the human nervous system that the intricate structure of our personalities, our identities, our values, and our communities are molded.

It is the dynamics of the knowledge structure—the total knowledge content of society, of what Pierre Teilhard de Chardin has called the "noosphere"—that really governs all other aspects of social life.[2] It is how this total knowledge structure is transmitted and increased from one generation to the next that determines the long run dynamics of society. All human knowledge is destroyed by death and has to be reestablished in new minds once every generation. An enormous number of agencies participate in this process of transmission: parents, teachers, peers, schools, books, conversations, mass media, sermons, speeches, jokes; every day a vast barrage of information is entering one's nervous system, modifying one's image of the world, one's values, and one's self-image. Every day, likewise, death, aging, and forgetting remove a proportionate part of the information deposit of the past. It is in this process that we must find the key to social change.

We may find, as McLuhan argues, that it is the medium, not the message, that matters, and it can certainly be argued that in our time the development of television outweighs all other factors in inducing social change by a high order of magnitude.[3] We may find also, however, that McLuhan, like everybody else who has a good idea, overdoes it, and there are some messages that are more important than the medium in which they are contained. There do seem to be great symbolic archetypes that are transmitted from generation to generation—the great myths, stories, symbols, proverbs, folklore, and now, of course, the great body of science—all of which are constantly transmitted from the old to the young in a relatively stable form. However, what it is that gives symbols their power we do not know, and until we know more about this we must constantly be prepared to be surprised by the rise of new symbolic systems.

One is almost tempted to intone a kind of litany of "Who would have thought. . .?" Who would have thought at the time that an itinerant teacher in a remote province of the great Roman Empire would have set in motion a movement that eventually became one of the world's great religions? Who would have though that a camel driver in Arabia would have set in motion a symbolic system that established a great civilization stretching from Spain to the Philippines? Who would have thought that a fiery old man with a beard in the British Museum would have set in motion a system that now governs a third of the human race? Considerations such as these should be at least a little humbling to the more grandiose pretensions of social science.

Need for Feedback Apparatus

Nevertheless, knowledge can increase even about social systems, and as one's knowledge increases, one's capacity to control the system toward the realization of one's deeper values increases likewise. It might well be that in social policy we are on the edge of a revolution as great as that which occurred in economic policy. At the moment large numbers of people are acquiring information about segments of the system in which they operate—people such as social workers, government officials, law enforcement officers, doctors, ministers, psychiatrists, teachers, counselors, and so on—all of whom are feeding information into the system and getting information back out. This information, however, is nowhere collected, indexed, and processed into a continuing and continually modified image of society. As a result, most of it is wasted. Decisions are constantly being made on the basis of misinformation, false images of the world, or simple absence of crucial information that exists somewhere in the system but is not available. We must not be deluded, of course, into thinking that the more information the better; indeed, a fundamental principle of epistemology is that knowledge is gained by the loss of information, not by its accumulation. However, if the collection and processing of information are informed and organized by theoretical models, which in their turn are modified by the information they generate, the result is a feedback process in the information system that is the essential secret of science and of the enormous expansion in human knowledge that the scientific subculture has produced. There would seem to be no reason why processes of this kind cannot be set up in the international system and in what might be called the integrative system with which social policy essentially deals. Until some process like this is established, however, social policy will continue to be ad hoc and haphazard and its practitioners will be continually frustrated.

It has been suggested by a number of people, notably by Dr. Bernard Gross of Syracuse University, that a council of social advisers should be established in the Office of the President, somewhat analogous to the Council of Economic Advisors.[4] There is a great deal of merit in this proposal.

The Council of Economic Advisors has provided a most useful focus for economic information and its application to economic policy. It represents, as it were, the "Establishment" of the economics profession within the framework of government, and exercises a constant pressure toward informed and sophisticated images of the economic system in the minds of the political decision-makers. This is not to say, of course, that the council is omniscient; it can and does make mistakes, which are inevitable in a system as complex as a total society. Even its mistakes, however, are fruitful, in the sense that there is some apparatus to foster learning from them. Perhaps the greatest significance of the council lies in the fact that it represents a process of two-way communication between the professional economist and government. As a result the professional economist himself develops a greater appreciation of the difficulties of political decision-making and becomes, one hopes, a little more humble about the advice he offers. On the other hand, whatever knowledge is contained in the minds of the professional economists is now much more accessible to the government than ever before. This factor has unquestionably played a role in preventing depressions and in increasing the rate of economic growth.

There is no such apparatus for feedback in the case of social policy. It is nobody's business to look at it as a whole; it is nobody's business to collect information about social variables on a comprehensive scale and an integrated basis. A council of social advisers might well meet a need of this kind, although we should not blind ourselves to the fact that the task would be in the first instance much more difficult than that of the Council of Economic Advisors. The latter has been able to rely on a large information collection and processing apparatus that predated it in the Department of Commerce and in other government departments. A council of social advisers would have to pioneer almost from scratch in developing an integrated information system about social variables even though here, of course, the raw material exists in almost every government department. The success of the Council of Economic Advisors was in no small measure due to the fact that important pioneering work had been done both in the conceptual framework and in the collection of data by certain private agencies such as the National Bureau of Economic Research in New York, which pioneered in the collection and interpretation of national income statistics. It may be that before a successful council of social advisers is to be set up in government there needs to be some well-financed private agency that will pioneer in the conceptual tasks involved and in the development of new methods of collecting and processing the enormous amount of information that is required, much of which exists somewhere in the system but is simply not available. In the absence of any such private agency, however, and in the absence of any support of such an agency from private foundations, it may be that government itself will have to do the pioneering work. One thing is certain—that a great intellectual task remains to be accomplished. How it is to be accomplished only the future will reveal.

Notes

[1]Kenneth E. Boulding, *Principles of Economic Policy* (Englewood Cliffs, N. J.: Prentice Hall, 1958).

[2]*The Phenomenon of Man* (New York: Harper & Bros., 1959).

[3]Marshall McLuhan, *Understanding Media: The Extensions of Man* (New York: McGraw-Hill Book Co., 1964).

[4]"The State of the Nation: Social Systems Accounting," in *Social Indicators,* Raymond A. Bauer, ed. (Cambridge, Mass.: MIT Press, 1966).

A Systematic Approach to Social Policy Analysis

David G. Gil

A Definition or Model of Social Policy

The study of any concept and the systematic analysis of processes and phenomena of which the concept is a referent are likely to be hampered as long as the concept remains undefined. As already suggested, the difficulties of students of social policy and of analysts of specific social policies may thus be due, in part, to the absence of a generally accepted definition of the term.

Many writers on social policy seem to assume that the concept is self-explanatory, that it conveys the same meaning to every reader, and that it therefore requires no definition. Many others who troubled to define the concept have, as noted above, limited it to social welfare programs or to the policies which shape these programs. This latter approach seems to lead into a dead-end street, since social policy is conceptualized as a reactive, ameliorative system for dealing with supposedly transitional short-comings of the "self-regulating free-enterprise economy." In other words, social policy is assumed to concerned with the "fall-out" of the economy, or of economic policies, pending adjustments which are hypothesized to result from constant growth of the GNP.

A number of authors, however, including Schorr, Burns, Wickenden, Boulding, Rein, and Bell in the United States, and Titmuss, Townsend and Abel-Smith in the United Kingdom have suggested conceptualizations of

Reprinted from "A Systematic Approach to Social Policy Analysis," Working Paper no. 1, Social Policy Study Program (Waltham, Mass: Brandeis University, 1970), pp. 1-16 and 25, by permission of the author and the *Social Science Review* vol. 20, no. 4, Dec. 1970, in which an edited version was published.

social policy which transcend the residual frame of reference of social welfare programs. These authors consider the reduction of social inequalities and the redistribution of resources and of social opportunities as the core function of social policy.[1] Yet, in apparent inconsistency with this broad conceptualization, these authors, too, seem to view social policy as apart from economic policy. Thus, in an attempt to differentiate social from economic policies Kenneth E. Boulding states that ". . . it is the objective of social policy to build the identity of a person around some community with which he is associated . . . ," and that "social policy is that, which is centered in those institutions that create integration and discourage alienation."[2]

Perhaps the most comprehensive view on social policy has been suggested by Macbeath[3] who stated that "social policies are concerned with the right ordering of the network of relationships between men and women who live together in societies, or with the principles which should govern the activities of individuals and groups so far as they affect the lives and interests of other people."

Pursuing to its logical conclusion the conceptualization of the functions and objectives of social policy as developed by the aforementioned writers, and avoiding the inconsistency of viewing social and economic policy as separate domains, leads to the following tentative definition or general model:[4]

> Social policies are the elements of a society's social policy system—a system of interrelated, yet not necessarily logically consistent, principles and courses of action which determine the nature of all intra-societal relationships among individuals, social units, and society as a whole, and which shape the quality of life or level of well-being of a society's members. Social policies operate by regulating:
>
> *a:* the development of life-sustaining and enhancing resources, goods and services;
>
> *b:* the allocation, to individuals and social units, of specific statuses within the total array of societal tasks and functions, involving corresponding roles and prerogatives;
>
> *c:* the distribution, to individuals and social units, of specific rights and right equivalents, through entitlements, rewards, and constraints concerning real and symbolic resources, goods and services;
>
> *d:* the extent to which the distribution of rights is linked to the allocation of statuses—the relationship between c and b above.

In accordance with the model suggested here, the domain of social policy includes all policies designed to regulate intra-societal relationships and the quality of life or level of well-being in a society. Economic measures are therefore not viewed as a separate policy domain but as important means for realizing the objectives of social policy. This comprehensive conceptualization of social policy differs substantially from a "residual" model according to which social policies are measures designed specifically for dealing with problematic social conditions such as poverty, which, contrary to widely accepted economic theories, continue to plague affluent societies in spite of unprecedented economic growth and development. In terms of a social planning orientation the proposed comprehensive model of social policy seems more appropriate than a residual one, since social policies are conceived to be potentially powerful instruments for planned social change, rather than corrective and reactive measures for compensating shortcomings of an economic system.

While, then, the proposed model of social policy includes economic policy as one of its instrumental components, the following policy domains, although interacting intensively with social policy, are conceived of as separate domains:

— foreign policy, which is primarily concerned with intersocietal relations; and
— religion, which deals with society's and man's relations to the supernatural.

Social policies derive from, are a dynamic expression of, and themselves support the structure and ongoing evolution of societies. They may be assumed to have originated at the dawn of societal history from man's collective response to certain apparently universal characteristics of the human condition:

— the bio-psychological drive for survival;
— the relative scarcity of life-sustaining resources available in the natural environment;
— the necessity for human labor without which life-sustaining resources could not be obtained from the environment;
— the necessity to devise systems for organizing and assuring the performance of these essential tasks, and for distributing the life-sustaining resources they procure.

Significant developments in man's collective response to these aspects of the human condition, and thus, in the evolution of social policy systems appear to have been the following:

— the evolution of division of labor as an organizing principle for the tasks to be performed;
— the evolution of systems of social stratification based on the differential statuses, roles and prerogatives resulting from the division of labor;
— the evolution of the principle of unequal rewards and rights linked to these differential statuses and roles;
— the emerging interest of individuals and groups in the perpetuation of advantages accrued to them as a result of the patterned inequalities in the allocation of statuses, roles, and prerogatives, and the distribution of rewards and rights;

— the evolution of the principle of storing and accumulating surplus rewards, and of inter-generational transmission of accumulated rewards and of rights.

These principles and tendencies, the inter-play between them, and reactions to them on the part of interest groups within a society, seem to constitute major dynamics in the ongoing evolutionary process of societies, and thus, of social policy. Once set in motion this process continues as a result of interaction among conflicting interests of individuals and diverse intra-societal groupings. The process of social policy evolution is also affected by, and in turn influences, a society's stage of development in cultural, economic, and technological spheres, its level of institutional complexity, its interaction with extra-societal forces, and its systems of beliefs, values, customs, and traditions.

Before presenting the derivation of a tentative analytic framework from the general model of social policy, certain core components of the model require further examination. Perhaps a good way to start these explorations is to define the terms "society," and "policies" as used in the model:

> A *society* is an aggregate of interrelated and interdependent human beings, living usually in territories over which they, collectively, hold sovereignty; a society's membership and ecological basis need not be fixed; a society functions to maintain itself, and to assure its continuity and its biological survival, while it also undergoes manifold changes over time in structure, membership, boundaries, values and functions.
>
> *Policies* are principles and courses of action adopted and pursued by established governments of societies as well as by various units within societies. They regulate or are intended to regulate specified domains of a society's, or a social unit's structure and functioning. Because of the interaction between various domains of societal structure and functioning, any policy may also affect aspects other than those with which it is primarily concerned. Policies tend to, but need not, be codified in formal legal instruments.

The model includes in social policies all policies, the primary function of which is to govern the nature of all possible sets of human relationships and to shape the quality of life or level of well-being, within a given society. The model conceptualizes all such policies as forming a single system, which means that no social policy is operating entirely independent of other social policies which constitute a given society's social policy system. However, while all social policies are conceived to be component parts of a system, the model does not view them as necessarily logically consistent with each other. On the contrary, it states specifically that internal inconsistency is a likely characteristic of social policy systems. Such internal inconsistency is, of course, a reflection of the conflicting tendencies which, as indicated above, underlie the process of social policy evolution.

The number of possible sets of human relationships within any society is likely to be large. However, they all fall within the following five reciprocal types:

individual member	individual member
individual member	social unit(s)
individual member	total society
social unit(s)	social unit(s)
social unit(s)	total society

The term "social unit" as used here refers to any type of social aggregate below the level of a total society. Policies, the primary function of which is the regulation of human relationships beyond the boundaries of a given society, do not belong to the domain of social policy as defined here, but to the domain of "foreign policy" although such policies are likely to interact with the social policy system.

Regulation of intra-societal relationships is reflected in the fact that interactions among members and units of a society are not random, but are patterned or "institutionalized," within normative, behavioral ranges. Members of a society usually know what behavior they may expect of others, and what others may expect of them in given social situations. While the regulation of behavioral ranges does not prevent all deviant behavior, it sets a framework for identifying deviance, and for patterned responses to it through mechanisms of social control. A society's system of social policy includes thus policies which facilitate normative behavior in social interaction, as well as policies geared to dealing with deviance.

"Quality of life or level of well-being" is a complex notion, the meaning of which can be grasped by way of common sense. Precise scientific definition and measurement of this concept is difficult, however, since it involves not only observable and measureable elements, but also subjective perceptions and value judgements. For purposes of analyzing effects of social policies on the quality of life or the level of well-being of members of a society, this concept will have to be represented initially by a set of social and economic indicators including:[5]

— demographic developments;
— physical and mental health and illness;
— educational and occupational achievement;
— developments in the sciences and the arts;
— production and consumption;
— wealth and income;
— conditions of housing;
— conditions of the natural environment;

— patterns of recreation;
— patterns of social participation;
— patterns of social mobility;
— social deviance and alienation.

Eventually valid and reliable indicators of subjective perceptions of the level of well-being will have to supplement measurements on these and other social and economic indicators.

Stating, as the definition does, that social policies determine the nature of all intra-societal relationships, and shape the quality of life or level of well-being of society's members, merely stakes out the domain and function of social policy systems, but does not specify through what mechanisms the regulation of these relationships and levels of well-being are accomplished. This necessary specification is contained in the operative section of the definition according to which these regulations are achieved by means of four basic societal mechanisms, the development of life-sustaining and enhancing resources, the allocation of statuses, roles and prerogatives, the distribution of rights, and the extent of linkage between the allocation of statuses and the distribution of rights. These four developmental, allocative, and distributive mechanisms are traceable to man's early collective responses to the universal characteristics of the human condition, which have been sketched above. The first mechanism—development of resources—derived from the condition of relative scarcity of life-sustaining resources available in the natural environment, and the necessity for human labor without which resources could not be procured from the environment. The second mechanism—allocation of statuses—evolved out of the principle of division of labor and the gradual stabilization of this principle through processes of social stratification.[6] The third mechanism—distribution of rights—evolved out of early mechanisms for the distribution of all life-sustaining resources, and the fourth mechanism—the extent of linkage between the distribution of rights and the allocation of statuses—originated in the time-honored principle of providing unequal rewards for incumbents of different statuses.

The major operative dimensions or variables of social policy systems appear thus to be the mechanisms of resource development, status allocation, and rights distribution; as well as the quality of interaction between these mechanisms. The possibilities for modifications in the way these mechanisms operate and in the manner of interaction between them are numerous, and correspondingly numerous are, therefore, the possible variations in social policy systems. According to the general model of social policy, each discrete social policy involves certain variations on one or more of these variables, and results in a unique configuration between them. Because of the central importance of resource development, status allocation, and rights distribution, and the quality of interaction between them, they constitute core components of the analytic framework which is being derived from the general model of social policy and which will be presented below. Some additional comments seem, however, indicated here with regard to these mechanisms and their interactions.

The first mechanism affects intra-societal relationships and the level of well-being in society by regulating the quality and quantity of all life-sustaining and enhancing resources, goods and services available to society. Since the totality of rights available for distribution to members and social units is a function of the totality of resources and services developed by a society, policy decisions concerning resource development, and priorities in that sphere, are likely to have important consequences for that distribution. Furthermore policies on resource development have a direct impact on the natural and physical environment of a society and in this way they influence the quality of life in that environment.

The second mechanism regulates the organization of the totality of tasks to be undertaken by a society, and the assignment of the society's members to these tasks. The term status as used here refers to a specific functional position within a society's array of tasks such as president, judge, soldier, farmer; thief, veteran; child, pensioner; female, father, wife, orphan, etc. The term does not refer to the prestige which tends to be linked closely with specific statuses in most societies, and which is an aspect of the rights distribution mechanism. A given individual occupies usually more than one specific status, and it is, therefore, possible to describe any individual in terms of the combination of statuses which he occupies at any given point in time, and throughout his individual career. Every society must devise mechanisms for recruiting individuals to fill the various statuses within the total array of societal tasks and functions which must be performed, and for allocating each individual to a specific combination of statuses. Some aspects of this allocative process are self-regulating as in the case of sex, life-cycle stages, and blood-relationships. Most other status allocation, however, tends to involve more complex selective criteria and processes.

The term "role" refers to the dynamic aspect of status, that is, the set of functions which the incumbent of a given status is expected to perform. It is important to note in this context that the role expectation is rarely fixed to the last detail. Rather the role defines a normative range of possible behaviors, and different incumbents of a given status will tend to interpret the role in their individual way within that range. This variability of role performance seems to be one important avenue of gradual social change. Role allocation is usually a function of status-allocation. However, occasionally the role content of given statuses may be changed during the incumbency of given individuals. In such situations the role allocation involves a certain degree of independence from the allocation of statuses.

Prerogatives are a specific type of rights which are attached to a status as a *sine-qua-non* of role performance, such as the right of a traffic policeman to stop traffic. Prerogatives are conceptually inseparable from status and role, and are thus considered to be allocated automatically along with the allocation of statuses rather than through the rights distribution mechanism. Prerogatives must be distinguished conceptually from other rights which are distributed as rewards for status incumbency or as entitlements, but which are not essential for the performance of roles. Prerogatives are, therefore, allocated through the status allocation mechanism, while all other rights including prestige are allocated through the mechanism dealing with the distribution of rights.

Summing up these comments on the status allocation mechanism and reducing them to the simplest possible terms, one may view its function as regulating the recruitment of individual members for, or their assignment to, the total array of tasks to be performed by society. This allocative mechanism is thus the "task and man-power" system of a society.

The third mechanism regulates right of access to the total array of life-sustaining and life-enhancing resources and opportunities within a society. A variety of methods are employed for this purpose—rewards, entitlements and constraints—all of which result in the distribution to every member of society and to social units of varying levels of rights to claim resources in the form of real and symbolic goods and services developed by society. Rewards are a specified level of rights provided in exchange for the performance of some role. Entitlements may be universal or categorical. They are specified levels of rights assigned by virtue of membership in a total society, or in a specified social unit. Thus, all members of society may be entitled to certain public services such as public health, education, recreation, sanitation, etc., and all children may be entitled to school meals. The boundary between rewards and entitlements is not a clear-cut and absolute one, since membership in specified social units or incumbency of certain natural statuses tends to involve certain task performance, and the entitlement may thus be interpreted as a reward in exchange for such task performance, rather than as a right by virtue of membership.

Constraints can be viewed as negative rewards or negative entitlements which take the form of limitations on the level of rights. They are an essential aspect of rights distribution since they define the limits of the rights which are distributed to members of society as rewards or entitlements. In this context one should remember that rights and freedoms in any society can never be unlimited or absolute. Constraints, like rights, tend to be distributed unequally in most societies.

In modern societies the rights to claims on resources are distributed partly indirectly through the money and market mechanisms. Specified quantities of money correspond to specified levels of rights which can easily be tranformed into a broad range of equivalent resources, goods and services.

However, a significant portion of rights, especially in the entitlement category, continues to be distributed directly, in kind.

Summarizing these comments on the rights-distribution mechanism, one could perhaps describe its function as organizing the social benefits and disbenefits.

One of the most crucial issues for social policy development, and therefore, for social policy analysis, seems to be the nature of the relationship between a society's mechanism of status allocation and its mechanism of rights distribution. Policy variations concerning this issue are reflected in varying degrees of independence between these mechanisms. Social policy systems can conceptually be classified along a continuum ranging from complete independence ($r = 0.00$) to complete dependence ($r = 1.00$).

Inequalities of status or of position in the task organization of society are an essential aspect of social organization once division of labor is adopted by a society. However, inequalities of rights are logically not an essential consequence of the division of labor. Most societies have, however, adopted the principle of inequality of rights as an apparent essential corollary of the principle of division of labor, and have institutionalized inequality of rewards for differential statuses. This situation is reflected in a high correlation between status allocation and rights distribution. It is of course entirely feasible, from a theoretical point of view, to distribute rights equally among all members of society irrespective of the different statuses they occupy, using the method of universal entitlement, rather than the method of reward for role performance. Such a principle of organization would be reflected in independence, or a near zero correlation between status allocation and rights distribution. Obviously, any intermediate level of correlation between these two systems is theoretically feasible, and could be designed in practice.

The relatively high correlation between status allocation and rights distribution, which is a dominant characteristic of most present day social policy systems, including systems of several societies which adopted socialism and communism as a political philosophy, is usually rationalized and justified by reference to, as yet insufficiently understood, concepts of incentives and human motivation. It is claimed, in axiomatic fashion, that in order to recruit personnel for the diversity of statuses in society, prospective incumbents must be attracted through incentives built into the reward system. While this may be a correct description of current human behavior it leaves several important issues unresolved. The descriptive statement that human beings are motivated to accept certain statuses by means of reward-incentives does not explain the forces underlying this behavioral response pattern, nor does it answer the question whether this response pattern is biologically given, and thus, the only possible behavioral alternative.

Without digressing into a thorough examination of this important issue, it seems nevertheless necessary to comment on it, since it is intimately linked to one proposition inherent in the model of social policy, according to which the correlation between status allocation and rights distribution is subject to significant variability as a major dimension for social policy change.

Biological, psychological, and sociological research seem to indicate that human motivation is rooted partly in biologically given factors and partly in socially learned tendencies. The relative importance of these two sets of factors is not known, but there seems to be little question that learned tendencies are a powerful aspect of human behavior. Based on these considerations, it seems that current motivation and incentive response patterns may reflect existing patterns of socialization, and that variations in socialization patterns could produce different motivational attitudes. One may, therefore, conclude that the premises which are used to justify the current system of social policy and the high built-in correlation between status allocation and rights distribution, are not fixed by nature, but are open to modification. The view that man responds primarily to the profit motive is not necessarily a correct indication of mankind's social and cultural potential.[7]

Summing up this discussion of the general model of social policy, its principal features may be restated as follows: the domain and function of social policy is the regulation of all intra-societal human relationships and the shaping of the quality of life or the level of well-being in society. This function is accomplished by regulating the development of resources, the intra-societal allocation of statuses, and distribution of rights. The degree of independence between the status allocation and rights distribution constitutes a major criterion in the analysis of alternative social policies and entire systems of social policy.

NOTES

[1]The following references are illustrative of the writings of the American and British authors referred to in this paragraph.

Schorr, Alvin L. *Explorations in Social Policy* (New York: Basic Books, Inc., 1968).

Burns, Evelyn M. "Social Policy: The Step-Child of the Curriculum," in *Proceedings, Ninth Annual Program Meeting, Council on Social Work Education* (New York: Council on Social Work Education, 1961).

Wickenden, Elizabeth. "Social Change Through Federal Legislation," in *The Social Welfare Forum* (New York: Columbia University Press, 1965).

Boulding, Kenneth E. "Boundaries of Social Policy," *Social Work,* vol. 12, no. 1, January 1967.

Rein, Martin and Marris, Peter. *Dilemmas of Social Reform* (New York: Atherton Press, 1967).

Rein, Martin. "Social Stability and Black Capitalism," *Transaction,* vol. 6, no. 7, June 1969.

Bell, Winifred. "Obstacles to Shifting from the Descriptive to the Analytic Approach

in Teaching Social Services," *Journal of Education for Social Work,* vol. 5, no. 1, Spring, 1969.
Titmuss, Richard M. *Commitment to Welfare* (New York: Pantheon Books, Division of Random House, 1968).
Townsend, Peter. "Does Selectivity Mean a Nation Divided?", in *Social Services for All?* (London: Fabian Society, 1968).
Abel-Smith, Brian "The Need for Social Planning," in *Social Services for All?* (London: Fabian Society, 1968).

[2]Boulding, Kenneth E. op. cit.

[3]Macbeath, A. *Can Social Policies by Rationally Tested?* (London: Oxford University Press, 1957).

[4]For an earlier definition see Gil, David G. "Research, A Basic Ingredient in the Study of Social Policy and Social Services," *Education for Social Work,* vol. 4, no. 1, Spring, 1968.

[5]U.S. Department of Health, Education, and Welfare, *Toward a Social Report,* (Washington D.C.: U.S. Government Printing Office, 1969).

[6]Duncan, Otis Dudley. "Social Stratification and Mobility" in *Indicators of Social Change,* Sheldon, E. B. & Moore, E. W. eds. (New York: Russell Sage, 1968).

[7]Macarov, David. *Incentives to Work* (San Francisco: Jossey-Bass, Inc., 1970).

3 Practical Policy Frameworks

It would seem that everyone who has thought about it has difficulties in establishing boundaries for examining policy. Reviewing public policy in 1970, Heclo, the political scientist, said:

> . . . Policy does not seem to be a self-defining phenomenon; it is an analytic category, the contents of which are identified by the analyst rather than by the policy-maker or pieces of legislation or administration. There is no unambiguous datum constituting policy and waiting to be discovered in the world. A policy may usefully be considered as a course of action or inaction rather than specific decisions or actions, and such a course has to be perceived by the analyst in question. . . . The study of policy . . . straddles a number of previously distinct academic disciplines. [Pp. 85-6]

But people do find convenient boundaries. Some have even become conventional. It may be useful to try to identify some of these.

Academic Frameworks for Analysis

The main distinction between academic frameworks seems to be whether they are:

1. descriptive and schematic, seeking to make patterns out of available data;
2. historically analytical, examining the causes of emergence of particular types of social structure and process; or
3. comparatively analytical, exploring effects of potential courses of action, consequences or impacts.

A Framework Based on a Single Discipline or a Multidisciplinary Approach?

It will be noted that Heclo argued the need for interdisciplinary approaches. This view was also taken by Yarmolinsky (1971) who, contrasting policy research with historical research, said the latter is conducted within a discipline which provides the historian with a generally accepted definition of his field and its subspecialties.

> The policy researcher has essentially none of these landmarks or navigational aids to rely on. Whatever discipline he has been brought up in, it is no longer the focus of his activities and interests. Indeed for some of the most effective policy researchers, their original disciplines served only to sharpen their minds and acquaint them with research methods generally, and they have since chosen a whole new set of navigational reference marks. [Pp. 197-98]

Effective at what? Yarmolinsky answers this question by listing five activities: trend measurement, policy choice, programme development, trouble-shooting and evaluation.

In discussing the study of policy, were Heclo and Yarmolinsky discussing the same activity? It seems not, for Heclo considered the value of case studies, described programmatic research and ended by saying that he thought policy studies were likely to make the most progress through developing greater understanding of the networks of interaction by which policies result. He recommended that policy researchers should take a perspective which viewed policy in terms of learning and adaptation in political life.

Yarmolinsky's approach and that of the programmatic researchers described by Heclo is not directed at the identification of causes or processes of decision making but at the investigation of future trends or alternative solutions to problems or the correction of present courses of action through evaluation and feedback. Both the intentions and frameworks differ, but because the word policy is used to describe both, confusions are likely to arise. By limiting his definition of policy to *impacts,* Yarmolinsky does not resolve the difficulties. It is useful to note, however, that American analysts tend to be more concerned with impacts, whilst British analysts have often concentrated on examining causes. Heclo, taking an international perspective, identified a wider range of approaches than Yarmolinsky, but still did not include the kind of social historical studies of policy making which are commonly adopted by English analysts.

The main distinction between one type of analysis and another is whether the analyst decides to rely upon a single discipline or, as Yarmolinsky proposed, to take an interdisciplinary approach.

The analyst of causes or structures or processes may find that he is well supported in his work by choosing the framework of an established discipline or one subsection of a discipline such as history, economics, sociology or social psychology. Bailey (1975), reviewing sociological theory for planning, has indicated that that discipline provides a rich choice of approaches. The readings following the chapters in this book will show examples of many of these different sociological approaches which have provided frameworks for different analysts—social change and evolutionary theory, systems theory, conflict theory and so on. As yet, some of these theoretical approaches may not have been sufficiently well developed to sustain an analysis in its totality. Mechanic (1976), who had used organization theory for his national studies of health services, complained that the development of interorganization theory was not yet advanced enough to cope with international comparisons of health care systems.

The analyst of policy alternatives may find that reliance on only one of the basic social sciences may not offer a sufficiently broad support for his researches (though economists may be heavily involved in impact-type research). It is for this reason that departments of applied social sciences such as political science and university business schools have developed. Health planning is being taught in emergent cross-disciplinary programs based on epidemiology, economics and organization theory. The products of these departments are less likely to ask why than how, and many are planning to go into government departments, business or social service organizations. But there is obvious need for many different kinds of analysis. On the following pages, figures 3–1 and 3–2 show available options in choosing disciplines and applications.

Descriptive/Schematic Analysis

Boulding's (1967), Gil's (1970) and De Miguel's (1975) frameworks are examples of descriptive/schematic analysis, so this chapter will be more concerned with causal and consequential approaches. However, one other useful schematic framework is that of Tropman and Vasey (1976), who were writing for American social work students. They tried to come up with an action framework so that their readers could decide where they could best have an input into policy making. The authors recommended that the policy maker who wished to make change should become involved in resource allocation, but they identified four other levels of analytic interest, namely, philosophy, ideology, scientific analysis "looking for the right answers" and backroom planning and suggested that many policy makers did not analyze at all, but were surprised when they had to take decisions.

In the final chapter (14), yet another schematic analysis is presented—that of development, organization and distribution of knowledge (Holzner and Marx, 1979).

FIGURE 3–1
Matrix Showing Approaches to Social Science Investigations

Philosophical and Ideological bases of study

Disciplines

Philosophical/Ideological Orientations	Anthropology	Sociology	Demography Epidemiology	Psychology	Economics
Political Science a) Study of Politics b) Study of Public Policies					
Commerce and Business Administration					
Social Policy and Social Administration					
Community and Regional Planning Social Work Training					
Health Services Administration					

See development in Figure 3–2.

FIGURE 3–2

THE TEACHING OF SOCIAL SCIENCE TO STUDENTS OF HEALTH CARE (available options)

Philosophical Orientations
The Basic Disciplines

		Physics	Chemistry	Biology	Anthrop.	Sociology	Psychology	Economics	Etc.
Political Science	Political science					political behavior			
	Policy					political policy development ———			
	Public Admin.					public administration ———			
Business Admin	Business science					organizational behaviour			
	Corporate policy					Health services ———			
	Admin. & Management					and Hospital Management ———			
Social/ policy admin. work	Social Science				medical anthropology	medical socilogy			
	Social policy					health and social service dev.		health and social service dev.	
	Public/ social admin.					health and social service organization		health and social service organization	
Health Care	Medicine/ hygiene			Epid. method.		organizational behaviour			
	Health policy			Planning	3rd wrld. policies	Health policy planning		Health economics	
	Health Admin.			Program Evaluation Clerkships	clerkships	Program Evaluation clerkships	Personnel Management clerkships	Program Evaluation clerkships	
Etc.									

It is suggested that 3 distinctive levels of education are emerging in professional schools: the scientific, the policy analysis level and the administrative skills levels.

CAUSAL RESEARCH

Those who are interested in philosophical and ideological or normative questions tend to be particularly interested in causal research. For example, Titmuss (1971) asked and answered the question why the organizations for the banking of blood differed in Britain and the U.S. by studying the different structures which had grown up and interpreting their growth in terms of national ideologies and the "theme of the gift." Much earlier, Tawney (1964) in *Religion and the Rise of Capitalism,* had described the development of the protestant ethic, a concept which Titmuss built upon in his study. Tawney traced the development of the complete change of attitudes in England which occurred after the Civil War, the Commonwealth and the Restoration in 1660, as Puritanism took over:

> The idea of economic progress as an end to be consciously sought, while ever receding, had been unfamiliar to most earlier generations of Englishmen in which the theme of moralists had been the danger of unbridled cupidity and the main aim of public policy had been the stability of traditional relationships. [The Englishman] found a new sanction in the identification of labour and enterprise with the service of God. The magnificent energy which changed in a century the face of material civilization was to draw nourishment from that temper. The worship of production and even greater production—the slavish drudgery of the millionaire and his unhappy servants—was to be hallowed by the precepts of the same compelling creed. [Pp. 247-48].

It was not until 1760 that the astonishing outburst of industrial activity took place which was the beginning of the industrial revolution. But English-speaking a societies were ready to move forward into this new era of resource development through commercial and industrial endeavour because of the development of the Protestant ethic in England in the previous century. It was not until much later that questions began to be raised about the effect of such developments upon English social relationships. These had been torn out of their traditional moulds and changed from solidary community relationships to those of a mass society. (For further discussion, see chapter 4.)

Another who has argued that historical analysis will increase understanding of western countries' social organization is Abel-Smith (1972), who has said that it is essential to appreciate nineteenth-century policies for dealing with poverty in order to understand why present day health service structures have developed as they have. It is not only Europeans who are interested in this kind of historical interpretation. Piven and Cloward (1971) have discussed the development of American legislation dealing with poverty in terms of social regulation of the "dangerous classes."

However, there are other disciplinary approaches in addition to the historians' analyses. Parsons (1952) and Freidson (1970) took sociologists' stances in examining the causes of present medical services organization within western societies. Their two different interpretations are summarized by the Ehrenreichs (1974).

The work of physicians in tracking down the causes of disease in society cannot be ignored. This has been an entirely different approach from the historians' or the sociologists' as it has been concerned more with the biomedical aspects of response to disease or disability. The gap between biomedical and social explanations of causes is beginning to be bridged by planner epidemiologists who, at one time, were mainly concerned with explaining the social patterns in the spread of infectious diseases or in examining the distribution of diseases across populations. They are now getting more involved in health planning because the questions arising out of their studies of disease distribution are political—are these disease distribution patterns a reflection of the outcomes which societies want? What are the causes of the present health status profiles which are emerging (McKeown, 1975)?

Consequential or Programmatic or Impact Research

These questions lead epidemiologists into consequential research, which seems more useful, these days, for practical guidance to governments. Biostatisticians and economists are also particularly active in this area. It may be helpful now to cite some examples of their work. Questions have arisen about the use of Pap tests for prevention of cervical cancer—when should these tests be given and what should be the expected results of a controlled programme (Knox, 1979)? Should multiphasic screening be funded by governments in order to improve early detection of disease (Pole, 1971; Australian National Health and Medical Research Council, 1972)? Is the introduction of a mammography likely to be useful in the early detection of breast cancer (Greenberg, 1976)? What kind of a dental program for children might there be developed in the Canadian provinces (Evans and Williamson, 1978)?

Whilst these are all difficult political questions for which rational answers are being sought, even larger issues need resolution such as the question of introducing a national health insurance scheme into the U.S.A. Is there any comparative experience in other countries which could provide useful guidelines to decision makers (Rein, 1976; Andreopoulos, 1975)? Heidenheimer et al. (1976) have discussed when it may be suitable to borrow concepts from other countries' experience and when they will be unlikely to work.

Inputs, Structures, Processes, Outputs/Outcomes

Whilst some analysts are concerned with looking at the whole cycle of policy development, others concentrate on one aspect as seeming most likely to yield results when exposed to their particular skills in analysis. So they are supportive of the approach suggested by Donabedian (1967), who said that in order to evaluate the provision of quality care, it might be useful to break down the policy cycle into its component parts: inputs, structures, processes, outputs or outcomes, for without such as analysis, it would be harder to identify factors in need of correction.

For some analysts the most important point in the policy cycle is the categorizing or labelling of *inputs.* Should the clients of a service be categorized by age or sex? By disease? By other types of social needs which deviate from the normal? Or should those who seek help be categorized by available types of service, such as often happens in institutional care where different levels of staffing meet different levels of need? In Saskatchewan (1969) six levels were identified, viz:

> Level I Care: Essentially independent but may need some guidance or supervision in the activities of daily living. . . .
> Level II Care: Supervision and assistance may be needed with personal hygiene and grooming. . . .
> Level III Care: All degrees of supervision and assistance may be needed in the activities of daily living. . . .
> Level IV Care: All patient care is carried out under continuing medical supervision and all nursing care is carried out under professional supervision. . . .
> Level V Care: Intended for persons with physical disabilities who require aggressive rehabilitation by a team of rehabilitation personnel to restore or improve function. . . .
> Level VI Care: Intended for persons requiring 24-hour medical/nursing supervision for emergency, diagnostic, obstetric, psychiatric, or surgical services. . . .

Warham (1974) has demonstrated that the same people may be classified in many different ways. Consequently, it is important to be clear about the principles underlying classification. This point is made in a different way by Gove (1975), who has presented a critique of the labelling of deviance, demonstrating how labelling may have negative effects for individuals. This stigmatization of the disabled or mentally ill has concerned many reseachers (e.g., Goffman, 1963). A study of the labelling of the mentally retarded in California by Mercer (1973) distinguishes between labelling directed towards solving individuals' problems and labelling devised by professionals anxious to find a method of disposing of difficult cases. And different professional groups may label differently. In reading reports by government departments, it is necessary occasionally to consider how much is hidden by language in this area. A report on Organized Community Health Services (Canada, 1966) reviewed rehabilitation services. Some provinces claimed that they had rehabilitation officers who were engaged in casefinding. At a quick glance, this gives the impression of an intensive search for those in need of help. In reality, however, it meant that the rehabilitation officers were more aware of the availability of scattered facilities and found suitable cases to fill slots in them.

Other analysts are interested in the effects (not the causes) of *structures.* Beckhard (1972) demonstrated the importance of structure for the delivery of community health services by comparing the traditional hospital organization and a new health care teamwork organization which had been developed in the Bronx. Brunet and Vinet (1978) examined the development of Community Health and Social Service Centres in Quebec and discovered that, despite efforts to develop strong community participation, all quickly reverted to professionally dominated organizations.

Hall (1977) described and analyzed the *process* of reforming welfare in England in an account of the way in which social workers were determined to become independent professionals with their own separate brand of learning, ethics and association and their own structures of organization. Hall's description of their leaders' actions in attaining this separation from other professional groups (including medical domination) is an interesting process analysis.

In other process studies, Laframboise (1973) and Klein (1974) looked at successful penetration of new initiatives into established systems. Laframboise was the architect of the Lalonde Report described in the introduction—the new expression of values about health as a basis for Canadian policy. His methods for persuading ministers and civil servants to adopt policies are described in a reading attached to chapter 13.

Klein, writing as an observer of the British scene, explained how difficult it is to make a disjunction in the incrementalism of policy development. He has been particularly interested in scandals, used by the public to force government to take notice and to make change, but which depend upon the climate being right.

The concept of examining policy *impacts (outcomes)* rather than intended *outputs* is explained by Cook and Scioli (1975), both academics concerned with the practical questions of applying research to short-term policy making. This orientation will be considered further in Coleman's paper attached to chapter 12.

The greatest emphasis an *outcome* measures occurs in epidemiological studies, though economists are also involved in this activity. Some of these have already been mentioned in the general discussion of consequential research, i.e., validation of PAP smear tests, multiphasic screening, mammograms, etc. Other work has been done by the McMaster University group on the use of nurse practitioners (Sackett et al. 1974; see references, chap. 13).

The most amusing exposition of this approach is that of Cochrane's *Efficiency and Effectiveness* (1972) in which he reviewed some studies made by epidemiologists for the British NHS on comparative methods of treatment of particular diseases.

The Blind Men and the Elephant

Klein has argued that no one has yet accepted a framework of analysis useful for understanding all aspects of policy making. Suggesting that different analytic concepts help to illuminate different aspects of policy making, he has illustrated his argument by choosing examples of policy development in the British NHS and applying three different theoretical schemes for their elucidation—elitist theory, pluralistic bargaining and incrementalism (see respectively chapters 4, 6 and 2 for further discussion of these theories).

In taking this approach, he was influenced by the work of Allison (1969), who examined U.S. government reactions to the Cuban Missile Crisis from three different standpoints—which he called the rational policy paradigm, the organizational process paradigm and the bureaucratic politics paradigm. He argued that interpretations of what went on in the decision making about that crisis could be set in one or the other of these frameworks and the conclusions drawn would be quite different because different kinds of evidence would be found to support the three analytic stances. In the rational policy paradigm, Allison said, "Governments select the action that will maximize strategic goals and objectives. These 'solutions' to strategic problems are the fundamental categories in terms of which the analyst perceives what is to be explained" (p. 694). In the organizational process paradigm,

> Governments perceive problems through organizational sensors. Governments define alternatives and estimate consequences as organizations process information. Governments act as these organizations enact routines. Government behavior can therefore be understood . . . less as deliberate choices of leaders and more as *outputs* of large organizations functioning according to standard patterns of behavior. [P. 698]

In the bureaucratic politics paradigm it has to be understood that

> The leaders who sit on top of organizations are not a monolithic group. Rather, each is, in his own right, a player in a central competitive game. The name of the game is bureaucratic politics: bargaining along regularized channels among players positioned hierarchically within the government. Government behavior can thus be understood . . . not as organizational outputs, but as outcomes of bargaining games . . . making government decisions not by rational choice but by the pulling and hauling that is politics. [P. 707]

Also using Allison's different stances as a model, Marmor (1970) reviewed the U.S. medicare crisis. He concluded that it was useful to apply these analytic paradigms sequentially—that is, the rational actor model was most helpful in explaining the origins of the medicare issue, the organizational process model in explaining what happened to the rational arguments during the period of discussion and consideration before legislation was passed (the legitimation period, as Hall et al. (1975) have called it) and the bureaucratic politics model in explaining the outcomes of the bargaining games to get the legislation passed and made feasible for implementation.

Klein, Allison and Marmor stand back and take the view of detached analysts anxious to find frames of inference. On the other hand, Alford (1972) was interested in what happens when an action group takes as its frame of inference one particular paradigm and bases its actions upon its beliefs in that paradigm. He considered the reasons for failure to reach agreement on the development of health services for the city of New York, concluding that three groups of participants were basing their actions on different ideologies and interests. He designated their perspectives those of "corporate rationalizers," "professional monopolists" and "equal health advocates." He argued that they were able to pursue their special interests because

> Little systematic knowledge exists about the ways in which the present system works or the alternatives that might be feasible. Not only are basic descriptive data scarce, but relevant research on the system as a whole has not been done. [P. 239] Different perspectives—pluralist, bureaucratic and class—on the possibility of health care reform are based on competing theories of the causes of the "crisis" in health care and, thus, alternative paths to reform. [P. 249]

Value-Free or Value-Laden Studies

In the 1950s, when strenuous efforts were being made to harden up the social sciences and make them as strong as the physical sciences in providing rational guidance to policy makers, many social scientists discussed the possibility of doing value-free research. It soon became clear that it was not possible to take this stance, that the social sciences deal with normative issues, not the "absolutes" of physical laws, as will be further discussed in chapters 6 and 14. However, since it is necessary to draw attention to it here, the following references may be reviewed (Benn and Peters, 1959; Kuhn, 1962; Pinker, 1971; Rein, 1976). The value-laden nature of studies of society (including health studies) means that what is selected for study is usually chosen because of the interest of individuals motivated to explore a particular subject or because of the funding of particular topic areas by governments and other financing bodies.

Coming full circle back to the start of this chapter, not only is there no unambiguous datum, there is no unambiguous way of analysing the data we do possess. Even the hardest of data relative to medical care, that about biomedical processes, is interpreted by Freidson (1970) as imputed by doctors.

If the ground is so shaky, is this a good reason for "muddling through," for taking a completely laissez-faire position in policy making? Most policy analysts would not think so. It may not be possible to realize the American Dream in all its complexities or to achieve complete social justice in Britain, but these are goals which have been pursued in these societies—goals which seem more worthwhile in recognition of the social contract between members of a society than complete free-for-all cutthroat competition or living at a medieval subsistence level. In order to achieve social goals, policy guidelines are required and policy processes need to be understood. Normative (i.e., value-laden) scientific interpretations seem to be better than no interpretations at all.

This book continues with an examination of some of these normative interpretations. That it is selective has always to be remembered. The interpretations apply to the four English-speaking liberal democracies unless specifically distinguished as belonging to one nation only, but they are unlikely to be valid in all other cultural settings because they have emerged out of one closely related set of traditions developed in sixteenth- and seventeenth-century England.

Discussion of the Readings and References

It is difficult to select a few readings to illustrate the wide range of policy frameworks discussed in this chapter; consequently, students will need to read reference material as well as the few selected reprints if they are to become aware of the many different approaches. What has been selected for reprinting not only illustrates frameworks but also raises broader questions discussed in other chapters.

The limited usefulness of Boulding's and Gil's frameworks was discussed at the end of the previous chapter. So it is with all frameworks. As De Miguel has pointed out, at the macro level of the scale there are too many variables to be comprehended and managed, at the micro end, too few to be of much use. His suggestion was that researchers should attempt to develop understanding at the micro-macro or middle-range level, and this has also been proposed by Merton (1957) and his followers, who have discussed the need for middle-range theories.

This chapter has explored a wide range of middle range paradigms which may be helpful to policy analysts working in different settings, for considering different stages of policy development.

1. There is a basic ideological difference between the approaches of the Marxists, exemplified by Navarro (1977) and the systems theorists, exemplified by Parsons (1952). Most of the frameworks considered in this book are broadly based upon Parsonian functionalist theory rather than the conflict

theory of Marx (though some radical analysts have attempted to reconcile the two approaches).

2. In order to try to bring some order into the many different systems approaches it may be useful to begin by considering De Miguel's eleven levels in the system of health care (see chapter 1 for this listing). Taking De Miguel's four subheadings: larger systems, society, institutions and individuals, the following readings can be recommended. At the larger systems level are Dr. Halfdan Mahler's annual reports (e.g., WHO, 1979). As Director-General of the World Health Organization, Mahler has been concerned with the health of the world at large, the health of all societies rather than one society. He has been anxious to develop a response among all nations to their wider environment, a concern for the world as a whole and not just their own ethnocentric problems. And the national figures on health outcomes published in WHO annual reports provide a basis for international comparisons of achievement of health standards.

At the next level, "Can the U.S. Learn from Canada?" was the title of a paper by Theodore Marmor [not reprinted here] which summarized a conference (reported by Andreopoulos, 1975) on the broad consequences of introducing a national health insurance scheme into Canada. This may provide a useful example of one nation's health policy-making activities.

Richard Beckhard examined policy making in one health service institution, the Martin Luther King Center, as a prototype of U.S. community health centre development. He laid special emphasis on structural factors in his analysis of "Organizational Issues in the Team Delivery of Comprehensive Health Care." This is also recommended as a model of structural analysis.

At the individual level, Jane Mercer has been concerned with health status issues in *Labelling the Mentally Retarded* and she has focussed upon inputs into the system of care and the policy implications of the labelling process.

3. Another way of analyzing levels of policy analysis is presented in chapter 10 in figure 10-2. This figure (which bears some relation to Tropman and Vasey's (1976) concept of levels of policy making) proposes seven types of policy analysis: philosophical, ideological, political, administrative, program development and evaluation, service delivery issues, and client involvement in policy making.

Beginning with philosophy, George Macbeath's (1957) approach to policy analysis seems to be the most frequently quoted (e.g., by Gil). Macbeath said "Social policies are the right ordering of social relationships between men and women who live together in societies, or with the principles which should govern the activities of individuals and groups so far as they affect the lives and interests of other people."

At the ideological level, Richard M. Titmuss has distinguished three western democratic societies' ideological approaches in his book on *Social*

Policy. These are discussed more fully in chapter 7.

Theodore Marmor's "Medicare: Social Policy and American Politics" (reprinted after this chapter) is concerned with the political policy making level. So is Rudolf Klein's "Policy Problems and Policy Perceptions in the National Health Service," also reprinted here (pp. 98–108).

For an example of administrative policy making: Hubert L. Laframboise's article "Moving a Proposal to a Positive Decision," which follows chapter 13, is concerned with the administrative processes of introducing a new policy into Canada. Phoebe Hall's book, *Reforming the Welfare,* is a much more comprehensive analysis of the introduction of a new administrative policy, relating to delivery of personal social services, into England.

At the program level, most institutions have policy manuals explaining the rules and regulations which have been agreed. But policies may appear in many other forms, such as clauses in union contracts, departmental budgets or even conventions about the use of cafeteria tables by different groups of workers. In the last few years the concept of program evaluation has become popular. A discussion of program evaluation in the NHS by Cochrane (1972) has raised questions about policy choices which are more (or less) efficient and effective at this level.

At the service level, where policies have to be translated into operational terms, the interstitial role of professionals or administrators who have to meet clients' demands have been considered both subjectively and objectively by a number of writers. To take one example, a particular problem at this level is how to ration professional time—this was usefully discussed by R.A. Parker in "Social Administration and Scarcity: The Problem of Rationing" in terms of social workers' behaviour, but the analysis could be applied to any service delivery group.

Finally, clients as individuals and as groups making demands on the health system are considered at many points in this book, but attached to chapter 5 is Aaron Wildavsky's discussion of "Doing Better and Feeling Worse" and attached to chapter 11 is a part of R. H. S. Crossman's lecture on "A Politician's View of Health Service Planning." Both of these are concerned with clients' impact, or lack of impact, on policy development—how consumers' ideas are fed back into the system.

4. Reprinted after chapter 12 is part of Avedis Donabedian's classic article on how to set about "Evaluating the Quality of Health Care" using a systems approach. He has suggested the importance of conceptualizing the stages of input—structure—process—output. It will be noted that some of the above readings deal particularly with one or other of these stages. Thus, Mercer stressed the importance of inputs, Beckhard of structures, Laframboise, Hall, Marmor and Klein have discussed processes and Cook and Scioli and Coleman focus upon outcomes (or impacts).

5. Another discussion in this chapter is concerned with the choice of disci-

plinary versus interdisciplinary approaches to policy analysis. Adam Yarmolinsky's discussion of historical (causal) and policy analysis (impact) research in his article on "The Policy Researcher" may help students to recognize these two different approaches to the examination of policy and reading of this reference is strongly recommended (not reprinted here). Hugh Heclo, in a review of policy analysis by political scientists up to 1970, also made this distinction. He thought that more progress has been made in interpreting frameworks of political structures and processes than frameworks for policy analysis. The analysts had been able to establish some acceptable paradigms to explain the functioning of the political system (e.g., Lowi's (1964) classification of government activities into distributive, regulative and redistributive actions) but the paradigms for analyzing cases or even programs were not then well developed. Since then, more work has been done.

Attached to this chapter is Brian Abel-Smith's chapter comparing the development of health services across a range of countries. It is not only a presentation of a causal analysis using history as a basic discipline, but rests on Richard Titmuss' ideological paradigm (discussed in chapter 7). Because it makes this bridge, it is an important reading. Equally, Thomas McKeown's paper (chapter 1) is more than descriptive history. It is also an epidemiological causal analysis of community health and disease.

Within each discipline there are a whole series of schools, and the analyst who chooses to work from a disciplinary base will likely need to select a particular theoretical way of examining the problems. Joe Bailey's book *Sociological Theory for Planning* (1975) seems to provide a quick means of reviewing the different theoretical approaches developed in that one discipline which might be used for finding paradigms relevant to policy making. The contents list in his book may provide a check list for those who read sociology in their degrees and may encourage others to explore sociological approaches. Similarly, there are different schools or orientations in economics, in history, in epidemiology and so on. One of the problems about taking a strict disciplinary approach may be in the communication of findings to others (see chapter 12).

6. It is argued by James Coleman (see chapter 12) and others, including Yarmolinsky, that policy analysts concerned with impacts should not confine themselves to one disciplinary approach, but should be eclectic, pragmatic and in touch with day-to-day decision making, otherwise their contribution will be too little and too late. These writers were concerned with policy evaluation in the U.S. context. Howard Glennerster in *Social Service Budgets and Social Policy* (1975) compared American and British processes of policy development, concluding that Americans evaluated and corrected whilst the British planned, implemented and corrected but did not evaluate before correcting. Correction followed expression of the general will for

change rather than scientific investigation and feedback. But Coleman and others have proposed a modified scientific methodology for evaluation. This is discussed in chapters 11, 12 and 13.

We are left with the conclusion that policy analysis can be many things to many men and varies from place to place and level to level of the system.

Is it worth doing? Subsequent chapters of this book attempt to show why it should be done.

The History of Medical Care

Brian Abel-Smith

There are extraordinarily few countries in the world where there has been less public control in the medical care market than in the United States. The phrase "public control" as distinct from "public regulation" is used here to cover two separate developments. The first is the ownership of medical care facilities by public authorities. The second is the use of tax or compulsory insurance financing.

Data collected by WHO shows the pattern of ownership of hospital facilities in different countries of the world. Though there may be occasional exceptions, I am confident that the data from Africa, Asia, Australasia and Europe as a whole will show that well over half the hospital beds for the physically sick are publicly owned. Among the high-income countries of Europe, with which the United States can most readily be compared, only the Netherlands has less than half its beds (about 30 per cent) owned by public authorities. While public authorities in the United States pay for the bulk of mental hospitals and offer services to the armed forces, veterans, Presidents and other categories, there is no compulsory health insurance. The vast majority of other high-income countries have some form of compulsory health insurance, and taxation pays for a considerable proportion, and usually a majority, of medical care services in the United Kingdom, Scandinavia, Eastern Europe, Africa and south-east Asia.

Why are the patterns of financing and organizing medical care services so different in the United States from those in other countries? It is only in recent years that this question has begun to be studied. And the answer is

---

Chapter 8 from *Comparative Development in Social Welfare,* E. W. Martin, ed. (London: George Allen & Unwin, 1972), pp. 219-39, reprinted with permission of the publishers.

beginning to emerge from detailed studies of the history of medical care organization. Most of my examples are drawn from high-income countries (particularly those in Europe) as it is thought that this experience is most relevant to the problems now facing the United States.

The philosophies which underlie systems of medical care organization cannot be understood without a knowledge of the history both of medical care and of wider social and political developments in each country. There is a danger of attributing systems of medical care organization to political ideologies of relatively recent origin—particularly to socialism or communism. Such notions can be dispelled only by a careful study of developments during the past two centuries and even earlier. This point can be made most forcibly by giving four quotations. They come from the same book.

> The majority of the population in England consider it not only not a disgrace, but the most natural thing in the world, when they fall ill, to demand and receive free treatment without question or delay.[1]
>
> Americans hold rightly that no person is entitled to occupy a free bed unless or until he can prove beyond dispute that he is unable to pay something for the treatment he receives in the hospital ward.[2]
>
> There is relatively little free medical relief anywhere in America.[3]
>
> The entire hospital system in Russia is now under the control of the State and municipal corporations.[4]

The quotations seem platitudinous until the date of publication is appreciated. They all come from a book published in 1893.

When comparing the history of medical care in the United States with that of Europe, it should be appreciated that for centuries it has been regarded as a public responsibility in Europe to make provision for the sick poor. And poverty has been interpreted generously. Just as the poor needed schools, so it was believed, to an extent varying in different countries and at different times, that the poor needed hospitals and medical care. In medieval Europe provisions were made by the Catholic Church. But gradually, or suddenly in the case of the French Revolution, many continental hospitals were transferred into the hands of public authorities either because of mismanagement, misappropriation of funds, or just the absence of adequate financial backing.[5] In both Denmark and Sweden it had by 1870 been made the duty of local authorities to provide hospitals.[6] Thus, in Scandinavia, the hospital services grew up almost entirely as a public service like the education service in the United States. In Britain up to 1948 charitable bodies provided the more costly acute hospitals, but this private sector was supplemented by public provision for the mentally ill, the chronic sick and cases of infectious disease. And where provision for the acute sick by charitable effort was inadequate to provide for all who needed care, the acute sector of hospital care was, from 1870 onwards, gradually supplemented by public authorities. For over a century the majority of the physically sick in institutional care in Britain have been in publicly owned institutions.[7]

Both charity and public authority hospitals set out to provide a service to the public—but mainly to the low-income public. The criterion for admission was medical need. The question of payment was not normally raised until after the patient had been admitted. If figures were available, I suggest that they would show that patient's direct payments unaided by insurance, have never contributed much to the running costs of European hospitals. In Britain, it was not until 1881 that any major hospital accommodated any paying patients at all. And even in 1938, paying patients were substantially less than 5 per cent of all hospital patients. In America hospitals have tended to be run on different lines. In 1893 Burdett reported that the majority of hospital beds were occupied by paying patients and that the managers would authorize a stated number of beds for the use of free patients, and this number could not be exceeded.[8]

The extensive development of public hospitals in Europe treating poor persons who made little or no payment for their care led to the employment of physicians on a whole-time or part-time salaried basis to look after them. Patients who had no physician could not be expected to be treated by their own physician when they entered hospital. Thus there emerged a separate class of hospital-based physicians who had every opportunity to specialize. This system became established before medical professions were effectively organized. And in the early days, few of the hospital patients could have paid much for any sort of medical services.

In Britain, the division between physicians working in the main voluntary hospitals and physicians working outside corresponded with an ancient class distinction within the medical profession. Similar traditional distinctions can be found in France, Sweden and Italy. While in the United States all purpose doctors preceded specialist doctors, in Britain specialists in the form of internists and surgeons preceded the emergence of general practioners out of the class of apothecary-tradesmen.

Indeed, I imagine that physician emigrants to the United States up to 1900 and beyond almost entirely consisted of general practitioners rather than the higher class of specialist. In Britain, the latter had a university education—an advantage not shared by general practitioners until much later. The internists and surgeons also charged much higher fees. It was this group of physicians who obtained a virtual monopoly of the principal hospital appointments. Having acquired it so early, the internists and surgeons have retained their hold over appointments in the principal hospitals in Britain. In the voluntary hospital days they did their work for virtually no direct payment, supporting themselves by private consultations, for which they charged about ten times more than a general practitioner. This system of charging and the etiquette of cases being referred by general practitioners to specialists helped to preserve a fairly sharp distinction between specialists and general practitioners in the main towns.[9] It also meant that specialist services to those who were not wealthy have been given at hospital departments where no payment is made to the doctor.

It was not only free hospital care which was made available to the poor, almost as a right. As part of the development of "poor law" or public assistance services, doctors were paid to give medical care to the poor either on a part-time or whole-time salaried basis. Such care was provided in London in dispensaries in the nineteenth century. Similarly, salaried doctors were employed to work in the outlying parts of Sweden, Norway and Switzerland. In the poorer parts of Europe at the end of the nineteenth century, salaried community doctors were engaged on a considerable scale to supervise the public health and give medical services to the poor. The system was extensively used in Poland and, similarly, "zemstvo" doctors were employed in the rural communities of Tzarist Russia.[10] Such doctors were often based upon dispensaries or polyclinics—a natural corollary of their salaried status. And extensive use of home visiting would have been wasteful of scarce doctors' time. The polyclinic system was extended by the Russians after the communist revolution under their system of compulsory insurance.[11] It was similarly used in neighbouring Poland and Czechoslovakia,[12] which were not under communist domination. The Eastern European system of polyclinics was adopted in the sick fund started by the Jewish immigrants to Palestine. It is still used in Israel today.

Thus, in Europe, salaried physicians were paid by government authorities to give service to the poor both in hospitals and dispensaries. When Europeans developed colonies in the even poorer countries of Asia and Africa, they introduced the same system. Originally the services were for the colonists themselves. In the same way as armed forces take with them their own medical services, so did the colonial services. But these services were gradually extended for the use of the local population, before and after independence. The physicians were paid by salary. These services were supplemented in some countries (e.g. India) by indigenous charitable effort and in all countries by medical missionaries. Thus, the low-income countries have developed a high proportion of publicly owned hospitals and salaried physicians.

Thus, government and charity played a much larger role, and indeed a different role, outside the United States, and this role was affected by the pattern of development of the medical and allied professions. In Europe, home-nursing services grew up alongside home medical services. For example, district nursing was organized as a charitable movement in Britain from 1859[13] and in time came to be heavily subsidized by or transferred to local authorities. Obstetric nursing developed in Britain, the Netherlands, France, Belgium[14] and some other countries as a separate independent profession which still takes a major responsibility for normal home confinements in Britain and the Netherlands. The experience of the United States has been different in this respect.

In the United States, provisions by public authorities for both the poor as a whole and for the sick poor in particular have tended to be less developed than in Europe. Several reasons can be suggested for this. First, the "poor" were often Negroes and new immigrants with whose needs older white settlers did not readily identify. Secondly, until relatively recently, land was available where it was thought the "poor" could settle and make a living. Thirdly, unmet need is more obvious in the large urban communities of a heavily industrialized nation: the latter were a later development in the United States than in Europe. Fourthly, there were many fewer hospital beds in nineteenth century America than in Europe and the general standard of medical care was lower. As few people received good medical care, it is not surprising that little was done for the poor. And finally, the more developed European countries (with the possible exception of France) developed strong working-class movements which became an important political force. Such a force came much later in the United States and has never been of the same character as in Europe.

It was the working-class movements, developing often out of earlier guilds, which pioneered the voluntary insurance movement out of which compulsory insurance was later to develop. In 1804, about thirty years before the British Medical Association was founded, there were about a million members of friendly societies in Britain, though systematic information about their activities in the health insurance field is not available. By 1900, there were, in Britain, seven million members of friendly societies—most of them entitled to invalidity cash benefits, the services of a doctor and the drugs he prescribed. The voluntary sickness insurance movement was also developed extensively in the Netherlands, Germany, Austria, Switzerland and Scandinavia during the nineteenth century. In the earlier schemes, it was common for physicians to be paid by capitation or salary as this simplified budgeting and administration for these somewhat amateur organizations which depended, during their early years at least, on the voluntary work undertaken by the members.

In Britain and Scandinavia,[15] the sickness insurance movement was primarily a movement run by consumers for their mutual benefit. In Britain it was a general and local working-class movement among the more skilled. Contributions were the same for all, though there were variations according to benefits provided. In Holland, Austria and Germany, it had more of an occupational basis. It was promoted in Germany by paternalist employers, and benefits were often related to wages. In some countries, prepayment systems were developed by individual physicians among their patients as a means of restricting the number of bad debts. This system of "provider-sponsored" pre-payment was to be found in the Netherlands, in Spain[16] and among middle-class patients in Britain, but consumer-sponsored prepayment was by far the larger sector.

The voluntary health insurance societies generally provided service benefits. In Sweden and France, however, benefits were mostly or exclusively given in cash. Thus, in many countries the consumers of medical care came to be organized before the physicians were effectively organized and they were in a position to dictate the terms of service of physicians who were engaged to provide services. There were many aspects of these terms of service which caused resentment among the physicians. The societies tended to appoint some physicians and not others to work for the fund: this damaged the practices of those excluded. Disciplinary matters were handled by lay committees which thus decided professional matters. And, finally, the level of remuneration fixed by the societies was held to be grossly inadequate. The societies were exploiting their quasimonopolistic position in each area. The resentment of doctors led to the development of medical organizations whose main activity was to fight the societies.[17]

The insurance of doctors' services came to Europe before hospital insurance. This was partly because hospitalization was much rarer than it is today and partly because both charity and public hospitals adjusted charges to means, thus making insurance unnecessary. The insurers adopted capitation and salary systems of paying doctors, whatever their advantages or disadvantages for securing good medical care, because they had the overwhelming advantage of enabling them to control and predict their expenditures. It was not long before this system of voluntary insurance was made compulsory for certain sections of the population. When legislation of this kind was passed in Germany, in 1883, and Britain, in 1911, it involved the extension of an existing system rather than the creation of a new one. It also brought the government into the disputes, which continued concerning levels and methods of remuneration, the control of medical services and other matters.

Often, the providers of services could persuade the government to force upon the insurers changes which they had refused to accept before they worked within a statutory framework.

In Germany, the administration of compulsory health insurance was left in the hands of local sick funds, and there were major protests from doctors about the "closed panel" restrictions extensively operated by them. Opposition was directed also at the capitation and salary systems of payment which were associated with the "closed panels." The universalization of fee-for-service systems of payment, which the German profession fought for and eventually won, was a means of establishing open competition between all physicians who wished to take part in the health insurance scheme.

In Britain the disputes which accompanied the establishment of compulsory health insurance in 1911 concerned, partly, levels of remuneration and, partly, the issue of who was to administer the system of medical benefit—the government, the friendly societies or the doctors.[18] Eventually *ad hoc* statutory bodies were set up in each locality in which all three took part and the principle was accepted that every doctor could participate in the scheme who chose to do so. The capitation system of payment was adopted and has retained the support of the profession. This might not have happened if the right of every doctor to take part in the scheme had not been conceded from the start. In a sense, the intervention of government in Britain had the effect of rescuing physicians from the control of friendly societies, while in Germany it initially enhanced the power which sick funds could exercise over the profession.

The capitation system, and the closed panels which were usually associated with it, have now been eliminated in Norway as well as in Germany, and their role has been substantially reduced in Denmark, Italy and Austria. In the latter, payment per three-monthly case—a modified capitation system—remains the most common way of paying general practitioners.[19] Capitation is still used in the towns of Denmark and in the rural areas of Italy and remains the sole way of paying physicians under the compulsory health insurance schemes of Spain and the Netherlands and in the British National Health Service. Where it exists, it has had the effect of protecting, promoting and crystallizing the concept of the general practitioner as the personal physician to whom the patient goes in the first instance whenever he needs medical care. The patient can, in fact, obtain "free" medical care only by approaching first of all the particular doctor with whom he has chosen to register for the time being. He cannot "shop around" among different physicians according to the particular disease he thinks he is suffering from. Thus, specialising within general practice does not give any obvious advantage to a physician hoping to attract patients from within the scheme. Specialists are seen on referral from a general practitioner who has to decide whether a specialist's opinion is required and, if so, what specialist. These decisions are much more likely to be taken by the patients themselves under fee-for-service systems of paying physicians. Specialization can, therefore, be used as a means of attracting additional consultations.

Thus, the trend toward fee-for-service systems of paying physicians under compulsory insurance has had the effect of fragmenting medical care at the point at which the patient originally consults the physician. Fewer patients have one personal physician who knows their whole medical history from having participated in its management—at least in its initial stages. This process has not occurred in those parts of Denmark where physicians are paid on a fee-for-service basis as there is an entrenched tradition of referral from general practitioner to specialist, which has been incorporated in the compulsory insurance regulations.[20] Fragmentation has gone furthest in Switzerland, where 53 per cent of practitioners in independent practice are "specialists."[21] It is also widespread in Stockholm and Oslo.[22] The trend has been the same in the United States, where compulsory health insurance does not exist.

All the insurance schemes established before the medical profession became effectively organized give service benefits. In other words, the scheme pays the physician directly for his services to beneficiaries. This is presumably what the consumers of medical care wanted. Systems of reimbursing patients for their medical care costs are to be found in those countries which were late in developing their insurance schemes. And in each case lobbying by the medical profession, often accompanied by "strikes" or threats of "strikes" has played an important role. Switzerland, which has little compulsory but considerable voluntary health insurance, is half one and half the other—representing a transitional stage in the history of health insurance. In France, voluntary insurance appears to have been restricted historically to cash benefits. Compulsory insurance was not introduced until 1930 and the reimbursement plan was adopted. New Zealand followed in 1938, Australia in 1950 and Sweden in 1956. In all these countries governments had originally tried to institute a service plan but were foiled by the profession. The option of a reimbursement system was eventually accepted by the Saskatchewan government after the stormy battles of 1962. Under most reimbursement plans, the physicians can negotiate levels of reimbursement and then charge patients additional sums if they wish to do so.

The "freedom of medicine" movement was influenced greatly by the desire to avoid the experiences of Germany which have been briefly described above. It crystallized in France in the twenties and in French-speaking Switzerland and had an important influence on the thinking of the profession in the United States at the same period. The opposition to "third parties" was essentially opposition to the German sick funds and generated the drive towards reimbursement systems of paying physicians. While reimbursement systems have given medical professions who operate under them more control of their economic destiny, they have not freed them from all controls. Indeed, reimbursement plans and straight fee-for-service plans have led to more interference with the clinical freedom of physicians than capitation plans because of the much larger possibilities of abuse at the expense of insurance funds. Thus, in France, 900 full-time control physicians and further part-time physicians are employed to check on the actions of individual physicians.[23] In Germany, the control of "abuse" is in the hands of the local medical profession. It involves extensive administrative work and discussions with individual physicians.[24]

Pharmaceutical benefits are normally included in compulsory insurance and public service health schemes. The usual system is for them to be purchased through local pharmacists, and either the pharmacist or the patient claims reimbursement from the sick fund or government. In the main sick fund of Israel, the drugs are issued through the sick fund. In the USSR patients have to purchase their own drugs for use at home. In Britain any drug may be prescribed for patients, though individual doctors may be required to account for their actions to their colleagues in the area, if their prescribing appears to be "excessive." The patient pays a standard charge of 20p for each preparation. In Australia, defined "life-saving" drugs are available free to the bulk of the population, with a more extensive list for pensioners.[25] There is a similar limitation to "essential" drugs in Sweden.[26] In the Netherlands doctors may not prescribe medicines which are in the experimental stage, or for which there is a less costly substitute of equal therapeutic value.[27] The development of health insurance inevitably raised the question of whether hospital services should be included among the benefits. In countries where hospitals made substantial charges for the higher classes of accommodation, and the means tests and treatment of indigents were regarded as humiliating, there was a strong incentive for hospital benefits to be included. Thus they are found among the benefits in most countries in Europe with compulsory or voluntary health insurance schemes. Where contributions are wage related and where the employer also pays substantial contributions, a much higher proportion of hospital costs can be, and has been, shifted on to the insurance scheme. Thus, a substantial part of hospital costs is paid for by social security funds in France, Belgium, Germany and Holland. In these countries the government also participates in hospital financing in some form. Either it adds a contribution to the social security funds or it meets the deficits of hospitals, as in Belgium and many cantons of Switzerland, or else it gives grants for capital construction, as in Germany.[28] In Sweden, Norway, Switzerland and Denmark the bulk of hospital costs are met by the local authorities which run them;[29] in the latter case the insurance funds pay only about a tenth of the cost of hospitals.

In Britain, when compulsory insurance with flat-rate contributions was introduced in 1911, it was rare for in-patients to pay anything for treatment and there was no obvious crisis in hospital financing. Thus, the case for a hospital benefit was not given priority: a restricted benefit for the treatment of tuberculosis was, however, introduced for a short period. When the whole system of health insurance was reviewed by a Royal Commission in the middle 1920s, it was decided that the contribution required would be more than wage earners could afford.[30] Potential increases in revenue from social insurance contributions were reserved for the extension of cash benefits for widows and old people. Instead of compulsory hospital insurance there developed in Britain a system of voluntary contributory schemes which did not pretend to be run on an actuarial basis. Workers contributed what they could afford—usually about a quarter of the actuarial cost of the risk of hospitalization—and the money collected was handed over to the voluntary hospitals in the locality. By 1938 these schemes raised about a third of the revenue of the voluntary hospitals and covered about ten million persons. Contributing bestowed no legal right to care in hospital. Some full-cost insurance of the "Blue Cross" type did, however, develop on a very small scale in the inter-war years among those who were comfortably off.

Thus, hospital insurance developed much earlier in Europe than in the United States and it took a completely different form. "Blue Cross" was a movement which was promoted by the providers of services.[31] The hospitals needed to have more "semi-private" patients who could pay the whole cost of the services they needed. Prepayment had, therefore, to begin among those with better than average incomes, and spread down the income scale as the country became more affluent.[32] In Europe, hospital insurance was part of the movement of mutual aid among the working classes. It was designed for those with "blue collar" incomes and often specifically excluded those who were more comfortably placed. The level of benefit was thus determined by the level of contributions which "blue collar" workers could afford, and not by the cost of providing the service. Any difference had to be made up by deductibles, charity and grants from public authorities: the latter subsidized hospital budgets directly, met deficits and often paid the deductibles of the indigent. The ultimate duty of society, to see that those who needed hospital treatment received it, had been tacitly accepted long before hospital insurance was started. It was this philosophy and the ability to pay contributions which have together determined the role which hospital insurance plays in different systems of medical care in Europe.

Once one accepts the citizen's right to receive medical care as a broad philosophy underlying a century or more of European history, the considerable difference in financing systems between the different countries become matters primarily of detail. The role of deductibles and national charges certainly varies greatly. So also does the role of insurance contributions. But it was not so wildly out of line with the arrangements of neighbouring countries for Russia to substitute a public service plan for the insurance method of financing in 1937, and for Britain to do the same in 1948. Lest it be supposed that there was some common political ideology shared by these two countries, it should be mentioned that the insurance method of financing is still retained in communist Poland and that in Scandinavia the bulk of hospital costs are in fact met on a public service basis without adopting the grandiloquent title of a National Health Service. The transition to a public service system usually involves extending the coverage of pre-paid health services to include the whole population. A high proportion of the population of European countries is, in fact, already entitled to pre-paid medical care under existing plans. The Norwegian insurance plan covers the whole population:[33] in Germany 85 per cent of the population is covered, and about three-quarters of the population is covered in Austria, Italy, the Netherlands and Switzerland.[34] In view of these figures and the early development of non-profit voluntary insurance, out of which compulsory insurance emerged, there has never been much room for profit-making insurance companies in the financing of medical costs. They play hardly any role in Europe.

The creation of Britain's National Health Service involved both an extension of the coverage of prepaid medical care from approximately one half to the whole population and also an extension of the range of benefits to include free hospitalization and dental, ophthalmic, home nursing and other services. A further major step was taken at the same time: the hospitals were nationalized. This was the solution chosen to deal with the problem of planning the size, function and location of hospitals. In Scandinavia, most of the hospitals were built by the large local authorities. Their siting has, therefore, always been planned. Similarly, continental local authorities have generally planned the development of the main hospital services in their area. Where they have not, hospital authorities have generally been powerful religious bodies of varying denominations. In Britain, the voluntary sector was large, uncoordinated and secular. Many haphazard influences had affected the size and location of the various units. Hospital beds were spread most unevenly round the country. Most hospitals were far too small to meet the needs of efficient modern medicine. The case for some system of planning was recognized first in London in the early eighteen-nineties,[35] just as it was recognized first in New York after the First World War. It was recognized as a national problem in Britain during the thirties,[36] just as it has become recognized as a national problem in the United States in the fifties and sixties.[37] Neither the voluntary hospitals nor the medical profession were prepared to accept a hospital system controlled by the local authorities. Both preferred national ownership. Britain's nationalized hospitals are not run on the pattern of the veterans' hospitals of the United States. Instead, they have been handed on to a battery of planning boards and management boards, to which are appointed representatives of the medical profession, ex-voluntary hospital trustees, local authority councillors and other persons drawn from the local community. Nationalization, paradoxically, has therefore led to an extension in the scope for voluntary work. Some five to ten thousand unpaid committee men and women meet at least once a month to control the affairs of their local hospitals.

Many aspects of the European pattern of organizing health services can be traced to developments which occurred long before compulsory insurance was invented, doctors were highly organized or commercial insurance had entered the field of financing health costs. For example, the split between hospital-based doctors and home-based doctors arose because hospitals developed apart from the private medical care market. It means that normally the European patient is looked after by a different physician when he is admitted to hospital. Those Americans who are used to a different system may see this is an undesirable break in continuity of care. Defenders of the European system would, however, argue that most admissions to hospitals require the services of a specialist and that physicians with hospital facilities are tempted to undertake more specialist work than their training warrants.[38] And as most illnesses do not require hospitalization, continuity of care in out-of-hospital treatment is more important than continuity between home care and hospital care.

While much of European medical care is the product of long tradition, the schemes of pre-payment found in different countries have affected the patterns of organizing health services. Countries with capitation systems of paying physicians have managed to combine the principle of free choice of physician with the principle of the personal physician who arranges all treatment, though he does not always provide it, and who has the advantage of continuity of relationships with particular patients and families. Protagonists of the system argue that the family doctor can practise better medicine in view of this continuity of relationship. It is true, however, that many patients in Europe, as in America, seem to like to choose their physician according to their diagnosis of their illness when they have the opportunity to do so within a compulsory health insurance scheme. Is the free choice of patients necessarily the best choice in this highly technical field? Similarly, private patients in Europe, as in the United States, like to have their own physician treat them in hospital. Will physicians always give the best advice about whether a specialist should be brought in when they have a financial interest in providing all the care themselves?

The principle of free choice of family physician is accepted in every Western European health scheme except that of Spain. In Eastern Europe, polyclinic physicians are given districts, as has been the practice since long before the communist revolutions. Special arrangements can be made for a particular patient to be attached to the physician responsible for another district, but this is seldom done. While this system may restrict the confidence of the patient in his physician, it has both epidemiological and economic advantages. And preventive medicine can be more systematically promoted in a salaried service. It may also be encouraged to some extent under the capitation system of paying physicians with the continuity of relationships it engenders. It is less likely to be encouraged when patients can shop around between different physicians for different illnesses. On the other hand, such a system clearly keeps physicians keen to attract and hold custom. But one means of doing so may be an excessive use of drugs.

Payment systems can affect or be deliberately used to influence the way in which medicine is practised. Thus, loading of the capitation fee and maximum list sizes can be used, as is the practice in both the Netherlands and Britain, to reduce the financial incentives of physicians to take on more patients than they can manage. Loading is also used in Britain to encourage physicians to work together in groups. This is, however, discouraged in Germany, where doctors are paid on a fee-for-service basis, because of the opportunities it would offer physicians to increase fees by passing patients around among the partners. It would be hard to draw the line between legitimate consultations and undesirable abuses. Teamwork, though desirable in modern medicine, is hard to accommodate in a pre-paid scheme where physicians are paid on a fee-for-service basis. The fee structures of both Germany and Sweden encourage the use of scientific diagnostic tests. There is not the same incentive for such tests where physicians are paid on a capitation basis. Fee structures can also be used to encourage referral in particular cases if a specialist is paid much more for a particular procedure than a non-specialist—particularly if the fee given to the latter barely compensates him for the time involved. Similarly, home calls and night calls can be encouraged if extra payment is given for them. All these features have been built into different health schemes.

How far physicians and patients respond to particular financial incentives, or become apathetic in the absence of them, is hard to assess. One might expect the number of times the average patient sees his physician to vary according to the system of payment. Thus, there would be a higher consultation rate under a fee-for-service system of payment than under a capitation or salaried system of paying doctors. The highest consultation rates reported in a recent international study were found in countries with a fee-for-service system—Germany with 10 consultations a year and Japan with 15 consultations a year.[39]

The lowest consultation rates (about 2 a year) were found in France and Sweden with their reimbursement systems. Belgium and Switzerland were about average (5 a year). The Netherlands with its capitation scheme of paying doctors had 5½ consultations a year, though pensioners are excluded from these figures. Spain, also a capitation scheme, had 7 consultations a year. Austria, with partly a fee-for-service scheme and partly a modified capitation scheme, had nearly 10 consultations a year, and Israel, with its salaried scheme, had about 8 consultations a year. Some of these variations may be explained by differences in the ratio of physicians in the countries studied and by differences in the level of health. For example, Israel is much more generously stocked with doctors than Sweden, but it makes it hard to generalize about the "inevitable" effects of remuneration systems. It may be that tradition, culture and medical education play the major roles. The subject deserves careful study. Such a study would have to take account of cost-sharing regulations and the availability of "free" drugs in the various schemes and the use of private consultations outside it.

The development and extension of systems of prepaying medical care have normally led to extensions in the use of services, but it does not follow that the countries where pre-payment systems or public health services are most developed spend the highest proportion of their national incomes on health services. The development of pre-payment not only makes medical care more readily available, it also introduces a third party which is in a position to bargain about the standards of care, particularly in its "amenity" aspects, which are thought to be reasonable: it can also negotiate collectively about levels of remuneration. The extent to which a "third party" performs its function depends on how far it is really representative of consumers and how far it needs to compromise when faced with the wishes and bargaining power of providers of services. The proportion of gross national expenditure devoted to health services (public and private, capital and current) was 4.7 per cent in Sweden (1956) and England and Wales (1960–1), 5.1 per cent in Israel (1959–60) and 5.2 per cent in the United States (1957–8).[40] An earlier and less through study estimated that public and private expenditure on medical care as a proportion of national income was 3.7 per cent in Denmark (1952–3), 3.8 per cent in the Netherlands (1953), 4.1 per cent in Belgium (1954) and in England and Wales (1953–4), 4.4 per cent in Canada (1953) and in France (1952), and 4.5 per cent in Norway (1955) and the United States (1953) and 4.6 per cent in New Zealand (1953).[41]

Thus when one looks around the high-income world, one can distinguish three essentially different patterns of providing medical care services. The first is the *American system,* where typically the patient chooses the physician for his illness, be he general practitioner or specialist, and that physician continues responsibility for that patient's care should hospitalization be necessary. This pattern is to be found extensively for *private* patients in Portugal and France and some other continental European countries, though the hospital to which such a patient is admitted in continental Europe is often owned and operated by the physician concerned, while in the United States the hospital is typically a non-profit and independent institution. Of course there is a growing number of closed hospitals and salaried physicians in the United States, but the general pattern is as I have described.

The second system is what I will call the *Western European system,* where physicians retain their private offices as in the United States but hospital care is normally the responsibility of a separate group of salaried physicians working mainly in governmental hospitals (usually local units of government). The compulsory insurance system pays the physician or reimburses the patient and pays the whole or part of the cost of the drugs which the physician prescribes. In many countries there are also home nursing services provided by local units of government. In Britain, these services are particularly well developed. For each general practitioner in the National Health Service there is a quarter of a health visitor (a public health nurse who devotes most of her time to preventive services among children and old people), a quarter of an obstetric nurse (midwife) and one-third of a qualified home-care nurse who provides basic and technical nursing services to patients sick in their own homes.

The third system I will call the *Eastern European system,* though it is to be found in Israel under the main sick fund and throughout the low-income countries of Africa and Asia. Here the physician is salaried and operates from an office (polyclinic, dispensary or health centre) which is provided by the service. This office is often sited beside the hospital, as is the growing pattern in North American. The district doctor, to whom patients are normally assigned, refers cases requiring hospitalization to a separate group of salaried physicians. A district doctor can be "promoted" to this group on passing the appropriate examinations. The epidemiological and preventive services work in close association with the other health services.

Thus, the major difference between the Eastern European and Western European systems is to be found in the independence of "out of hospital" physicians. They are private contractors in Western Europe and salaried officials in Eastern Europe. In other respects the services are more similar though there is much more centralized control and national planning in Eastern Europe than Western Europe. In the latter systems the planning of hospital services tends to be the responsibility of local rather than central government. In Eastern Europe "posting" of physicians and especially high salaries for the less-popular posts are used to try and secure even coverage of the country with physicians. In Western Europe basic salaries and systems of mileage allowances and loading of remuneration systems are used to attract physicians to work in the less populous areas. Britain also uses a system of *negative* control over the location of general practitioners: a physician cannot get a contract under the national health service in certain scheduled "over-doctored" areas unless he has some special family or other claim to work there. Britain's hospital service is more like that of Eastern Europe in so far as it is centrally and regionally planned, but no posting of physicians occurs and both the planning and management of hospitals is done by bodies which are composed of both local lay and local medical representatives.

I have argued that the fundamental differences in the organization and financing of medical care between the United States and other high income countries have been greatly influenced by long-established differences in attitudes to medical care. In Europe the provision of medical care has always been regarded more as a collective responsibility and different institutions have been developed to undertake it. Hospitals were started to serve the needs of the poor rather than to meet the needs of paying patients. In most European countries hospitals started in the hands of mainly religious charitable bodies but have been increasingly transferred to public authorities. American short-stay hospitals have remained primarily non-profit community services. They always took paying patients and the role of charitable support has gradually declined.

In America prepayment has been primarily a movement generated by providers of services, though particularly in the last ten years the field has been entered by the profit-making insurance organizations. In Europe prepayment has always been primarily a non-profit movement sponsored and controlled by consumers. When government has entered the field it has usually been to extend by compulsion the membership of these consumers' organizations rather than to supersede them. Thus it has found itself cast in the role of mediator in what previously had been the private disputes between producers and consumers. And the sick funds of Europe and particularly of Israel are powerful bodies. In the United States there have hardly ever been any consumers' organizations in this field. With the possible exception of the unions, whose interests are large and diffused, there is virtually no organized countervailing power to balance the demands of providers of services—of the hospitals and the physicians. Thus, when government has intervened in the medical care market, it has had to initiate, not to mediate. And there is never much incentive for a government to challenge organized and articulate interests on behalf of less articulate and largely unorganized opinion, unless it is compelled to do so.

In any review of the emergence of medical-care systems throughout the world, there is a danger of over-emphasizing the extent to which each country has been a slave to its own culture and tradition. It is so much easier to detect after the event the forces which have led to particular developments. The alternative courses which history might have taken are much harder to identify. Governments and consumers' organizations can influence and have deliberately influenced patterns of health care, not only in Britain and Eastern Europe but throughout the world. The fact that usually intervention has been slow and gradual has perhaps been largely because we know so little about what constitutes good medical care. Governments act and, in a democracy, the public demands action more readily when indisputable facts are available to support the need for action. Each country tends to shroud its medical system in complacent praise. In an age when tools of research have never been so readily available, argument by assertion can no longer be tolerated. Instead, we need facts. In particular we need to measure the quality of medical care under different systems of financing and organization.

NOTES

[1]Henry C. Burdett, *Hospitals and Asylums of the World* (1893), vol. 3, p. 56.
[2]Ibid.

[3]Ibid., p. 55.
[4]Ibid., p. 613. The author makes two relatively minor exceptions to this general statement.
[5]Ibid., pp. 76, 423, 454, 618.
[6]Ibid., pp. 448–57, 662.
[7]Brian Abel-Smith, *Hospitals 1800–1948* (1964).
[8]Burdett, p. 56.
[9]Abel-Smith, op. cit.
[10]Mark G. Field, *Doctor and Patient in Soviet Russia* (1957).
[11]Sir Arthur Newsholme, *International Studies on the Relations between the Private and Official Practice of Medicine* (1931), vol. 2, p. 216
[12]Ibid., p. 241.
[13]Mary Stocks, *A Hundred Years of District Nursing* (1960).
[14]Newsholme, p. 31, vol. 2, pp. 26, 57.
[15]James Hogarth, *The Payment of the General Practitioner* (1962), p. 392.
[16]Newsholme, Vol. 1, p. 24.
[17]Brian Abel-Smith, "Paying the Family Doctor," *Medical Care, 1* (1963), p. 30.
[18]R. M. Titmuss, "Health" in *Law and Opinion in England in the Twentieth Century,* ed. M. Ginsberg (1959). Reprinted in *Commitment to Welfare,* London 1968.
[19]Hogarth, p. 346.
[20]Op. cit., p. 401.
[21]Op. cit., p. 282.
[22]Op. cit., p. 62, 100.
[23]Op. cit., p. 149.
[24]Op. cit., pp. 243–8.
[25]Ministry of Health, *Final Report of the Committee on Cost of Prescribing* (1959), p. 38.
[26]International Social Security Association, *Volume and Cost of Benefits in Kind and Cash* (1961), p. 382.
[27]Ministry of Health, op. cit., p. 38.
[28]Abel-Smith, "Changing methods of financing hospital care," *The Changing Role of the Hospital in a Changing World,* published by the International Hospital Federation (1963).
[29]Hogarth, op. cit., pp. 52, 94, 272, 389.
[30]Abel-Smith, *Hospitals 1800–1948.*
[31]H. and Anne Somers, *Doctors Patients and Health Insurance* (1961), p. 292.
[32]Ibid., p. 291.
[33]Hogarth, op. cit., p. 94.
[34]Ibid., p. 328.
[35]Abel-Smith, *Hospitals 1800–1948,* op. cit.
[36]Ibid.
[37]Somers, op. cit., pp. 83–90.
[38]See, for example, Ray Trussell, *The Quantity, Quality and Costs of Medical and Hospital Care Secured by a Sample of Teamster Families in the New York Area* (undated).
[39]The figures quoted in this paragraph come from International Social Security Association, op. cit., p. 392.
[40]Abel-Smith, (1963), "Health Expenditure in Seven Countries," *The Times Review of Industry and Technology* (March 1963), p. vi. The final report appeared in *An International Study of Health Expenditure,* Public Health Papers No. 32, W.H.O. (1967).
[41]International Labour Office, *The Cost of Medical Care* (1959), pp. 76–7.

Medicare: Social Policy and American Politics

Theodore R. Marmor

The Origins of Medicare: The Rational Actor Model

In dealing with the origins of Medicare, the question [is] why government elites *chose* in the early 1950s to narrow the focus of federal health insurance bills from the general population to the aged, and to restrict benefits to partial hospitalization coverage. Why, in short, did the Truman Administration decide to adopt the Medicare strategy?

The unit of analysis used . . . [is] a strategic political decision. The explanation given for the strategic choice [is] in the form of a set of reasons why sensible men could agree on a new but less dramatic course of action. This type of explanation should be distinguished from an account of why the shift in strategy took place. Useless debate is furthered without care for such distinctions. The reasons men give for a course of action may differ widely from the fundamental causes for a course of action—in this case, a shift in political strategy.

The fate of the Truman health insurance proposals provided the immediate backdrop for strategic choice. The perception that the aged were more acceptable to the general public as a deserving group was the major reason they were the chosen target of concern. Likewise, the restriction of Medicare benefits to social security beneficiaries was explained by the observation that social insurance programs enjoy considerable legitimacy while public assistance programs that use the means test do not. The principal pattern of inference [is] to show what goals the reformers were pursuing in deciding to

---

opt for the Medicare rather than the national health insurance strategy.

Thinking about a government as if it were a single rational actor is perhaps the most common analytic orientation of U. S. political scientists. The vocabulary of "choice," "purposive action," and "rational calculation" is so common in national policy studies that its users are not typically self-conscious about the assumptions on which their conceptual orientation depends. For many purposes, political occurrences may be properly characterized as the purposive acts of national governments, to summarize the varied activities of governmental representatives as the nation transforms "unwieldy complexity into manageable packages" (Allison, 1968, 1). But this productive shorthand has the capacity to obscure as well as aid; it does not take into account that what we call the government is in fact a loose congerie of large organizations and political bargainers.

According to the rational actor model, the happenings of national politics are "the choices of domestic actors." Policy is understood as the action of the rational decision-maker. The choices and actions of the nation are thus "viewed as means calculated to achieve national goals and purposes." Such actions are interpreted as solutions to domestic problems such that the "explanation of rational action consists of showing what goal the nation was pursuing in committing the action and how in the light of that goal the action was the most reasonable choice." The implication is that important policy decisions have big causes, that large organizations perform important actions to serve substantial purposes. Analysts employing this framework may disagree sharply on which causes, which reasons, and which purposes are associated with particular governmental decisions, but the similarity of their purposive analytic orientation is striking (Allison, 1968, 1 ff.).

The basic unit of analysis in such work is the government's choice of strategy. The central concepts include the government as actor, governmental goals, alternative solutions, calculation, and consequences. These characteristic concepts are employed in a distinctive pattern of inference.

As Allison suggests, "if a nation or state or city has specific objectives, it will choose the optimal means towards those objectives." Conversely, if the "nation chooses an action or makes a decision, its goals can be inferred by calculating what are the ends towards which those acts constitute optimum means" (1968, 9). The result is a type of explanatory logic in which the knowledge of either goals or actions leads to an explanation of the other. Portraying governments as rational actors thus involves a characteristic model of description, explanation, and (one could show) prediction and evaluation.

Had the question of Medicare's origins been raised in organizational or bargaining terms, both the formulation and solution of the puzzle would have been different. From an organizational perspective, the question of Medicare's origins would have focused on the process by which health insurance for the aged arose as a political issue. Such an analysis would have characterized the relevant organizational units concerned with health and the aged, their standard ways of receiving, generating, and interpreting information, and their ordinary rules of decision for political strategy. Also, [it] would have dealt extensively with the organizational setting of the Medicare strategy; the central issue would have been "How is it that the shift in health insurance strategy took place?" The relevant answer would have been not so much reasons why that decision made sense but rather why those reasons made sense to the organizational actors and how that led them to take this different posture toward the problems and possibilities of health insurance in American politics. Organizational analysis would emphasize that information on the aged was more readily available to organizations like the Federal Security Agency, a group charged with responsibility for the aged generally, and social security beneficiaries particularly. The reasons for concentrating on the aged would, from this view, be very different from the reasons why the aged warranted, in an objective analysis, special health concern.

My purpose here is not to treat alternative analytic frameworks as mutually exclusive. They are less discrete than that, and the analysis of a topic like Medicare's origins inevitably mixes elements of a number of analytic approaches. But I do want to emphasize the focus of attention. . .on the decision to adopt a Medicare strategy [which] differs from the organizational analyst's interest in how a particular set of complex events takes place. Students of bureaucratic bargaining would. . .raise still different questions about Medicare's origins as a public issue. They would treat the Medicare strategy decision as part of an ongoing policy contest in which the most stubborn advocates of the Truman health proposals were defeated by the proponents of incrementalism. Detailed information about the actors involved and the governmental atmosphere in which the Ewing plan emerged would be required for this type of analysis. Very little appears [here] about the structure of the Federal Security Agency, its relations with the Truman staff, and its connections with congressional health insurance advocates.

It is precisely that sort of evidence which permits characterizing a bargaining game out of which a strategic choice emerges. Such a view not only stresses political victors and losers, but treats decisions as part of an ongoing struggle. The shift to a Medicare approach is but one stage in a fluid policy development; the incentives of key actors to promote or oppose this shift would be part of an overall portrait of the health-politics field. . . . The prominent position within the Federal Security Agency of such long-time social security experts as Wilbur Cohen and I. S. Falk helped to explain the availability of a social insurance alternative to the Truman plan. (It should be remembered that both these officials were advocates of general health insurance, but less sanguine than others as to its political feasibility.) The access Cohen and Falk had to Oscar Ewing constituted a crucial bargaining advantage for those seeking a limited, but more politically appealing health insurance initiative. The difference between explaining why health insurance for the aged made sense and why that decision was adopted should by now be more apparent. . . .

THE RESPONSES OF MEDICARE, 1952–64: THE ORGANIZATIONAL PROCESS MODEL

The second topic of this [selection] is the fate of Medicare proposals *after* the Ewing-Truman decision. We were interested in the contestants about Medicare and the nature of the contest over time. Here our concern for describing and accounting for a *pattern* of organizational behavior makes the rational actor framework less useful. The immediate organizational problems of concerned pressure groups at this point took precedence over the social problems of the aged to which the advocates of Medicare have drawn attention. In discussing this aspect of the problem, we were less interested in Medicare as a rational response to the problems of the elderly and more concerned with the use made of their woes by pressure group antagonists. In characterizing the Medicare contest, we concentrated on the major organizational units concerned and, implicitly, employed some of the characteristic features of what has been called the organizational process model (Allison, 1968, 3).

According to the organizational process model, what the rational policy analysts call *choices* and *acts* are in fact outputs of organizations functioning according to standard patterns of behavior. To explain a particular occurrence, one "identifies the relevant organization" (or organizations) and "displays the pattern of procedures and conventions out of which the action emerged." The basic unit of analysis is the organization, and the focal concepts include routine behavior, standard operating procedures, biased information, incremental change, and organizational perspective (Allison, 1968, 3).

Explanations in organizational terms typically "focus on the pattern of statements, directives, and actions of relevant agencies and departments." A central assumption is that organizations change slowly, that behavior in time $t + l$ will resemble that of time t. Predictions thus are based on the "structure, programs, and past behavior of the relevant organizations" (Allison, 1968, 22). Throughout, our central concern is how certain patterns of activity take place in the special organizations we call government.

. . . Both the contest and the contestants over Medicare remained remarkably stable in the period 1952–64, "two well-defined camps with opposing views, camps with few individuals who were impartial or uncommitted" (c.f.

Wildavsky, 1962, 304). The breadth of the conflict over Medicare was illustrated by the large number of concerned groups (often otherwise not involved with health issues) and their ideological polarization. The disputes over Medicare had recurring, predictable features even as the specific proposals in question changed substantially. The disputants—like adversaries in open class conflict—called upon crystalized attitudes and positions and expressed them in distinctive ways to identify problems and frame remedies. The stability in Medicare demands and reactions permitted a relatively static description of group conflict on this issue.

The stereotypical and static quality of the fight over Medicare is more readily understandable when one considers the size and character of the parties to it.* Large national associations like the AMA and AFL-CIO have widely dispersed component parts; they function in part as Washington lobbyists for issues affecting the interests of widely disparate members. Hence, they must seek common denominators of sentiment that will satisfy the organization's leading actors without antagonizing large bodies of more passive members. Such large organizations are specialized, with full-time staffs devoted to preparing responses to public policy questions when the occasion arises and in the direction dictated by past organizational attitudes. These attitudes are slow to change and help account for the predictable way in which sides were taken on various Medicare proposals over time. Intelligence and research were weapons in a long struggle between groups that distrusted each other. Hence, it is not surprising that the debate was stable; mutally incompatible positions on health insurance arose in part from the maintenance needs of large-scale organizations (and their leaders).

An organizational perspective was appropriate for analyzing the *pattern* of Medicare debates and debaters. In dealing with that pattern it was useful to concentrate on the predictable behavior of the large pressure groups involved. Students of organizations know that such collectivities do not behave like individuals. Organizations filter information in ways persons do not. They seek means to maintain themselves over time not characteristic of individual behavior. The conjunction of the routine behavior of many individuals in organizational settings has results in public policy for which one cannot account by looking only at the activities of isolated individuals.

Other questions could . . . [be] raised about the long fight over Medicare.

---

*It might be objected that stereotypes and simplified images of opponents are characteristic of most political disputes. But any one who has, for example, surveyed the hearings of regulatory bodies will recognize an attention to evidential canons never present when Medicare antagonists aired their views, whether in the press or during congressional hearings. Part of the reason, of course, is that Medicare actors were directing their remarks to a much wider audience and naturally relied on compelling symbols where complex factual presentations would have been confusing or boring.

[If] one [were to] concentrate on explaining a particular response to a particular proposal (the 1961 congressional battle, for instance), it would . . . [be] more appropriate to stress individual actions and the individual bargaining that characterized that episode. That was precisely the approach used in discussing 1961 events, and, in particular, the 1965 legislative outcome.

The 1965 Legislation: The Bureaucratic Politics Model

The enactment of Medicare was . . . primarily . . . the result of a bargaining game in which none of the relevant executive, legislative, or pressure-group players could fully control the outcome. The key actors—Mills and Byrnes of the Ways and Means Committee, Cohen of HEW, Long and Anderson of the Senate Finance Committee, the AMA and the labor leaders—all had different conceptions of the problem at hand. They had different stakes in the outcome of the legislative struggle and different terms on which they were willing to compromise.

Not only was bargaining stressed—both explicit and tacit—but also the decentralized nature of the American political process. It was never clear at what stage in the legislative process major alterations were or were not possible. The statutory result could not be interpreted solely as the product of the Administration's intentions. Rather, it emerged as the outcome of a long, complicated struggle and the law in its final form was not one which any of the major actors intended at the outset.

The bureaucratic politics framework considers "domestic policy to consist of *outcomes* of a series of overlapping bargaining games" arranged heirarchically within the national government. Two descriptive emphases are involved: that governments are made up of disparate, decentralized organizations headed by leaders with unequal power, and that such leaders, in the course of policy-making, engage in bargaining. These players, operating with different perspectives and different priorities, struggle for preferred outcomes with the power at their disposal. Explanations in this third model proceed from descriptions of the "position and power of the principal players" and concentrate on the "understandings and misunderstandings which determine the outcome of the game" (Allison, 1968, 3).

The basic unit of analysis is the decentralized bargaining game played by relatively autonomous actors. The focal concepts include bargaining strategies, roles, moves, stakes, trade-offs, tactics, and conventions (or rules of the game). Explanations that employ this framework typically draw upon the stakes and interests the actors bring to disputes about particular policy issues. The decisions and actions of governments constitute outcomes in the "sense that what happens is not chosen as a solution to a problem" but is rather the result of "political bargaining among a number of independent players, of compromise, coalition, competition, and confusion among government officials many of whom are focusing on different faces of the issue." The actions of government—the sum of the "behavior of representatives of a government" involved in a policy issue—"is rarely intended by any individual or group." From this characterization of policy-making come distinctive patterns of inference, rules of explanation such as "where you stand depends on where you sit." Moreover, important government decisions are not viewed as the result of a single game. Rather, what the government does is a "collage of individual acts, outcomes of minor and major games, and foulups." The understanding of that cumulative process requires piece-by-piece disaggregation of the policy-making. What moves the process, in any event, is not simply the "reasons which support a course of action, nor the routines of organizations which enact an alternative, but the power and skill of proponents and opponents of the action in question" (Allison, 1968, 26 ff.).

Treating statutes as bargaining outcomes requires [a] detailed characterization of individual styles, interests, and positions. . . . Actors like Mills, for instance, no longer asked in January, 1965, whether it was preferable that the U.S. Government provide hospital and nursing home insurance for the aged under social security. That much was a foregone conclusion which shaped the behavior of an adaptive committee chairman like Mills. He could in 1965 be a reluctant bystander or an adroit manager of legislation which in another setting he would have preferred to block. Mills has always adjusted to legislative certainty and tried to take charge of the form which the inevitable takes. Cutting back on the Administration's proposal in 1965 was an extraordinarily difficult alternative, given that the problems of the aged had been identified in a way for which the "input" of H.R. 1 was at best a partial solution. Moreover, scrimping on the aged when legislation was imminent was more difficult than preventing any Medicare action whatsoever in the period before 1965. . . . The bargaining which took place should not be allowed to obscure the vital fact that the election of 1964 had given all the actors less to bargain about.

We have thus far concentrated on showing how different analytic approaches lead to distinguishable sets of questions about public policy developments like Medicare legislation. It should be added that they also make a difference in the evaluations, recommendations, and predictions one makes about public policy. Consider some of the predictive and prescriptive differences that would emerge from alternative approaches to the explanation of the Medicare statute. The analyst who viewed Medicare legislation as the national solution to a pressing social problem would expect (and predict) that periodic adjustments would be made to make the program a more efficient instrument to cope with the health and financial problems of the aged. He would expect monitoring of the program as part of the effort to increase the level of achievement of the original national goal.*

Contrast these predictions with those a bargaining analyst would make. . . . He would expect future outcomes to vary with what one might call the deal of the electoral cards. Since the innovations of 1965 were so much the result of the atypical partisan makeup of the 88th Congress, he would predict less innovation in more typical Congresses. He would not expect the Committee of Ways and Means, for instance, to preoccupy itself with improving the program, or to seek aggressively alternative means to meet the health needs of other Americans not assisted by Medicare.

Political recommendations would be equally different. One could imagine problem-solvers trying to convince the congressional committee that new difficulties, such as higher medical prices, have arisen for the aged, or that more serious health and financial problems are being felt by the disadvantaged and poor. The emphasis here would be on identifying the social ills for which national action is required. Students of bargaining would offer different recommendations. They would stress continued efforts to reshape the Committee on Ways and Means, taking cues from the "packing" of the committee after 1961. They would advise political investments of this kind, rather than a search for problems, as the best means of insuring action on health problems we are already aware of. Viewed from the anti-Medicare perspective, bargaining students would firmly recommend prevention of these long-term investments. These illustrations—admittedly brief and elliptical—are examples of the differences which analytic lenses may make in what we see, predict, and recommend about public policy.

Processes and Policy in American Politics: The Case of Medicare

. . . Political scientists have expended great efforts in recent years trying to specify the ways by which different issues are raised, disputed, coped with, and sometimes "solved." Lowi (1964) has provided a typology for discriminating among public policies which usefully categorizes the Medicare case. He describes three major patterns of political conflict which are said to be associated with three different types of public policies—*distributive, regulative*, and *redistributive*. Distributive policies, which parcel out public bene-

*This follows from the assumption that the problem was financial inability of the aged to manage their health costs. If the "problem" had been defined as coping with the demand by unions, the aged, and others for "some" health care assistance, the legislation of 1965 might well be considered a rational (and nearly complete) solution.

fits to interested parties, provoke a stable alliance of diverse groups that seek portions of the pork barrel. Regulative policies, which constrain the relations among competing groups and persons, provide incentives for shifting coalitions, pluralistic competition, and the standard forms of compromise. Redistributive policies, which reallocate benefits and burdens among broad socioeconomic population groups, foster polarized and enduring conflict in which large national pressure groups play central roles.

References

Allison, Graham T. 1968. Conceptual Models and the Cuban Missile Crisis. *American Political Science Review*, Sept. 1969.

Wildavsky, Aaron. 1962. *Dixon-Yates: A Study in Power Politics*. New Haven: Yale University Press, 5–6, 305–4.

Lowi, Theodore J. 1964. American Business, Public Policy, Case-Studies, and Political Theory. *World Politics* 16:677–715.

Policy Problems and Policy Perceptions in the National Health Service

Rudolf Klein

The development and discussion of theories of policy-making,[1] analytical and prescriptive, has in recent years acquired new impetus. But how helpful are the various theories when applied to a specific field of activity? This paper looks at a number of policy areas in the National Health Service in an attempt to provide some answers to this question. However, the way in which the question has been formulated in itself carries a warning both about the limitations of the available theories and about the assumptions which have prompted the inquiry. To ask whether a theory is "helpful" is to concede that it is not specific enough to be tested in a rigorous manner: that it can only be judged by its operational usefulness in helping to explain what happens or does not happen. To talk about theories in the plural presupposes that different modes of explanation are not necessarily mutually exclusive, and that their explanatory power may vary with the situation to which they are applied: in other words, it assumes a sort of intellectual pluralism.

The rest of this paper will try to justify this characterisation of the available theories and the assumption about their differing usefulness in various situations. Its starting point is the discovery, when trying to apply

---

The original version of this paper was prepared for the Anglo-American conference on policy studies, organised by Professor Peter Self at Birmingham in September 1973. My thanks to Phoebe Hall, A. R. Isserlis and Mayer Zald for their constructive comments on the first draft. Permission to reprint from *Policy and Politics* 2(1974): 219–20, 226–34, 235, has been granted by the author, the journal and the School for Advanced Urban Studies, University of Bristol. Footnotes have been renumbered and removed to end of text.

them in practice to policy-making in the NHS, that the various tools of explanation are too helpful in a sense. They tend, as it were, to explain too much and too little. All seem to explain *something;* none explains everything. Collectively they make up a useful analytic toolkit; individually they are far from being universal in their application. To support this assertion this paper examines a number of policy areas in the NHS without, however, attempting to be in any way comprehensive. First, it looks at the usefulness—in terms of providing insight into policy-making—of what might be called macro-theory; modes of explanation which concentrate on the distribution and organisation of power in a particular society (in contrast to micro-theory which concerns itself chiefly with the processes of policy-making).

[Klein then discusses elitist theory, pluralist bargaining theory, and the incrementalist approach.]

The National Health Service Experiment: Care of the Mentally Ill

. . . I shall now look at some specific policy areas and policy decisions. The choice is inevitably arbitrary since we lack a typology of policy situations[2] which would allow an analysis based on criteria of selection; indeed in as much as this paper has a positive theme, it is the importance of trying to develop a more sophisticated and precise classification of policy situations. And the examples chosen from the NHS have been picked because, in my view, they tend to emphasise some rather neglected aspects of such situations.

In 1953 the then Minister of Health, Iain Macleod, announced that he was giving priority to the mentally ill, a theme to which he frequently returned.[3] In 1962, much the same theme was taken by Enoch Powell who put particular emphasis on the care of the mentally sub-normal; indeed looking back subsequently on his period of office, he gave extra expenditure on provision for the mentally sub-normal as an example of his ministerial influence.[4] Yet only a few years later a series of scandals revealed that little had effectively changed in this whole area of NHS. When the NHS was launched in 1948, the care of the mentally ill, handicapped and sub-normal, of the chronically ill and of the elderly was the neglected sector of the NHS. Two decades later, the picture had hardly changed: for instance the relationship between the expenditure per patient in the favoured acute hospitals and in the under-privileged chronic sector had remained virtually constant.[5]

At this point, in 1969, there was a change in policy. Richard Crossman, as Secretary of State for Social Services first sought to switch resources from the acute to the chronic sector.[6] In this attempt, he failed. And the reason for this failure is significant. He failed but not because the medical profession acted as an organised pressure group to stop him; there were no protests from the BMA, no campaign by the organised medical interests. It was, however, made clear to Crossman by his civil servants and by the chairmen and officers of the regional hospital boards that a diversion of existing resources was unacceptable to the profession. And since the profession formed part of the fabric of the NHS—since it is represented at all the administrative levels of the organisation as well as being responsible for the delivery of the service—he had no option but to abandon his attempt. Instead, he adopted a strategy of allocating some *extra* resources to the under-privileged sector and ear-marking them specifically, so moving from the hortatory or symbolic policy-making of his predecessors to effective policy-making.

The episode is instructive. It shows the irrelevance of much of pressure group or pluralistic bargaining theory in the context of an organisation like the NHS. It suggests that in analysing policy-making we ought to pay much more attention to the policy-deliverers: the power exerted by those who interpret and implement decisions (and where the recognition that this power exists can already help to determine the decisions that are taken, since there will be a realisation that certain types of decisions will simply not be accepted and implemented). It indicates the importance of organisational factors or bureaucratic politics: the civil servants were much more reluctant to risk a confrontation over resource allocation with the medical profession than Crossman (so limiting his options), not necessarily because they disagreed with his policy aims but because, unlike politicians who move from office, they tend to put a higher value on maintaining good relations with the doctors as a form of investment for the future. It also raises some interesting questions. In the case of the NHS, does the power of the doctors reflect their professional strength, their membership of an elite to which civil servants also belong, or the peculiar organisational characteristics of the NHS itself as a virtual monopoly public service? And, to return to an earlier point, if it is the professional strength of the doctors, does this in turn rest on organisational characteristics like control over entry and professional discipline or on the nature of their professional expertise and mystique?[7]

There is another interesting aspect of this particular policy issue. In the outcome, it seems almost custom-built to illustrate the incrementalist thesis. The final policy change involved only a minor readjustment; the inherited resource distribution was accepted as a baseline. Analytically, the incrementalist mode of explanation is amply vindicated. Prescriptively, though, can the final outcome be described as rational? Here it is important to distinguish between the different dimensions of rationality. The decision may have been politically rational, in the sense that any other outcome would have meant an excessive investment of political capital.[8] It may have been administratively rational, in the sense that all Ministers must give priority to keeping the NHS running as distinct from changing it (and therefore are peculiarly vulnerable to threats of non-co-operation). But was it rational in any other sense? Did it not mean the acceptance of the medical profession's priorities over other priorities, and is there any reason for thinking that the former's were the right ones?

These questions underline the difficulty of making policy in the NHS. Changing policies in the NHS depend on changing values: altering perceptions, modifying the "mental set"[9] towards the health service—engineering a new consensus, (to return to an earlier point), about the NHS which puts less emphasis on professional priorities and more on social, human and other considerations. The importance of how a situation is perceived (a massively neglected aspect of the policy-making process) can be further illustrated, still drawing on this particular area of policy-making. After all, nothing in the available modes of explanation tells us why there should have been a shift in policy precisely in 1969. Nothing had changed in the actual situation of the chronic sector of the NHS: quite possibly things had even been improving (though of course the improvements may have been lagging behind expectations). There had been a change of Minister, and no doubt Richard Crossman's own views and personality played a crucial role.

Still, it is possible to identify one other factor exploited, but not wholly created, by Crossman; a shift in how the situation was perceived. In 1967, the Association for the Elderly in Government Institutions (a small agitational pressure group) published *Sans Everything,*[10] a highly coloured account of conditions in various institutions caring for the elderly, alleging both specific acts of cruelty and a general tendency to treat the old as dehumanised objects. The charges were investigated by Committees of Inquiry.[11] These Committees dismissed the specific charges of cruelty and ill-treatment. . . . Yet the reports were widely regarded as a white-washing exercise. The extent of the criticism was largely ignored because the expectation had been that the committees would find cruelty as alleged.

Eight months later there was published another report:[12] that of a Committee into allegations of ill-treatment of patients at Ely Hospital for the mentally ill and subnormal. Not only did this find many of the allegations of ill-treatment substantiated. It also criticised the quality of the nursing and medical care, and made recommendations for change going well beyond the specific institution under examination: in particular, it recommended the creation of an "independent inspectorate."

The Ely report precipitated action. Mainly this was, as already noted, because Richard Crossman had taken over at the DHSS. He not only insisted on having the Ely report published, he deliberately exploited it as an opportunity to take a policy initiative, using it as a weapon to force change on his own department and on the profession. Partly, though, the reasons, which help to explain why Crossman succeeded must be sought elsewhere. Here it seems helpful, and revealing, to draw on the findings of social psychologists—in particular, the theory of cognitive dissonance.[13] To sum up a very complex argument, this suggests that information inconsistent with existing attitudes will tend to be ignored: there may be an attempt to discredit its sources, there will certainly be a readiness to exploit any ambiguities which justify holding on to one's present views. This was indeed the reaction to the *Sans Everything* charges (assisted perhaps by the over-dramatic way in which the charges were put). But then the Ely Report came out. The dissonance or discomfort caused by this information was such as to force a change in attitudes. There was not just an incremental change in attitudes, but a reversal: the situation was seen in a new way, and additional information tended to be interpreted in support of new rather than old attitudes.

This example not only suggests, I think, that policy-making studies could usefully lean on the work of social psychologists much more than at present. It also indicates that policy-making may have something in common with scientific research:[14] that for most of the time it will be incremental, based on an agreed consensus model of the nature of the problems being tackled and of the policy-tools available for dealing with them, but that occasionally the incongruity between the model and experience will prove too great and lead to a change in perception and a search for new models. The effect of Keynesian economic theory on policy-making would seem to be a good illustration of the Kuhn thesis as applied to policy-making. This may be a rare, exceptional event: indeed it is bound to be since the sheer number of policy issues that have to be dealt with in a complex organisation like the NHS dictates that routine methods of dealing with them must be used for most of the time. But it is important that in analysing policy-making in search of patterns and regularities, we do not overlook—or try to explain away deterministically—evidence about creative policy-making; that is a readiness to invent new models or, if not to invent them, at least to try out ideas hitherto outside the pale of the acceptable or conceivable. There is every reason for arguing with Dror[15] that a positive effort should be made to encourage such creativeness.

Just how easy it is to under-play this element is shown by events subsequent to the Ely Report. As a result, Crossman set up the Hospital Advisory Service whose functions are:—

1. by constructive criticism and by propagating good practices and new ideas, to help improve the management of patient care in individual hospitals (excluding matters of individual clinical judgment) and the hospital service as a whole.

2. to advise the Secretary of State about conditions in hospitals.[16]

This was certainly a major innovation: it did not build on any existing institutions. But it had to be introduced incrementally, as it were. Any suggestion that HAS would act as an inspectorate (enforcing central standards as distinct from generating professional self-criticism) had to be abandoned in the face of resistance from the medical profession. Its activities have been limited so as not to impose too great a strain on the administrative machinery's capacity.[17] So far, incrementalism would seem to be a helpful tool of analysis. So would pressure group theory, at least to the limited extent that the HAS is confined to that area of the NHS—the hospitals for the mentally ill, the mentally handicapped and the chronic sick—where the professionally least powerful doctors work. (And, it's worth pointing out, where the professional element is chiefly provided by the nurses whose apparent lack of influence in policy-making was noted at the beginning of this paper: this raises the question, though, of whether this lack of influence should be put down to weakness of organisation, difference in social background and/or lack of expertise). All this seems to suggest that the explanatory power of various explanatory modes may vary in the different stages, as well as in different situations, of policy-making—that the same factors may not be as important at the stage of policy-initiation as during the process of policy-implementation.

Planning Medical Manpower

The policy area discussed so far is a non-technical one, in the sense that the issues involve questions of social priorities, professional independence and institutional innovation. By way of contrast it is illuminating to discuss briefly what may at first sight seem a completely different sort of policy area, that of planning medical manpower, where the problems would appear to call more for the application of suitable techniques than for judgment or bargaining. The question of how many doctors a country needs would seem to be, at first sight at any rate, one which calls primarily for rational analysis, involving essentially non-political and non-value judgments.

Here it is instructive to consider the report of the Royal Commission on Medical Education,[18] published in 1968, a majority of whose members (ten out of sixteen) were doctors. The Commission was set up at a time when there was considerable alarm about the exodus of British-trained doctors and the increasing reliance of the NHS on Commonwealth doctors. Ten years earlier, in 1957, the Willink Committee had advised a reduction in the number of medical students, to avoid the risk of a surplus of doctors. Not surprisingly, therefore, the Royal Commission recommended a massive expansion in the number of doctors produced by Britain's medical schools: an increase of about fifty per cent over twenty-five years.

How did it reach this conclusion? The difficulty facing the Commission, as it acknowledged, was that there is no "absolute or optimum level of health services which can be measured and towards which we should aim." It was therefore thrown back on using some fairly rough and ready methods, though using some quite elaborate statistical analyses, for assessing future requirements. It looked at population trends, and changes in the population structure (such as a higher proportion of the elderly) which might increase the demand for medical services. It examined, and extrapolated from, past trends showing the relationship between rising standards of living and medical manpower. It compared the number of doctors in Britain with that in other countries.[19]

The Commission's exercise is interesting from a number of different points of view.[20] It shows just how difficult policy-making is in an area where aims cannot be clearly defined. Equally, and perhaps more significantly, it shows the crucial importance of what might be called problem definition. The Royal Commission defined the problem facing it as being to decide how many doctors were needed. It did not define the problem as being to decide what services were required. Consequently, it did not examine the scope for substituting non-medical skills for medical ones.[21] Far less did it examine the scope for substituting non-medical services for medical ones: to what extent for instance, the NHS could be relieved of many of its tasks by developing community services (although by the time the Royal Commission was at work, the concept of community care was becoming increasingly fashionable, if only because this was seen as a means of cutting rising costs). In short, the way the Royal Commission defined the problem largely determined its policy recommendations.[22]

It is only fair to point out that if the Royal Commission had adopted a different, and wider definition of the problem, it would have faced a number of difficulties. The technology of medical manpower forecasting is not particularly well-developed, and there are a variety of difficulties about the methods that have been used in different countries.[23] Further, it is by no means clear how far skills and services of different kinds can be substituted for each other. Research might well answer some of the questions about substitutability, but the Royal Commission was working at a time when there was little British work to draw on. In other words, the policy time-table and the information time-tables were not synchronised: a recurring problem in policy-making, and one which supports the case for cautious incrementalism so as to allow for changes in direction when the information does eventually become available.

The example of the Royal Commission also raises another general point: the danger of looking at the experience of one country in isolation. This particular example could be used to illustrate the power of the medical profession in the context of the British NHS. But this could be misleading. Other countries—for instance, France—are also planning to expand their medical manpower.[24] The appropriate conclusion could therefore be that the British experience of policy-making in this area reflects not the particular circumstances of the NHS but a more general phenomenon: the ability of the medical professions to define the policy problems of health services, irrespective of their methods of organisation and institutional character. Or they may point to a wider conclusion still: to the danger of looking at the experience of one profession in isolation. It may be that all professions responsible for providing a public service with ill-defined aims are in a particularly strong position to define their own policy problems: education—and higher education in particular—would seem to be another internationally applicable instance of this.

The point about the dangers of parochialism in policy analysis can be reinforced by a further example. The debate about the reorganisation of the NHS has been largely dominated by the questions of whether it is too managerial in character: the emphasis on managerial accountability has been cited as an example of Conservative ideology.[25] The vocabulary of managerial accountability is exemplified by the following quotation:

> Health services are now being seen as part of the basic social services of a country and it is increasingly the intention to ensure that they are effectively and efficiently organised . . . to achieve this objective, management principles will have to be applied to health services. Limited needs and competing demands make it certain that systematic planning, careful monitoring and critical evaluation will be required.

As it happens, this quotation does not come from any of the NHS reorganisation documents, but from a report published by the World Health Organisation,[26] compiled by an expert committee including a Russian, an Argentinian, a Ghanaian, a Bulgarian, an American and a Briton. In short, it is essential to distinguish those elements in policy-making which spring from problems of providing a particular sort of service from those which spring from the organisation of that service in a particular country or from the policy perceptions of a particular Minister. It is essential to draw an analytic distinction between the structural elements (technological and economic factors), the organisational superstructure (machinery of administration, routines of decision-making) and perceptions of policy options (party ideologies, personal commitments, shifting social values), all of which may, however, contribute to the way a specific situation is resolved in terms of policy-making.

Conclusion

[. . .] The evidence reviewed in this chapter suggests that, in the case of health service policy in Britain, the various modes of explanation examined are all useful, but that their explanatory power varies considerably from situation to situation. . . .[27]

The other general conclusion suggested by a study of the NHS is the need to develop a way of conceptualising policy-making as a sort of multi-dimensional chess. There may well be some self-contained policy areas and policy issues (indeed in some cases it may be in the interests of the protagonists to keep them so). But in a field like health services, it is the interrelatedness of areas and issues which seems to be the norm. If the medical profession adopts a particular stance on issue X, it may well be because section A of the profession wants to enlist the support of section B on issue Y. Similarly, governments may well give in to the demands of the medical profession on issue Z, because it wants to conserve its political and administrative resources for the coming conflict over issue W. Hence conclusions drawn on individual case studies can be positively misleading unless they can be fitted into some larger framework.

To vary the metaphor, decision-making in complex and heterogeneous policy areas like health services can be usefully analysed in terms of capital appreciation and depreciation and their opportunity costs:[28] whether they build up the capital of good-will, prestige or administrative capacity of the policy-makers, and whether their opportunity costs in these same currencies are greater or larger than those of alternative courses. The same is true when policy-making in the health system spills over into policy-making in the political system as a whole: thus in 1970 the Labour Government refused to implement the recommendations of an independent review body in favour of a large pay increase for doctors, apparently because the costs in loss of good-will among the medical profession were thought to be outweighed by the political costs of seeming to give in to a privileged group and the economic costs of encouraging emulative pay demands.

This paper has raised many questions without answering them. This is because, to return to the main theme, all the modes of explanation seem to be useful to varying degrees in different situations. Indeed, why should this be otherwise? There is no reason for assuming, *a priori,* that any one theory should have equal explanatory powers irrespective of the situation to which it is being applied. Hence, in my view, the most urgent requirement in policy-making studies—whether these are analytic or prescriptive—is to develop a more precise descriptive vocabulary capable of delineating policy environments, areas and issues with more accuracy than is at present possible. Only then should it, hopefully, be possible to assess the relative contributions (which, in any case, need not be mutually exclusive) of the various tools of explanation.

NOTES

[1]I have not attempted to define policy-making, nor to draw a distinction between policy-making and decision-taking. See Desmond Keeling *Management in Government* (London: Allen and Unwin, 1972), 23–26, where he argues that it is impossible in practice to draw any sharp distinction between policy and implementation, and that policy is often defined during the decision-making process.

[2]Various attempts have been made to devise such typologies. One such typology is that proposed by Theodore J. Lowi in "American business public policy case-studies and political theory." *World Politics,* 1964, where he distinguishes between distributory, re-distributory and regulatory policy issues. Another scheme is that proposed by Emmette S. Redford in *Democracy in the Administrative State* (New York: Oxford University Press, 1969), where she distinguishes between micro-politics, subsystem politics and macropolitics. Finally Lewis A. Froman Jr. in "The categorization of policy contents," in A. Ranney, ed. *Political science and public policy* (Chicago: Markham Publishing Co., 1968), addressed himself to the question of whether categories of policy can be related to variations in political processes. However, I have not found it useful to apply any of these schemes to policy-making in the NHS, though many of the ideas are stimulating.

[3]N. Fisher, *Iain Macleod* (London: Andre Deutsch, 1973), 93–95.

[4]J. Enoch Powell, *Medicine and Politics* (London: Pitman Medical, 1966), 48–9.

[5]Nicholas Bosanquet, "Inequalities in health," in P. Townsend and N. Bosanquet, eds., *Labour and Inequality* (London: Fabian Society, 1972).

[6]This section draws on the private, unpublished diaries of Richard Crossman. I am most grateful to him for allowing me access to them and Janet Morgan, the custodian of the diaries, for help and guidance. In addition, the paper draws on conversations with civil servants and others who prefer to remain anonymous.

[7]It would be instructive, for example, to compare the power exercised by doctors with that exerted by scientists, as described by Don K. Price, *The Scientific Estate* (Cambridge, Mass: Belknap Press, 1965). If one were to classify the various professions on a continuum running from expertise to mystique, physicists and some doctors would come at the expert end, while lawyers and most doctors would be nearer the mystique end. How does this affect their role in the policy-making process?

[8]For a discussion of political costs—related to Neustadt's reputation costs—see Aaron Wildavsky, in "Political science and public policy," op. cit., 80–81.

[9]For a discussion of the importance of the mental set in another context, see Aaron Wildavsky, *The politics of the budgetary process* (Boston: Little Brown and Company, 1964), p. 29.

[10]Barbara Robb ed., *Sans Everything* (London: Nelson, 1967).

[11]*Findings and recommendations following enquiries into allegations concerning the care of elderly patients in certain hospitals, Cmnd 3687* (London: HMSO, 1968).

[12]*Report of the committee of inquiry into allegations of ill-treatment of patients and other irregularities at the Ely Hospital, Cardiff, Cmnd 3975* (London: HMSO 1969).

[13]Leon Festinger, *A theory of cognitive dissonance* (Evanston, Illinois: Row Peterson and Co., 1957). See also Harold L. Wilensky, *Organisational intelligence* (New York: Basic Books, 1967). But, as so often, some percipient insights come from novelists. See for example the account of the interpretation of information in the Dreyfus affair in Marcel Proust, *A la recherche du temps perdu* (Paris: Pleiade, 1954), 2, 241–2.

[14]Thomas S. Kuhn, *The structure of scientific revolutions* (Chicago: University of Chicago Press, 1970), 2nd edition.

[15]". . . quite new kinds of ideas and knowledge are among the necessary requisites for building up the needed novel policy-making system—and the supply of such new kinds of ideas and knowledge is the main longer range mission of policy sciences," Y. Dror, *Prolegomena to policy sciences,* Rand Corporation, P–4283, January 1970.

[16]National Health Service Hospital Advisory Service, *Annual Report for 1969/70* (London: HMSO, 1971).

[17]Hospital Advisory Service, *Annual Report* 1972 (London: HMSO, 1973).

[18]*Royal Commission on Medical Education, Cmnd 3569* (London: HMSO, 1968). Op. cit.

[19]"(The passion for figures did not merely result from the help which they gave in deciding issues of policy, but also because figures gave the processes by which decisions were reached an apparent air of scientific rationality. A document which contained statistics was nearly always considered superior to one which was mere words." Ely Devons, *Planning in practice: essays in aircraft planning in wartime* (Cambridge: Cambridge University Press, 1950), p. 156.

[20]For a study of policy making by Royal Commissions, see Sir Geoffrey Vickers, *The art of judgment* (London: Chapman and Hall, 1965), chapter 3.

[21]Here there is an interesting contrast between Britain and the United States. In the latter, there has been much more emphasis on substituting auxiliaries and aides for medical manpower. Why is this? Is this because the American medical profession is weaker than the British? The success of the American medical profession in moulding the development of health services hardly suggests that this is the explanation. Perhaps the answer may be found in the fact that the US spends a much higher proportion of its GNP on health than Britain, 6.8 percent as against 4.8 percent in 1969 and rising at a faster rate. So there is much more of an incentive to push for change, with professional power limited by economic forces (a warning again against trying to assess the power of pressure or interest groups without looking at the other side of what may be a constantly changing equation).

[22]I am grateful to my former colleague, Phoebe Hall, for allowing me to see a draft of her forthcoming study of the Seebohm Committee which documents the importance of initial problem definition.

[23]The various methods have been reviewed by Herbert E. Klarman, "Economic aspects of projecting requirements for health manpower," *Journal of Human Resources* 4, 3, (Summer, 1969).

[24]*Sixième Plan de développement economique et social* (Paris: Imprimerie des Journaux officiels, 1971), 309.

[25]*Parliamentary Debates,* vol. 853, nos. 85 and 86, 27 and 28 March 1973. (London: HMSO, 1973).

[26]*Statistical indicators for the planning and evaluation of public health programmes,* World Health Technical Health Report Series, no. 472 (Geneva: World Health Organisation, 1971), p. 37.

[27]In adopting this approach, I have been much influenced by Graham T. Allison's *Essence of decision* (Boston: Little, Brown and Company, 1971). But instead of applying different modes of explanation to the same situation I have tried, in a very tentative and preliminary way, to apply them to different situations. I have also used a rather different categorisation of the modes themselves.

[28]Raymond A. Bauer, Ithiel de Sola Pool and L. A. Dexter, *American business and public policy* (New York: Atherton Press, 1963), pp. 480–481.

PART II

The Social Order

4 Maintenance and Change

Policies as Guidelines for Social Development

If policies are guidelines for social development, as most analysts seem to believe, then it seems to be important to try to understand the forces of maintenance and change in society. Where will resistance to change be encountered? What are the likely prospects of bringing about change?

Most people are reluctant to make large changes in existing patterns of social relationships in western democratic societies. They value social order, they like to know where they stand in society.

Societies are not static. They have to respond to internal and external pressures. Revolution from within, or conquest from without are concepts which are very threatening to many people; and if not for most people, at least for those with some power. They are anxious to preserve the social order, to ensure that change comes slowly enough so that it is evolutionary rather than revolutionary. Before going on to examine social change processes, it may be useful to consider the mechanisms for preserving social order.

Social Control

Philosophers and sociologists have been greatly concerned to explore the workings of society, to conceptualize how the social order is created and maintained. Watkins' (1975) review of these theories explains that there are two conceptions of the social order—the first, the Hobbesian view that "there are certain tensions between people and groups that have to be resolved, something that becomes a political tension when there is some awareness of differences of interest and view and [the other] the conception of a society as a set of relationships which are natural, normatively guided and deviance from which is the puzzling factor . . . Our key concepts for the understanding of these problems are legitimation and solidarity" (p. 21).

What is meant by these last two terms? Legitimate, in this sense, is defined in the Concise Oxford Dictionary as "lawful, proper, regular, conforming to standard type," whilst solidarity is "holding together, mutual dependence, community of interests, feeling and action."

Legitimacy

It is clear that health policy analysts and policymakers profit from having an awareness that social organization is normative. What is lawful, proper, regular and conforms to standard type is decided by a particular society to meet its own purposes of holding together. Benn and Peters (1959) have described how social laws differ from the laws of nature which are studied by physical scientists. They are negotiated in societies through political processes, therefore it becomes important to understand some of the tensions arising from differences of view and the mechanisms for resolving them.

Individuals usually wish to be regarded as normal (or, if deviant, better than normal) members of their community. If health is complete physical, mental and social well-being, then knowing one's position, its acceptable roles and their acceptable norms is of great importance for health.

Individuals have been expected to adjust to society rather than society to individual differences, although now, with more resources available, societies are becoming more tolerant of deviance. They are widening the bounds of normal behaviour and accepting redefinitions of social relationships. Societies are constantly changing as these redefinitions continue to be made.

Gil (1970) has explained that the mechanism of social allocation of power and authority "evolved out of the principle of the division of labour and the gradual stabilization of this principle through processes of social stratification. . . . This allocative mechanism is the 'task and manpower system' of a society."

With the allocation of responsibilities there was a corresponding allocation of authority and prerogatives—a legitimation of privilege.

Solidarity

From existence in small groups of hunters and farmers who survived through solidarity, giving mutual aid to one another, societies have become structured into modern national groupings. Gradually, as these larger groupings have developed, the need for formally approved laws and other types of regulation have seemed to be necessary to govern social relationships.

But as societies move away from simple social groupings where all can see the mutual efforts of others, tensions arise over the distribution of tasks and authority and prerogatives assumed by those who are in power positions: the legitimacy of privileges begins to be challenged.

In Watkins' view, the central questions relating to social control were "who aligns with whom, why these alignments are as they are, who or what they may be in tension with and what the conditions of the maintenance and breakdown of these relationships are . . ." (p. 20–21).

Political history is concerned with the struggles of societies over the allocation of political responsibilities and prerogatives; and political philosophy with the different interpretations of men's rights to exert power over others. Obviously, within the scope of this reader, it is not possible to examine whole fields of study. However, it is important to appreciate the major differences in the approaches of political analysts who will be quoted here and these will be given consideration in this and the next five chapters. To take one example, Watkins begins his exposition by discussing the differences in interpretation of the issues by those who support social equilibrium theories (e.g. Parsons, 1952) and those who take other positions (e.g. Marxists and radicals).

Ruling Classes and Elites

Sociologists have said that it is important to distinguish between ruling classes and the elites of society. The ruling classes are likely to be numbered in the hundreds, whilst elites may be quite large in resource-rich societies where there have been more opportunities to become entrepreneurs, managers or professionals and to move from working class to middle class occupations (from the proletariat to the bourgeoisie). Ruling classes and ruling elites are complementary concepts referring either to different types of political systems or different aspects of the same system.

The reason for trying to make this distinction clear is because of semantic and ideological confusions which have arisen. Elites have been studied mainly by those in the liberal tradition, whilst the class struggle is of particular importance to Marxists. Bottomore (1966) has proposed a threefold classification of class/elite structures ranging from a tightly articulated ruling class to a multiplicity of elites without a cohesive group of powerful individuals or families. Giddens (1974) has extended this to a fourfold grouping: ruling and governing classes, power elite, leadership.

The importance of studying ruling classes and social elites, relative to social control, is that in all societies there is an unequal division of wealth and power. Those who have more of both will seek to maintain their advantages by aligning themselves with others like themselves and adopting behaviour which will preserve their prerogatives—their positions of authority in the stratified societies which exist today by virtue of ever-increasing division of labour into more and more specialist activities.

Before considering their behaviour, one must decide who are the ruling classes or the elites and by what criteria they are identified. Many social scientists equate the rulers with those who have economic and political power.

In *The Vertical Mosaic,* Porter (1965) described those he considered to be at the top of Canadian society, calling them the economic elite, the labour elite (heading up the unions), the political elite (the federal cabinet and the senior judiciary), the bureaucratic elite (the federal bureaucracy), senior executives of the mass media and the elites of higher learning and the clergy (including the men of science). It will be noted that, apart from scientists, who may or may not be interested in biomedical or health care research, there are no health professionals in this group.

There have been a number of studies of the elite groups in the liberal democratic societies with which we are concerned, because elitism seems to be a denial of the democratic principle of political equality. Porter concluded that, "The nineteenth century notion of a liberal citizen-participating democracy is obviously not a satisfactory model by which to examine the processes of decision-making in either the economic or the political contexts." A new country is not necessarily able to free itself from its historical roots. In his view, Canada, like other western industrial nations, was dominated by elite groups who had taken over power from the colonizing British authorities. These elites were able to make major decisions and to determine the shape and direction of development of the country. Given the complexities of modern societies, he thought it was unlikely that widespread democratic participation could develop without very great changes and institutional experimentation.

Like Porter, Encel (1970) in Australia was concerned at the inability of his compatriots to achieve greater equality in that new country, but like the Canadians, Australians are burdened with a history of colonization and learned responses to authority. Unlike the Americans, who rebelled against the authority of George III and his government, overthrowing the colonizing power's ruling class and establishing a local one, the Canadians and Australians have inherited rulers. Like the British, they have chosen to make changes in their societies by evolution, not revolution, and this is often slow.

Mechanisms of Social Control

Other analysts have been more interested in explaining the mechanisms of social control used by power groups. Lasswell (1948) examined the practices of what he called the ruling elites at the top of a country's social structure and tried to answer the question: who gets what, when, how? He explained the mechanisms which were used to hold on to power, authority and prerogatives and discussed who aligned with whom and why the alignments were as they were.

Lukes (1974) summarized the work of social scientists who had been interested in the question of legitimation of issues for consideration by the public and added his own contribution. He proposed that power should be considered in three dimensions—firstly, developing issues overtly; secondly, covering them up and easing them out of view; thirdly, not even being aware that an issue might exist when someone from another culture is only too aware that it does.

As Watkins has shown, power groups are particularly concerned to maintain and transmit their value system to others. He has quoted Moore to show some other ways of doing this. Moore has tried to shock his readers into realizing how members of a society may be socialized or controlled, "... human beings are punched, bullied, sent to jail, thrown into concentration camps, cajoled, bribed, made into heroes, encouraged to read newspapers, stood up against a wall and shot, and sometimes even taught sociology" (p. 10). He extends the normal view of the socialization process, for most writers are content to discuss socialization through family interactions, schooling and the disciplines of employment, and to consider the provisions for correcting deviance through the obvious forces of law and order, but few reveal the hidden mechanisms of social control as Moore does.

One of the few others who looked below the surface was Parsons, who, in his interpretive description of homeostatic social systems, identified personal service professionals as the principal controllers for society. Among those professionals, he considered physicians to be key figures in maintaining social order. Parsons developed the concept of the "sick role" as a mechanism which enabled people to drop out temporarily from their normal activities in their allocated roles. They could move into a holding pattern which was acceptable to others if duly authorized by a licensed physician who was responsible for guiding them back to "health." This idea has stimulated a great deal of research and there have been a number of important critiques of the Parsonian approach in recent years. Watkins is specifically interested in the social control aspects but others (e.g., Gallagher, 1976; Levine and Kozloff, 1978) have reviewed all the researches stemming from the "sick role" paradigm and their comments are of interest. Gallagher has suggested that

> further theoretical development is necessary to account for significant health-illness phenomena which the deviance conception cannot encompass. The phenomena under consideration are: (1) chronic illness, wherein there is no possibility of the patient's return to health; (2) patient self-help and self-treatment; (3) the acquiescent posture of the medical profession in the face of widespread health-risking behaviour; (4) the failure of many health institutions

> to promote maximum rehabilitation in patients; and (5) the contradiction between the high position of personal health in the hierarchy of American values and the extent of preventible ill health. Later Parsonian formulations which view illness as impaired adaptive capacity rather than deviance, and which attribute less importance to social control and to medical instrumentality, offer a fruitful prospect for a more thoroughgoing conceptualization. [P. 207]

Levine and Kozloff, whilst accepting Gallagher's criticisms of Parsons' "medico-centred" framework, have made their own list of difficulties with the paradigm whilst acknowledging that it has been "remarkably provocative."

> First, there is an underestimation of the impact of family and other lay supportive systems. . . . Second, Gallagher suggests that the Parsonian scheme "does not give sufficient scope to the social structure of medical care." Consequently, "the question may be raised as to whether the role of the patient is indeed the same throughout the health care system. . . ." A third issue is that of the latent functions and iatrogenic consequences of the sick role. . . . Fourth, several writers have suggested that we begin to look beyond traditional variables in searching for a more complete understanding of illness behaviour. . . . The problems of the physically disabled are not to be understood only in terms of the social norms they appear to violate. Because of the social stigma assigned to the disabled and the social incapacities attributed to them, they are characteristically denied various opportunities afforded to others in society. [Pp. 337-39]

The study of Freidson (1970) of professional dominance (growing out of Parsons' work) has also had an important influence on medical sociologists' views. (In the readings attached to chapter 3, the Ehrenreichs have compared the work of Parsons and Freidson.) Again, some critics have thought his approach was too medico-centric and have argued the necessity to examine the doctors' place in promoting the general ideological objectives of their society in order to understand better their functioning. McKinlay (1977), for example, listed four levels of analysis which he thought were necessary for understanding doctors' positions in society, namely, their contribution to capitalist power, to capitalist state power, to medical power and to public power.

Radical and Marxist Views of the Doctors' Gatekeeping Functions

It is McKinlay's argument that doctors in the U.S.A. are the "willing tools of big business," so that it is necessary to examine their part in promoting the social purposes of American capitalist society as well as their role as social controllers for that society.

A number of other American radicals became concerned about the uneven distribution of services to the rich and the poor in their country in the late sixties and various interpretations began to be offered in explanation of this.

The Ehrenreichs (1975), who claim to be radicals but not Marxists, have been interested specifically in the medical profession's part in American society's concern to control the "dangerous classes." A summary of their thesis by Mandell (1975) is that

> Although [they] do not believe that doctors are engaged in a conscious conspiracy [against the laity], their look at doctors' practices in the United States leads them to conclude that doctors' power to affect even non-medical aspects of the society has vastly expanded. By holding down their numbers whilst holding on to their power, doctors have increased their income spectacularly. Further, they have invaded the consciousness of Americans through extensive media coverage so that few people are free from some passive acquiescence in accepting the doctors' pronouncements. . . .
>
> The most prestigious and highly paid professionals in the U.S. have shaped a service through tightly organized pressure and control of the medical schools. Their power may be used to exclude some people from the services the doctors provide or to vastly increase the range of services to other people; both patterns involve shuffling the label "sick". . . .Disciplinary control occurs when some doctors force sterilization on poor women; expansionary (cooptive) control occurs when some doctors enter eagerly into lucrative abortion practice.
>
> [The Ehrenreichs] argue from the assumption that class, sex, and race strongly influence people's attitudes and practices. Because doctors belong to the upper middle class and are predominantly white and male, they often help to perpetuate society's dominant ideology, thereby helping to reinforce existing class and caste patterns or dominance-submission. Most human-service professionals have faced the same charge, and there is a good deal of research evidence to document it.
>
> There are two sides to the coin of authoritarianism. Authority is legitimate to the extent that people accept it as legitimate. When people attribute magical power to doctors—or to any authority— they give up some of their own autonomy. In *The Brothers Karamazov,* Dostoevesky had the Grand Inquisitor show how the Church maintained control over people by maintaining an aura of mystery and claiming ultimate authority. Doctors use the same elements of control; perhaps they have become our new priests. [Pp. 138-39]

Whilst the Ehrenreichs have emphasized the need to reconsider the legitimacy of the doctors' mandate in their discussion, Navarro (1976) was more concerned with the lack of solidarity—the divisions in modern society between the rulers and the ruled—by the way in which the rulers may exploit the ruled through the treatment of illness. He has interpreted the Marxists' viewpoint about the haves and have nots and aligns personal service professionals with the haves who keep the have nots in their place.

It will have been noted that McKinlay distinguished between capitalist and capitalist state societies. Health care services may be provided almost entirely by free enterprise within capitalist nations (e.g., U.S.A.) or they may be provided almost entirely by the state (e.g., U.S.S.R.). Most other countries fall somewhere between the extremes—Australia, Canada and Great Britain being more entrepreneurial and less state-controlled in that order.

Navarro (1977), taking a black and white view, regarded all four western democratic societies as exploitative capitalist societies whilst others (e.g., Abel-Smith, 1972 (see selection in chapter 3), Titmuss, 1974) have distinguished between unrestrained capitalism and welfare state capitalism. There are other Marxists (e.g., Wilding and George, 1974-5), who have argued that welfare states, by modifying social insecurities through state social insurance schemes and other capitalist state interventions, have compounded injustice through making it more difficult for the have nots to identify the practices of the ruling groups to keep them "in their proper place."

Social Change

Just as some members of society are conservative by nature and are more anxious to maintain the social order, others are reformist and wish to promote social change. It is useful to have some conception as to whether much change may be brought about.

Change theorists are interested in the conditions which produce alterations and the forms which these alterations take—the types of events which occur.

Varieties of Change

Smith (1976), taking the historical long view, defined change as

> A succession of events which produce, over time, a modification or replacement of particular patterns or units by other novel ones. This places events at the centre of our analysis of change mechanisms, and at the same time allows for partial as well as total substitution of either the patterns or the units which are alleged to change. [P. 13]

Events are short-term changes, clusters and sequences of events are *processes* and *trends* may last over millenia.

By focussing upon *events,* an analyst can see whether individuals can influence change. It is also possible to examine *processes* over a middle-range time period (Smith suggested a decade might be chosen) and *trends* over the long term. But these become impersonal movements.

It is possible to chart major events in health policy development over the past two centuries since democratic governments took office. It would seem that, in liberal democratic countries, major political events occur about once in a generation or less often, rather than every decade. Titmuss (1950) and others have pointed out that wars greatly influence social policy, bringing all sectors of society together in mutual defence. They permit questions about the weaknesses in society to be raised and values to be reconsidered. Once national values have been restated and legitimized, steps can be taken to restructure the situation, to explore the feasibility of new approaches. Figure 4–1 pinpoints the times when values and structures have been reexamined since the 1840s in the western democracies. Dates of events can be shown precisely, processes are indicated by the cyclical flow and trends are outlined at the foot of the chart. This chart is very simplistic, for of the three types of change, Smith specified *socioeconomic, political* and *cultural,* it shows only political change. Political change, that is, the distribution of power and authority, the formulation of public policy and the institutionalization of power in organizations may come faster than other forms of change, especially if there are revolutions. Socioeconomic change, that is, change in patterns of resource allocation, production, economic interests of various groups and in the prestige associated with property and class, is slow. In the cultural sphere, content is likely to change faster than style. These three regions of change can be analyzed separately, although they may interact with one another.

It is particularly important for health policy makers to be able to understand these distinctions—that making political changes which affect the socioeconomic or cultural interests of others may be resisted because they are not worked through with these groups—are not legitimized in their eyes or the eyes of their supporters. Accounts of the changes which governments in Australia (Hunter, 1966) or in Saskatchewan (Badgley and Wolfe, 1967) or Quebec (Taylor, 1972) tried to bring about against the will of the medical profession, and with which they had only partial success, can be considered in the light of Smith's tripartite classification. Similarly, political changes affecting different ethnic groups have to be assimilated into their economies and cultures. Indigenous groups in North America and Australia have had particular difficulties in accepting western ideas.

Human Initiative in Making Changes

Smith has argued that it is only when one views *events* that human initiative in making changes can be observed. Individuals' efforts are unlikely to succeed unless the times are ripe for change and supporters come forward. Viewed over the long term it seems likely that change does not happen unless it is part of a *trend.* Smith has distinguished between active and passive change and has suggested that not enough is yet known as to "whether or not human beings actually intervene in initiating the events, in providing the channels of their impact and in furnishing novel forms for embodying the changes" (p. 23). However, mankind likes to consider that it is in control of developments, that human initiatives are of importance. Smith has suggested that change analysts can help others to understand better what is going on if they can identify *sources, channels* and *repertoires of forms* (which distinguish between *active* and *passive* change), for these can

FIGURE 4–1

THE CYCLICAL DEVELOPMENT OF SOCIAL/ HEALTH POLICIES

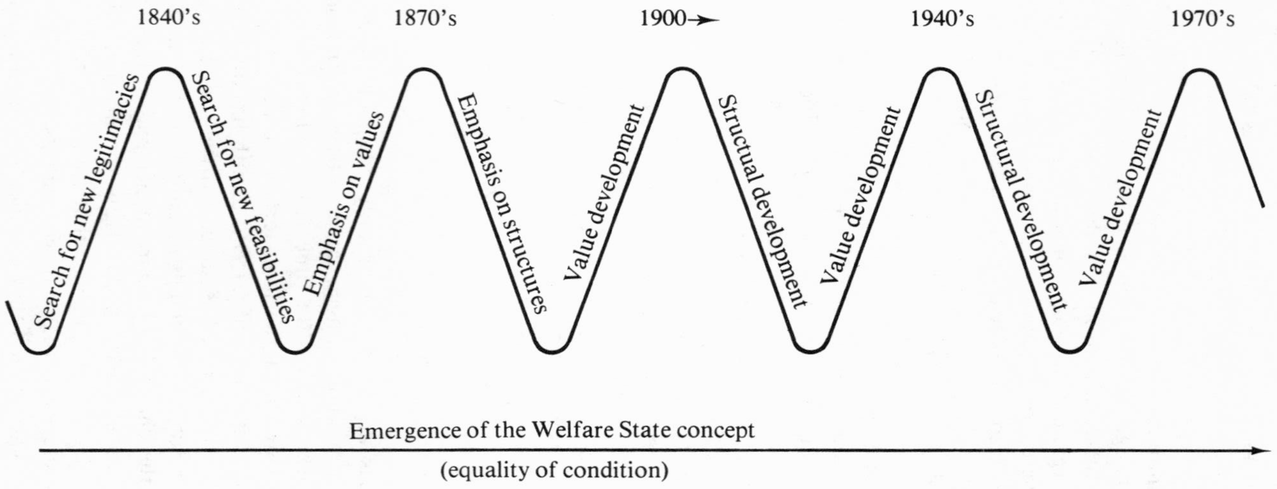

1840's
1870's
1900→
1940's
1970's

Search for new legitimacies
Search for new feasibilities
Emphasis on values
Emphasis on structures
Value development
Structual development
Value development
Structural development
Value development

Emergence of the Welfare State concept
(equality of condition)

be differentiated according to the peculiar mode appropriate to the presence or absence of human intervention at each of the points along the chain leading to change.

In an attempt to illustrate different kinds of human initiatives in social change, Etzioni and Etzioni-Halevy (1973) have reviewed five articles on change processes: (1) Lindblom's incrementalism (or, as they describe it, laissez-faire); (2) Dahrendorf's planned change; two types of evolutionary change through (3) educational processes and (4) social movements; and finally, (5) revolutionary change. For health policy makers it is important to understand all these forms of change, even revolutionary change.

(1) Lindblom's "The Science of Muddling Through" has already been reviewed in chapter 2. (2) Much of the last part of this volume will be concerned with planned change, so discussion of planning is postponed to chapters 11 and 12. (3) So far as educational change is concerned, some readings are suggested—one on the socialization of physicians (Hughes, 1958); and (4) one on the career pattern of social movements (Wilson, 1973). Social movements seem to be an important channel for introducing new forms of health and social service institutions, such as specialist voluntary health agencies, into a society. (5) Lee (1979) has described the evolution of Quebec's health and social services during the period 1967–77. In 1964, as part of the Quiet Revolution in that province, provincial government representatives informed Ottawa that they wished to organize their own affairs according to the francophone culture (not the anglophone) and a block grant was negotiated (Newman, 1966). This enabled the government to begin planning for major changes in the provision of services. Lee has discussed the development of these revolutionary changes, which, in fact, had to take notice of existing political and social institutions and so were modified as implementation proceeded. But the priorities in planning and resource allocation were changed. Health services have begun to be provided as a right to poorer francophone Quebecois.

Social Movements

The apparent failure of democratic political systems to provide for citizens' participation in policy development for social change in the post-World War II years led to considerable questioning of decision-making processes and the structures for introducing changes into the political system. The Quiet Revolution in Quebec has been a successful challenge to existing power in Canada, developing from a social movement into organized political opposition and then becoming a provincial government in office, but most social movements have fewer supporters and are less ambitious in intention. For these, in the late 1960s there were developed practical guide books on how to become more involved in decision making, advocacy, confrontation with existing power groups and so on. Sociologists began to examine the rise and fall of social movements—the development of mutual aid or mutual interest groups—solidary organizations with a purpose to achieve. For those intending to embark on encouraging such developments, this kind of analysis is helpful, for it generalizes from many experiences and may provide guidelines for action or understanding of the reasons for failure to succeed.

Wilson has explained the stages in the career of a social movement, how it becomes structured and how it ends. Social movements are dynamic and therefore cannot continue indefinitely. They accomplish change and become established or reach a position of stalemate or fail. If a movement succeeds and becomes institutionalized,

> it changes its identity and [according to its mission] becomes a welfare organization, or a pressure group, an interest group, a denomination, an educational or philanthropic association or a political party. . . [but] few social movements enjoy the feeling of having completed their mission and contentedly disband. . . . Frustration is the fate of all social movements. [Pp. 359–60]

In listing these organizations which take over when social movements succeed, Wilson has drawn attention to other mechanisms developed by democratic societies for dealing with social control or social change, some of which have been reviewed above. It may be useful now to consider the function of pressure groups and interest groups (called interest intermediation by Schmitter) in effecting social change.

Interest Intermediation

Schmitter (1977) has explained that, with the development of industrial societies and the division of labour, groups with shared interests began to evolve and get together to pursue these interests in their context.

There were, he said, different explanations for the emergence of these groups during the nineteenth century according to the political philosophical stance taken. When political scientists first began to examine the phenomenon of pressure groups in the post-World War II period, they were influenced by the American or British context and saw interest groups as evidences of pluralism in western democratic political life. Schmitter is critical of their simplistic descriptive approaches, yet it is helpful when Eckstein (1960) makes a distinction between attitude groups which are concerned with legitimation of their own ideas and changing others' values, and interest groups which are concerned with pursuing selfish advantage, even though the two activities may be carried out, consecutively or concurrently, by one pressure group.

Schmitter has developed a typology of interest intermediation activities. After specifying the three modes most appropriate for identifying differences in interest politics viz: pluralism, corporatism and syndicalism, he has argued that there are two variants in each of the modes.

> As statically specified above, the three generic modes of interest intermediation could have come into being by two radically different processes and, hence, may embody diametrically opposed relations of power and influence. They could have emerged "from below" in more-or-less spontaneous response to prior changes within civil society and the associational sphere itself; or they could have been imposed "from above" as a matter of deliberate public policy contrived and controlled by preexisting authority groups. [P. 10]

Schmitter's model used western Europe as the basis of discussion because the early writers on pressure groups in England and America

> uncritically accepted the pluralist paradigm and its assumptions for analytic purposes. They failed to notice that the existing structure and behavior of interest associations in most Western European systems hardly exhibited the spontaneous, overlapping, chaotic, and competitive properties said to characterize their U.S. analogs, or where there was evidence of such pluralism, that it was rooted in polarized ideological conflicts and/or ethnic-religious-linguistic diversity and so hardly conducive to the same consensual, moderate, equilibrated outcomes. [P. 17]

However, by examining western European developments, Schmitter has extended the North American view of pressure group activities into those areas described by Lukes as the second and third dimensions of power which often remain hidden areas in democratic societies (see also Porter's comment about power in democracies). Schmitter has cautioned against the use of his typology in too simplistic a manner, for whilst it may be useful to discuss national units in generic terms,

> all interest intermediation systems of Western Europe are mixed. They may be predominantly of one type but different sectors and subsectors, classes and class factions, regions and sub-regions are likely to be operating simultaneously according to different principles and procedures. [P. 14]

From developing the typology, Schmitter went on to try to elucidate the relationship between interest intermediation groups and societal change but he regarded his efforts as only partially successful. Using structural differentiation, historical materialism and political economy as three different frameworks for analyzing the art of association, he found that no one of these frameworks was adequate by itself. However, he suggested that, taken together in juxtaposition or synthesis, they might be able to provide a satisfactory basis for analysis.

Discussion of Readings and References

Within the scope of this book it has not been possible to include all the readings which would have been useful. In pursuing the issues raised in this chapter, the only reading selected, that of Barbara and John Ehrenreich on

"Health Care and Social Control," should follow on a series of preliminary readings which are discussed below.

1. There are several series of introductory sociology texts which may be used to gain a quick insight into the general issues of social control and social change. For the purposes of this chapter, the Longman series was used as a guide to the territory. C. Ken Watkins' *Social Control* and Anthony Smith's *Social Change* are both part of this paperback series of useful summaries of work done up to the mid-1970s.

Since they were written specifically for those interested in sociology, the language used is not simple, but health policy makers will find it worthwhile to follow the writers' arguments. These may help them to view health issues in a different way—to realize why the Ehrenreichs are concerned about the doctors' position as social controllers.

2. It was suggested in the discussion following chapter 3 that social analysts tended to range themselves along a political continuum from Marxists on the left to liberals on the right. Talcott Parsons took a right wing liberal stance in developing his ideas of *The Social System.* An important chapter in that book is concerned with the "sick role" and the doctors' gatekeeping function for society. Since much of medical sociology has stemmed from Parsons' formulation, it is important to read chapter 10 of this book. Again, the language and style of writing may be complex and turgid but it is a classic presentation which needs to be read and understood. Levine and Kozloff (1976), reviewing work done on the sick role, found over one hundred research studies which had used the concept as a basic idea which is some indication of its importance.

Eliot Freidson, some twenty years later than Parsons did his work, has produced a series of studies of doctors' activities in the U.S.A. In this book it has been decided to refer only to the two most influential of these studies, *The Medical Profession* and *Professional Dominance.* In the latter, Freidson considers the controlling activities of doctors in a different way from Parsons. This, too, is very important reading for those interested in health policy since Freidson has been an influential thinker.

The Ehrenreichs' article which is reprinted in part here, compares and contrasts the way in which Freidson and Parsons view the doctors' gatekeeping.

3. In addition to Smith's historical analysis of social change, readers may find it helpful to consult a reader edited by Amitai Etzioni and Eva Etzioni-Halevy on *Social Change.* This reader provides quick access to the topic area and its main analysts. One section is concerned with Human Initiatives in Social Change. It suggests that there are five main methods of introducing change: incrementation, planning, socialization, social movements and revolution. The editors have selected readings giving examples of each.

Incrementation, first discussed by Lindblom, has also been considered by many of the writers whose works are reprinted in this book (e.g. Klein, Donnison).

Planning is reviewed in some detail in chapters 12 and 13.

It is not possible to go into detail on socialization for this is broad territory. However, it may be useful to read some of the studies on socialization of health care providers (e.g., part 2 of Freeman, Levine and Reeder, 1963 provides an overview up to that date). Radicals in Canada (e.g., Allentuck, 1978) and America (e.g., Ehrenreich and English, 1973) have been concerned with issues in the socialization of consumers and have endeavoured to alert those whom they consider to be exploited by the health system as presently organized. Whilst John Wilson's *Introduction to Social Movements* draws most of its examples from religious sects, it is also a good guide to evolution of health care movements. To read this summary alongside a history of a developing health organization such as Mary Pack's story of the Canadian Arthritis and Rheumatism Society, *Never Surrender,* enables one to analyze the stages in the development of the society, and perhaps, to predict similar developments in other emergent societies.

4. This chapter has also been concerned to explore the structures and processes of power. As Watkins said, the central questions are: "who aligns with whom, why these alignments are as they are, who or what they may be in tension with and what the conditions of the maintenance and breakdown of the relationships are" (pp. 20–21). Stephen Lukes has enlarged on the pluralistic liberal view of how political and social issues are dealt with (or fail to be dealt with). He has described how social structures facilitate or prevent issues being raised overtly and covertly. Harold D. Lasswell was concerned with the same questions about power. He described the processes of maintaining power in the U.S.A. Others have wanted to explain interest group activities (e.g., Eckstein, 1960 or Blishen, 1969). But up till recently, analyses have been simplistic. Now, just as Lukes has revealed hidden power structures in decision making, so Schmitter has revealed a range of interest groups not considered by earlier writers on this topic.

Health Care and Social Control

Barbara Ehrenreich and John Ehrenreich

The formal description of the medical system as a system of social control comes largely from the work of Talcott Parsons and Eliot Freidson.[1] One sees the medical system as chary in its favors ("exemptions"); the other sees it as recklessly indulgent. One excites moral concern over what it may *not* do, whom it may *not* care for, in its caution lest "sickness" sap the moral fiber of the nation; the other excites concern for what it *does* do, whom it *does* care for, in its drive to be caretaker for more and more of the nation's ills.

The picture of the American "sickness system" that emerges from Parsons's work resembles the American welfare system. Welfare too holds out exemptions, particularly from the requirement to seek gainful employment. But these exemptions are offered only to the "legitimately" poor (those certified as eligible); moreover they are only offered on the condition that the recipients recognize their status as undesirable and cooperate with "competent helpers" (social workers) to overcome the "character defects," "family pathology," etc., that have led to it. Like the sick role, the welfare role puts the recipient under the supervision of certain nonpoor people (caseworkers). And even more obviously than in the case of sickness, a variety of measures (low payments, degrading procedures) are taken to make sure that the welfare role will not be too tempting to the mass of working people. Concern for the sick or the poor, it seems, must always be held in check by the fearful possibility of *contagion*.[2]

Singularly absent from Parsons's description is any sense of agency. What

---

From *Social Policy* vol. 5 no. 1 (May-June, 1974): 27–30, 40, published by permission of *Social Policy* and the authors. The most complete radical treatment of the health system is *The American Health Empire,* a report from the Health Policy Advisory Center, prepared by Barbara and John Ehrenreich (New York: Random House, 1970).

determines the "social construction of sickness" he describes? In the homogeneous and seemingly middle-class America of Parsons's medical writings, the answer is simply "our values," and these appear to arise out of some deep cultural consensus. The first thing that strikes us as important about Freidson's work is that he identifies the actual architects of our "social construction of sickness": it is the medical profession which defines illness in theory (i.e., determines what biological syndromes admit one to the sick role and which can be considered as minor, psychosomatic, or otherwise ineligible for special treatment). And it is the doctors who identify illness in practice (i.e., determine who is eligible for sick roles), and undertake to supervise those identified as "sick."

> They [professionals] are not merely experts but incumbents in official positions. . . .Given the official status of the profession, what happens to the layman—that is, whether or not he will be recognized as "really" sick, what the sickness will be called, what treatment will be given him, how he will be required to act while ill, and what will happen to him after treatment—becomes a function of professional rather than lay decision. . . .Thus the behavior of the physician and others in the field of health constitutes the objectification, the empirical embodiment, of certain dominant values in a society.[3]

Where Parsons is concerned with a culturally diffuse "sickness system" (our term), Freidson is concerned with the actual medical system. He describes it as an agency of social control on a par with the legal system or organized religion. Each of these institutions is concerned with the prevention, detection, and management of social deviance: criminality in the case of the law, sin in the case of the organized religions, and illness in the case of the medical system. In his understanding of deviance Freidson makes a significant departure from Parsons. Parsons sees deviance as motivated behavior or deliberate idiosyncracy—more a matter for psychiatry than for sociology to comprehend. Freidson's approach is operational; he describes deviance as a state *imputed* by the relevant officials. The courts label certain people as "murderers" or "shoplifters"; doctors label certain others as "cancer cases" or "neurotics." Once so labeled, the person is required to enter the social role appropriate to the label: to undergo certain types of treatment, to modify his behavior in ways seen as therapeutic, perhaps to abandon all other social roles and enter an institution filled with similarly labeled people (cancer ward, jail, mental hospital).

While the aspect of the sick role which seems to concern Parsons is the exemptions it entails, and the allure these might exercise on the nonsick, the aspect of the sick role which concerns Freidson is the requirement that the sick person cooperate with the agencies and personnel set up to deal with his sickness. Freidson's moral concern is aroused not by the power of the medical profession to manage the sick but by its power to define what is meant by "sick." He describes the medical system as continually expanding its definition of "sickness" to embrace more and more forms of social deviance, thus advancing the frontiers of its jurisdiction and recruiting more and more patients into sick roles. Sin is going out of style along with the church; the courts are losing ground to the psychiatric establishment; and "the hospital is succeeding the church and the parliament as the archetypical institution of Western culture."[4]

We emphasize this difference in perspective because the same apparent contradiction runs through the radical critiques of the medical system: on the one hand we blame the system for being too chary and exclusionary ("there are not enough services; what services there are, are too costly, uninviting, etc."); on the other hand we, to a less extent, blame the system for being expansionist (for claiming ever more areas for its jurisdiction and endlessly expanding its institutional apparatus). Nowhere is this contradiction closer to the surface than in the critiques of "medical empires."[5] Some empires were criticized for being conservative and failing to expand their services to needy communities. Others were criticized for being expansionist and seeking to expand their services, i.e., their "control" over community health resources. Some were criticized for having *both* tendencies.

We do not wish to make too much of this apparent inconsistency. As activists in the health movement learned, the medical system does have both exclusionary and expansionist faces, and neither is wholly benign or even "neutral." In fact we can now draw on the sociological thinking we have so hastily surveyed and postulate that the exclusionary and expansionist aspects of the medical system correspond to two different forms of social control exerted by the medical system, which we shall call *disciplinary* social control and *co-optative* social control.

Types of Medical Social Control

Disciplinary Control

Exclusionary sectors of the medical system, which exert disciplinary control, are characterized by high barriers to entry (high costs, geographical inaccessibility) and/or socially repellent treatment of those who do enter (discourtesy, extreme impersonality, racism, fragmentation of care, long waits). The impact of exclusionary sectors on the populations they are supposed to serve is to discourage entry into sick roles, either because of the visible barriers to entry or because of public knowledge of the treatment experienced by those who do enter, or in some cases both. Such services exert disciplinary social control in that they *encourage* people to maintain work or family responsibilities no matter what subjective discomfort they may be experiencing.

Disciplinary social control operates primarily on those who are not "sick" (in the sociological, not the medical, sense). At times it has been used quite consciously to maintain industrial discipline in the work force. Foucault describes the combined poor-houses/insane asylums of eighteenth-and nineteenth-century Paris and London, which were maintained as *public spectacles* to remind the populace of what awaited them if they opted to "drop out" into pauperism or madness.[6] In much the same way today, exposés of conditions in state mental hospitals serve to discourage "madness" as an out, and public knowledge of the indignities inflicted on welfare recipients serves to discourage willful unemployment. Doctors also may function quite explicitly to keep people out of sick roles and in work roles, rather than to detect and cure disease. Consider the company doctor whose role is to pressure the injured worker to return to his station, thus minimizing production losses and saving the company workmen's compensation benefits. The widespread requirement of a "doctor's note" to excuse absence from work or school similarly reflects the "anti-malingering" function of the medical system.

Co-optative Control

Expansionary sectors, which exert co-optative control, are characterized by relatively low barriers to entry and acceptable, even sympathetic, treatment of those who do enter. Such services encourage people both to enter sick roles and to seek professional help in a variety of nonsick situations (preventive care, contraceptive services, marital difficulties). In so doing they bring large numbers of people into the fold of *professional management* of various aspects of their lives. It is this situation of professional management—whether all-inclusive, as in the case of a cancer patient, or partial—which allows for the exercise of co-optative control. It should be clear that co-optative control, unlike disciplinary control, operates on those who do gain entry into the system, to whatever degree. The important question is, what is the nature and ideological content of co-optative control? In other words, what is the impact of professional management on the patient's ideology, self-image, acceptance of work and family roles, etc.? We will devote a major section of this article to a discussion of these questions.

First, however, it is important to emphasize that the exclusionary and expansionist aspects of the medical system are often closely intermingled. A given agency, or even physician, may present exclusionary or expansionist faces at different times, in different situations, to different groups of patients. At the same time, as we all know, there are certain consistent patterns in the kind of care experienced by different groups in our society—classes, sexes, races, age groups. For example, the overwhelming historical experience of the poor is of an exclusionary system. Thus the different forms of social control we have distinguished are exerted differentially on different groups in society. History provides a striking illustration of the differential social control functions of the medical system.

Consider the kinds of medical care experienced by the urban poor and by the urban upper and upper-middle classes in late nineteenth-century America. (This period is interesting not only because it provides such vivid contrast but because this is the period of the formation of the American medical profession.) The urban poor—mostly first- and second-generation immigrant workers—faced a grossly exclusionary system. Aside from a few dispensaries located in the ghettos, professional outpatient care was virtually unavailable: doctors were not interested in serving people who could not pay or could not pay well. Institutional care in the few municipal hospitals of the time was avoided for good reasons: sanitary conditions in the hospitals were atrocious; nursing care was minimal until quite late in the century; and medical science had little to offer anyway.

"Legitimate" sick roles were simply not available to the poor. Grinding poverty and the brutality of employers meant that if you were sick enough not to work, you were probably sick enough to die, and poor conditions in the hospitals meant that if you were going to die, you were better off dying at home. *Disease* of course *was* readily available to the poor: TB, cholera, typhus and typhoid fevers, malnutrition, and untreated complications of childbirth were rampant. But without a social and medical system willing to identify the diseased and offer exemptions to them, disease does not become sickness, and the diseased go right on working. Thus to the extent that the nascent medical system of the time had any effect on the poor, it was to enforce industrial discipline.

Meanwhile the urban upper classes—families of wealthy businessmen, bankers, etc.—faced a medical "system" which was expansionary to a degree experienced by very few Americans today. Relative to today, there was an *excess* of doctors serving the better-off. At least it appeared so to the AMA at a time when doctors were reduced to running newspaper ads and other less-than-professional tactics to drum up business. One of the medical profession's most successful business strategies was the exploitation of affluent women patients. First, medical theory maintained that women—or at least "ladies"—were inherently sick: puberty, menstruation (with or without irregularity) pregnancy, and menopause were described as morbid conditions requiring close medical management. To fill in the time between these reproductive crises, doctors found a host of vague disorders—"nerves," "chlorosis," "hysteria"—also requiring diligent treatment. Medical neglect of poor women, who also suffered from the supposedly baneful effect of uterus and ovaries, was justified on the grounds that the poor were constitutionally tougher than the rich, consistent with their "coarser" natures.

Sickness became so stylish among upper-class women that it is hard to say where the sick role ended and the approved social role of women began. Fainting and nervous delicacy were signs of good breeding; lengthy rest cures and visits to health spas were definitely "in"; invalidism was virtually a way of life for many; the doctor was an almost constant companion. The woman who yearned for a more active life ran into stern medical admonishments: higher education could cause the uterus to atrophy; political involvement, even voting, could be an invitation to hysteria. Rebelliousness was itself pathological and indicated the need for a medically managed return to "normalcy."[6]

Whether the doctors were motivated by greed, misogyny, or a benevolent concern for the "weaker sex" does not concern us here. There can be no question that medicine operated as a key agency in the social control of women, enforcing passivity and a childlike dependency on men, particularly on doctors and on the husbands who paid the bills. It is true that these women were *objectively* dependent on men anyway: they had few rights and no means of self-support. But medical theory provided a "scientific" justification for their dependency; and medical practice served in effect as an intimate surveillance system ready to detect female discontent when it was still at the stage of "nerves" or "hysteria," and to intervene at once with a regime for "recovery."[7]

Thus the emerging medical system exerted two different kinds of social control on the two groups we have considered: services for the poor served as a warning to the poor not to get "sick" (and possibly to the rich as a warning not to get poor). This is what we have termed *disciplinary* control, and was aimed at the not-yet sick, the working poor. Wealthy women, on the other hand, experienced *co-optative* control. This form of control was latent in the services themselves and directed at those labeled "sick" (a category which, in medical theory of the time, included all affluent women).

The Evolution of the Medical System

The differential pattern of social control which prevailed in the late nineteenth century cannot, of course, be simply extrapolated to the present. The class structure of society has changed dramatically; sex roles have changed in all social classes. Even more important, for our analysis, the medical system itself has undergone profound changes not only since 1900 but since 1930. Two broad changes in the medical system seem particularly relevant: (1) the vast expansion of the system in all dimensions; and (2) the rapid rise in status and class position of the medical profession. The first is related to an expansion of the co-optative social control exerted by the medical system; the second is related to changes in the ideological content of that control. . . .

Notes

[1]Talcott Parsons, *The Social System* (New York: Free Press, 1951), pp. 428–479; and "Definitions of Health and Illness in the Light of American Values and Social Structure," in E. Gartly Jaco, ed., *Patients, Physicians and Illness,* 2d ed. (New York: Free Press, 1972), p. 107. Eliot Freidson, *The Profession of Medicine* (New York: Dodd, Mead, 1970), especially pp. 203–331.

[2]Frances Fox Piven and Richard A. Cloward, *Regulating the Poor* (New York: Pantheon, 1971), pp. 33–36.

[3]Freidson, op. cit., p. 304.

[4]Philip Rieff, *Freud: The Mind of the Moralist* (Garden City: Doubleday, 1961), p. 360, cited in Freidson, op. cit., p. 248.

[5]A concept advanced by Health-PAC to describe the increasing centralization of urban medical services around medical schools and major teaching hospitals. Strictly speaking, an "empire" would include the core controlling institution (medical school or teaching hospital) plus all its affiliated lesser hospitals and health centers of various types. Usually, though, the word "empire" has been used in reference to the core institution only. Cf. *The American Health Empire,* prepared by Barbara and John Ehrenreich, chaps. 3–6.

[6]Michel Foucault, *Madness and Civilization* (New York: Pantheon, 1965), pp. 46–63, 68–70.

[7]Cf. B. Ehrenreich and D. English, *Complaints and Disorders: The Sexual Politics of Sickness* (Old Westbury, New York: Feminist Press, 1973).

PART III

An Overview of Policies: Social Goals and Their Attainment

5 Resource Development

Until relatively recently in the world's history, most men have lived short, uncomfortable lives. Gradually, they have learnt how to organize themselves to exploit the earth's natural resources so that they can live longer and more comfortably.

At first, resources were developed mainly through men's manual labour, but gradually social groups learnt how to use mechanical aids to help themselves to exploit the riches which were available for the taking. It was not until the seventeenth century, however, that technology began to advance more rapidly.

Technology may be defined narrowly or widely. A useful broad definition is that of Dubin (1958), who described it as implying more than "tools, instruments, machines and technical formulas whose employment is necessary to its performance." Technical ideas are also part of technology because they guide technical behaviour, i.e., "the body of ideas which express the goals of the work, its functional importance and the rationale of the methods employed."

The Protestant Ethic

It was after the Reformation that the body of ideas changed direction in western Europe. Tawney (1938), has explained in his *Religion and the Rise of Capitalism* how, gradually, attitudes began to alter in protestant countries. The changes in social attitudes began to gain momentum in the late seventeenth century as the Puritans established their place in English society. They "repeated the ancient maxim *laborare est orare* (to work is to pray) with a new and intenser significance" (p. 240). Because the Puritans (or Dissenters) were excluded from social advancement because they did not conform to the state religion, they turned their attention to succeeding in business. At this point, "the questions which excited them were neither those of production nor of social organization, but of commerce and finance" (p. 241). They were interested in capturing world markets from the French and the Dutch, with the expansion of trade. This commercial or mercantilist revolution led to the industrial revolution a century later. It was after 1760 that productivity and social organization in England began to change, but these changes could not have occurred without the earlier development in attitudes during the commercial and financial revolution. And the merchants of England worked out many of the ideas about capitalism which were taken up with enthusiasm by the American colonies and other European countries later.

The four countries of this study have emerged out of this seventeenth-century Puritan tradition. They adopted the "Protestant ethic" of working to develop resources to increase the world's wealth and their individual citizens' advancement, and if some fellow countrymen fell by the wayside, this was a social cost which they felt had to be accepted. As Tawney pointed out, the acceptance of individual responsibility as the principal value led to a redefinition of what was acceptable in social relationships and consequently to changes in the social order. Where earlier generations had maintained solidarity in society by emphasizing responsibility towards fellow men and the stability of human relationships, there was now perceived to be an individual responsibility to advance oneself and devil take the hindmost.

Of course from the start, some were concerned about the implications of such rapid technological development for society's solidarity—yet the importance of the rise of capitalism and the development of resources is pointed out by Benn and Peters (1959), who began a discussion on human rights by saying,

> With the enormous expansion in wealth since the seventeenth century, expectations have been greatly extended. Men have become more aware of how one another live, not only as between class and class but as between continent and continent. They have been led to challenge the fairness of privileges formerly taken for granted. Moreover, the sense that poverty, disease and ignorance need not be the inevitable lot of most of the world's inhabitants, and that they might be remedied by deliberate action, has led to the recognition of claims to certain minimal economic and social conditions as "human rights." [P. 98]

So, there is a paradox here. Should resources continue to be exploited to the fullest extent in order that there will be more to distribute? Or should there be a more limited rate of development?

The Open Question: Is Small Beautiful?

The failure of the capitalist societies to cope with the depression of the 1930s and their propensity to engage in wasteful world wars led to considerable questioning by social philosophers some fifty years ago. Some of their doubts were voiced by Tawney:

> Few can contemplate without a sense of exhilaration the splendid achievements of practical energy and technical skill, which from the latter part of the 17th century were transforming the face of material civilization, and of which England was the daring, if not too-scrupulous pioneer. If, however, economic ambitions are good servants, they are bad masters. Harnessed to a social purpose, they will turn the mill and grind the corn. But the question to what end the wheels revolve, still remains; and on that question the naive and uncritical worship of economic power, which is the mood of unreason too often engendered in those whom that new Leviathan has hypnotized by its spell, throws no light. Its result is not seldom a world in which men command a mechanism that they cannot fully use, and an organization which has every perfection except that of motion. [P. 276]

The questions became even more searching in the 1960s when economists, such as Galbraith (1966) and others, exposed the wastefulness of postwar affluent societies and discussed the rapid exhaustion of the world's nonrenewable resources. And the differences in wealth between the industrialized and the so-called developing countries were shown to be increasing, not diminishing. Schumacher (1974) described his view of these developments before pleading for consideration of substitution of an intermediate technology in lieu of the large-scale technology of today, particularly in the developing nations, in his book, *Small Is Beautiful.*

> In the excitement over the unfolding of his scientific and technical powers, modern man has built a system of production that ravishes nature and a type of society that annihilates man. If only there were more and more wealth, everything else, it is thought, would fall into place. Money is considered to be all powerful: if it could not actually buy nonmaterial values, such as justice, harmony, beauty or even health, it could circumvent the need for them or compensate for their loss. The development of production and the acquisition of wealth have thus become the highest goals of the modern world in relation to which all other goals, no matter how much lipservice may still be paid to them, have come to take second place. The highest goals require no justification: all secondary goals have finally to justify themselves in terms of the service their attainment renders to the attainment of the highest. [P. 246]

But, how can nations reverse the gears, organize for a more leisure-oriented society? Are societies ready and willing to abandon excessive resource exploitation? Possibly, as Iran's revolution would seem to indicate, when the social disruption caused by industrialization goes too far. But other developing countries still seem anxious to move into rapid resource exploitation in order to increase their wealth as quickly as possible, and the people of developed countries find it hard to slow production voluntarily. The problem of leisure distribution in advanced societies is as difficult as wealth distribution. Some work too hard and others are forced to take unwanted leisure as unemployed, forcibly retired or half-time employees, for working is highly prized.

Doing Better and Feeling Worse

Affluence creates other problems as Hirsch (1976) has pointed out.

> So long as material privation is widespread, conquest of material scarcity is the predominant concern. As demands for purely private goods are increasingly satisfied, demands for goods and facilities with a public (social) character become increasingly active. These demands in themselves appear both legitimate and attainable . . . but, there is an "adding up" problem. Opportunities for economic advance, as they present themselves serially to one person after another, do not constitute equivalent opportunities for economic advance by all. What each of us can achieve, all cannot. [Pp. 4-5]
>
> The compelling attraction of economic growth in its institutionalized modern form has been as a superior substitute for redistribution. Whereas the masses today could never get close to what the well-to-do have today, even by expropriating all of it, in the conventional view, they can get most, if not all of the way there with patience, in a not too-distant tomorow, through the magic of compound growth. But . . . generalized growth then increases the crush. . . .Thus, the frustration in affluence results from its very success in satisfying previously dominant material needs. [P. 7]

It is Hirsch's conclusion that

> Over an increasing sphere of economic and social activity, action taken by individuals in response to their own preferences and needs in the situation they face has become an inefficient and ineffective way of achieving the objectives on which these actions rest. . . . Collective means may be necessary to implement individual ends. [Pp. 178–79].

Similarly, Wildavsky (1977) has discussed the political pathology of health policy in the U.S. He posed these questions for consideration:

> If most people are healthier today than people like themselves have ever been, and if access to medical care is now more evenly distributed among rich and poor, why is there said to be a crisis in medical care that requires massive change? If the bulk of the population is satisfied with the care it is getting, why is there so much pressure in government for change? Why, in brief, are we doing better but feeling worse? [P. 106]

Wildavsky discussed the paradoxes which have been created by the past successes of medical technology and social organization and how the goals which were once the most important ones have been displaced and replaced. Thus, health outcomes as the goals, have given place to access to care. He has argued that this access to care is a double displacement: caring is substituted for health and access for caring. And this has become the new goal because equality of access is an objective criterion which can replace the elusive goal of health, particularly for an aging population.

Individualism and Collectivism

Both Hirsch and Wildavsky conclude their discussions by raising the matter of the mixed system of individualism and collectivism and the problems of planning better economic and social policies in the present world.

This is the central issue for Shonfield (1965) for whom the changing balance of public and private power is the challenge facing *Modern Capitalism.* Shonfield assessed the astonishing revival of Europe after the Second World War and put forward explanations for the successes and failures of different nations to adapt to pressures for change.

He argued that international pressures were such that all industrialized countries were forced to engage in planning their economies. This might be a limited kind of planning (which seems to have been the approach taken by Anglo-Saxon countries) or a more broadly based attack.

> One is struck by the Anglo-French contrast—the willingness of the French authorities to assume a tutelage role in the division of prizes which result from a more efficient management of the economy, whilst British planning in the early 1960s was concerned exclusively with enlarging the aggregate volume of supplies; so far, at any rate, it has recoiled from any attempt to plan demand. The French Fourth Plan insisted vigorously on its objective of achieving a more complete view of man. . . .This frank emphasis not on what people want now but on what they will want (or ought to be wanting) in the future is characteristically French in style. But, leaving aside the transcendental overtones, it is, in practice, closely in line with the thinking of the growing body of planners elsewhere in the western world. Increasingly the realization is forced upon us that the market, which purports to be the reflection of the way in which people spontaneously value their individual wants and efforts, is a poor guide to the best means of satisfying the real wishes of consumers. That is because market costs generally fail to measure either social costs or social benefits. In our civilization, these constantly grow more important. . . .Unless the state actively intervenes, and on an increasing scale, to compel private enterprise to adapt its investment decisions to considerations such as these, the process of economic growth may positively impede the attainment of things that people most deeply want. [Pp. 226–27]
>
> It is the individual in his private capacity who is most vulnerable to the erosion of old style capitalism—which allowed him considerable freedom so long as he had a bit of money and a steady job—and to the crowding in of more and more public power. That this power often has a beneficent purpose does not make it any less awkward to deal with. [P. 385]
>
> It is noticeable that some of the nations which made the most complete and successful adaptation to the political problems of the earlier era of capitalism

> seem to be stuck with especially inefficient and stumbling political machinery when they apply themselves to the new problems. This is outstandingly true of the Anglo-Saxon countries. [P. 398]

Shonfield has pointed out that, in Europe, the countries which have developed most efficiently since World War II are France and Germany where administrators are not only strong but also as responsible to the public as politicians have been.

Political invention is part of the technology required for economic growth. Marchak (1975) has discussed the liberal view of government in her book on Canadian ideologies, a view of keeping government in its proper place so that it might regulate the situation for resource development to take place while holding back from other forms of intervention. Since Canada, Australia and the U.S. adhere strongly to the liberal ideology, they must undergo a considerable change in attitude before accepting Shonfield's views.

Discussion of Readings and References

In stating the arguments presented in this chapter, quotation has been used extensively. Two readings only are attached.

1. The first reading from M. Patricia Marchak's *Ideological Perspectives on Canada* is concerned with identifying the dominant ideology in western liberal societies. How this ideology of development emerged from earlier western traditions was traced by Richard H. Tawney in his classic *Religion and the Rise of Capitalism.*
2. The implications of technological progress have been examined by many economic historians who have shown the uneven distribution of the resources and the sufferings of many people who laboured in the lower strata of western societies and who came to be exploited. Benn and Peters, however, make the important point that with the development of resources over the past two centuries there is more to distribute and more people can expect to get a share of this wealth.
3. However, the new affluence has brought with it a number of paradoxical questions. How is the wealth to be distributed fairly? For the wealth is not only money but access to all kinds of things that money can buy, such as education, personal services and some kinds of power. However, as Fred Hirsch pointed out in his *Social Limits to Growth,* the privileged are not only privileged because they have more wealth in an absolute sense but because they are relatively better off. When everyone has education, then those who had positional advantage in the past no longer have this advantage.
4. The second selection is part of Aaron Wildavsky's article on "Doing

Better and Feeling Worse: The Political Pathology of Health Policy" (taken from a collection of articles going by the same general title and edited by John H. Knowles). Wildavsky took up some of the same issues as Hirsch and some others specific to the health field. He also dealt with the matter of displaced objectives.

5. From the start the development of capitalism and modern technology seemed to proceed without giving enough attention to humanitarian needs. E. F. Schumacher's book, *Small is Beautiful,* was hailed by many who questioned the dominant ideology of continuing resource development of affluent societies in spite of the fact that Schumacher directed his prescription specifically towards India and other developing nations. Andrew Shonfield examined the advanced societies of modern Europe and proposed that *Modern Capitalism* must consider planning not only for humanitarian reasons but also for survival. Schonfield's discussion of planning is particularly recommended.

Free Enterprise in (Relatively Moral) Nation States [I]

M. Patricia Marchak

The liberal ideology rests on three distinctive organizational features of the societies in which it is held. The first is that those societies support one or another form of representative government within the framework of the nation-state. This support involves periodic elections of members of a government by the population inhabiting a given territory. The second is that their economies are not directed exclusively or even mainly by the governments, and profits from economic transactions may be legally retained—subject only to taxation laws—by private citizens or privately owned corporations. The third is that judicial courts evaluate the merits of individual, corporate and government actions with reference to legislation provided by governments, when any two individuals or other entities disagree on the nature of their prerogatives.

The first of these conditions underlies a range of beliefs and values widely held. One of these is that majority rule is achieved when governments are elected through majority votes of the people, and that rule by majority vote is both democratic and just. In part this belief in justice reflects the further belief. . .that there is general equality of condition among the people, so that a government's decisions will equally affect all members. The majority and the minority are assumed to belong to the same, homogeneous population. Also involved is the belief that, since all people have the same single vote, a government does not represent the interests of any one sector of the population, including the wealthy sector. Since there are no classes, parties cannot

---

From M. Patricia Marchak, *Ideological Perspectives on Canada* (Toronto: McGraw-Hill Ryerson Ltd., 1975), 35–37.

be class organizations nor governments the means of promoting class interests.

There is a certain contradiction at the core of the liberal view of government. On the one hand, governments are the managers of the system, subject to the wishes of the majority and acting in their interests. On the other, the economy is not directed or managed by governments. Governments, to be sure, are able to enact various kinds of legislation that affect the economy, but such legislation is expected to be regulative and to restrict in no fashion the rights and privileges of the owners and directors of the major economic institutions. Free enterprise means, essentially, private business or business not directed by governments. It is assumed, and often argued, that where a large number of people pursue private profits through individual initiative, the net result is a prosperous and free society. The corollary of this belief is that those societies in which governments own or control large segments of the economy are neither prosperous nor free.

The contradiction is not resolved by the functional model of society postulated within the liberal ideology: a model of independent but interacting institutions, each balancing the others and responding to actions taken in the other sectors. The difficulty lies in the fact that only one of these institutions is subject to electoral vote, and the institutions of the economy are neither required nor expected to subject themselves to majority control. The managers of the system, then, must respond to the directors of the economy and must account for their responses to the citizens; the directors may or may not respond to the managers and are not accountable to the citizens. To the extent that economic institutions influence the daily lives of citizens independent of government management, governments do not govern. Their independent actions are restricted to other spheres, or to responses rather than initiatives in the economic sphere. Majority government, then, does not mean—as it is assumed to mean—direction and control of the society by representatives of the majority.

The precise role of governments is not altogether clear, but the general direction of their actions is, according to the ideology of the liberal state, to provide the framework of legislation by which individuals may pursue their private objectives successfully. As stated by a former prime minister of Canada:

> [the problem] is posed in the necessity of preserving the independence and self-reliance of the individual, driving home the realization that he stands above the state, which is the essence of liberalism, with the obligation, in the complicated organization of society which we have today of the state to protect the individual when protection is required.[1]

The belief in the rights of the individual and the supremacy of the individual over the state are intimately linked to the restriction on government action in the economic sphere. The assumption, then, is that government control of the economy would restrict private freedom, independence, and individual self-reliance. The assumption lies behind the words of John Stuart Mill in 1849:

> "There is a limit to the legitimate interference of collective opinion with independence. . . ."[2] and, "The sole end for which mankind are warranted, individually or collectively, in interfering with the liberty of action of any of their number, is self-protection."[3]

It is more explicitly stated by Lester Pearson in 1958:

> "No intervention of the State in the affairs of the individual is justified if it doesn't liberate and release the forces of the individual so he will be better able to look after himself."[4]

Mill talked to recent converts and lingering skeptics in an England torn between the remnants of a land-based class system and the needs of an industrial and urban society. Sentimental attachments to the feudal aristocracy remained. Ideologies do not die easily, and Edmund Burke's eloquent defence of the past written half a century earlier bespoke a passionate attachment to stability, order, and community still felt by many English workingmen as well as by Lords.[5] Yet the conditions had irrevocably changed, and the change predated Burke's appeal. Burke might rail at the pettiness of the commercial entrepreneurs, at the tragedy of Marie Antoinette's pretty head, at the loss of religion and sense of propriety signalled in the French Revolution. But it was Mill who caught the flavour of the new industrial state. It was a flavour of motion rather than stability, freedom rather than control, personal salvation rather than the collective good. Let a man choose his way of life, he preached, and the collective good will result; let a man act as he pleases, and it will please him to serve his community; let a man serve himself and all men will be well served. Enlightened self-interest—a catchphrase for the laissez-faire economic doctrine of the eighteenth-century philosopher Adam Smith—became an exciting new venture as Bentham, Mill, and others of the school called "the Utilitarians" preached the new ideology of individualism and efficiency.

The liberal state of the 1970s expresses little admiration for the feudal aristocracy. It has labelled "good" those events of history that brought it to an end: the industrial revolution in Britain, the French Revolution, and American War of Independence, the development of colonies, the extension of the franchise, the creation of a landless and mobile labour force, and the establishment of public schools. Individualism is so well entrenched, indeed, that those who called themselves revolutionaries in the 1960s were able to do little more than proclaim the virtues of this creed. To do one's own thing was thought of as remarkably novel, though it was precisely what the leaders of the liberal revolution were doing two centuries earlier.

The threat to individual freedom in this long-developing creed is from governments; governments, therefore, must be restricted. The question, however, is whether governments are the only source of threat. To deal with that question, it is essential to gain some understanding of the economic conditions—which are basic to the society, and of the economic framework within which governments of nation-states must operate.

NOTES

[1]Lester Pearson, *Canadian Liberal 10* (September, 1958) p. 2.
[2]John Stuart Mill, "On Liberty" (1849) in *The Utilitarians* (Garden City, N.Y.: Doubleday, 1961), p. 479.
[3]Ibid., p. 484.
[4]Lester Pearson, *Canadian Liberal* 10 (September, 1958) p. 2.
[5]Edmund Burke, *Reflections on the Revolution in France* (1790) (Harmondsworth, England: Penguin Books, 1968).

Doing Better and Feeling Worse: The Political Pathology of Health Policy

Aaron Wildavsky

According to the Great Equation, Medical Care equals Health. But the Great Equation is wrong. More available medical care does not equal better health.

Paradoxes, Principles, Axioms, Identities, and Laws

The fallacy of the Great Equation is based on the Paradox of Time: past successes lead to future failures. As life expectancy increases and as formerly disabling diseases are conquered, medicine is faced with an older population whose disabilities are more difficult to defeat. The cost of cure is higher, both because the easier ills have already been dealt with and because the patients to be treated are older. Each increment of knowledge is harder won; each improvement in health is more expensive. Thus time converts one decade's achievements into the next decade's dilemmas. Yesterday's victims of tuberculosis are today's geriatric cases. The Paradox of Time is that success lies in the past and (possibly) the future, but never the present.

The Great Equation is rescued by the Principle of Goal Displacement, which states that any objective that cannot be attained will be replaced by one that can be approximated. Every program needs an opportunity to be successful; if it cannot succeed in terms of its ostensible goals, its sponsors may shift to goals whose achievement they can control. The process subtly

---

From *Doing Better and Feeling Worse: Health in the United States,* ed. John H. Knowles (New York: W. W. Norton and Co., Inc., 1977), pp. 105–114, 121.

becomes the purpose. And that is exactly what has happened as "health" has become equivalent to "equal access to" medicine.

When government goes into public housing, it actually provides apartments; when it goes into health, all it can provide is medicine. But medicine is far from health. So what the government can do then is try to equalize access to medicine, whether or not that access is related to improved health. If the question is, "Does health increase with government expenditure on medicine?," the answer is likely to be "No." Just alter the question—"Has access to medicine been improved by government programs?"—and the answer is most certainly, with a little qualification, "Yes."

By "access," of course, we mean quantity, not quality, of care. Access, moreover, can be measured, and progress toward an equal number of visits to doctors can be reported. But better access is not the same as better health. Something has to be done about the distressing stickiness of health rates, which fail to keep up with access. After all, if medical care does not equal health, access to medical care is irrelevant to health—unless, of course, health is not the real goal but merely a cover for something more fundamental, which might be called "mental health" (reverently), or "shamanism" (irreverently), or "caring" (most accurately).

Any doctor will tell you, say sophisticates, that most patients are not sick, at least physically, and that the best medicine for them is reassurance. Tranquilizers, painkillers, and aspirin would seem to be the functional equivalents, for these are the drugs most often prescribed. Wait a minute, says the medical sociologist (the student not merely of medicine's manifest, but also of its latent, functions), pain is just as real when it's mental as when it's physical. If people want to know somebody loves them, if today they prefer doctors of medicine to doctors of theology, they are entitled to get what they want.

Once "caring" has been substituted for (or made equivalent to) "doctoring," access immediately becomes a better measure of attainment. The numbers of times a person sees a doctor is probably a better measure of the number of times he has been reassured than of his well-being or a decline in his disease. So what looks like a single goal substitution (access to medicine in place of better health) is actually a double displacement: caring instead of health, and access instead of caring.

This double displacement is fraught with consequences. Determining how much medical care is sufficient is difficult enough; determining how much "caring" is, is virtually impossible. The treatment of physical ills is partially subjective; the treatment of mental ills is almost entirely subjective. If a person is in pain, he alone can judge how much it hurts. How much caring he needs depends upon how much he wants. In the old days he took his tension chiefly to the private sector, and there he got as much attention as he could pay for. But now with government subsidy of medicine looming so large, the question of how much caring he should get inevitably becomes public.

By what standard should this public question be decided? One objective criterion—equality of access—inevitably stands out among the rest. For if we don't quite know what caring is or how much of it there should be, we can always say that at least it should be equally distributed. Medicaid has just about equalized the number of doctors' visits per year between the poor and the rich. In fact, the upper class is showing a decrease in visits, and the life expectancy of richer males is going down somewhat. Presumably, no one is suggesting remedial action in favor of rich men. Equality, not health, is the issue.

Equality

One can always assert that even if the results of medical treatment are illusory, the poor are entitled to their share. This looks like a powerful argument, but it neglects the Axiom of Inequality. That axiom states that every move to increase equality in one dimension necessarily decreases it in another. Consider space. The United States has unequal rates of development. Different geographic areas vary considerably in such matters as income, custom, and expectation. Establishing a uniform national policy disregards these differences; allowing local variation means that some areas are more unequal than others. Think of time. People not only have unequal incomes, they also differ in the amount of time they are prepared to devote to medical care. In equalizing the effects of money on medical care—by removing money as a consideration—care is likely to be allocated by the distribution of available time. To the extent that the pursuit of money takes time, people with a monetary advantage will have a temporal disadvantage. You can't have it both ways, as the Axiom of Allocation makes abundantly clear.

"No system of care in the world," says David Mechanic, summing up the Axiom of Allocation, "is willing to provide as much care as people will use, and all such systems develop mechanisms that ration. . .services." Just as there is no free lunch, so there is no free medicine. Rationing can be done by time (waiting lists, lines), by distance (people farther from facilities use them less than those who are closer), by complexity (forms, repeated visits, communications difficulties), by space (limiting the number of hospital beds and available doctors), or by any or all of these methods in combination. But why do people want more medical service than any system is willing to provide? The answer has to do with uncertainty.

If medicine is only partially and imperfectly related to health, it follows that doctor and patient both will often be uncertain as to what is wrong or what to do about it. Otherwise—if medicine were perfectly related to health

—either there would be no health problem or it would be a very different one. Health rates would be on one side and health resources on the other; costs and benefits could be neatly compared. But they can't, because we often don't know how to produce the desired benefits. Uncertainty exists because medicine is a quasi-science—more science than, say, political science; less science than physics. How the participants in the medical system resolve their uncertainties matters a great deal.

The Medical Uncertainty Principle states that there is always one more thing that might be done—another consultation, a new drug, a different treatment. Uncertainty is resolved by doing more: the patient asks for more, the doctor orders more. The patient's simple rule for resolving uncertainty is to seek care up to the level of his insurance. If everyone uses all the care he can, total costs will rise; but the individual has so little control over the total that he does not appreciate the connection between his individual choice and the collective result. A corresponding phenomenon occurs among doctors. They can resolve uncertainty by prescribing up to the level of the patient's insurance, a rule reinforced by the high cost of malpractice. Patients bringing suit do not consider the relationship between their own success and higher medical costs for everyone. The patient is anxious, the doctor insecure; this combination is unbeatable until the irresistible force meets the immovable object—the Medical Identity.

The Medical Identity states that use is limited by availability. Only so much can be gotten out of so much. Thus, if medical uncertainty suggests that existing services will be used, Identity reminds us to add the words "up to the available supply." That supply is primarily doctors, who advise on the kind of care to provide and the number of hospital beds to maintain. But patients, considering only their own desires in time of need, want to maximize supply, a phenomenon that follows inexorably from the Principle of Perspective.

That principle states that social conditions and individual feelings are not the same thing. A happy social statistic may obscure a sad personal situation. A statistical equilibrium may hide a family crisis. Morbidity and mortality, in tabulating aggregate rates of disease and death, describe you and me but do not touch us. We do not think of ourselves as "rates." Our chances may be better or worse than the aggregate. To say that doctors are not wholly (or even largely) successful in alleviating certain symptoms is not to say that they don't help some people and that one of those people won't be me. Taking the chance that it will be me often seems to make sense, even if there is reason to believe that most people can't be helped and that some may actually be harmed. Most people, told that the same funds spent on other purposes may increase social benefits, will put their personal needs first. This is why expenditures on medical care are always larger than any estimate of the social benefit received. Now we can understand, by combining into one law the previous principles and Medical Identity, why costs rise so far and so fast.

The Law of Medical Money states that medical costs rise to equal the sum of all private insurance and government subsidy. This occurs because no one knows how much medical care ought to cost. The patient is not sure he is getting all he should, and the doctor does not want to be faulted for doing less than he might. Consider the triangular relationship between doctor, patient, and hospital. With private insurance, the doctor can use the hospital resources that are covered by the insurance while holding down his patients own expenditures. With public subsidies, the doctor may charge his highest usual fee, abandon charitable work, and ignore the financial benefits of eliminating defaults on payments. His income rises. His patient doesn't have to pay, and his hospital expands. The patient, if he is covered by a government program or private insurance (as about 90 per cent are) finds that his out-of-pocket expenses have remained the same. His insurance costs more, but either it comes out of his paycheck, looking like a fixed expense, or it is taken off his income tax as a deduction. Hospitals work on a cost-plus basis. They offer the latest and the best, thus pleasing both doctor and patient. They pay their help better; or, rather, they get others to pay their help. It's on the house—or at least on the insurance.

Perhaps our triangle ought to be a square: maybe we should include insurance companies. Why are they left out of almost all discussions of this sort? Why don't they play a cost-cutting role in medical care as they do in other industries? After all, the less the outlay, the more income for the company. Here the simplest explanation seems the best: insurance companies make no difference because they are no different from the rest of the health-care industry. The largest, Blue Cross and Blue Shield, are run by the hospital establishment on behalf of doctors. After all, hospitals do not so much have patients as they have doctors who have patients. Doctors run hospitals, not the other way around. Insurance companies not willing to play this game have left the field.

What process ultimately limits medical costs? If the Law of Medical Money predicts that costs will increase to the level of available funds, then that level must be limited to keep costs down. Insurance may stop increasing when out-of-pocket payments exceed the growth in the standard of living; at that point individuals may not be willing to buy more. Subsidy may hold steady when government wants to spend more on other things or when it wants to keep its total tax take down. Costs will be limited when either individuals or governments reduce the amount they put into medicine.

No doubt the Law of Medical Money is crude, even rude. No doubt it ignores individual instances of self-sacrifice. But it has the virtue of being a powerful and parsimonious predictor. Costs have risen (and are continuing to rise) to the level of insurance and subsidy.

Why There Is a Crisis

If more than three-quarters of the population are satisfied with their medical care, why is there a crisis? Surveys on this subject are inadequate, but invariably they reveal two things: (1) the vast majority are satisfied, but (2) they wish medical care didn't cost so much and they would like to be assured of contact with their own doctor. So far as the people are concerned, then, the basic problems are cost and access. Why, to begin at the end, aren't doctors where patients want them to be?

To talk about physicians being maldistributed is to turn the truth upside down: it is the potential patients who are maldistributed. For doctors to be in the wrong place, they would have to be where people aren't, and yet they are accused of sticking to the main population centers. If distant places with little crowding and less pollution, far away from the curses of civilization, attracted the same people who advocate their virtues, doctors would live there, too. Obviously, they prefer the amenities of metropolitan areas. Are they wrong to live where they want to live? Or are the rural and remote wrong to demand that others come where they are?

Doctors can be offered a government subsidy—more money, better facilities—on the grounds that it is a national policy for medical care to be available wherever citizens choose to live. Virtually all students in medical schools are heavily subsidized, so it would not be entirely unjust to demand that they serve several years in places not of their own choosing. The reason such policies do not work well—from Russia to the "Ruritanias" of this world—is that people who are forced to live in places they don't like make endless efforts to escape.

Because the distribution of physicians is determined by rational choice—doctors locate where their psychic as well as economic income is highest—there is no need for special laws to explain what happens. But the political pathology of health policy—the more the government spends on medicine, the less credit it gets—does require explanation.

The syndrome of "the more, the less" has to be looked at as it developed over time. First we passed Medicare for the elderly and Medicaid for the poor. The idea was to get more people into the mainstream of good medical care. Following the Law of Medical Money, however, the immediate effect was to increase costs, not merely for the poor and elderly but for all the groups in between. You can't simply add the costs of the new coverage to the costs of the old; you have to multiply them both by higher figures up to the limits of the joint coverage. This is where the Axiom of Inequality takes over. The wealthier aged, who can afford to pay, receive not merely the same benefits as the aged poor, but even more, because they are better able to negotiate the system. Class tells. Inequalities are immediately created within the same category. Worse still is the "notch effect" under Medicaid, through which those just above the eligibles in income may be worse off than those below. Whatever the cutoff point, there must always be a "near poor" who are made more unequal. And so is everybody else who pays twice, first in taxes to support care for others and again in increased costs for themselves. Moreover, with increased utilization of medicine, the system becomes crowded; medical care is not only more costly but harder to get. So there we have the Paradox of Time—as things get better, they get worse.

The politics of medical care becomes a minus-sum game in which every institutional player leaves the table poorer than when he sat down. In the beginning, the number of new patients grows arithmetically while costs rise geometrically. The immediate crisis is cost. Medicaid throws state and federal budgets out of whack. The talk is all about chiselers, profiteers, and reductions. Forms and obstacles multiply. The Medical Identity is put in place. Uncle Sam becomes Uncle Scrooge. One would hardly gather that billions more are actually being spent on medicine for the poor. But the federal government is not the only participant who is doing better and feeling worse.

Unequal levels of development within states pit one location against another. A level of benefits adequate for New York City would result in coverage of half or more of the population in upstate areas as well as nearly all of Alaska's Eskimos and Arizona's Indians. The rich pay more; the poor get hassled. Patients are urged to take more of their medicine only to discover they are targets of restrictive practices. They are expected to pay deductibles before seeing a doctor and to contribute a co-payment (part of the cost) afterward. Black doctors are criticized if their practice consists predominantly of white patients, but they are held up to scorn if they increase their income by treating large numbers of the poor and aged in the ghettos. Doctors are urged to provide more patients with better medicine, and then they are criticized for making more money. The Principle of Perspective leads each patient to want the best for himself, disregarding the social cost; and, at the same time, doctors are criticized for giving high-cost care to people who want it. The same holds true for hospitals: keeping wages down is exploitation of workers; raising them is taking advantage of insurance. Vast financial incentives are offered to encourage the establishment of nursing homes to serve the aged, and the operators are then condemned for taking advantage of the opportunity.

Does anyone win? Just try to abolish Medicare and Medicaid. Crimes against the poor and aged would be the least of the accusations. Few argue that the country would be better off without these programs than with them. Yet, as the programs operate, the smoke they generate is so dense that their supporters are hard to find.

By now it should be clear how growing proportions of people in need of medicine can be getting it in the midst of what is universally decried as a crisis in health care. Governments face phenomenal increases in cost. Administrators alternately fear charges of incompetence for failing to restrain real financial abuse and charges of niggardliness toward the needy. Patients are worried about higher costs, especially as serious or prolonged illnesses threaten them with financial catastrophe. That proportionally few people suffer this way does not decrease the concern, because it *can* happen to anyone. Doctors fear federal control, because efforts to lower costs lead to more stringent regulations. The proliferation of forms makes them feel like bureaucrats; the profusion of review committees threatens to keep them permanently on trial. New complaints increase faster than old ones can be remedied. Specialists in public health sing their ancient songs—you are what you eat, as old as you feel, as good as the air you breathe—with more conviction and less effect. True but trite: what can be done isn't worth doing; what is worth doing can't be done. The watchwords are malaise, stasis, crisis.

If money is a barrier to medicine, the system is discriminatory. If money is no barrier, the system gets overcrowded. If everyone is insured, costs rise to the level of the insurance. If many remain underinsured, their income drops to the level of whatever medical disaster befalls them. Inability to break out of this bind has made the politics of health policy pathological.

Political Pathology

Health policy began with a laudable effort to help people by resolving the polarized conflict between supporters of universal, national health insurance ("socialized" medicine) and the proponents of private medicine. Neither side believed a word uttered by the other. The issue was sidestepped by successfully implementing medical care for the aged under Social Security. Agreement that the aged needed help was easier to achieve than consensus on any overall medical system. The obvious defect was that the poor, who needed financial help the most, were left out unless they were also old and covered by Social Security. The next move, therefore, was Medicaid for the poor, at least for those reached by state programs.

Even if one still believed that medicine equaled health, it became impossible to ignore the evidence that availability of medical services was not the same as their delivery and use. Seeing a doctor was not the same as actually doing what he prescribed. It is hard to alleviate stress in the doctor's office when the patient goes back to the same stress at home and on the street.

"Health delivery" became the catchword. At times it almost seemed as if the welcome wagon was supposed to roll up to the door and deliver health, wrapped in a neat package. One approach brought services to the poor through neighborhood health centers. The idea was that local control would increase sensitivity to the patients' needs. But experience showed that this "sensitivity" had its price. Local "needs" encompassed a wider range of services, including employment. The costs per patient-visit for seeing a doctor or social worker were three to four times those for seeing a private practitioner. Achieving local control meant control by inside laymen rather than outside professionals, a condition doctors were loath to accept. Innovation both in medical practice and in power relationships proved a greater burden than distant federal sponsors could bear, so they tried to co-opt the medical powers by getting them to sponsor health centers. The price was paid in higher costs and lower local control. Amid universal complaints, programs were maintained where feasible, phased out where necessary, and forgotten where possible.

By now the elite participants have exceeded their thresholds of pain: government can't make good on its promises to deliver services; administrators are blamed for everything from malpractice by doctors to overcharges by hospitals; doctors find their professional prerogatives invaded by local activists from below and by state and federal bureaucrats from above. From the left come charges that the system is biased against the poor because local residents are unable to obtain, or maintain, control of medical facilities, and because the rates by which health is measured are worse for them than for the better off. Loss of health is tied to lack of power. From the right come charges that the system penalizes the professional and the productive: excessive governmental intervention leads to lower medical standards and higher costs of bureaucracy, so that costs go up while health does not.

As neighborhood health centers (NHCs) phased out, the new favorites, the health-maintenance organizations (HMOs), phased in. If the idea behind the NHCs was to bring services to the people, the idea behind the HMOs is to bring the people to the services. If a rationale for NHCs was to exert lay control over doctors, the rationale for HMOs is to exert medical control over costs. The concept is ancient. Doctors gather together in a group facility. Individuals or groups, such as unions and universities, join the HMO at a fixed rate for specified services. Through efficiencies in the division of labor and through features such as bonuses to doctors for less utilization, downward control is exerted on costs.

Since the basic method of cutting costs is to reduce the supply of hospital beds and physician services (the Medical Identity), HMOs work by making people wait. Since physicians are on salary, they must be given a quota of patients or a cost objective against which to judge their efforts. Both incentives may have adverse effects on patients. HMO patients complain about the difficulty of building up a personal relationship with a doctor who can be seen quickly when the need arises. Establishing such a relationship requires communication skills most likely to be found among the middle class. The patient's ability to shop around for different opinions is minimized, unless he is willing to pay extra by going outside the system. Doctors are motivated to engage in preventive practices, though evidence on the efficacy of these practices is hard to come by. They are also motivated to engage in bureaucratic routines to minimize the patients' demands on their time; and they may divert patients to various specialties or ask them to return, so as to fit them into each physician's assigned quota. In a word, HMOs are a mixed bag, with no one quite sure yet what the trade-off is between efficiency and effectiveness. Turning the Great Equation into an Identity—where Health = Health Maintenance Organization—does, however, solve a lot of problems by definition.

HMOs may be hailed by some as an answer to the problem of medical information. How is the patient-consumer to know whether he is getting proper care at reasonable cost? If it were possible to rate HMOs, and if they were in competition, people might find it easier to choose among them than among myriads of private doctors. Instead of being required to know whether all those tests and special consultations were necessary, or how much an operation should cost, the patients (or better still, their sponsoring organizations) might compare records of each HMO's ability to judge. Our measures of medical quality and cost, however, are still primitive. Treatment standards are notoriously subjective. Health rates are so tenuously connected to medicine that they are bound to be similar among similar populations so long as everyone has even limited access to care.

If health is only minimally related to care, less expertise may be about as good as more professional training. If by "care" many or most people mean simply a sympathetic listener as much as, or more than, they mean a highly trained, cold diagnostician, cheaper help may be as good as, or even better than, expensive assistance. Enter the nurse-practitioner or the medical corpsman or the old Russian *feldsher*—medical assistants trained to deal with emergencies, make simple diagnoses, and refer more complicated problems to medical doctors. They cost less, and they actually make home visits. The main disadvantage is their apparent challenge to the prestige of doctors, but it could work the other way around: doctors might be elevated because they deal with more complicated matters. But the success of the medical assistant might nonetheless raise questions about the mystique of medical doctors. In response the doctors might deny that anyone else can really know what is going on and what needs to be done, and they might then use assistants as additions to (but not substitutes for) their services. That would mean another input into the medical system and therefore an additional cost. The politics of medicine is just as much about the power of doctors as it is about the authority of politicians.

Now we see again, but from a different angle, why the medical system seems in crisis although most people are satisfied with the care they are receiving. At any one time, most people are reasonably healthy. When they do need help, they can get it. The quality of care is generally impressive; or whatever ails them goes away of its own accord. But these comments apply only to the mass of patients. The elite participants—doctors, administrators, politicians—are all frustrated. Anything they turn to rebounds against them. Damned if they do and cursed if they don't, it is not surprising that they feel that any future position is bound to be less uncomfortable than the one they hold today. Things can always get worse, of course, but it is not easy for them to see that.

Governmental Legitimacy: Curing the Sickness of Health

Why should government pay billions for health and get back not even token tribute? If government is going to be accused of abusing the poor, neglecting the middle classes, and milking the rich; if it is to be condemned for bureaucratizing the patient and coercing the doctor, it can manage all that without spending billions. Slanders and calumnies are easier to bear when they are cost-free. Spending more for worse treatment is as bad a policy for government as it would be for any of us. The only defendant without counsel is the government. What should it do?

The Axiom of Inequality cannot be changed; it is built into the nature of things. What government can do is to choose the kinds of inequalities with which it is prepared to live. Increasing the waiting time of the rich, for instance—that is, having them wait as long as everybody else—may not seem outrageous. Decreasing subsidies in New York City and increasing them in Jacksonville may seem a reasonable price to pay for national uniformity. From the standpoint of government, however, the political problem is not to achieve equal treatment but to get support, at least from those it intends to benefit. Government needs gratitude, not ingrates.

The Principle of Goal Displacement, through the double-displacement effect, succeeds only in substituting access to care for health; it by no means guarantees that people will value the access they get. Equal access to care will not necessarily be equated with the best care available or with all that patients believe they require. Government's task is to resolve the Paradox of Time so that, as things get better, people will see themselves as better off. . . .

Let us summarize. Basically there are two sites for relating cost to quality—that is, for disciplining needs, which may be infinite, by controlling resources, which are limited. One is at the level of the individual; the other, at the level of the collectivity. By comparing his individual desires with his personal resources, through the private market, the individual internalizes an informal cost-effectiveness analysis. Since incomes differ, the break-even point differs among individuals. And if incomes were made more equal, individuals would still differ in the degree to which they choose medical care over other goods and services. These other valued objects would compete with medicine, leading some individuals to choose lower levels of medicine and thus reducing the inputs into (and cost of) the system. This creative tension can also be had at the collective level. There it is a tension between some public services, such as medicine, and others, such as welfare, and a tension between the resources left in private hands and those devoted to the public sector. The fatal defect of the mixed system, a defect that undermines the worth of its otherwise valuable pluralism, is that it does not impose sufficient discipline either at the individual or at the collective level. The individual need not face his full costs, and the government need not carry the full burden.

6 Social Organization

Without a social contract, said Hobbes, there would be "no arts; no letters; no society; and which is worst of all, continual fear and danger of violent death; and the life of man, solitary, poor, nasty, brutish and short."

By getting together in groups men help each other to survive. Some are very prosperous whilst others remain poor and downtrodden—the wretched of the earth. Some of the reasons for these differences in achieving access to resources were explored in the chapter on resource development: some countries have positive philosophies about development, some have more resources to develop and capital to invest in development and some have acquired more skill and experience in organizing their communities for the purposes of development and distribution of wealth.

This chapter will be concerned with the organization of western liberal democratic societies for the task of surviving and flourishing.

Social Reciprocities

Early on, mankind found that the principle of the division of labour was the key to survival. As a result of organizing small communities and, later, larger complex societies according to this principle, occupational differences were built in from the start. In the small communities the mutual aid was obvious, the reasons for differences in allocating prerogatives were accepted, and the reciprocities were understood (Gouldner 1960). It was only when societies became more complex that social exchange networks became disorganized and distorted. The emphasis upon individual responsibility and the Protestant ethic facilitated the rise of capitalism because it broke through the old reciprocity traditions and freed men to pursue their own ends, but this was very often at the expense of others.

As societies became more complex, the simple one-to-one reciprocities had to give way to networks of support, to "reciprocal altruism" or giving help to others now in the hope of being helped oneself at a time of need. This network of support worked quite well in preindustrial societies but as the Protestant ethic took over and mass societies began to emerge, the old arrangements broke down and these societies failed to ensure that their networks provided for the weak.

THE ORGANIZATION OF THE TASK AND MANPOWER SYSTEM

What is at issue was what Gil (1970) described as the allocation of statuses and prerogatives and the organization of the task and manpower system of a society. What manpower is required to carry out tasks regarded as necessary? How can this manpower be given rewards which are adequate for motivation? What margin is necessary for adjustment to future developments? How can these adjustments be made whilst maintaining the social order? How can resistances to change be managed?

In the past (and, for some countries, in the present) the task and manpower system was organized by conquerors and their successors in power. In England, the feudal system of military service and work organization persisted long after the Normans landed but was gradually eroded as the towns grew and a merchant class emerged. Gradually, the forces of the market challenged the established landowners' power. But both landowners and entrepreneurs combined to use the mechanism of social control to keep the lower socioeconomic or "dangerous classes" at bay and to ensure that traditions did not change too quickly.

NEW OCCUPATIONAL GROUPS

Several groups emerged which were of great importance for the new tasks of societies moving from traditional to modern forms of existence. Two of these were the merchants and the entrepreneurs. These two groups have continued to claim concessions from the rest of society because of their developmental function on behalf of society. They are the groups which pressure governments to develop distributive policies which favour their interests, making the case that economic support is necessary for their risk-taking. (These are Schmitter's corporatist interest intermediaries.)

As technology has become more complex other groups have joined with the merchants and entrepreneurs to persuade society that their members have a special contribution to make. An example are the scientists and academics who are responsible for developing ideas and techniques for applying the ideas. But scientists and academics seldom identify with merchants and entrepreneurs. They envisage themselves as professional people. Professional groups emerged as strong interest groups during the nineteenth century. Scientists and academics are small subgroups of this important socioeconomic stratum.

Johnson (1972) has identified three stages in the relationship between the professions and the rest of society—patronage, self-regulation, and mediation—capitalist or state intervention. This classification can be used to explain the behavior of the medical profession in the nineteenth century and their resistance to changes now, for they prefer to be self-regulating groups rather than subject to patronage or state control.

In the nineteenth century, in publicly financed hospitals (charity or municipal or Poor Law), the doctors did not, at first, select their patients, who were there because they were the poor who needed institutional care. Abel-Smith (1964) has described the struggle to restructure the English hospitals in the nineteenth century from places where the poor were sent for care to places where the sick were sent for treatment. The history of Royal Melbourne Hospital (Inglis, 1958) is similarly concerned with the redefinition of the relationship between medical staff and patrons. It was not until 1900 that the doctors could select patients and choose their colleagues. Equally, the history of medical payment schemes is concerned with the doctors' struggle to avoid becoming contractors to Friendly Society or union groups which set conditions of practice in return for guaranteed payment for services.

After the Medical Act of 1858 was passed in England, the doctors were able to get themselves organized into one exclusive group. The Parrys (1976) have stressed the importance of this move to bring together physicians, surgeons and apothecaries into one medical profession which might still be divided internally, but which was able to maintain a strong external boundary. Medicine and law became the models for aspirant professionals because these occupations had managed to become self-regulatory associations of practitioners during this century.

The argument for being permitted to take up this stance was that no one but another professional could judge whether work had been done properly and so the groups must become self-policing. The groups asked for the right to control entry and to impose their own ethical codes. It was thought that group discipline over colleagues' standards and patients' free choice of doctor and fee-for-service would provide a satisfactory system of control. There was no other mechanism which could have been used to regulate doctors' work in the mid-nineteenth century except control by boards of public trustees, for at that time bureaucratic organizations had not become established. (It was not till the 1860s that the British civil service was reformed from patronage to entry through examination and similar reforms came much later elsewhere.)

As doctors and lawyers managed to acquire prerogatives, so other people thought they would like to become professionals too. Etzioni (1969) in America and others elsewhere (Vollmer and Mills, 1966) have made a study of quasi or semiprofessional groups aspiring for higher status: teachers, nurses and social workers. Wilensky (1964), noting the interest of many occupations in the concept of professionalism wondered whether American society was moving towards the professionalization of everyone.

In a later chapter of his discussion of social control, Watkins (1975) considered the way in which personal service professions emphasize their technical skills but seem to want to underplay their other professional activities, to keep them indeterminate. These are the gatekeeping activities which they undertake for society—the social control functions which Parsons (1952) discussed, the rationing and allocating of services, which Parker (1967) commented upon, and the caring on behalf of society identified by Halmos (1965).

They are seen to be members of society who make day-to-day adjustments between general social policies and individual citizens' needs. In return for their services, they anticipate that society will value their contribution and allocate special prerogatives.

They are also members of Schmitter's syndicalist interest intermediary groups; that is, they are organized to look after the economic and social interests of their members. Whilst the merchants and entrepreneurs got in first with their challenges to traditional social organization, professionals were not prepared to continue to be patronized or exploited and they took action to accent their demands for a share in prerogatives. Their actions were of two kinds: one, to get legislation changed in order to permit self-regulation, and two, to challenge any employers' or potential employers' efforts to exert control in any other way (e.g. patronage or mediation).

In reviewing the development of occupational groups which claim prerogatives in mass societies, it is important to recognize the growth of government bureaucracies and other bureaucracies in industry and commerce (what Burnham (1941) called the Managerial Revolution). In considering the development of the health care industry, they must be regarded as an important group. As students of bureaucracy have pointed out (Gerth and Mills, 1946), it is, at least in theory, a more efficient and effective way of organizing society's services to bureaucratize them, for a bureaucracy is characterized by:

(a) defined rights and duties, which are prescribed in written regulations;
(b) authority relations between positions which are ordered systematically;

(c) appointment and promotion which are regulated and are based on contractual agreement;
(d) technical training (or experience) as a formal condition of employment;
(e) fixed monetary salaries;
(f) a strict separation of the office and incumbent in the sense that the employee does not own the means of administration and cannot appropriate the position;
(g) administrative work as a full-time occupation.

But bureaucracies and bureaucrats have earned a bad name for themselves through their occasional inflexibility, and they are under constant challenge in liberal democracies because they appear to restrict the initiative of the entrepreneurs and professionals. However, so far as government bureaucracies are concerned, Porter (1965) puts the top civil servants into his elite membership group. Like professionals, top civil servants have been struggling for greater professional independence through establishing administrative expertise.

Carr-Saunders and Wilson (1933), writing one of the first studies on the professions, spent some time in making out a case for English administrative civil servants to be regarded as professional persons with an independent view, not totally dependent upon the politicians' whims but experts in their own right.

Johnson's third category of professionals, those in the state mediative stage, are not dissimilar to senior bureaucrats since they are obliged to recognize that there are strict rules which govern their contracts of service. They are not entirely free to make their own decisions but must acknowledge broad guidelines for their activities. The lower one goes down bureaucracies, however, the less discretion given the staff, but they are not expected to deal with the kind of contingencies that their superiors have to face.

Occupational Groups as Interest Intermediary Groups

From the early nineteenth century onwards, other occupational groups have struggled to assert their rights to be rewarded properly for their contribution to the task and manpower system of a society. It is not possible in a book on health policy to examine the development of trade unions but only to refer to standard texts on this movement. Organization differs from one country to another, and from one union to another. The development of trade unionism in the health services and the rights to collective bargaining will be discussed further later in the book. However, it is necessary to mention briefly the development of employee power in an overview discussion of allocation of statuses and prerogatives since this movement has changed the way in which demands for prerogatives are now made.

The Ubiquity of Stratification

"The ubiquity of stratification in every society has led some students to claim that there must be something inevitable and valuable in social inequality. Otherwise, they argue, how could stratification be so persistent and widespread?" (Tumin, 1967, p. 106) In reviewing the work of sociologists on the subject, he dismissed the question as meaningless.

> Ultimately, the argument for stratification, which appeals to the requirements for survival notion, rests upon premises regarding human motivation. These premises, usually left unstated, maintain that one can't get people to do unequally difficult or unequally unskilled tasks without distributing evaluations and rewards unequally. The unequal compensation serves as the motivating force. [P. 107]

Tumin examined the evidence for the need of such motivating incentives and concluded

> We must seriously question whether a claim can be made for the necessity of differential rewards as a motivational system. If differential rewarding is *not* inevitable as a motivational scheme, and if there are serious doubts regarding its relative efficacy, the whole issue of the *inevitability* of social stratification is called in question. For if we cannot rest the case for the inevitability of stratification on inescapable facts about human motivation, we cannot rest it upon anything at all. We must, therefore, face the likelihood that we are dealing with something optional rather than inevitable in human affairs. This being the case, we are forced to confront once again the question, why is stratification ubiquitous in human societies. . . ? [P. 108] Neither the ubiquity nor the antiquity of a phenomenon may be cited as grounds to consider it inevitable or of positive value. Focussing alone for the moment on questions of inevitability, the principal argument in support of the claim holds that no society could survive without some form of institutionalized inequality in evaluation and reward. . . . [P. 106]
>
> The most obvious fact about any system of stratification is that it produces greatest benefit and gain for those who rank high and receive the greatest rewards. Furthermore, those who benefit most from the system will usually do whatever they can to preserve their privileges, whatever effort they may make from time to time to spread the benefits of the system more widely. [P. 108]

Tumin then reviewed the recent efforts made to change the social order in democratic societies—by increasing social mobility through educational opportunity—and concluded, "To substitute an aristocracy of talent for one of lineage is hardly praiseworthy as a feature of democratic society." He was not alone in this conclusion. Young (1958) in Britain has also deplored this post-World War II trend. References on social stratification in the four countries are provided.

The Negotiated Order

Can societies ever hope to work towards complete equality? Tumin's comments raise but do not answer that question, but others would not think it to be possible. Strauss (1978) has argued that stratification in societies can be explained as a process of negotiations in great variety, with alternative approaches which include persuasion, appeal to authority, coercion and force. He has developed a paradigm to explain how macro and micro social relationships form a web. (It may be of interest to health policy makers that the paradigm was developed out of Strauss' [1963] studies of mental hospital organization.)

Reviewers have said that Strauss' paradigm may not be elegant but have commended its practical applications. They are convinced that negotiations are a central feature of social organization. Maines (1979) summarized the argument thus:

> Several key concepts form the structure of the [Strauss] paradigm. The first, obviously, is *negotiations.* What is the nature of the interaction, the types of actors, the strategies and the tactics used and the consequences of negotiation? Also what are the sub-processes of negotiation, such as making tradeoffs or obtaining kickbacks? Second is the notion of *structural context,* or the structural parameters within which negotiations take place, what are the structural properties that bear on negotiations? The third concept is *negotiation context*. . . . Negotiation contexts are affected or "surrounded" by the larger and more encompassing structural contexts and refer to those conditions which enter directly into and shape the course of negotiations. Furthermore, negotiation contexts themselves contain many properties which can combine in multiple ways to direct specific negotiation trajectories. [P. 525]

Maladjustment of the Task and Manpower System and Allocation of Prerogatives

The fit between the supply of manpower and the demand for it has never been perfect because of the lags in adjustment. It has become more imperfect as the rate of technological and social change has increased.

Whilst some occupational groups were emerging within western industrial societies and laying successful claim to prerogatives, others were not so fortunate in negotiating their case. The allocation of statuses and prerogatives became more and more complex and less obviously related to social tasks, particularly since interest intermediaries became better organized and better able to look after specific groups' wants.

The two open frontiers of the U.S.—free entrepreneurial endeavour and westward drift—enabled it to avoid some of the pressures for change arising in the old countries. Wave after wave of immigrants ensured continuing supplies of cheap labour and there were vast reservoirs of untapped natural resources. Similarly, Canada and Australia had open frontiers and natural resources to be developed. It is in the older countries that the maladjustments have been felt most acutely because there have not been the potentialities for escape that existed in the new lands.

The Poor as a Social Responsibility

In England, the church and the landowners took the responsibility for helping those in need in pre-Reformation times. The first change brought about by Protestantism was the dissolution of the monasteries in the sixteenth century, and the reorganization of the church as a Protestant establishment. There were extensive land enclosures in the eighteenth century which removed the rights of the country people to use common lands and led to absentee landlordism. Meanwhile, in the mid-seventeenth century the mercantilist revolution, initiated by the dissenters, had led on to the industrial revolution in the eighteenth and nineteenth centuries with its demand for labour and the drift of the country people into the towns.

The conditions of work were grim indeed and so were the conditions of living in the towns. Hewitt (1958) has described how the women who worked in the Victorian cotton mills of England had little conception of what were good child-rearing practices, for they had often been separated from their families at an early age. Infant mortality was very high and the babies that survived were kept quiet with laudanum and gin-soaked bread.

Because of the belief in individual responsibility which had now become predominant, it was assumed that the poor were to blame for their indigent state. If they had worked hard, shown more responsible attitudes, then they need not have been in want. Consequently, the policies for coping with the demands of the poor for subsistence were unsympathetic. And because there was fear of revolution in England after 1789, policies became particularly repressive. People were expected to deal with shortages of resources by seeking extended family support or mutual aid from neighbours. There was still some philanthropic charity from rich to poor in some areas, but it was uneven in its distribution—charities, some very eccentric, were supported by rich men's legacies; soup was given out by the "ladies bountiful" of the neighbourhoods (by the rich men's wives with social consciences); and there was some redistribution of wealth by churches (mainly the noncomformist sects) which preached the virtues of Samaritan charity.

The disruptions to social organization which resulted from the social revolutionary changes of the mercantilist and industrial revolutions were very considerable, resulting in an alienation of "haves" from "have nots" and a complete lack of understanding about the causes of poverty (Mencher, 1967). However, by the 1870s some efforts were being made to develop more effective ways of coping with the problems of poverty. Philanthropists, such as Octavia Hill, provided counselling—in her case through using rent collectors to advise working class women on housing management. Josephine Butler concerned herself with the causes and consequences of prostitution. And public servants, such as John Simon, recognizing that sanitary installations were only part of the solution to public health problems, encouraged the growth of a cadre of health visitors to provide advice on health care to working class mothers.

After a time, extended family patterns reestablished themselves. As Young and Wilmott (1957) have shown, the grandmother was the most important force in holding together working class families in East London in the mid-twentieth century. Neighbourly relationships also had to become reestablished. The old patterns of mutual aid between the social classes were replaced by aid given within the urban working classes. Instead of looking for aid from the upper strata of society in times of distress, workers began to develop new class solidarities. English artisans first got together to develop Friendly Societies to protect themselves in time of social insecurity and later they joined with the labourers to advance their efforts to establish a trade union movement. The mateships of Australian working men are another example of the development of mutual aid in a different setting.

Public Poor Relief

By the mid-nineteenth century in England, there was concern that the philanthropic charities were being exploited by a permanent group of undeserving poor who knew how to work the system rather than the deserving poor in need of temporary help, for, clearly, there was not enough voluntary charitable help to provide for all the needs of the poor. These needs could not be met by the best intentioned extended families, neighbours, workmates and charitable resources.

Another form of poor relief was given by public authorities. This public relief had first been necessary in the fourteenth century to meet the disruptions of wars and widespread epidemics when families, neighbours, landlords, and charities could not cope with the magnitude of the problems arising. Earlier legislation was considered and recodified in 1601 when the Elizabethan Poor Law was enacted. The policy set down in that Act was to be the accepted basis for dealing with the publicly assisted poor in the western English-speaking countries thereafter until the twentieth century. Poor relief was to be given only after all else had failed, on the principle of less eligibility—that is, under conditions of degradation and with deliberate stigmatization of recipients.

Gradually, over the next two centuries, (the seventeenth and eighteenth) the original conditions of the English Poor Law were modified. Indoor relief in workhouses was replaced by outdoor relief and, later, by the Speenhamland system of subsidizing low wages. By the early nineteenth century, there appeared to be need for reform. However, instead of recognizing that the poor were not masters of their own fate but victims of changing technology and social reorganization, the new Poor Law of 1835 returned to the Elizabethan principles, reinstating the harshest conditions of that legislation.

It was not until the 1870s in England that there began to be agitations for change, for the break up of the Poor Law into component parts, recognizing that different social risks might need to be considered separately, that blame for falling into pauperism should be removed from many categories of persons who sought (or, in many cases, dared not seek) help from public funds. In the 1890s in England, workmen's compensation was taken out from the Poor Law and dealt with under separate legislation and in the first decade of the twentieth century, old age pensions were provided separately. From 1910 onwards, insurance against widowhood, orphanhood, unemployment, and ill health began to be introduced. However, it was not until the dirty thirties that there came a general realization that it was not a matter of individual character weakness that led to poverty so much as the disruptions caused by economic cycles running out of control. Later still, it was recognized that poverty was not only an absolute matter of subsistence levels but also a matter of social relativities in a society—thus, for example, one finds the people of Quebec comparing their position with other Canadians and pointing out that they live in a poor province, when by international standards they are part of the excessively rich North American culture.

References are given at the end of the chapter to recent commentaries on poverty in the four countries.

Present Day Recognition of Social Reciprocities

Developments in exchange theory have recently been reviewed by Emerson (1976) (who has said it is not really a full blown theory but rather a frame of reference for looking at social relationships). That it has not been a common frame of reference until recently in thinking about health care matters was demonstrated rather dramatically by two books which appeared at about the same time. Starting from empirical evidence and looking for ways to interpret it, both Fox and Swazey (1974) and Titmuss (1972) decided that exchange theory was the only way to make sense of the organization of organ and blood donation. Titmuss developed this theory, too, to explain medical student-patient relationships and the time lag effects. Meanwhile, Strauss (1970) and his colleagues were using social transaction theory to explain the failures in the U.S. medical system. Social transaction theory has begun to be of special interest to social workers and a model developed by Lawrence (1968) to explain the concept may prove helpful.

Discussion of Readings and References

1. In the first reading attached to this chapter Melvin Tumin has noted that social stratification is ubiquitous. It is important for students to become aware of social differences and there are available many national studies of this phenomenon, e.g., United Kingdom: Kelsall, R. K. and Kelsall, H. M. *Stratification* (London: Longmans, 1974). United States: Reissman, Leonard. *Inequality in American Society* (Glenview, Ill.: Scott Foresman, 1973). Canada: Forcese, Dennis. *The Canadian Class Structure* (Toronto: McGraw-Hill Ryerson, 1975). Australia: Encel, Sol. *Equality and Authority* (Melbourne, Cheshire, 1970).

See bibliography for references to other studies of stratification, such as Wedderburn, 1974 (U.K.); Porter, 1967 and Hiller, 1976 (Canada).

2. The implications of social stratification for health policy makers are that persons in the higher social strata have better access to resources, and this has implications for health. Both affluent and poor groups have health problems. The problems of an affluent society are discussed in later chapters of the Lalonde Report. The wide distribution of illness associated with affluence is a recent problem. Of greater concern to many nations is ill health arising out of poverty. When the health indicators for different socio-economic groups in societies are compared, the lower strata are usually worse off than the higher strata. Some nations have taken steps to redistribute health services to all groups in society. Rein (1976) attributed better health in Britain in the mid-sixties to increased access to health care after the introduction of the National Health Service, and Kohn (1967) demonstrated that the poorer citizens of the Swift Current region of Saskatchewan (who had been provided with universal health services under a pilot scheme) were not differentiated by health status according to socioeconomic strata as other Canadians were. However, if we are to accept McKeown's view that medical care is relatively unimportant compared with other factors such as nutrition in creating a healthy population, it is necessary to learn more about poverty and national attitudes to its management.

Parkin (1971) has discussed the way in which, in western capitalist societies, the poor have frequently been regarded as a threat to the social order, an idea also explored by Piven and Cloward (1971) and Mandell (1975). They were the "dangerous classes" who threatened others' privileges, particularly those which had been gained hardly by entrepreneurial effort. At the same time the poor ought to be provided wth Christian charity as tradition dictated. Mencher (1967), de Schweinitz (1961), and others have traced the evolution of social security programs from the days of the supplementation of voluntary charity by the Elizabethan Poor Law 1601, to the welfare state provisions of the 1940s. Some regard welfare state provisions as a means of increasing social equality and social justice (e.g., R. M. Titmuss in *Social Policy*) others regard welfare states as compounding injustice (Wilding and George, 1974-5) because they bring about some change but only just enough to maintain social control and to keep the same groups in power as before.

A further list of references on poverty and poverty and health is attached to this chapter.

3. Two of the new middle class groups which emerged in the developmental stages of capitalism were first the entrepreneurs and, later, the professionals. They claimed status and prerogatives in society in return for their special contributions to social development on one hand, and preservation of the social order on the other. They formed special interest groups which were successful in getting governments to give them a mandate to regulate social conditions in favor of their group's growth and establishment as part of the social fabric. Of special interest for health policy makers is the development of the health professions. Rosemary Stevens has made historical studies of the British and American medical professions and the Parrys have developed a more radical interpretation of British developments. Abel-Smith's analysis of health services attached to chapter 3 stressed the importance of understanding who got there first among the groups of consumers or providers contending for status and power in nineteenth century societies.

4. A second reading attached to this chapter is a short piece from Terence J. Johnson's *Professions and Power* which is an important analysis of three stages in professional groups' development from patronage, through self-regulation to mediative control. It is hoped that reading this selection will encourage students to seek out Johnson's short book which is full of insightful observations on professional groups' behaviour.

5. In simple societies reciprocal relationships are well understood but with the growth of more complex capitalist societies, the exchange network often fails to function satisfactorily: those in lower strata are not usually considered to be as important as those with greater social status and so get fewer privileges. What they do give to society tends to be downplayed and often needs to be reconsidered as R. M. Titmuss made clear in *The Gift Relationship.* Medical care providers' failures to recognize reciprocities have been criticized by other writers, such as Strauss et al. in *Where Medicine Fails.* R. J. Lawrence has developed "A Social Transaction Model for the Analysis of Social Welfare Activities," which is concerned with exploring more fully social exchange relationships for the purpose of educating professional service providers and is recommended reading.

6. Returning to Tumin's observation that all societies are stratified, we note that Gil has related this to the task and manpower system which has been developed. The powers and privileges of groups within society bear a close relationship to their abilities to negotiate status differences. The third read-

ing is a review by David Maines of a book by Anselm Strauss called *Negotiations.* This review summarizes and critiques Strauss's formulation of the concept that societies are negotiated orders.

Further References on Poverty

Abel-Smith, B. and Townsend, P. *The Poor and the Poorest.* London: Bell, 1965.

Townsend, Peter. *The Concept of Poverty.* London: Heinemann, 1970.

Marris, Peter and Rein, Martin. *Dilemmas of Social Reform.* New York: Atherton, 1967.

Harp, John and Hoffley, John R., eds. *Poverty in Canada.* Scarborough, Ontario: Prentice-Hall of Canada, 1971.

Caskie, Donald. *Canadian Fact Book on Poverty.* Ottawa: Canadian Council on Social Development, 1979.

Australia, Commonwealth Government. (Henderson) Commission of Inquiry into Poverty. Canberra: Australian Government Publishing Service, 1974.

References on Poverty and Health

Townsend, Peter. *The Social Minority.* London: Allen Lane, 1973.

Kosa, John, Antonovsky, Aaron and Zola, Irving Kenneth, eds. *Poverty and Health.* Cambridge, Mass.: Harvard University Press, 1969.

Beck, R. Glen. "Economic Class and Access to Physicians' Services Under Public Medical Care Insurance." *International Journal of Health Services* (3) (1973): 341–355 (Canada).

Australia, Commonwealth Government. (Martin) *Social Medical Aspects of Poverty in Australia:* Commission of Inquiry into Poverty. Canberra:Australian Government Publishing Service, 1976.

Social Stratification: Some Theoretical Problems

Melvin M. Tumin

The ubiquity of stratification in every society has led some students to claim that there must be something inevitable and valuable in social inequality. Otherwise, they argue, how could stratification be so persistent and widespread? Stated in these terms, the argument is obviously meaningless: Neither the ubiquity nor the antiquity of a phenomenon may be cited as grounds to consider it inevitable or of positive value. Focusing alone for the moment on questions of inevitability, the principal argument in support of the claim holds that no society could survive without some form of institutionalized inequality in evaluation and reward. The following evidence has been brought forth:

1. Inequality in power is a necessary condition for the management of any multi-person enterprise.
2. Under some conditions of culturally-specific motivation and training, it is easier to distribute rewards unequally.
3. Under similar conditions, it is more suited to the interests of those who control matters to distribute rewards unequally.
4. Under the same conditions, it is less of a wrench with previous history to continue unequal distributions of shares than to institute equality.

It can readily be seen, however, that none of these findings is decisive with regard to the inevitability of stratification. Inequality in task-specific powers is not the same as inequality in rewards or evaluation. And what is culturally

---

From Melvin M. Tumin, *Social Stratification* (Englewood Cliffs, N.J.: Prentice-Hall), pp. 106–11. Reprinted by permission of the publisher.

convenient, given certain traditions, may have nothing to do with what is necessary or unavoidable.

Ultimately, the argument for stratification, which appeals to the requirements for survival notion, rests upon premises regarding human motivation. These premises, usually left unstated, maintain that one can't get people to do unequally difficult or unequally skilled tasks without distributing evaluations and rewards unequally. The unequal compensation serves as the motivating force.

The evidence about motivation from the actual conduct of human affairs is worth examining. However ubiquitous inequality may be, one cannot but be equally struck by the fact that all over the world men and women work extremely hard and conscientiously at a variety of tasks without thought or consideration for unequal evaluation and reward. Similarly, human laziness is widespread both under conditions of relative equality and great inequality of rewards. Variations in the quality of human effort are found not only between societies but within any society. Even where unequal rewarding is pervasive, one finds people working conscientiously at equally strenuous tasks without any promise of differential rewards. Contrast, for instance, the main motivational themes that characterize the occupational and the family spheres of life in America today. Stratification is a dominant theme in the former and is absent in the latter. Yet it would be extremely difficult to demonstrate that most people act less conscientiously in one than in the other.

It may be argued that the values and norms that govern family life cannot be easily extrapolated to conform to the occupational sphere, and that however sufficient the family themes may be for family tasks, they simply won't work in the occupational sphere. The same argument points to the difficulties raised by the impersonality of the occupational world, the large numbers of people who must be organized in large-scale bureaucracies, the inherent strains in such bureaucracies, and so on.

If we ask how American family life evokes conscientious behavior without promise of differential reward, it is clear that identification by every family member with one another's welfare is a crucial element. Everything that happens to one's children is consequential; parents cannot evade responsibility for their families.

If occupations could be constructed so that workers felt more identification with the final product, along with responsibility for that product, one might secure a great increase in conscientious, skilled performance without having to employ differential rewards. Indeed, one has perhaps to use differential rewards as inducement for effective performance precisely in proportion to the absence of self-determination and identification with the product.

One must also reckon with the likelihood that the use of differentials in rewards to induce conscientious work introduces a spirit of calculation that undercuts the spirit of voluntary giving of an employee's time and efforts. When differential rewards are calibrated to effort, then it is most natural that everyone concerned give just as much as, but no more than, he is being paid for, and that he compare how much he is giving, relative to his pay, with how much others are giving relative to theirs. In such circumstances the least efficient and least conscientious worker is likely to set the pace by which others measure how much they should give.

Yet in view of the fact that men can be highly motivated by a sense of identification with a product and a feeling of moral responsibility toward their work, we must seriously question whether a claim can be made for the necessity of differential rewards as a motivational system. If differential rewarding is *not* inevitable as a motivational scheme, and if there are serious doubts regarding its relative effficacy, the whole issue of the *inevitability* of social stratification is called in question. For if we cannot rest the case for the inevitability of stratification on inescapable facts about human motivation, we cannot rest it upon anything at all. We must, therefore, face the likelihood that we are dealing with something optional rather than inevitable in human affairs. This being the case, we are forced to confront once again the question, why is stratification ubiquitous in human societies.

Specifically with regard to social stratification, we may once again aver the following: (1) people can be motivated to high effort in a number of different ways; (2) each way involves its own balance of price and profit so far as human desires and values are concerned; (3) in and of itself none seems more natural or fitting than any other; (4) the number of people benefitted or harmed by various schemes of motivation is likely to be variable—some schemes will surely benefit a few and work adversely for many, while the reverse will be true for other schemes.

The most obvious fact about any system of stratification is that it produces greatest benefit and gain for those who rank high and receive the highest rewards. Furthermore those who benefit most from the system will usually do whatever they can to preserve their privileges, whatever effort they may make from time to time to spread the benefits of the system more widely. It is also predictable that in a society stressing maximum acquisition, most men will try to obtain increasingly more of whatever is available. When the main emphasis of a society urges everyone to maximize his material well-being and to achieve maximum invidious distinction over others, how could one expect any other motivational scheme to be easily learned and followed?

Is stratification useful then? Yes, certainly, in direct proportion to one's height on the ladders of rank and reward. However much high rewards may motivate the elite members of a work force to extra effort, the lower rewards received by the majority are just as likely to *demotivate* them and induce them to lower levels of effort. If, as is often observed, men work hard and give their best in spite of low rank and reward, this is primarily because of other cultural themes to which they are educated, because they do not perceive alternatives, or because they fear the alternatives. It can hardly be due to inspiration from their relatively lower ranks and rewards.

In response to this argument, those who see positive values in stratification maintain that however adversely affected the motivations of the less rewarded may be, the positive effects on the most talented, highest rewarded are the maximum possible, and that the net balance yields a higher social product than would be possible under other arrangements. But again, this argument begs the issue. Unequal rewards for an elite may produce a kind of net yield that the *elite* judges to be the highest possible, but those less rewarded may find the net yield quite unsatisfactory compared to alternative possibilities.

Still another version of the defense of stratification states that the drive to fame and distinction—the quest for greatness—is an indispensable ingredient in the motivation of men who do achieve greatness. But this argument fails to make the important distinction between the urge to *do* something great, on the one hand, and the urge to *be considered* great, on the other.

Biographies often suggest that there is a mixture of both these motives, but that the motives are nonetheless quite distinct from each other. The desire to write a great novel is one thing; the desire to be known as a great novelist is quite another. Both desires may be present in the same man, but we must inquire whether the desire for personal fame may not impede the kind of commitment and perspective required to produce greatness. In any event, it seems quite clear that the dynamics of great cultural achievement are variable and that such achievement is due to the confluence of many complex factors; this in itself precludes a facile assumption of the clear and dominant importance of invidious distinctions and unequal rewards.

One must also reckon with the likelihood that a great deal of individual talent remains forever dormant and that one of the most important factors that obscures or prevents the discovery of talent is the lack of opportunity for the vast majority of people in the world, who live in limited material and spiritual circumstances. We cannot know for sure how much scientific or humanistic talent is actually present in a given population, but we do know that every time the doors of opportunity have been opened to segments of a population previously denied such opportunity, there has been an unexpected outpouring of talent. This is not to say that the world is full of hidden geniuses, but only that there is probably much more talent of all kinds than is ever evident at a given time, and that the systems of unequal opportunities in stratified societies are in large part responsible for the muting of these potentials.

These remarks about talent and its utilization have implied a very special meaning for the term. The reference has obviously been only to a limited number of all possible human talents, namely, to those which happen to be most in demand and most honored at the moment. In America today there is great concern about the country's attempt to discover, recruit, and train those talents considered important to industrial and military technology. There is a commensurately lower concern for other kinds of talent—artistic, humanistic, political, familial, and literary. The majority of the people may agree that this is as things should be. But the fact remains that most talents are being relatively ignored while a few—specifically relevant to certain very limited purposes—are being emphasized.

Stratification—considered as unequal evaluation and rewarding—produces mixed consequences wherever it is found. Its effect upon one segment of a population differs from the effect upon other segments. Its implications for social and eocnomic development are also quite varied and involve very different strategies of short-range vs. long-range benefits and harms, depending on which segments are chosen for the momentary advantage and whose interests are held in abeyance. The kind of product that can be achieved by a well trained elite and a relatively poorly trained mass is different from that which results from a middle level of training for the majority. The net yields in loyalty, participation, conscientiousness, sense of social duty and responsibility, and general acceptance of a society's values are likely to vary substantially, depending on how the society rewards its various contributors and how much effort it expends to incorporate its members into satisfying occupations.

The obligation of the social scientist is to examine the consequences of various structures of opportunity and privilege for the lives of the people concerned and for the general conduct of the society. In the course of such an examination the social scientist must remember the elementary fact that the more unequally a society distributes wealth and distinction, the fewer are the people who accept and respect the values of that society and who are willing to contribute their talents to it. The moral implications of these consequences are significant for the social scientist, for if it is true, as most sociologists assume, that men act in terms of what they believe, and if unequal evaluation and rewarding lead many men to believe their society is unfair, then that society will suffer accordingly. In short, the moral reactions of lowly rewarded or degraded people become important elements in the final outcome of stratification.

The most finely argued defense of stratification in current writings appeals to the greater sacrifices individuals experience in training for the highly rewarded positions—doctor, lawyer, business executive, and the like. But one can conceive of these prolonged training periods as important and gratifying advantages enjoyed by a small elite: chances to have their minds and sensibilities trained, their tastes refined, and their perspectives enlarged. Surely whatever elements of sacrifice may be involved in professional training, these advantageous elements are also present. It is therefore difficult to characterize this period as predominantly one of sacrifice.

As for the relative importance of different occupations, we must be cautious in making such judgments. Society decides what is important, but it is plausible to maintain that all jobs, however, simple or complex, are equally important to the society. In the long run all of a society's "necessary" tasks must be performed or the society suffers. For the moment let us view importance in terms of ranges of consequences incurred from adequate or inadequate performance of a task. Let us assume further that we can get perfect measurement and unanimous agreement on these matters. We cannot proceed from this definition and these "perfect" measurements to any conclusion about how rewards *should* be made. Unavoidably, we would still be involved in making a value judgment to the effect that those who perform more important work ought to be rewarded more handsomely.

Moreover, at the bottom of this judgment is a crucial but concealed fact: Assuming perfect equality of opportunity, the talents required to perform such more important work occur as accidents of birth. For example, a special dexterity is required to become a skilled surgeon, and if only a few people are born with this talent, to argue that surgeons should receive high level rewards is to argue on behalf of the accident of birth. For even if we agree that the work of the surgeon is in some ways far more important than the work of others, we could not justify extra rewards for the surgeon except on the grounds that he is lucky enough to have been born with this rare talent. The only other conceivable basis for rewarding the surgeon disproportionately would be that he has made greater sacrifices than others in the course of his training or that he won't be motivated to use his talents. But we have seen that both these arguments are dubious.

These observations entail certain important conclusions. In the first place, it is clear that the main determinants of what kind of work one will be able to do are: (1) native talent, and (2) social opportunities for discovery, training and utilization of that talent. It is equally clear, secondly, that to be born with desired and valued talents is a matter of accident, and that the children of the elite have considerably greater opportunities to have their talents trained and utilized. The chance to get into positions that receive higher rewards for performance of more skilled tasks is often a function of accident and unequal opportunity. In a democratic society neither of these grounds is meritorious. To substitute an aristocracy of talent for one of lineage is hardly praiseworthy as a feature of democratic society.

All moral considerations aside, we are left with the question concerning the possible positive contributions of unequal ranking and rewarding to social systems. The evidence regarding the mixed outcomes of stratification strongly suggests the examination of alternatives. The evidence regarding the possibilities of social growth under conditions of more equal rewarding are such that the exploration of alternatives seems eminently worthwhile. In short, there are many more possible ways to organize societies and to motivate people to conscientious use of their talents. If man seeks for ever more effective ways to maximize his social yield, not to mention his personal gratifications, it might very well pay him to examine these alternative possibilities. There seems to be a great deal of possible gain and very little possible loss in prospect.

Types of Occupational Control

Terence J. Johnson

Attempts to develop the concepts of professionalisation and professionalism in order to account for observed differences between occupations which are conventionally regarded as professions have concentrated attention on the instutional orders which have grown up around occupational activities. In general, they have ignored the prior problem of distinguishing between occupational activities as such. In identifying the nature of occupational activities we must first look at the general consequences of the social division of labour. In all differentiated societies, the emergence of specialised occupational skills, whether productive of goods or services, creates relationships of *social and economic dependence* and, paradoxically, relationships of *social distance.* Dependence upon the skills of others has the effect of reducing the common area of shared experience and knowledge and increases social distance; for the inescapable consequence of specialisation in the production of goods and services is *un*specialisation in consumption. This consequence flows from the crystallisation and development of all specialised occupations. While specialisation creates systematic relationships of interdependence, it also introduces potentialities for autonomy. It is social distance as a product of the division of labour which creates this potentiality for autonomy, but it is not to be identified with it. Rather, social distance creates a structure of uncertainty, or what has been referred to as indeterminacy,[1] in the relationship between producer and consumer, so creating a

Reprinted with permission of the British Sociological Association and the author, from Terence J. Johnson, *Professions and Power* (London: Macmillan 1972), pp. 41–47. Footnotes have been renumbered and transferred to the end.

tension in the relationship which must be resolved. There is an *irreducible but variable* minimum of uncertainty in any consumer-producer relationship, and depending on the degree of this indeterminacy and the social structural context, various institutions will arise to reduce the uncertainty. Power relationships will determine whether uncertainty is reduced at the expense of producer or consumer.

The fact that the level of indeterminacy is variable has important consequences for the relative autonomy of various occupations and the resources available to one occupation as against another in imposing their own definitions of the producer-consumer relationship. The resources of power available to any single occupational group are rarely sufficient to impose on all consumers its own definitions of the content of production and its ends, except where these resources are articulated with other and wider bases of social power. The major exception to this rule is the modern professional army, whose technological and organisational resources are often sufficient to achieve this. A significant element in producing variations in the degree of uncertainty and, therefore, the potentialities for autonomy is the esoteric character of the knowledge applied by the specialist. However, this is not to follow the usual stress in the literature upon systematic theory as a basis for professionalism and professional authority. First, the term "esoteric" is used advisedly, as it refers neither to the degree of the complexity of knowledge nor to the level of specialisation involved in an occupational activity. For example, while certain skills may increase in complexity, as measured by the level of training necessary for their application, it is not inconceivable that the general level of understanding of such skills could also increase with educational advance on a broad front. Social distance does not, therefore, automatically increase. Also, social distance is not in all circumstances a direct consequence of specialisation, as high levels of specialisation may expose an occupation to fragmentation and routinisation as a result of which it is more easily understood and controlled by non-practitioners. However, the technological conditions for routinisation within a given occupation will not necessarily lead to such fragmentation where, for example, the practitioners already control and define the content of practice. Accountants are already struggling against the consequences of routinisation heralded by the computerisation of a number of their activities, while printers are another well-known example of a group which has successfully retarded the introduction of technologies reducing the skill content of production.[2] The power relationship existing between practitioner and client may be such, then, as to enable the practitioner to increase the social distance and his own autonomy and control over practice by engaging in a process of "mystification." Uncertainty is not, therefore, entirely cognitive in origin but may be deliberately increased to serve manipulative or managerial ends.

The assertion made that an occupation group rarely enjoys the resources of power which would enable it to impose its own definitions of the producer-consumer relationship suggests that *professionalism* as defined in the literature is a peculiar phenomenon. It is only where an occupational group shares, by virtue of its membership of a dominant class or caste, wider resources of power that such an imposition is likely to be successfully achieved, and then only where the actual consumers or clients provide a relatively large, heterogeneous, fragmented source of demand. The polar opposite of this situation is where there is a single consumer—a patron who has the power to define his own needs and the manner in which he expects these to be catered for. In order to determine the variations which are possible in forms of institutionalised control of occupational activities, then, it is necessary to take account of the wider resources of power which are available to an occupational group and also to focus upon the producer-consumer relationship in so far as this is affected by the social composition and character of the source of demand.

While each of these factors will help to explain why certain institutional forms of control of an occupation arise, there remains the fact that occupational activities vary in the degree to which they give rise to a structure of uncertainty and in their potentialities for autonomy. It is this factor which provides an explanation of why it is that some occupations rather than others achieve self-regulation and even why they draw recruits from groups who already command alternative resources of power. Certain occupations are associated with particularly acute problems of uncertainty, where client or consumer judgement is particularly ineffective and the seeking of skilled help necessarily invites intrusion of others into intimate and vulnerable areas of the consumer's self- or group-identity. Medical practice, for example, intrudes into areas of social taboo relating to personal privacy and bodily functions as well as areas of culturally defined ritual significance such as birth and death. In a similar way, the functions of a specialised priesthood may be regarded as fundamental to the well-being of a group. Such occupations involve social relationships of potential tension, where the provision of specialised services is threatening and uncertainty compounded. The greater the social distance, the greater the "helplessness" of the client, then the greater the exposure to possible exploitation and the need for social control. It is clear that a number of occupations conventionally regarded as professions are of this kind. Two points must be made here. First, while it is suggested that certain occupations are potentially threatening and exploitative, we do not need to conclude that this will be equally so for all groups in a society, nor that the service is equally valued. In short, the functionalist reification of a "central societal value" must be avoided. As pointed out above, the values associated with law are not equally shared, and the apparatus of a legal order has functions for the maintenance and legitimation of a dominant group and explains why law should be regarded as a "fit" occupation for members of or aspirants to an upper class.

Secondly, an occupation may undergo changes in its skill content and cultural significance over time. As a result its potentialities for autonomy will also vary. The decline in the significance of the priesthood in England is a case in point. The decline in its cultural significance during the twentieth century has led to a decline in status and income and a reduction in the number of recruits from upper-class backgrounds.[3] It is also true that in mass-consumption societies new occupations have emerged which give rise to acute problems of control as a result of their cultural significance in such societies. The servicing mechanics are a case in point—a series of occupations which give rise to new forms of exploitation and need for social control.

Historically, various social mechanisms have arisen to "manage" these areas of social tension which present problems of social control. A characteristic form of traditional control is where the quality of a good or service is guaranteed by a blood relationship only. For example, with the rise of large-scale business houses in Renaissance Italy, the initial means of controlling the operations of a factor or agent in distant markets was to send a family member or to tie him to the family by marriage.[4] In more modern times, the contract, the free market, and even branded goods have all fulfilled similar functions. They are an expression of moral orders associated with the existing division of labour and they consist of rules and conventions about who can do what and to whom and when. They are aspects of institutionalised forms of control which vary not only in association with changes in the content of knowledge and skills associated with an occupation, but also in response to emerging social problems and needs which are to a large extent the product of changing power relations. Those occupations which are associated with peculiarly acute tensions, as described above, have given rise to a number of institutionalised forms of control, "professionalism" being one. Professionalism, then, becomes redefined as a peculiar type of occupational control rather than an expression of the inherent nature of particular occupations. A profession is not, then, an occupation, but a means of controlling an occupation. Likewise, professionalisation is a historically specific process which some occupations have undergone at a particular time, rather than a process which certain occupations may always be expected to undergo because of their "essential" qualities. In order to place this peculiar form of occupational control in context, a typology of institutionalised orders of control will be suggested and the various characteristics of each order and the conditions for their emergence discussed.

While the typology presented below is expected, in a more developed form, to apply to all occupations, for the purpose of the present argument the discussion will be restricted to those occupations conventionally regarded as professions. In drawing up a typology it has been found useful to focus on the core of uncertainty—the producer-consumer relationship. There are three broad resolutions of the tension existing in the producer-consumer relationship which are historically identifiable:

1. In which the producer defines the needs of the consumer and the manner in which these needs are catered for. This type will be referred to as *collegiate* control and is exemplified by the emergence of autonomous occupational associations. Identifiable sub-types of *collegiate* control are *professionalism,* which in its most fully developed form was the product of social conditions present in nineteenth-century Britain, and *guild* control which emerged as one of the phenomena associated with urbanisation in late medieval Europe. The following discussion will be restricted to professionalism, which followed the rise to power of an urban middle class and attained its most extreme expression in the organisation of law practice in England.

2. In which the consumer defines his own needs and the manner in which they are to be met. This type includes both oligarchic and corporate forms of *patronage* as well as various forms of *communal* control. *Oligarchic patronage* has arisen in those traditional societies where an artistocratic patron or oligarchy was the major consumer of various types of services and goods—where the artist and craftsman, architect and physician, were tied to the great houses. *Corporate patronage* refers to the condition in which occupations such as accountancy find themselves in present-day industrialised societies, where a major part of the demand for their services comes from large corporate organisations. Communal control refers to a situation where a community as a whole or a community organisation imposes upon producers communal definitions of needs and practice. This has occurred in isolated pioneering communities, but finds more modern expression in the development of consumer politics, whereby consumer organisations deliberately set out to control the quality and eventually the organisation of the production of goods and services.

3. In which a third party mediates in the relationship between producer and consumer, defining both the needs and the manner in which the needs are met. There are various institutional forms of this *mediative* type also, perhaps the most conspicuous example being *capitalism*, in which the capitalist entrepreneur intervenes in the direct relationship between the producer and consumer in order to rationalise production and regulate markets. No less significant, however, is *state mediation,* which will be the example discussed below, in which a powerful centralised state intervenes in the relationship between producer and consumer, initially to define what the needs are, as with the growth in Britain of state welfare policies. A further historical example was the role of the medieval church in Europe in regulating the practice of a large range of occupations.

There are many more possible resolutions of the basic tension in the producer-consumer relationship. For example, the needs may be defined by one party, while the manner in which the needs are catered for is controlled by another. Whereas it can be argued that the state defines who is to receive medical services in Britain today, by and large medical practitioners continue to determine the manner in which these needs are catered for. A "nationalised" occupation would exist only where the state defined both "needs" and "manners." In accepting that there are variations in the control of "needs" on the one hand and "manner" of production on the other, we can take into account relatively subtle differences in the organisation of occupations which have created some difficulties in the literature on the professions.

It must be kept in mind that the impact of a prevailing system of control upon individual occupations will vary as a result of the prior historical development of the occupation. For example, an occupation which emerged in nineteenth-century Britain may bring with it into the twentieth century many of the symbols and organisational characteristics of *professionalism* (used in the sense indicated above), even though *professionalism* may be in decline and new institutional forms of control emerging. However, where a given set of social conditions is influential in affecting the development of occupations, there will emerge dominant institutional forms of control which will in turn vary from occupation to occupation in accordance with the potentialities for autonomy which a developing occupation exhibits. . . . The . . . analysis of each of the types outlined . . . will [include] a discussion of such factors as the nature of the consumer, the producer-consumer relationship, the conditions and characteristics of recruitment, colleague relationships, knowledge and ideology.

Notes

[1]This term is used by Jamous and Peloille in *Professions and Professionalization,* ed. J. A. Jackson (Cambridge: 1970), pp. 111–120.

[2]See A. J. M. Sykes, "Unity and Restrictive Practices in the British Printing Industry," *Sociological Review* 8 (Dec. 1960):239–54.

[3]See B. Wilson, *Religion in a Secular Society* (Harmondsworth, 1969).

[4]Max Weber, *A General Economic History,* trans. F. H. Knight (London, 1923).

Mesostructure and Social Process

David R. Maines

. . . Negotiation as a form of interpersonal and intergroup interaction is a fact of social existence. [Some sociologists assert that] we live in a rapidly and ever-changing world in which the normative components continuously must be reconstituted, debated, and negotiated. Nothing ever is fixed once and for all. . . .

The position taken by Anselm Strauss in *Negotiations,* however, is a more fundamental and ultimately a farther reaching view. Strauss is concerned with the relation of negotiation to social order. . . . [He] maintains that the structures of social orders to some extent are always breaking down and being reconstituted, and even when they are maintained in relatively stable forms, negotiation is one of the processes contributing to that maintenance. Strauss' point of departure for the analysis of negotiation, therefore, is that "A social order—even the most repressive—without some forms of negotiation would be inconceivable" (p. ix). As "ways of getting things accomplished," negotiations are processes present in both stable and unstable social orders. They are as important for understanding permanence, in other words, as they are for understanding change. In this sense, it is misleading to think of negotiation merely as a distinctive feature of contemporary society. Rather, it is an ongoing mechanism which variously operates in all social orders, and which when appropriated as an analytical framework can pro-

---

Adapted from a review of *Negotiations: Varieties, Contexts, Processes, and Social Order,* by Anselm Strauss, which appeared in *Contemporary Sociology,* July 1979, vol. 8, no. 4, pp. 524–527. Reprinted with permission of the American Sociological Association. The notion of "mesostructure" as it is used in this essay is borrowed with permission and appreciation from an unpublished manuscript by Fritz Schuetze.

duce significant understanding of social process and social structure as well as their interdependence. . . .

The impetus for *Negotiations,* is derived from several sources and represents several thrusts. It is a systematic attempt to formulate a paradigm for examining negotiation and social orders which itself is grounded in a body of research findings. It is an attempt to selectively utilize the strengths of abstract negotiation theory as well as those studies with narrower topical foci. It represents a contribution to the history of social thought insofar as its intellectual antecedents are so clearly spelled out. And, because it is a paradigmatic analysis, it represents a major turning point in the development of the negotiated order perspective. . . .

Strauss examines a number of major works by some very influential scholars with several questions in mind concerning the use or lack of use of a negotiation perspective. The purpose of this examination is not to critique the analyses *per se* but to assess how and in what respects those analyses might differ if the problem of the relation of negotiation and social order had been central to them. . . .

Strauss' discussion of these cases is interesting. In particular, it attempts to answer the question of whether a conceptual framework focusing on negotiation and social order makes any difference. Strauss argues that it does and that the differences are indeed major ones. Thus, this section of the book might be thought of as a sort of critical test of the perspective. More generally, Strauss is saying that while each of the works he examines had raised valid theoretical problems, it is unlikely that those problems could have been adequately answered without an analysis of multiple interlocking processes, including that of negotiation. This raises the larger question of whether social orders can be properly analyzed at all without taking negotiation processes into account.

Part Two ("Paradigm and Case Analysis") is the heart of *Negotiations,* and constitutes fully one half of the entire volume. It is here that Strauss maps out an analytic scheme and then applies it to the analysis of eleven research reports of negotiation. The paradigm is basically intended to provide three things: a way of incorporating the existing literature into a single framework, a guide for analyzing and researching negotiation processes and social orders, and a systematic set of cues for future work which could modify and refine the paradigm itself.

Several key concepts form the structure of the paradigm. The first, obviously, is *negotiations.* What is the nature of the interaction, the types of actors, the strategies and tactics used, and the consequences of negotiation? Also, what are the subprocesses of negotiation, such as making trade-offs or obtaining kickbacks? Second is the notion of *structural context,* or the structural parameters within which negotiations take place. What are the structural properties that bear on negotiations? The third concept is *negotia-*

tion context, which is similar to Glaser and Strauss' (1964) earlier concept of "awareness context." Negotiation contexts are affected or "surrounded" by the larger and more encompassing structural contexts and refer to those conditions which enter directly into and shape the course of negotiations. Both concepts refer to structural units used to relate negotiation processes to the social orders in which negotiation takes place. Furthermore, negotiation contexts themselves contain many properties which can combine in multiple ways to direct specific negotiation trajectories. Among these properties are the number and experience of the negotiators; whether negotiations are one-shot, sequential, multiple, or serial; the power distributions among negotiators; the nature of the stakes involved; whether the negotiations are covert or overt; the complexity of the issues; available options other than negotiation; and how clear is the legitimacy of the boundaries of the issues. Strauss emphasizes that these properties are not logical constructs but are grounded in empirical work and were selected chiefly on the basis of their relevance rather than logic. The paradigm, as I see it, is an attempt to develop practical theory—theory that works and which can be applied to diverse settings—rather than aesthetically appealing theory. On that score, Strauss is very clear. "Their various permutations and clusterings constitute the explanations for the specific kinds of negotiators, interactions, tactics, strategies, subprocesses of negotiations, and consequences that will be discussed" (p. 100). Thus, these permutations allow for an analysis of the developmental character of negotiation processes, and the focus on structural and negotiation contexts (and their properties) allows that analysis to be lodged in considerations of social structure.

In applying the paradigm, Strauss uses six dimensions or general issues raised by the scheme and analytically discusses comparative research cases. The first dimension is *continuous working relationships in organizations* in which experimental psychiatric wards and industrial firms are compared. Matters of legitimacy were seen as important here—in terms of defining the boundaries of new work roles and functions in the former case, and in terms of organizational continuity in the latter. The second is the *interplay of legal and illegal negotiations.* The case of a corrupt judge reveals much about the interlocking relationships of judiciary and business systems, while that of a political machine portrays the social order of a city as an inherently negotiated order. A significant point made in this comparison pertains to the distinction between nonnegotiated agreements (involving coercive conditions) and negotiations. The third issue, *building cooperative structures,* deals directly with negotiation and historical process. Paired here are an account of an attempt to establish an economic union among several European countries which involved long term, sequential, multi-issue negotiations and an account of the setting up of the legal and procedural framework for the Nuremberg Trials, which were short term, sequential, multi-issue, but essentially one-shot. *Negotiating compromises within social orders* is the fourth dimension. In comparing bargaining over bridewealth and the bargaining between insurance companies and claimants, Strauss shows the relevance of structural and negotiation contexts. In the first case, for instance, the negotiations taking place within clan and family relationships are preceded and will be succeeded by a history of previous and future negotiations, while the second case involves one party (the claimant) that is rarely engaged in such transactions, the other party (the insurance company) that engages in many such transactions, and a negotiation process that terminates once a settlement is reached. In the fifth set of comparisons, Strauss discusses antagonistic negotiations within changing structural contexts. The contrasting cases include international negotiations between the United States and the Soviet Union over the Balkans and the power struggles among various ethnic groups in Kenya. The importance of this dimension is in showing how changing structural contexts can affect negotiations and how antagonistic parties engaged in an adversary relationship attempt to take advantage of those changing conditions. The final dimension, *limits, silent bargains, and implicit negotiation,* leads to a critical discussion because two very important topics are explicitly examined: the limits of negotiation and the kinds of interactions to which the concept of negotiation can legitimately refer. Whether violated or not, laws can remain unchanged and thus have consequences for people's actions with regard to a given law; the limits of laws can be tested through violations and/or public campaigns which do not involve negotiations; or laws can be temporarily suspended through negotiations with the police. Furthermore, there is the important matter of tacit agreements and implicit negotiations. These agreements can be long or short standing and may or may not have been reached through negotiation. Their presence, however, often gives rise to minimum negotiations. The general point of this discussion is that not all of the dynamics of freedom and constraint automatically involve negotiations.

In concluding this essay, it might be useful to return to the original position taken in *Negotiations.* The central contention is that there is no social order that is not also a negotiated order; negotiation is inherent in any social order. This is not the same as saying, however, that negotiation theory can explain everything about social order. As Strauss explicitly states, "To assert that would be not only merely presumptuous but patently foolish" (p. 251). . . .

Strauss, then, has proposed a paradigm for engaging in structural analysis, but it is a paradigm that insists that social structure should not be viewed merely as "something out there." It seeks to specify exactly in what respects a "structure" is a structure. . . . It seeks to show, furthermore, that important social structural phenomena *are* negotiable in certain respects. Contrary to some views, such as Marxism, which maintain that the really important features of a society are hardly ever if at all negotiable, it is apparent that a number of the case analyses in *Negotiations* demonstrate quite the opposite. While the institutional structures of any social order do indeed have material and tacit underpinnings, those very institutional arrangements must be maintained in part through negotiation processes (Freidson, 1976). It is in this respect that the paradigm gives one a sense of the "mesostructural" realm of social orders, in which the overlap of social constraint and individual voluntarism operates and in which multiple webs of interaction fill the interstitial arenas that exist between what otherwise would be referred to as the macro and micro levels of society.

Other Literature Cited

Freidson, Eliot. 1976. "The division of labor as social interaction." *Social Problems* 23:304–13.

Glaser, Barney and Anselm Strauss. 1964. "Awareness contexts and social interaction." *American Sociological Review* 29:669–79.

Maines, David. 1977. "Social organization and social structure in symbolic interactionist thought." *Annual Review of Sociology* 3:235–59.

Strauss, Anselm, Leonard Schatzman, Danuta Erlich, Rue Bucher, and Melvin Sabshin. 1963. "The hospital and its negotiated order." Pp. 147–69 in Eliot Freidson (ed.), *The Hospital in Modern Society*, New York: Free Press.

7 Human Rights

"Man is born free but is everywhere in chains," said Rousseau in 1762 in his discussion of *The Social Contract.* This sentence became a rallying cry for many people who had become disturbed about the organization of European societies in the eighteenth century. It was a potent force in the French and American Revolutions.

The concept of human rights is a continuing theme challenging modern social organization. It is the theme underlying attempts to remind those who have power that they must attend to social reciprocities, to ensure that all those who have membership in a society are given proper recognition.

The concept was embodied in the American Bill of Rights: "We hold these truths to be self evident that all men are created equal, that they are endowed by their Creator with certain inalienable rights. . . ." It was assumed by the revolutionaries that "social goals could be assumed empirically as natural laws" (Donnison, 1972, p. 97) but as Benn and Peters (1959) have pointed out, it was not until 1777 that Hume's work distinguished between natural laws and social conventions. This distinction helped people to see thereafter that societies were constituted according to the rules social groups had set up for themselves and did not follow absolute rules such as governed physical matter.

> Words like "rights," "duties," "ought," and obligation belong primarily to normative discourse; they are used, that is, in prescribing conduct according to rules, and have a descriptive force only if we assume the rule to be in force, i.e. widely observed, when to know what rules require of people is to know what they are likely to do. . . . [P. 88]

Benn and Peters have explained how this normative approach affects the interpretation of "rights" and "duties"—these words possess meaning only in the context of rules. Many social philosophers have not appreciated this context and have equated "rights" with "powers" or with "expectations" or "with some kind of mystical bond with other members of their community."

Yet it is felt that setting down statements of rights has strong moral force and may result in contexts being changed. It was for this reason that the Universal Declaration of Human Rights was prepared and adopted by the Plenary Session of the General Assembly of the United Nations in 1948 by 48 votes to nil with 8 abstentions (the Soviet Union, Poland, Czechoslovakia, Yugoslavia, the Ukraine, Byelorussia, South Africa and Saudi Arabia). In a preamble, the origins of this Declaration are revealed. It was the disregard and contempt for human rights manifested in the Second World War by barbarous acts which "outraged the conscience of mankind." It was thought that if man is not to be compelled to have recourse to rebellion against tyranny and oppression, then human rights should be protected by the rule of law.

The Preamble goes on to relate the Declaration to the reaffirmation by the peoples of the U.N. in their Charter of their own "faith in fundamental human rights, and in the equal rights of men and women, and to their determination to promote social progress and better standards of life in larger freedom." These statements are followed by 31 Articles setting out the rights in detail. However, the Declaration has not had any binding force, and subsequent world history has indicated that it has had little, if any, effect in states which did not already observe its principles.

Rights and Justice

Liberté, Egalité, Fraternité; Life, Liberty and the Pursuit of Happiness. These were the slogans of the French and American Revolutions. As Benn and Peters have pointed out, the early declarations of rights were statements of grievances against governments, but times have changed:

> Since the 18th Century we have come to regard the state less as a hostile, if necessary, intruder in private affairs, and more as an instrument for promoting welfare. Accordingly, the duties imposed by more recent declarations require positive action, not merely non-interference [with personal autonomy]. . . . The presumption is that if the right is not otherwise implemented, the duty rests on the government by default. [P. 102]

Can all the eighteenth-century revolutionary objectives be realized or were these just good rallying cries?

From Moral to Legal Rights

"Human rights should be protected by the rule of law," said the Declaration. Benn and Peters explain that there are two kinds of rights, the first, customary or legal and the second, moral rights. Moral rights, once recognized, may then be developed into laws such as the Sex Discrimination Acts which provide for men and women to be treated equally in specified circumstances, such as job-hunting activities.

> Legal rights may be particularistic, that is, they may refer to contracts made between individuals or groups, or may be universal, that is, necessarily, benefits conferred by the state. Moral rights are not specific or particularistic, but general: "the rules purport to apply to all men, not to creditors, debtors, landlords, tenants, doctors, etc., but universally. . . . [P. 100]
>
> [Legal and customary rights] raise no philosophical problems beyond understanding what is meant by saying that a man has such a right. Concepts like "human," "natural" and "fundamental" rights, however, are more puzzling because they are not so clearly related to rules. Statements of rights of this type are statements of moral principles of a very high order of generality. No particular consequence of action ever follows as a necessary consequence of such a principle. Nevertheless, they draw attention to important interests which are shared by most men, like the interest in living and being let alone, in security of person and security of property. To recognize these interests as "natural rights" is to lay down that they can rightly be impaired only for very special reasons—that the onus of proof rests heavily on whoever would set them aside. [P. 104]

The struggle for human rights began as a struggle against arbitrary treatment by rulers against the ruled, against imprisonment without trial, or taxation without representation.

> Formal declarations of rights are mainly directed not to the regulation of relations between private citizens, but to the duties of governments and legislatures. Where private relations are involved, the duty is laid on the legal authority concerned to make positive law conform to the standards prescribed. [P. 102]

Difficulties in Definition of Rights

One of the problems of implementation is the conflict which appears to exist between liberty and equality. There is a political tension in any society which proposes to provide both.

One of the problems is that of interpretation. The relationship of the two concepts may be interpreted differently by different individuals and groups. If men are to be permitted to have complete liberty, how then can attempts be made to ensure equality? It took many years before this question was examined fruitfully. Either liberty was emphasized or equality. But the western democracies have gradually worked on the issues and have made positive moves towards implementation of both together. Particularly, different political parties interpret the concepts of liberty and equality in different ways. Donnison has compared the views of the right with the views of the left—should the emphasis be put on economic growth and development of more resources or should it be put on redistribution? It is the right wing group which makes more claim to protect liberty and the left wing to be interested in equality.

Tawney (1931) wrote, "Liberty and equality have usually, in England, been considered antithetical and since fraternity has scarcely been considered at all, the famous trilogy has easily been dismissed as a hybrid abortion. . ." (p. 164). After consideration, he concluded that,

> When liberty is construed, realistically, as implying not merely a minimum of civil and political rights, but securities that the economically weak will not be at the mercy of the economically strong, and that the control of those aspects of economic life by which all are affected will be amenable in the last resort to the will of all, a large measure of equality, so far from being inimicable to liberty is essential to it. [P. 164]

Donnison has argued that the important thing is to recognize that both parties are searching for liberty, the former for one group of individuals, the latter for another. The search for liberty needs to be related to the search for equality, he said. Liberty implies equality.

> When policies are to be decided, top priority should normally be given to the extension of liberty, particularly among those who have least of it, the people whose lives are most severely stunted by economic, social and political restraints. [P. 114]

And in his book on social justice, Rawls (1972) argued that each individual should have the right to the most extensive liberty compatible with similar liberty for others.

But liberty tends to have been associated with maintaining prerogatives and equality with developing human rights and Donnison's reinterpretation of the concept of liberty is not a common interpretation. The proponents of each cause see themselves as defenders forced to make concessions to the other side.

Warham (1974) has examined the concept equality and its implications for policy development. As a philosophical concept

> equality may be analysed as a logical rule or formal principle, or in relation to an existing state of affairs, or as a moral or political principle, or as an ideal. [P. 5]
>
> Wilson (1966) suggests that we can make meaningful distinctions between categories of words associated with "equality" some of which are purely descriptive and some of which carry an element of value. Amongst the first are "similar," "identical," "uniform," and "level" and amongst the second are "fair," "just," and "equitable." Hobhouse (1958) refers to the attitudes which the very use of the term may invoke: "Justice is a name to which every knee will bow. Equality is a word which many fear and detest." To be meaningful, the statement that "all men are equal" must be modified to read "all men are equal in respect of their rights. . . ." [P. 7]

Warham went on to consider equality as a moral concept (that is, making the basic assumption that men will be treated as ends and not means).

> The principle of universalizability is that we cannot make different moral judgments about similar cases, for that is merely to express preferences. This principle provides a basis for that of impartiality, which means that, morally, the reasons for treating one person differently from another must be the existence of a significant difference between them. . . . Differences in treatment must be based upon rationally diagnosed differences in situation or in condition. . . . The only universal right is the right to equality of consideration; that is to impartiality. . . [for when it comes down to the real situation, it may be judged that some men ought not to have the same rights, e.g., murderers]. It is more realistic, Hobhouse suggests, to conclude that equality of rights should apply within categories and relationships and that these categories, having been at any point determined, rights should apply impartially to all who fall within them. . . . The promotion of equality through social policy requires the identification of categories of persons to whom particular rights or entitlements may justifiably be ascribed. [And] rights themselves may be categorized [into moral, social, administrative, legal, esteem/status rights]. . . ." [Pp. 9–12]

But categories are not distinct and so individuals may have problems in realizing a particular set of rights. And there are conflicts of interest about realization of rights.

> Clearly associated with the philosophical concept of rights is justice [but it is different]. The emphasis is on the individual: "justice is a rule of treating like persons (not cases) alike in the distribution of benefits or burdens" (Raphael, 1970). In social policy, this raises the question of the circumstances in which services should be administered impersonally to categories of persons (as is done with Family Allowances and Social Insurance benefits in Britain) and when "personally" to individuals within categories (as is the case of the personal social services offered in Britain by local authorities). . . . The idea of justice is often made equivalent to those of fairness and equity. . . . Equality is a controversial objective, whereas justice, equity, fairness are terms of praise. And yet if we go back to first principles, justice and equity as values appear to be grounded in the right to consideration. . . . [Pp. 13–16].

Warham discussed two ways of interpreting equality, namely, equality of condition and equality of opportunity which have been particularly important in Britain and America respectively. The former describes a redistribution of the national income in order to ensure that all citizens have a minimum standard of living. It provides a safety net for those in difficulties. The latter is concerned with socialization through equal educational opportunity to minimal achievement levels and beyond. The former emphasizes equal citizenship through equal social security, the latter equal citizenship through socialization into the society. Both kinds of intervention seem to be necessary if real change is to occur.

Time Lags in Achieving Social Change

The social ordering—the allocation of statuses—in the established English society which had adopted the Protestant ethic did not change overnight. Those who had power were not prepared to give it up; they wanted to retain and increase their prerogatives. Although an entrepreneurial middle class began to emerge, earlier patterns of social organization persisted and were strengthened by such actions as enclosures of common lands by the landowning classes. Those who had gained power through their risk-taking activities found it difficult to break into the closed circles of the landowning elites—they were kept out because they were "in trade." In the discussion of ruling classes and elites in chapter 4, mention was made of the persistence of established power even across national frontiers—the inheritance by the U.S., Canada and Australia of some of the British colonizers and their agents as their rulers.

But social mobility has been much easier to achieve in the societies with open frontiers, such as these three countries have had until recently. In the settled east, of all three countries, established landowners also resisted invasions, but the removal of titles and honors in the U.S. made it easier for monied men to become accepted. In an attempt to escape from European obsessions with rank, it became customary for ordinary Americans to deny the existence of social classes. However, sociologists have demonstrated that these still exist, even if they are redesignated socioeconomic status groupings. Whatever they are called, social stratification is present and those in the lower strata of every society have fewer prerogatives.

As an alternative to social climbing within established communities in the new lands, aspiring status seekers could "go west" to seek their fortunes and might become members of the elite of new isolated communities. There was more room to start afresh where communications were slow and difficult. Gouldner (1957–8) has suggested that there are people with cosmopolitan orientations and people with local orientations. Some aspiring people have no desire to become smaller fish in bigger ponds—they prefer to remain closer to local life and be part of the elite of their community—others take a national or international view.

However, England was not like the new lands where every person's contribution was valued in frontier settlements. With the enclosures of common lands and the migrations into the towns to meet the demands for labour in the factories, a physical and social separation had occurred between the landowners, the entrepreneurial and professional middle classes and the labouring classes. Describing this separation, Tawney (1964) said:

> It was partly that, in an age which worshipped property as the foundation of the social order, the mere labourer seemed something less than a full citizen. It was partly that in spite of a century of large-scale production in textiles, the problems of capitalist industry and of a propertyless proletariat were still too novel for their essential features to be appreciated. [P. 266]

Gradually, however, working class men made their needs for acceptance into citizenship felt. The leaders of the liberal cause anticipated a general desire to attain middle class standards and Marx forecast the rebellion of the proletariat against the bourgeoisie. However, the reality of social aspiration and concepts of social justice seem to be more complex than either of these anticipations.

For some working-class families in Britain, particularly in Scotland and Wales, entry into the professions (or semiprofessions) was regarded as entry into greater social security in the nineteenth and early twentieth centuries. Because some working-class people had striven for upward social mobility, it was assumed by Liberals in the mid-twentieth century that English workers would want to join the middle classes, to aspire to their cultural standards. By the end of the Second World War, however, Goldthorpe (1968) found that affluent workers who had become accustomed to living in the style of the working-class culture did not wish to assume middle-class behavior patterns. They were well protected by the welfare state. Dahrendorf (1979) has pointed out that class structures in different countries may be more permeable than in others. They are certainly very impermeable in Britain.

Runciman (1966) demonstrated that members of British society compare themselves with others with whom they interact closely rather than with all of society. Thus, deprivation is a relative concept and negotiation tends to be about relativities, not absolutes. Social justice, then, is not often perceived as a matter of providing equal treatment for everybody, but as a matter of negotiating suitable differentials on the basis of some acceptable rationale.

As resources have been developed further, there has been more to distribute. Absolute poverty has largely disappeared in the western world, though relative poverty continues to exist. Although differences between those with rank and those with money have been disappearing in recent years, those in the upper reaches have still been able to retain many of their advantages.

Whilst wars always bring members of national groups more closely together to consider their strengths and weaknesses, improved communication of ideas and greater development of resources have also been of the greatest importance in lessening differences within societies, particularly in the twentieth century. In the period before radio and TV arrived, national solidarity was maintained mainly through the educational process, but this was not such an effective leveller as the media have been. Meanwhile, another form of communication—the automobile—had the opposite effect. Its use led to changes in the organization of the towns, particularly, in America, changes which were disruptive of social solidarity because of the separation of social strata into distinct neighbourhoods. In terms of general knowledge about the world and how to get access to resources, the upper, middle and lower classes are now less clearly distinct, but there are other barriers to equality, such as urban and suburban housing and differences in neighbourhood quality which cannot so easily be altered. In addition, sex differences, ethnic differences and racial differences make it hard for some people not only to attain higher status in societies but even to be treated equally with the dominant groups when seeking services from commercial or social service organizations.

Nowadays, it is not only the ruling elite at the top of the national pyramid which has privileges to preserve, almost everyone is afraid that if the social order is forced into rapid change, he may lose the advantages he now possesses. It has been said that inflation/deflation is an indicator of maladjustment and the need for change. It is not hard to observe the fear of inflation in advanced societies.

The last major economic depression forced western countries into national redistributive policies. The U.S. developed its New Deal in the late 1930s and after the Second World War the British moved to bring in the Welfare State. On the surface the latter was a levelling move resulting from the shared experiences and the camaraderie built up during the war, but it has also been interpreted as a move on the part of the middle classes to preserve their privileges. The takeover of social services by the state for the whole community meant that the costs of health care and other services did not go out of reach of middle income groups. As well, vast numbers of jobs were created for professionals and semiprofessionals.

The present recession and inflation may force nations into rethinking international redistributive policies, but that is not the topic of this book, which is concerned only with the four countries' health and social policies in the years up to 1980.

A Comparative Assessment of Social Stratification and the Achievement of Equality, 1963

A study by Lipset (1963) attempted to compare moves towards equalization of power—equality—in the four countries of our study. Lipset focused on what he called pattern variables (a concept borrowed from Parsons), viz: elitism-egalitarianism, ascription-achievement, particularism-universalism (i.e., differential treatment of groups as against universal standards for the whole community) and specificity-diffuseness (i.e., individuals regarded as members of groups as against an all-embracing community). He found that the countries followed the ranking in which they appear above from least to most in the last three of the areas. In the first, Australia had achieved greater egalitarianism than the U.S., but otherwise this rank order remained.

Encel (1970), an Australian sociologist, was not convinced that Lipset's study of pattern variables is a valid method of comparing the four countries. He has suggested that the differences between them are more likely to be presented meaningfully through an analysis in terms of class, status and power, such as the studies made by Mills (1959) in the U.S.A., Porter (1965) in Canada, in the numerous analyses of British social structure and, of course, his own of Australia. (References to these texts on social stratification were given in the previous chapter.) However, Encel concluded that "the ability of entrenched positions of inequality to resist or absorb change remains the outstanding characteristic of Anglo-American societies, as it does of other industrial societies" (p. 194).

Despite Encel's doubts, Lipset's pattern variables are a useful way of breaking down the vague concept of equality into more specific ways of assessing equalization policies for study by policy analysts.

Some comments on elitism-egalitarianism were made in chapter 4 and earlier in this chapter.

Ascription and achievement are sociological terms used to describe how positions are allocated in a society. "Born to the purple" is a way of describing the ascribed position of noble birth, but one can become a professional person only through achievement. Lipset's assumption was, then, that the more ascribed positions, the less equal the society, for ascription blocks those who wish to achieve higher statuses. Bates (1956) has explained how positions are made up of roles which may also be ascribed or achieved. And role theorists (Biddle and Thomas, 1966) have shown that it is impossible to escape from some social roles imposed by age, sex and other physical characteristics. Consequently, although attempts continue to be made to redesignate positions as achieved rather than ascribed, there are strong resistances. So far as ascription-achievement is concerned, Porter's listing of the Canadian elites, or cosmopolitan ruling classes, gives some indication of ascription in a new society and possible routes to achievement: the economic elite, the political elite, the bureaucratic elite, the elite of the media, the higher learning and the clergy.

Methods of Operationalizing Rights

The idea of just treatment is one of great antiquity and the method of ensuring that justice was done and seen to be done in England from early times was to bring civil complaints or apprehended criminals before the courts. An impartial judge, often with a jury, would try the case under the rules of common law. Blackstone, who codified the law in the eighteenth century, took the conservative view that this provided sufficient protection for customary and legal rights.

As Benn and Peters point out, the interpretation of the common law is not fixed but changes with the times—it is normative. In the nineteenth century, trade unions in Britain had to fight for recognition to make contracts without restriction and their fight was successful in such matters as being able to form trade unions, not to have to buy at the company store, being able to have the coal they had mined weighed by an independent arbitrator and so on. In the twentieth century, blacks in America have been fighting for reinterpretation of the laws regarding their rights.

As times change, the common law is reinterpreted through new case law. In America, reinterpretations of the Bill of Rights may also be made after challenges in the Supreme Court, and constitutional amendments may be introduced. Benn and Peters have pointed out that this makes the Supreme Court a place where political battles about policy development are fought between the judges and, in consequence, their appointments are of key importance to the nation because they move towards change through reinterpretation of rights, whereas only the cabinets of parliamentary governments in Great Britain, Canada and Australia can undertake this function of making change in the laws through presenting new statute legislation.

The first attempts to introduce statute legislation in England were not altogether successful. It is not only a matter of having rights in law. These rights may exist but some people may not be able to realize them through poverty or ignorance or intimidation. Humanitarians thought that all that was necessary was to pass the law, but gradually the operational issues which follow regulation became clearer. The early history of public health services is a case in point. A Public Health Act passed in 1848 was relatively ineffective because it could not be implemented properly until there were sanitary inspectors with technical skills to enforce the law, health educators to improve understanding of its implications, and local government authorities to pay them and to ensure their accountability (Briggs, 1968). Similarly, in the other countries, attempts to introduce new legislation or new programs without securing adequate resources for implementation have resulted in setbacks.

Changing legislation may help, but it may not be able to alter the reciprocity of social relationships into a positive transaction. Much has to be changed by altering conventions. The status of women is not only a matter of legal rights but of personal confidence, an altering of reciprocities in behaviour of those in responding roles, and getting community support for change. Before women can have greater equality there has to be a liberation from traditional norms of behaviour and legitimation of different societal relationships. Similarly, other groups are discriminated against—orientals, the elderly, children and so on. They too have expected reciprocal roles to play in society—conventional behaviors which may be difficult to change.

Organizing Operationalization of Services

Warham distinguished between the two types of redistributive social service to increase equality of condition in Britain—the universal social insurance service organized quite impersonally, and the particularistic personal social services departments (including medical care and social work) which are expected to give individual attention. Though all men are equal in theory, they are patently unequal in fact, except in their rights to consideration. Some of their wants can be met by universalistic schemes of protection or redistribution, others can best be dealt with through particularistic services, but both need to be kept in proper balance, and there will be constant pressures for change.

A related problem is that of diffuseness versus specificity—should the national resources available for government's purposes be redistributed to all citizens or to particular high risk groups or to particularly pressing interest intermediary groups? Already privileged groups in society tend to be more articulate, better informed about how, why, where and when to press their case for differential (better) treatment.

So how, then, should services be organized? Like the social order, they tend to evolve. Having been set up in the nineteenth century, they have had to be accepted or rejected, but in either case, developed from what they have been.

In the nineteenth century the services were started by entrepreneurs on the one hand and voluntary organizations or the Poor Law on the other. The British NHS was set up because the entrepreneurs—doctors and insurance companies—and the voluntary organizations and local government heirs of the Poor Law were not providing a sufficiently comprehensive medical care system. Despite voluntary coordinating bodies being set up, the inability of these delegated authorities to resolve universalistic redistributional questions became clear in wartime (Titmuss, 1950). The health services of the U.S., Australia and Canada are regulated by the state(s) in terms of quality control and, to some extent, coverage, but are delivered by individuals and institutions which are not directly controlled by the state(s).

In the past there was considerable room for exercising wide discretion in service delivery. Now, attitudes have changed. On the one hand, whilst there are strong pressures to maintain personal, particularistic care, on the other, there have been strong pressures towards depersonalization and universalization so that services can be distributed more equally or more widely. One reason for defending entrepreneurial and voluntary organizations' services is that they are personalized, but Zald (1971), Mechanic (1976) and others have described the steady bureaucratization and depersonalization of all services in a mass society. One basic right which is claimed in a right-wing liberal society is to have the least possible intervention by government (Marchak, 1975). From this arises the dilemma of ensuring effectiveness and efficiency in delivery of other universal legal rights such as rights to health care. Those who take the strain of this conflict between universalistic or selective services are the professionals and clerks who are at the point of delivery.

All kinds of questions arise. Are there greater advantages in permitting particularistic services to continue or to develop? There may be, but then key questions about resource allocation and professional direction and control emerge.

From Moral to Legal Rights: One Example of Change

The disabled have only recently begun to seek recognition as a pressure group. From early times, disabled individuals were expected to sue at common law for any wrongs they might have suffered. But not every disabled person has been able to identify an adversary who did him wrong—he may have dived into an empty pool or been born handicapped.

In the nineteenth century many had to resort to the Poor Law. Gradually, through humanitarian pressures, this was felt to be wrong and they were pulled out into separate programs of Workmen's Compensation, chronic invalids' assistance, etc. Later, when welfare state legislation was enacted, it gave the disabled safety net support for certain aspects of their problems—some income security, some medical care, some educational opportunity, and possible help with housing or vocational reeducation. But as Albrecht (1976) has pointed out, utilitarianism is the underlying philosophy in liberal social policies and the tension between utilitarianism and humanitarianism affects the development of long-term policies for such a group. The assumption that they will return to work after temporary sickness may be quite unjustified, for they may never be fit to work again.

In the 1960s, New Zealand began the process of legitimating a new view of their situation by reviewing how well the rights of the disabled were met in those sectors which were covered by common law, or by statute law, or ignored. Problems were found particularly in the common law sector where, depending on the judge and jury and the lawyers' and clients' abilities, individuals were liable to get very different kinds of settlements. Some were able to get high benefits out of an adversary situation, others were less fortunate. Others could identify no adversary. In New Zealand, new statute law was enacted to provide comprehensive support to all disabled persons.

This investigation (New Zealand, 1967) triggered off similar studies in Australia (Australia, 1974) and in Britain (Great Britain, 1978). But in all these countries, there has been some hesitation in moving from investigation to action—from recognizing particularistic claims to redistributing resources to this group. As the level of legitimacy of their claims increases, so steps begin to be taken to make implementation feasible, to move from a universal welfare state scheme which provides minimal help towards a particularistic program to meet the special needs of the group.

Discussion of Readings and References

1. The challenge to the dominant privileged classes by the less privileged is known as the human rights movement and is given moral support by those nations who are signatories to the Universal Declaration of Human Rights, 1948, that is, all but eight of the member nations of the United Nations. (This document is readily available in libraries.) S. I. Benn and R. S. Peters have discussed the distinction between moral and legal rights in their *Social Principles and the Democratic State*. This is an important book, helpful for understanding the difficulties in organizing a just society.

2. They begin by pointing out that early writers on human rights failed to distinguish natural law from the laws governing societies—that is, value free from value laden concepts about rights. It is important to recognize that all concepts about social organization are value laden. A number of social analysts have discussed the difficulties arising from this, e.g., Rein (1976), Gouldner (1973), Pinker (1971).

3. The discussion of human rights tends to be concerned with two issues raised in the seventeenth and eighteenth centuries: liberty and equality. How can these ideals be operationalized?

Much depends upon the definitions attached to these words. What does equality mean? How are liberty and equality to be related to each other? What is social justice as compared with individual justice? A number of references are given in the text and may be followed up. The work of John Rawls on *A Theory of Justice* has had particular appeal to supporters of welfare state (i.e., redistributive) solutions.

David Donnison, writing from a British perspective, has explained how liberty can be reconciled with equality through redistribution of resources in a reading attached to this chapter.

4. In a review of achievement of equalization by the citizens of Britain and its former colonies, the U.S.A., Canada and Australia, Lipset used four pattern variables suggested by Parsons to rank the four societies. Whilst Lipset's study has been criticized, the drawing of attention to these four variables is useful. They are: elitism-egalitarianism, ascription-achievement, particularism-universalism, specificity-diffuseness.

Using these four concepts as guidelines, students will find it possible to identify ways in which the idea of equality has been operationalized as a policy in different countries and to what extent the operationalization has been successful.

5. Liberal societies which are concerned with resource development will be more sympathetic to the concept of utilitarianism than humanitarianism. Gary Albrecht in "Social Policy and the Management of Human Resources" has discussed the way in which the priority given to utilitarianism affects the structuring of humanitarian services provided for the disabled. Dropouts

from liberal societies are stigmatized unless they assume the sick role, although the needs of such people may be much less for medical care than for other support services.

However, a number of countries are beginning to question the way in which they have been managing the problems of the disabled as a group. A paper by Crichton (1980) has reviewed stages in development of disablement policies.

Social Issues [I]

David Donnison

FRATERNITY, THEREFORE EQUALITY

The division between advocates of growth and of equality may be easier to understand if we ask why people want more equality. It is to social philosophers of the Left that we must look for an answer to this question—and first to the continuing influence of Richard Tawney. (One of the latest American books on poverty still relies wholly upon him; "In this book we do not argue the reasons why inequality should be reduced. For one, it is difficult to be more eloquent and moving than R. H. Tawney."[1]) That great and Christian teacher based his case for equality upon man's need for fellowship. "What a community requires, as the word itself suggests, is a common culture, because, without it, it is not a community at all . . . But a common culture cannot be created merely by desiring it. It rests upon economic foundations . . . It involves, in short, a large measure of economic equality. . . ."[2] Twenty-five years later Anthony Crosland went further, saying: "if we want more equality, the case for it must rest on statements largely, if not entirely, unrelated to economic welfare."[3] Although economic arguments—about wasted talent, for example—do appear in it, most of his chapter on "The Case for Social Equality" is devoted to sociological, psychological and moral

From David Donnison, "Ideologies and Policies," *Journal of Social Policy* 1 (1972): 111–17, by permission of the Cambridge University Press and the author. Footnotes have been renumbered and given at the end.

Much of this section has already been printed in *The Three Banks Review* (no. 88, Dec. 1970, pp. 3–23), where some further discussion of its themes may be found. It is repeated here at the invitation of the editor of this journal and with the kind permission of the editors of *The Three Banks Review*.

argument about industrial conflict, personal envy and social justice. More recently Lord Balogh concludes on a similar note: "without greater equality in consumption, that consensus of opinion will never be reached which is needed to safeguard the steady progress of this country."[4]

Tawney was not the first to use these arguments. They appear much earlier in discussion of another type of equality: the equality of relationships between people who live and work alongside each other in a non-deferential society. Ebenezer Howard echoed the utopian writers of a century and more when he condemned, in 1898, "the large cities of today" because they were not "adapted for the expression of the fraternal spirit" and called for "garden cities of tomorrow" which would "silence the harsh voice of anger, and . . . awaken the soft notes of brotherliness and good-will."[5]

No civilized person could deride human aspirations for fellowship. Without the good Samaritan's capacity to perceive strangers as sentient, suffering human beings, we have no way of making judgements about social policies: we literally do not know what we are talking about.[6] But it is an altogether different matter to say with Crosland that "the first argument for greater equality is that it will increase social contentment and diminish social resentment."[7] Societies that grow more equal may prove to be not more, but much less, fraternal—at least for a time.[8] (Something like this appears to have happened in Ulster and in the American ghettos.) Liberals who lose their nerve at this discovery are apt to turn against equality, and liberty too. Fraternity, moreover, comes in many forms, some of them much less attractive than Tawney's. There is a cosy, conservative brand, which seeks protection from new ideas, disturbing people and competition of all kinds; and there is a harsh, authoritarian brand: *Ein Reich! Ein Volk! Ein Führer!* was a call for fraternity of a sort. A free world will be full of conflict: it cannot be a fellowship of friends, ruled by love, because the search for friends soon degenerates into the exclusion of enemies, the suppression of conflict and, ultimately, rule by hate.

Liberty, therefore Equality

This line of argument leads the advocates of equality away from advocacy of growth, not because the two ideas conflict but because they do not seem to have much relevance to each other. I believe both ideas had robuster and more closely related origins.

In Britain egalitarian aspirations have a long and honourable history. But intellectual analysis of the case for a more equal urban society begins with the Utilitarians.[9] In essays published in 1859 and 1861 John Stuart Mill gave us the clearest and most comprehensive statement of the Utilitarian point of view. By then the doctrine was already in decline, encrusted with the qualifications that bereft liberalism of its cutting edge. But the vigour of the original faith still shines through his exposition. Shorn of the encrustations, this is what it amounted to:

1. A government which must decide what to do should not look for guidance to history, religion, the ruling classes, or a mythical social contract. It should consider the consequences of the different courses of action open to it, and the essential consequences to ask about are those that affect people.
2. People should, so far as possible, be enabled to attain their own ends, for each of us "is the person most interested in his own well-being . . ." and "with respect to his own feelings and circumstances, the most ordinary man or woman has means of knowledge immeasurably surpassing those that can be possessed by anyone else."[10]
3. It is not enough to abolish monopolies and arbitrary powers, and to extend political rights and religious toleration. We must also protect individuals from "the tyranny of the majority" which may be exercised not only "through the acts of the public authorities" but also through "a social tyranny more formidable than many kinds of political oppression, since . . . it leaves fewer means of escape, penetrating much more deeply into the details of life, and enslaving the soul itself."
4. When the interests of different people conflict, as they often will, we should try to follow "Bentham's dictum, 'everybody to count for one, nobody for more than one'," for Utilitarianism "is a mere form of words without rational signification, unless one person's happiness. . . is counted for exactly as much as another's."[11]
5. This "equal claim of everybody to happiness . . . involves an equal claim to all the *means* of happiness. . . ."[12]
6. Restrictions on liberty can only be justified if they are necessary to protect other people's liberties.

This philosophy is regularly shot full of logical holes in lectures to first-year students (which seldom offer anything half so interesting in its place). My concern is not with its moral logic, but with the mix of ideas it presents. Utilitarians sought liberty and *therefore* equality. Bentham, their founding father, was confident that the trinity of liberty, equality and industrial progress went naturally together: "if the laws do not oppose (equality), if they do not maintain monopolies, if they do not restrict trade and its exchanges, if they do not permit entails, large properties will be seen without effort, without revolutions, without shock, to subdivide themselves by little and little."[13]

In its day this philosophy moved men to poetry. When, in *Prometheus*

Unbound, Shelley's "Spirit of the Hour" proclaims man's release from injustice it is to a paradise of liberty, and *therefore* equality, that he is admitted.

> . . . thrones were kingless . . .
> None fawned, none trampled . . .
> . . . the man remains
> Sceptreless, free, uncircumscribed, but man
> Equal, unclassed, tribeless and nationless,
> Exempt from awe, worship, degree, the king
> Over himself . . .[14]

The poets of revolutionary liberalism and the capitalist creators of the industrial revolution were not "really on the same side": had they been, the poets would not so often have died young, poor or exiled. But they were inspired by a common intellectual tradition—more robust than our own.

We set out from a world in which educated, liberal people believed that economic and social progress could both be achieved, and could only be achieved, in a society that was both freer and more equal. We have arrived in a world where guardians of the conventional wisdom assert that there are inherent and possibly insoluble conflicts between social justice and economic growth, and between equality and freedom.

A Reformulation

It would take two centuries of history to explain how that happened, and I shall not attempt the task here.[15] But since the change has not been convincingly argued out, and the evidence for it is mostly erroneous, it may be worth dusting off the old liberal creed, as I try to do in the numbered paragraphs that follow. Even if it proves to be no longer roadworthy, the exercise may draw our attention to questions we should examine more carefully.

1. When policies are to be decided, top priority should normally be given to the extension of liberty, particularly among those who have least of it—the people whose lives are most severely stunted by economic, social and political constraints.

I use "liberty" in a general sense, describing what others might call freedom, choice, opportunity or accessibility—recognizing there will often be conflicts between aspirations of these kinds. This starting point commits us heavily to trusting in people's capacity to choose better for themselves than anyone else could choose for them (a faith that will be bitterly disappointed from time to time). It precludes the construction of utopias because the future character of a free society cannot be precisely forecast or planned:

people will use their freedom in unpredictable ways. It is based on confidence in our technical and political capacity to solve the problems which arise when freedom produces chaos, as it sometimes will (such as the congestion and pollution caused by the unforeseen growth of motor transport).

This approach will sometimes provoke dilemmas uncomfortable to liberals—when religious or racial groups within a city decide to live in separate streets and send their children to separate schools, as they are doing in Northern Ireland. Fraternity may follow, when security and equal rights are assured; it cannot be achieved sooner.

2. To be freer, our society must be less deferential and therefore less constrained by social hierarchies. That is unlikely to happen unless its distributions of status, living standards and security become more equal.

An English-speaking country which may enter the Common Market offers its people exceptional and growing opportunities for migration. Until we have international policies for incomes, our scope for modifying the distribution of earnings will therefore be limited. The scope for change will be greatest among groups suffering (or gaining) from discrimination that owes little to market forces—racial minorities and qualified women, for example. It is difficult to say how much scope there will be for redistribution of income and wealth, because we have devoted little research and less experiment to the problem. In all countries, as a United Nations study shows, "income policies have been seen as one among several possible instruments for countering the forces of inflation, rather than as policies directly concerned with improving the distribution of income."[16] We should particularly beware of our tendency to devote resources to the underdog in ways that preserve intact the hierarchies of an earlier social order: separate and segregated schools, housing estates and pension schemes will not go far to dissolve those hierarchies.

3. In a peace-time democracy, the greater equality and the expansion of opportunities which we seek are unlikely to be achieved unless we maintain a higher rate of economic growth.

Redistribution to help poorer people calls for more and better buildings (houses, schools . . .), capital equipment (factories, transport . . .) and public services (teachers, doctors . . .) in places where they are most urgently needed. We cannot shift the buildings and equipment from the more prosperous areas where they are now concentrated. The professional staff are almost as difficult to move. Expanding (and therefore more prosperous) areas will in any case secure new houses and schools, newly trained teachers, and other benefits. The most deprived areas will never catch up with them unless the output of these resources grows fast enough.

Selective downward mobility can be healthy, but it wastes potential talent if it becomes massive. With slow downward mobility, upward mobility must depend mainly on the rate at which opportunities expand—opportunities for better jobs, better houses, better education and so on. (A great deal of research has been done on the contribution education makes to economic growth and social change, but we forget that the reverse relationships may also hold: a society in which economic and social opportunities grow very slowly will not encourage rapid advances in learning and attainment—which may help to explain why young people in Britain's slowly growing economy leave school sooner than in almost any other urban, industrial society.[17])

4. We should ensure, wherever possible, that our towns grow in ways that make it easier, not harder, for people to seize new opportunities, and to encounter and learn from others of different ages, races, classes and incomes.

We should not assume, with Ebenezer Howard, that this will "awaken the soft notes of brotherliness and goodwill," or be discouraged if it does not. Although fraternity is desirable, liberty is more important. We still know very little about the "psychological neighbourhoods" which determine the opportunities people perceive as coming within their reach; they are clearly more complex than a spatial neighbourhood—the simple pursuit of "social mix" will not create an open society, although it may help.

We should bear in mind that although the human race can endure incredible hardships it tolerates very little failure. Thus we ought to ask ourselves why children should be expected to devote long hours to homework and do their best at school unless their older brothers and neighbours—people just like themselves—thereby achieve recognized academic success. Likewise, why should they forego freedom and money to stay on at school and take public examinations unless they have good reason to believe they will thereby get better jobs and wider opportunities in the labour market? How can they attempt new things in school or at work, with all the risks of failure involved, unless others who know them believe they can succeed? Why should they work the longer hours, take the further training and bear the heavier responsibilities which better jobs often entail unless they are convinced this will bring them more money or higher status? What use will the money be to them unless it enables them to get better housing for their families, a new car, a more venturesome holiday or other things they want? And why should they help encourage their own children to learn unless their own experience of learning was enjoyable, successful and rewarding?

We have too often tolerated or unwittingly exacerbated social traps of the sort to which these questions direct our attention; cities have replaced one-class slums with remoter, one-class council estates, served by one-class (and possibly one-denomination) schools and readily accessible only to one-class jobs. If rents are then increased to levels which compel the more successful to escape to owner-occupied estates, leaving behind only those who get special help from rent and rate rebates and the Supplementary Benefits Commission, social segregation may grow more destructive. Developers may fear with good reason that rents on such estates will be pushed to a level that only leaves tenants enough to buy the essentials of life. Hence they will not be prepared to provide shopping and recreational opportunities in their vicinity and the horizons of aspiration for tenants and their children will be restricted as a result. Meanwhile if older neighbourhoods are cut up by raised or fenced highways and public transport services wither, their people too may be excluded from the opportunities for work, education and recreation which the city could offer.

These are questions posing hypotheses for study, not confident assertions. Clearly, too, they are questions about the orgnization of government. For social traps are more likely to be created where urban areas are divided by municipal boundaries which make no economic or social sense, and housing, planning, highways, education and personal social services are administered as separate and unrelated programmes. "Disjointed incrementalism" is a philosophy not chosen but dictated by such administrative structures.

5. Liberty will not have been effectively extended unless it provokes new demands, and unlocks new talents for meeting them. The "virtuous circle" we seek to create would extend freedom, and thus encourage innovation, which hastens economic and social growth, which furnish the resources for further progress towards equalization of attainments and living standards, which again extends freedom. . . .

These beneficent conjunctions do not follow automatically. In Britain we are usually in the grip of a vicious circle which runs the opposite way: slow growth and the resulting strain on the balance of payments inhibit governments from developing the social services or moving towards greater equality; thus we preserve a divided and deferential society in which talent is wasted, innovation is difficult and the economy stagnates. It is the job of governments to get things moving in the opposite direction—if that is what the country wants.

But is it? Many would reject this ideology—and reject it with greater conviction the sounder these speculative assertions proved to be. They do not want to turn the economy round. They fear that a society which grows too free, too equal or too rich will become coarsened, congested and quarrelsome, and their point of view is a respectable one which deserves to be more frankly stated. Freedom and growth bring unforeseeable changes, and every change is a kind of bereavement. Such questions cannot be conclusively settled, but they can be constructively discussed—more constructively than most of the questions our political debates deal with.

NOTES

[1]S. M. Miller and Pamela Roby, *The Future of Inequality* (New York: Basic Books, 1970), p. vii.
[2]*Equality* (London: Allen and Unwin, 1931), p. 41.
[3]*The Future of Socialism,* (London: Cape, 1956), p. 190.
[4]Thomas Balogh, *Labour and Inflation,* Fabian Tract no. 403, p. 61.
[5]*Garden Cities of Tomorrow* (London: Faber, 1965), pp. 146 and 150.
[6]See Brian Abel-Smith, "Whose Welfare State?" in *Conviction,* ed. Norman MacKenzie (London: MacGibbon and Kee, 1958), p. 68.
[7]*The Future of Socialism,* p. 205.
[8]W. G. Runciman, in *Relative Deprivation and Social Justice* (London: Routledge and Kegan Paul, 1966), suggests some of the reasons why this may occur.
[9]The Levellers' claim to this distinction is discussed in *The Three Banks Review,* op. cit.
[10]*On Liberty* (Everyman edition), p. 133.
[11]*Ibid.* p. 68.
[12]*Utilitarianism* (Everyman edition), p. 58; my italics.
[13]Bentham, "Principles of the Civil Code," *Works,* 1843, vol. I, chapter 12 quoted in *Equality,* p. 133.
[14]*Prometheus Unbound,* Act III, lines 131 and 193.
[15]Parts of the story were briefly outlined in *The Three Banks Review,* op. cit.
[16]UN Economic Commission for Europe, *Incomes in Postwar Europe. A Study of Policies, Growth and Distribution,* Geneva, 1967, chapter 1, p. 1.
[17]The proportions of British seventeen-year-olds still in school are roughly one third of those for Belgium, one quarter of those for Japan, and one fifth of those for the U.S.A. Second Report of the Public Schools Commission (London: HMSO, 1970) p. 23.

8 Prerogatives and Rights

Major changes in the existing social order come about only when strains become so intolerable that something has to give. Some of those in privileged positions entrench themselves and wait for the revolution, others, recognizing the inevitable, work to bring about change by evolution. However, "Those who benefit most from the system will usually do whatever they can to preserve their privileges, whatever effort they may make from time to time to spread the benefits of the system more widely. . ."(Tumin, 1967, p. 108). As Lasswell (1948) pointed out, the groups in power have found many ways of defending their privileged positions.

In chapter 6 the emergence of the middle classes was noted—the entrepreneurs and freely elected politicians, professionals, bureaucrats, scientists and technologists, managers, and others. Members of these groups have challenged traditional privileges, then sought privileges for themselves not open to the citizenry generally. These may take many forms—tax reliefs for risking their money, tax free expenses, professional titles and professional respect, influential power, queue jumping and so on.

The middle classes are in the classical "interstitial" position, looking up and looking down. The entrepreneurs and the scientists and technologists seem to be less divided in mind than others such as politicians and personal service professionals who have to respond to their constituents or clients. Politicians have party platforms to provide general guidance but professionals are pulled between their own, their individual clients' and society's interests. Because of these pulls they tend to be inconsistent. In one role they want to maintain their personal advantages, but in others they may feel the pressure of conscience to promote human rights. It may be the same people in different social roles who back conflicting social policies or who fail to recognize Hirsch's paradox (see chapter 5). For example, it is common for professionals to want to maintain their occupational groups' prerogatives yet at the same time to press for increased educational opportunity for their own and others' children. And they may want to do their very best for individual clients within a cost limited resource program which implies exclusion or reduction of services for somebody else.

Ideologies—Guides to Negotiation?

Blishen (1969) made a study of one privileged subgroup's attitudes in 1963 when he was research director of the Canadian Royal Commission on Health Services. He found that the ideology developed by the Canadian medical profession was very conservative and, in his view, maladaptive in meeting the increasing pressures which were being felt by that professional group as a result of the bureaucratization of health services. Blishen interpreted the elaboration of a professional ideology to be a reaction to strain rather than a deliberate pursuit of self-interest without thought of others. Geertz (1964) had said:

> There are currently two main approaches to the study of the social determinants of ideology: the interest theory and the strain theory. For the first, ideology is a mask and a weapon; for the second, a symptom and a remedy. In the interest theory, ideological pronouncements are seen against the background of a universal struggle for advantage; in the strain theory, against the background of a chronic effort to correct psycho-sociological disequilibrium. In the one, men pursue power; in the other, they flee anxiety. As they may, of course, do both at the same time—and even one by means of the other—the two theories are not necessarily contradictory; but the strain theory (which arose in response to the empirical difficulties encountered by the interest theory), being less simplistic, is more penetrating, less concrete, more comprehensive. [P. 52]

Geertz identified four ways in which ideologies could help to deal with psycho-social strain:

(1) by catharcism—through using a safety valve or a scapegoat. Some other group is identified as the object of hostility, and by projecting his hostility, the man or group under strain may be able to continue to function;

(2) by morale sustainment in face of chronic strain—". . . Ideology bridges the emotional gap between things as they are and as one would have them be, thus insuring the performance of roles that would otherwise be abandoned in despair and apathy";

(3) by knitting a group together in solidarity;

(4) through advocacy—"ideologies state the problems for the larger so-

ciety, take sides on the issues involved, and 'present them in the court' of the ideological marketplace." [P. 55]

Maps of Problematic Social Reality

Geertz thought that ideologies did more than enable individuals and groups to deal with psycho-social strains, they were important mechanisms for dealing with cultural strains:

> It is a loss of orientation that most directly gives rise to ideological activity, an inability, for lack of usable models, to comprehend the universe of civic rights and responsibilities in which one finds oneself located. The development of a differentiated polity (or of greater differentiation within such a polity) may and commonly does bring with it severe social dislocation and psychological tension. But is also brings with it conceptual confusion, as the established images of political order fade into irrelevance or are driven into political disrepute. . . . And it is, in turn, the attempt of ideologies to render otherwise incomprehensible social situations meaningful, to so construe them as to make it possible to act purposefully within them, that accounts both for the ideologies' highly figurative nature and for the intensity with which, once accepted, they are held. . .Whatever else ideologies may be. . .they are, most distinctively, maps of problematic social reality and matrices for the creation of collective conscience. . . . [P. 64]

The maps of problématic social reality (and the reader should also see the discussion of the sociology of knowledge in Chap. 14) which are held by individuals, groups or nations are like the mental maps described by Gould and White (1974)—enormously variable in scope and content. These two geographers discovered that the way in which people's knowledge of the physical world developed was partly a function of exposure to communication, partly a function of their ability to receive it and structure it and partly a function of their motivation to use it. Similarly, with ideologies, there is exposure to communication, but structuring and use of ideas also depends on intelligence and motivation. Geertz's listing of the functions of ideology: to provide for catharsis, to counter strains on morale, to develop solidarity and to present concerns through advocacy seems to widen the scope and content of the ideological map with each item on the list. Some people are able to take only a limited view, others a much wider one. As Gould and White have pointed out, too much communication may overstimulate and lead to breakdown, but some people are exposed to very limited amounts of communication (the news coverage in much of Canada and the U.S. is far less than in Europe), some have no concept that they have a choice in structuring the communication they do receive (they accept the prevailing ideology without questioning it), some have no motivation to think about change.

Smith (1976) suggested that change took place in three main sectors—

socioeconomic, political and cultural—thus one might expect to find ideologies to cope with strains in these sectors and indeed there are national, group and individual ideologies which offer support to those involved in the unending negotiation processes in these areas.

National Ideologies

As Geertz pointed out, there are a variety of ideologies within countries at national, group and individual levels, some more admirable than others. These become particularly visible at a time of special cultural strain such as a war or economic depression but they continue to exist at other times, too. They are constantly being modified to deal with new situations but there is usually a continuity in their main features.

Political Ideologies

Men had begun to challenge the status allocation patterns of England in the seventeenth century, in France and America in the eighteenth century, and elsewhere in the nineteenth century. Some confrontations were more successful in achieving change than others, some changes were temporary or affected only a small stratum of society. By the mid-nineteenth century, however, the forces of change were growing stronger in Europe. The emphasis in the American revolution had been on liberty as a principal objective, the emphasis in Europe was put more strongly on equality. It seemed to many that those who had prerogatives and power should share these more fairly.

At first, entrepreneurs in eighteenth-century England were quite unrestrained in their harsh treatment of labour as a commodity. They were subsequently persuaded to recognize that a labour force was made up of human beings by two influences: the humanitarian and utilitarian. The humanitarians, usually strong Christians, persuaded international society that slavery should be outlawed and British society that restrictions were necessary to protect women and children from undue exploitation by employers.

The utilitarians, whose spokesman first was Bentham (1789) and, at a later period, Mill (1859), convinced entrepreneurs that it was to their advantage to ameliorate conditions, to consider the greatest good of the greatest number and enlightened self-interest as guiding principles.

These two philosophies are combined in different proportions in the English-speaking western liberal democratic societies. Marchak (1975) has explained, however, that utilitarian ideas are dominant, but are always being challenged by the humanitarians in a liberal society. It is Marchak's view that liberalism has survived because of its pragmatism and it is clear that, in North America, liberal policies have been strongly influenced by socialist concepts and have adopted these when they appeared expedient.

The development of socialist ideas in the nineteenth century was part of this movement to assert human rights and reestablish social reciprocities. The first pressures had been for political rights, now there were demands for more even sharing of other resources: "from each according to his ability, to each according to his needs." To the established authorities, all who sought for change were radicals—the Chartists who wanted more political power; the Christian socialists who wanted more humanitarian treatment of the working classes (such as Kingsley, who campaigned for the boy chimney-sweeps in *The Water Babies*); the cooperative movement for groups combining together to market their produce, for buying wholesale and selling retail more cheaply, and for increasing educational opportunity among the working classes; Marx and his revolutionary propaganda; the anarchists who made negative protests by planting bombs.

The four countries of the study reacted to socialism in different ways. England set out on the path of the "inevitability of gradualness" towards the post-World War II welfare state.

In the U.S.A., the open frontiers in the nineteenth century allowed people to escape the need to react to humanitarian or socialist philosophies (Abel-Smith, 1972), for the belief in equality of opportunity and in the American melting pot assumed upward mobility, if not for the immigrant himself, at least for his children. There was a Civil War in the 1860s to right the differential status of slaves so that they, too, could become part of this society in which liberty and equality are held in tension. In the thirties, the New Deal came as near to socialism as the U.S. has ever come and through some collectivist policies a modified approach to welfare statism was initiated. It was the Second World War which precipitated strong negative reaction to socialism in its communist form, anti-East block attitudes which spread down through society because of fears of treason and betrayal of the American Dream. Collectivism became confused with socialism, and all government interventions for the purposes of redistribution were regarded as socialist. There is no effective socialist party in the committed liberal democratic society of the U.S. (Dolbeare et al., 1973). As Marchak has pointed out, the radical confrontations of the 1960s and 1970s were neither socialist nor anti-collectivist but individualistic reactions of disappointment with the achievements of western democratic societies. The radicals stressed individual or subgroup self-determination as the principal objective, not social class advancement.

In Canada, there is a socialist party, the New Democratic Party (NDP), which emerged out of an agrarian socialist movement in the prairie provinces, and later combined its rural cooperative socialism with that of the labor movement. It is not a strong national force yet, being the third party at the federal level, although the NDP forms the government or opposition in several provinces. In order to keep Canada together as a small group of people spread over vast territories, the Liberal federal government in office for 45 out of the last 50 years felt obliged to adopt welfare state policies for the nation—the Liberals stealing some of the socialists' collectivist clothes. However, the dominant ideology of the country is liberal in the utilitarian tradition. Its humanitarian conscience is expressed in the challenging welfare state ideologies of the NDP and philanthropic endeavours supported by Liberals and Conservatives (Kilbourn, 1970).

In Australia, the Labour Party represented the lower socioeconomic classes, many of whom were immigrant Irish Catholics. In consequence, the clash between the Church and the Marxists took place within the party in the 1960s (Murray, 1970). Other countries' socialist parties have well formulated policies for regulation and redistribution, but the Australian Labour Party tends to be more pragmatic in its approach than, for example, the British and Canadian parties. Radical policies are weak and uncoordinated because what is perceived and understood is limited by distance and lack of experience of many of the kinds of strains felt in other countries. When Labour attains power, about once in a generation, its programs are not well worked out in terms of legitimacy or feasibility, its experts are inexperienced and reforms are easily overturned by conservative forces within a few years. Politics tend to become emotional confrontations because adequate support for challenging issues is not properly established before legislation is enacted.

Other references to political parties in the four countries are given at the end of the chapter.

Social Ideologies

None of these countries has chosen revolutionary socialism; instead, all have preferred to support an evolution in the social order from aristocratic dominance, through laissez-faire capitalism to modern capitalism in Shonfield's sense, (1965)—a modification of the existing social relationships with moderate amounts of reform.

Does it really matter that there are wide social differences? In theory, Marxists would argue that they affect social solidarity. In practice, communist countries which are industrialized are also highly stratified. But socialists are always concerned about unnecessary social differences and the effect of these differences upon life chances. Some nations are more concerned about these differences than others. All become concerned when law and order is really threatened, or when the effect of the differences leads to weaknesses which may be exploited by international rivalries.

In order to counter the strains within their social organization, the four nations have developed social ideologies stemming from their political ideologies. Titmuss (1974) has argued that there are three models which can be observed in the western democracies: "the residual welfare model" (U.S.), "the industrial achievement performance model" (West Germany) and "the institutional redistributive model" (Great Britain).

"All three models involve consideration of the work ethic and the institution of the family in modern society." The American model relies upon the private market and the family for meeting individuals' social needs. "The true object of the welfare state is to teach people how to do without it" (pp. 30–32). The West German model holds that social needs should be met on the basis of merit, work performance and productivity. The British solution, Titmuss said, has been to develop a social model incorporating systems of redistribution in command-over-resources-through-time.

Up until the 1930s the United States was expanding and was able to manage its strains through citizens using its open frontiers. However, the depression, the additional strains set up by two world wars and the closing of the western frontiers (other than Alaska) led to modifications of the totally free enterprise system and some redistribution of the national income. It was not until the late 1960s that the Vietnam War precipitated action to end discontents which were brought to notice when American radicals challenged the dominant ideology and forced some changes, particularly in race relations—ethnic groups previously excluded from common law justice were now included. However, the dominant ideology persists. America is still predominantly a country which believes in equality of opportunity or seizing chances whilst young, and developing adult self-sufficiency.

The German model will not be discussed further here. Some follow up references are given (Maynard, 1975; Heidenheimer et al., 1976; Altenstetter, 1974).

In Britain, the disruptions of the industrial revolution in the 18th and 19th centuries were followed by the disruptions of wars which ended the imperialist ventures, and resulted not only in loss of colonial wealth but in loss of commercial and industrial leadership in the world. There are many books which describe the evolution of the British welfare state (e.g., Gilbert, 1966; de Schweinitz, 1961) which was legislated into existence in the 1940s when a concerted effort was made to ensure that there would be equality of condition, by which it was meant that no one would be permitted to fall below a minimum level of social support. As well, revision of state school organization was intended to promote more equality of opportunity, but considerable numbers of independent schools were permitted to continue to exist. Later, there were even some programmes of reverse discrimination introduced to assist people living in decaying communities to catch up with the rest of society. Efforts were also made to improve equality before the law.

Canada, too, was subjected to severe strains in the 1930s. To meet some of the strains, the federal government committed the country to extensive resource development and redistribution in the 1940s. A hybrid of British and American models of social policy have emerged, the former at the federal, the latter at the local level (Meilicke and Storch, 1980). This model tends towards an institutional redistributive approach across the provinces for social security and health services, but it takes (more or less) a residual welfare approach to those not defined as "sick" who apply for help at the local level. "Equality of condition" has been pursued quite forcefully by the federal government. "Equality of opportunity" follows the American pattern in promoting advance through public education at the local level.

Australia, too, was hard hit by the depression of the 1930s and the war, but since then it has not felt any major strains. Motivation to change is low. However, there have been international pressures and some internal pressures (Roe, 1976) to develop redistributive social security provisions (Kewley, 1973) and medical care services (Dewdney, 1972).

Cultural Ideologies

Early chapters of this book were concerned with changes in cultural ideologies—with the rise of capitalism. Less has been said about nationalism. In this book, four countries stemming from the same cultural background have been considered. Mention has been made of their efforts to escape from colonization, political and economic.

The four countries have felt it to be important to establish separate cultural identities whilst sharing in general advances of English-speaking societies. Britain and the U.S. are both sure of their national identities as is the distant Australia; but Canada, particularly, has felt pressured, first by Britain and, more recently, by the U.S.A., to be a dependent colonial country.

Canada's strains are related to its problems of identity and survival as a nation, strung, as it is, across a wide geographic area in close proximity to the U.S., peopled by immigrants from many different nations, and with two main contenders for cultural dominance—English- and French-speaking Canadians.

The particular forms of response in nationalism are related to the overall dominant political and socioeconomic ideology—liberalism—and challenges to that ideology. Much of this book has been concerned with tracing the development of liberalism and its challenges. But the case of Canada is interesting because, in its efforts to be different, it has had to try to develop its own particular cultural and social policies. The former are perhaps less central to our consideration (although still important because of the challenge by French Canadians to Anglo-Saxon habits of thinking). The latter, however, are of special interest. It seems that Canada, pushed far into "welfare statism" through its close association with Britain in the Second World War, is really not convinced about "institutional redistribution" to the degree that Britain is, but is more ideologically committed to "residual welfare." However, once started on the path towards national health insurance, it has adopted this social policy as its special national pride. In addition to a general social security program, such a program meets a number of Canada's needs. In a country colonized in the economic sphere, it is important to have a distinctive national social policy of one's own and a well developed health insurance scheme is a justifiable utilitarian and humanitarian social policy. It deals with those in the "sick role" rather than other, less "deserving" welfare services applicants, and provides employment for large numbers of Canadian citizens across the country.

Group Ideologies

There were three types of interest intermediary groups identified by Schmitter (1977)—pluralist, corporatist and syndicalist. Alford (1975) thought that, in the New York health scene, there were those with pluralist or market perspectives, those with bureaucratic and planning perspectives and those with institutional or class perspectives. Obviously, there are many more ways of classifying and interpreting groups' orientations. Of particular concern to the health policy maker are those taking the roles of providers or of consumers of health care.

Ideologies of Health Care Providers

The development of the professions during the nineteenth and twentieth centuries was described in chapter 6. Numerous studies of professionals and professionalization are important for the health policy analyst, for the arguments about professionalization are, largely, arguments about the right to claim the professional prerogative of having freedom to control one's own work in return for giving services to the community. Since the nineteenth century, it seems to have been the goal of accepted and aspiring professional groups to freeze their position in society in the self-regulatory model. Whilst the mediative model of the twentieth century (Johnson, 1972) developed in Britain and to some extent in Canada, has provided steady income and good working conditions, American and Australian medical professionals seem to have achieved at least equal, if not better, rewards by refusing to accept it.

An alternative form of organization was chosen by Florence Nightingale for nurses. They were selected only if they had a "vocation" to serve patients and were willing to conform to institutional rules. Hospitals were one of the early bureaucracies modelled along military lines. Etzioni (1969) has argued that nurses, like teachers and social workers, are not truly professional because they are not "in control" of their own standards, but subject to others' initiatives.

Why is it important to identify with self-regulatory professionalism? Do not bureaucrats have good terms and conditions of employment? Yes, but they must obey their masters. The ideal model of the professional is that of self-regulating persons whose standards of technical skill and personal conduct are beyond reproach (with very few exceptions). If they are expected to be competent to make the judgments on behalf of society about personal needs or organizational development, then they think they should be given a wide mandate to do so. As Watkins (1975) has pointed out, technical competence is only one aspect of professional activity and professional persons like to keep their other activities indeterminate. They think they would not be able to do so easily in a bureaucracy, though scientists and others have been pioneering new forms of bureaucratic organization (Toren, 1976).

The established "free choice of doctor" and "fee-for-service" relationships set up for the middle classes in the nineteenth century were not designed to serve the poor. The doctors had given their services as honoraries to charity hospitals or had worked out a Robin Hood relationship with their private patients, charging the rich more than the poor. This is, of course, patronage by the professionals who, themselves, had rebelled against patronage.

The questions about prerogatives and rights of professionals were put by Shaw (1906) in his play, *The Doctor's Dilemma,* and they remain the same today. The first question which he raised is whether the professionals are meeting societies' needs, as society has defined these needs rather than the professionals themselves (more specifically, individuals within the professions who are pursuing "justice" on behalf of their individual patients). For, by permitting the professions to become self-regulating and by educating professionals to follow their individual consciences, society has delegated a responsibility. Shaw, the socialist, asked these questions in his play: Who shall live? and who shall decide who shall live? He was challenging the responsibility and authority of medical professionals to answer these questions on behalf of society. He made one of his characters phrase it this way, "All professions are conspiracies against the laity".

These same questions have been pursued up to the present time by social policy analysts such as Fuchs (1974), who has demonstrated that medical services are very unevenly distributed because doctors and their clients are involved in a large area of elective decision making and doctors have chosen to work where people can pay for elective work. Freidson (1970) put the responsibility for poor health care organization on the doctors. He considered the problem of medical dominance—the inequality of power between doctors and patients (and others without technical knowledge) and the way in which that power might be used to advise and persuade their unknowing clients.

The development of the mediative model of government/professional relationships came about as nations began to consider the consequences of ill health for their national interests. France became concerned with maternity and child welfare after defeat in the Franco-Prussian War, 1870, and this interest spread to other countries in Europe. England decided to develop a school health service after revelations of ill health of volunteers for the Boer War, 1899–1902, and, shortly afterwards, a national health insurance service, using Bismarck's social security plans as a comparison, was started in 1911, so the government began to extend medical services down into the lower levels of the social strata. The question of prerogatives and rights began to be raised as soon as England started to consider providing health services to this wider range of citizens. Battles were fought from the start on whether these were to be insured services or services funded out of taxation. Out of taxation meant that doctors would become salaried and accountable to municipal authorities (like public health officers) whilst services funded out of insurance meant that they remained independent contractors who would negotiate their willingness to take on each patient individually. The Liberals who introduced the NHI scheme into England and Wales in 1911 supported insurance for other reasons—it was a levy separate from income tax, very visible to the contributors and thus a permanent reminder of their rights and responsibilities (as well as being politically more acceptable to Liberal voters than a tax scheme at that time).

These issues have been fought all over again in each country when governments have attempted to increase their involvement in health policy making.

The Australian doctors have taken the strongest line against state intervention, challenging an act passed in 1946 which proposed that they should prescribe subsidized drugs for their patients according to a formula. They won a suit charging the government with "civil conscription" against the terms of the Australian constitution. Subsequently, they fought successfully against the introduction of the Medibank scheme from 1973–78. This scheme would have ended the concept of charity care for those uninsured in private prepayment schemes or unable to pay fees out of income. It is clear that the doctors are not against government intervention but only government control, for the profession accepts state subsidization of all hospitals where they do complex work.

The American medical profession has accepted Medicare and Medicaid schemes brought in during the 1960s after some initial opposition (Marmor, 1973) and has subsequently agreed to cooperate in improving quality control, but it is adamant about defending the principles of fee-for-service and free choice of doctor.

Canadian doctors came out on strike against the introduction of Medical Care (i.e., government payment of doctors for all medical services) in Saskatchewan in 1962, and the specialists withdrew their services in Quebec in 1970. However, having got into the national scheme and having preserved the principles of fee-for-service and free choice of doctor, physicians in these two provinces seem to have accepted Medicare and, like the American doctors described by Marmor, accepted that they had moved to a new stage where the negotiations were about feasibility not legitimacy (Hall et al., 1975). However, in Ontario and Alberta challenges are now being presented again about doctors' remuneration. It seems that the issue of legitimacy of this program is not settled in all provinces.

Because doctors have been able to migrate across national frontiers, it has been difficult for governments to devise strong policies to curb their prerogatives. However, it seems likely that the increased supply of doctors will soon be equal to the demand for them in Britain, Canada and Australia, and these countries have said that they have reached the limits of their ability to pay for health care. It is not so much the remuneration of the doctors themselves as the costs which are incurred by adding to the group of practitioners licensed to prescribe and allocate services that has begun to worry governments.

There is another broader group which is beginning to become important in the negotiations about privileges and rights in the health services—the unionized workers who are now making their power known. As the nurses were controlled by the concept of vocation, so were other groups of workers in the industry up till about 1970, but in the last decade they have begun to negotiate more fiercely. Abel-Smith (1960) and McCarthy (1976) have traced the rise of trade union action among nurses and their aides in Britain, and others have begun to examine industrial action in the U.S. (Boyer et al., 1975; Chaney and Beech, 1976) and Canada (Bean and Laliberty, 1977). As yet, Australia has not been faced with the issue of health workers' militancy, possibly because it had developed a structure for dealing with militancy in industrial relations much earlier than other countries (Moore, 1974).

In addition to pressing for more rewards for themselves, hospital employees in England staged a strike against the existence of private wings in 1974 and forced the government to agree to a phased withdrawal (a decision which has been reversed by the Conservative government elected in 1979). Lower level hospital workers have tried to make various interventions into doctors' control over work flows in recent years with variable rates of success. These interventions are a symptom of their dissatisfaction with the processes of decision making and a protest about the need for consultation. They are particularly vocal in the mental hospitals where unions were formed earlier than in general hospitals.

Ideologies of Health Service Consumers

In the last decade when nations have been reviewing their goals, reviewing the organization of services which might meet these goals and examining the functions of professionals who have to implement policies, it has become clear that it is not only the individual doctors who have led to the spectacular increase in cost of health services in recent years. Individual consumers have also contributed.

In an earlier chapter, Wildavsky's review (1977) of displacement was considered. He asked, is it health, health care or access to health services that is important? Because it is not possible to measure the first two of these goals very easily, there is increasing pressure for access, which is equated with rights to health. But since access is not health, this equation leads to problems in relating individual satisfactions and national needs for health promotion.

The pressures for access may also be pressures for reorganization and integration of services. How does a patient know whether he is likely to get access beyond the first stage unless the system is well coordinated? With the rapid developments in technology, will he get through to the services he really needs to have? Are the professionals who act as gatekeepers and rationers of services impartial in making their judgments?

Conservative pressures in all countries have prevented the emergence of a completely equal system of access to health care. These pressures are partly from consumers and partly from producers of services, as well as from established institutions which are not anxious for change.

Middle class consumers have been anxious to retain and develop their privileges in getting access when they want it and to the professional providers of their choice. Lower class consumers have usually been quick to use new opportunities of access to services.

In England, Bevan (Foot, 1973) was able to introduce the NHS because he negotiated with the specialists an agreement whereby they could provide private service alongside their public service commitments.

It is clear that Bevan, in giving way to the specialists' demands for a private service alongside the NHS, thought that the concession was quite unimportant in the long run compared with getting a national integrated service provided for all citizens. But in order to do private work, one must have a demand from consumers. The specialists knew the demand was there for their services (as it was not for the general practitioners' to the same degree). Nonprofit insurance was moved in to help the middle classes to prepay specialists' services and private wing hospital accommodation. It is argued that citizens should have a right to spend their spare money in buying advantages if they wish. However, this gives them more opportunities of access than other citizens not in the scheme. The health through choice issues are considered by Titmuss (1956) and Lees (1961).

Ideologies of Governments about Health Services Organization

Lowi's concept (1964) of distributive, regulative and redistributive functions of a government for its community is a useful one for focussing upon the differences in health services organization from one country to another. If the country's government is more concerned with distribution of prerogatives than redistribution of rights, then the kind of services which will emerge are very different ones, as can be seen by comparing the American system with the British. But both are concerned with matters of regulation of quantity and quality. The U.S. has more problems in deciding how to proceed and how far to proceed with regulation because bureaucratic government is mistrusted; the British know more or less how they want to proceed but have to get agreement from the parties involved and are embroiled in bargaining; the Australians have both problems; the Canadians are more like the British.

Whilst it is accepted that health services are necessary in modern societies and attracting doctors to man them is of great importance, many questions still need to be answered: how many doctors are needed, what is to be their distribution over geographic space and over specialties, their levels of payment vis à vis other nationals, the methods of payment and their effect upon effective and efficient performance, what working conditions should be provided for them or by them, what delegation of work can be permitted or encouraged. The answers to these questions are very complex and relate to the goals of the society, the structures developed to move society towards these goals, the processes of decision making and the constraints which exist to prevent the attainment of the desired outcomes (Marmor and Thomas, 1971).

General Trends in Relating Prerogatives and Rights in Health Care

Because of the advances in technology and organization of health services which have come in the twentieth century, there is no longer a simple one-to-one relationship of doctor to patient, a privately negotiated reciprocity licensed by government. Now there exists a complex network of health services in every country. The old personal guidelines (within which the doctor made extensive efforts for his individual patient's well-being) are being challenged. Are doctors giving too much care to those who make excessive demands on public resources because there is a very limited amount of financial control over both parties to the relationship since third party payment systems have been introduced? How can individual patients' wants be linked into national priorities for health care? Should these priorities be reconsidered in terms of group rights versus individual justice? Will individual citizens, essentially selfish about their own health problems, allow the priorities to be reconsidered?

Policy makers are now being forced to reexamine what health services are for. The first issue is the general health of the population. Since it is clear that the people of liberal democratic countries "have never had it so good" as in the post-World War II period and that poverty is now a matter of relative deprivation rather than the desperate pauperism of Victorian times, how far is it necessary to be concerned about the effects of social stratification on health?

Greater mortality and morbidity are still associated with lower social class status and this fact has been an important weapon in the armoury of advocates for a national health service programme financed from taxation (e.g., Kosa et al., 1969; Australian federal government (Henderson), 1974). Rein (1976) made a study of the impact of the British NHS on different social classes and concluded that since its inception the lower classes had become able to get better access to care and that this had been of profit to them in the treatment of physical conditions.

On the other hand, Hollingshead and Redlich (1958) showed that the treatment of lower socioeconomic groups in the U.S. public mental health service was discriminatory, that they were given different care from middle class patients, partly because they related differently to the diagnosticians and therapists. There is no doubt that the British middle classes are able to make better relationships with doctors and to do some queue jumping by playing off the private and public systems against one another.

However, it is not only lower social class groups which show evidences of different health problems and communication difficulties in relating to treatment personnel. Medical sociologists have discussed the issues of ethnicity, gender, urban/rural differences and more (Skipper and Leonard, eds., 1965).

Clearly, national concerns about health indicators show up more clearly in wartime when a strong defence force needs to be recruited and the rate of rejection of conscripts becomes a visible sign of failures in health care of citizens. But nations are also concerned about having a satisfactory labour force (utilitarianism) and a caring health service (humanitarianism).

The second issue is the health of individual citizens. As a result of developments in modern technology, new questions about mortality and morbidity are beginning to arise. How can health care organizations ensure that patients' rights are protected and that justice is done and seen to be done? What is the point of prolonging existence in quantity when quality is not there? Who shall live? Is the Protestant ethic the right ethic for the twentieth century? Should those who will never work be cared for as well as those who will be producers? (Crossman, 1972).

Other questions are about the costs of health care and its place in national priorities. What is the right amount of GNP to allocate to health services? If growth is not the right answer to their future development, then how can they be reorganized? How can those with the greatest prerogatives be persuaded to accept a reduction in privileged status when there are pulls towards higher paying and technically better equipped institutions in other parts of the world? Can teamwork be made acceptable to those in power?

What kinds of adjustments are possible within health service organizations where lower socioeconomic groups of workers have awakened to the fact that they have been badly paid in comparison with similar groups not in health service employment?

In subsequent chapters we shall explore how policy makers can anticipate these challenges and make plans to react to them.

Discussion of Readings and References

1. The chapter begins by considering the way in which groups and individuals organize their values into a structured collection of ideas known as an ideology which is used as a general guide to behaviour. In the translation of social philosophies into policies and services, the development of ideologies forms an intermediate stage.

The first reading is part of an article by Clifford Geertz on "Ideology as a Cultural System" in which he considered two interpretations of the reasons for the development of ideologies—the interest and the strain theories.

2. For most people today, political ideologies are of great importance since political territoriality and citizenship of a country affect so many aspects of daily living. National states have become regulators of the boundaries of individual and group activities and other major distributors or redistributors of wealth and power.

Since this book is concerned with four countries which have developed within the liberal ideology, it is important to understand its implications and how it has been modified in different settings. A second excerpt from M. Patricia Marchak's book, *Ideological Perspectives on Canadian Society,* advances the ideas of the first reading attached to chapter 5. However, within the scope of this book it is not possible to go into any depth on that or any other political ideology. A list of references on national political ideologies follows this chapter.

One feature of Marchak's book is that it has discussed dominant and challenging ideologies. It is important to try to assess the dominance of one party's ideology over the others in each nation being studied. This may be done by considering who gets power and how long they are able to keep it when challenged by an opposition party.

As well as discussing the weighting of political approaches to maintenance or change, Marchak has also pointed out that liberalism is not so deeply committed to a philosophy as socialism or conservatism. Liberals develop strategic responses to political pressures—thus the countries with a dominant liberal ideology tend to borrow from other parties' programmes when it has seemed appropriate to do so (e.g., in introducing welfare state redistributive policies, they were influenced by socialist ideas).

3. A short excerpt from David Donnison's article on "Ideologies and Policies" compares and contrasts the operationalization of the dominant political philosophies of Great Britain and the U.S.A. by exploring the development of two towns, Milton Keynes and Houston. Donnison examined documents relating to the planning of these urban developments and showed how each collection reflects a different philosophy of social organization.

It is important for health planners to recognize the ideological differences between countries because there are frequent attempts to borrow ideas across international frontiers and it is important to consider which ideas will be able to travel and which will not. Heidenheimer et al. in "Comparative Public Policy" have given some consideration to this issue.

Why has the reorganization of mental health services been so easily transferable across boundaries whilst health insurance has not? Readings on attitudes to social control may help to illuminate reasons for the former. Christa Altenstetter has compared social insurance in West Germany and the United States. In *Social Policy,* R. M. Titmuss developed a classification of national ideologies relating to social welfare which should provide illumination on the difficulty of transferring West Germany's social insurance scheme to the United States.

Some institutions, such as hospitals, were conceived before national boundaries became so important. In *Social Settings and Medical Organization,* William A. Glaser has made an interesting study of religious ideologies and their influence upon the development of medical care institutions. The Judeo-Christian approach to health care is very different from the Moslem, for example. This may be an important realization for students considering international social service.

4. A second reading from David Donnison's article outlines the main issues with which societies must be concerned, namely, growth and distribution. These are the central themes. He identifies the contrasting standpoints of the tough-minded, economically oriented Right and the tender-minded, socially oriented Left.

5. For health policy analysts it is important to know about the ideologies of health professional groups. Building on Geertz's ideas that ideologies are a response to strain, Bernard Blishen examined the attitudes of the Canadian medical profession to the introduction of publicly financed Medical Care in Canada in the 1960s. He concluded that the ideology developed by the profession was maladaptive, faced as the group was by considerable pressures for change.

Terence J. Johnson's book on *Professions and Power* was mentioned in the previous chapter and is again recommended.

In an article which is difficult but rewarding to read, Philippe Schmitter's analysis of interest intermediary groups may help in understanding the orientations of pressure groups. He discusses three types of groups: those with pluralist (i.e., political), corporatist (i.e., entrepreneurial) and syndicalist (i.e., occupational group) interests.

In the last few years occupational groups organized into professions or trade unions have been emerging as a force in western societies. The health services, previously governed by a vocational (or normative) ideology, promoted by such influential figures as Florence Nightingale, are moving away from this orientation towards what Amitai Etzioni (1961) has called utilitarian approaches. Health care workers are organizing more effectively to demand their share of power and wealth. And the doctors are struggling to maintain their prerogatives vis à vis society generally and these other groups in the health services. Some references to health workers' trade union developments are given in the bibliography, e.g., McCarthy, 1976; Boyer, 1975; Chaney et al., 1976; Bean and Laliberty, 1977.

6. The position of health care consumers remains confused and disorganized partly because they are still dependent on professionals to relate policies to their needs through service delivery, and partly because no consumers previously privileged wish to lose the advantages they have had. A series of references from Victor Fuchs' *Who Shall Live?* which sets out the issues of professional choice to Dennis Lees' *Health Through Choice,* which sets out the issues of consumers' buying privileges in health care, may be consulted. They are discussed in the chapter and listed in the bibliography.

7. Further reading of David Donnison's "Ideologies and Policies" is recommended because it makes a helpful connection between ideological thinking, planning and decision taking. Donnison argued that a Standing Plan (see A. J. Kahn's "Theory and Practice of Social Planning," for example) can be drawn upon by decision takers to meet their immediate needs for rational guidance in deciding on the incremental moves which they are required to make in a particular content area of choice.

Further References on Political Ideologies

Utilitarianism

Bentham, Jeremy. *An Introduction to the Principles of Morals and Legislation,* 1789.

Borson, John M., ed. *John Stuart Mill: A Selection of His Works.* Toronto: Macmillan, 1966.

Mill, John Stuart. *On Liberty,* 1859.

Viner, Jacob. "Bentham and J. S. Mill: The Utilitarian Background." *American Economic Review* 39(1949): 360–83.

Fabian Socialism

Crossman, R. H. S., ed. *New Fabian Essays.* London: Turnstile Press, 1972.

Mackenzie, N., ed. *Conviction.* London: McGibbon and Kee, 1959.

Marxism

Maximilien, R., Meyer, A. G. and Bottomore T. *International Encyclopedia of the Social Sciences,* vol. 10, pp. 34–52.

National Ideologies

Marshall, T. H. "Value Problems in Welfare Capitalism." *Journal of Social Policy* 1 (1972): 15–32.

Oakeshott, M. *Rationalism in Politics.* London: Heinemann, 1962.

Friedmann, M. *Capitalism and Freedom.* Chicago: Chicago University Press, 1962.

Dolbeare, Kenneth M. and Dolbeare, Patricia with Jane A. Hadley. *American Ideologies.* 2nd. ed. Chicago: Rand McNally, 1973.

Bell, Daniel. *The End of Ideology.* Glencoe: Free Press, 1960.

Apter, David E., ed. *Ideology and Discontent.* New York: The Free Press, 1964.

Fox, Paul W. *Politics: Canada.* 3rd ed. Toronto: McGraw-Hill, 1970.

Kilbourn, William. *Canada: A Guide to the Peaceable Kingdom.* New York: St. Martins Press, 1970.

Engelmann, F. C. and Schwartz, M. A. *Canadian Political Parties: Origin, Character, Impact.* Scarborough, Ontario: Prentice-Hall of Canada, 1975.

Thorburn, Hugh G., ed. *Party Politics in Canada.* 3rd ed. Scarborough, Ontario: Prentice-Hall of Canada, 1972.

Davies, A. F. *Australian Democracy.* Melbourne: Longmans, 1964.

Crisp, L. F. *Australian National Government.* Hawthorn, Victoria: Longman, 1965.

Sawer, G. *Australian Government Today.* 10th ed. Melbourne: Melbourne University Press, 1964.

Atkins, R. and Graycar, A. *Governing Australia.* Sydney: John Wiley and Sons: Australasia Pty. Ltd., 1972.

Mayer, Henry and Nelson, Helen, eds. *Australian Politics: A Third Reader.* Melbourne: Cheshire, 1973.

Ideology as a Cultural System

Clifford Geertz

There are currently two main approaches to the study of the social determinants of ideology: the interest theory and the strain theory.[1] For the first, ideology is a mask and a weapon; for the second, a symptom and a remedy. In the interest theory, ideological pronouncements are seen against the background of a universal struggle for advantage; in the strain theory, against the background of a chronic effort to correct sociopsychological disequilibrium. In the one, men pursue power; in the other, they flee anxiety. As they may, of course, do both at the same time—and even one by means of the other—the two theories are not necessarily contradictory; but the strain theory (which arose in response to the empirical difficulties encountered by the interest theory), being less simplistic, is more penetrating, less concrete, more comprehensive.

The fundamentals of the interest theory are too well known to need review; developed to perfection of a sort by the Marxist tradition, they are now standard intellectual equipment of the man-in-the-street, who is only too aware that in political argumentation it all comes down to whose ox is gored. The great advantage of the interest theory was and is its rooting of cultural idea-systems in the solid ground of social structure, through emphasis on the motivations of those who profess such systems and on the dependence of those motivations in turn upon social position, most especially social class. Further, the interest theory welded political speculation to political combat by pointing out that ideas are weapons and that an excellent way to institutionalize a particular view of reality—that of one's group, class,

From *Ideology and Discontent,* ed. David E. Apter (N.Y.: The Free Press 1964), pp. 52–57, 60–65. Footnotes have been renumbered and placed at the end.

or party—is to capture political power and enforce it. These contributions are permanent; and if interest theory has not now the hegemony it once had, it is not so much because it has been proved wrong as because its theoretical apparatus turned out to be too rudimentary to cope with the complexity of the interaction among social, psychological, and cultural factors it itself uncovered. Rather like Newtonian mechanics, it has not been so much displaced by subsequent developments as absorbed into them.

The main defects of the interest theory are that its psychology is too anemic and its sociology too muscular. Lacking a developed analysis of motivation, it has been constantly forced to oscillate between a narrow and superficial utilitarianism that sees men as impelled by rational calculation of their consciously recognized personal advantage and a broader, but no less superficial, historicism that speaks with a studied vagueness of men's ideas as somehow "reflecting," "expressing," "corresponding to," "emerging from," of "conditioned by" their social commitments. Within such a framework, the analyst is faced with the choice of either revealing the thinness of his psychology by being so specific as to be thoroughly implausible or concealing the fact that he does not have any psychological theory at all by being so general as to be truistic. . . .

On the other hand, the view that social action is fundamentally an unending struggle for power leads to an unduly Machiavellian view of ideology as a form of higher cunning and, consequently, to a neglect of its broader, less dramatic social functions. The battlefield image of society as a clash of interests thinly disguised as a clash of principles turns attention away from the role that ideologies play in defining (or obscuring) social categories, stabilizing (or upsetting) social expectations, maintaining (or undermining) social norms, strengthening (or weakening) social consensus, relieving (or exacerbating) social tensions. Reducing ideology to a weapon in a *guerre de plume* gives to its analysis a warming air of militancy, but it also means reducing the intellectual compass within which such analysis may be conducted to the constricted realism of tactics and strategy. The intensity of interest theory is—to adapt a figure from Whitehead—but the reward of its narrowness.

As "interest," whatever its ambiguities, is at one and the same time a psychological and sociological concept—referring both to a felt advantage of an individual or group of individuals and to the objective structure of opportunity within which an individual or group moves—so also is "strain," for it refers both to a state of personal tension and to a condition of societal dislocation. The difference is that with "strain" both the motivational background and the social structural context are more systematically portrayed, as are their relations with one another. It is, in fact, the addition of a developed conception of personality systems (basically Freudian), on the one hand, and of social systems (basically Durkheimian) on the other, and of their modes of interpenetration—the Parsonian addition—that transforms interest theory into strain theory.[2]

The clear and distinct idea from which strain theory departs is the chronic malintegration of society. No social arrangement is or can be completely successful in coping with the functional problems it inevitably faces. All are riddled with insoluble antinomies: between liberty and political order, stability and change, efficiency and humanity, precision and flexibility, and so forth. There are discontinuities between norms in different sectors of the society—the economy, the polity, the family, and so forth. There are discrepancies between goals within the different sectors—between the emphases on profit and productivity in business firms or between extending knowledge and disseminating it in universities, for example. And there are the contradictory role expectations of which so much has been made in recent American sociological literature on the foreman, the working wife, the artist, and the politician. Social friction is as pervasive as is mechanical friction—and as irremovable.

Further, this friction or social strain appears on the level of the individual personality—itself an inevitably malintegrated system of conflicting desires, archaic sentiments, and improvised defenses—as psychological strain. What is viewed collectively as structural inconsistency is felt individually as personal insecurity, for it is in the experience of the social actor that the imperfections of society and contradictions of character meet and exacerbate one another. But at the same time, the fact that both society and personality are, whatever their shortcomings, organized systems, rather than mere congeries of institutions or clusters of motives, means that the sociopsychological tensions they induce are also systematic, that the anxieties derived from social interaction have a form and order of their own. In the modern world at least, most men live lives of patterned desperation.

Ideological thought is, then, regarded as (one sort of) response to this desperation: "Ideology is a patterned reaction to the patterned strains of a social role."[3] It provides a "symbolic outlet" for emotional disturbances generated by social disequilibrium. And as one can assume that such disturbances are, at least in a general way, common to all or most occupants of a given role or social position, so ideological reactions to the disturbances will tend to be similar, a similarity only reinforced by the presumed commonalities in "basic personality structure" among members of a particular culture, class, or occupational category. The model here is not military but medical: An ideology is a malady (Sutton, *et al.,* mention nail-chewing, alcoholism, psychosomatic disorders, and "crotchets" among the alternatives to it) and demands a diagnosis. "The concept of strain is not in itself an explanation of ideological patterns but a generalized label for the kinds of factors to look for in working out an explanation."[4]

But there is more to diagnosis, either medical or sociological, than the identification of pertinent strains; one understands symptoms not merely etiologically but teleologically—in terms of the ways in which they act as mechanisms, however unavailing, for dealing with the disturbances that have generated them. Four main classes of explanation have been most frequently employed: the cathartic, the morale, the solidarity, and the advocatory. By the "cathartic explanation" is meant the venerable safety-valve or scapegoat theory. Emotional tension is drained off by being displaced onto symbolic enemies ("The Jews," "Big Business," "The Reds," and so forth). The explanation is as simple-minded as the device, but that, by providing legitimate objects of hostility (or, for that matter, of love), ideology may ease somewhat the pain of being a petty bureaucrat, a day laborer, or a small-town storekeeper is undeniable. By the "morale explanation" is meant the ability of an ideology to sustain individuals (or groups) in the face of chronic strain, either by denying it outright or by legitimizing it in terms of higher values. Both the struggling small businessman rehearsing his boundless confidence in the inevitable justness of the American system and the neglected artist attributing his failure to his maintenance of decent standards in a Philistine world are able, by such means, to get on with their work. Ideology bridges the emotional gap between things as they are and as one would have them be, thus insuring the performance of roles that might otherwise be abandoned in despair or apathy. By the "solidarity explanation" is meant the power of ideology to knit a social group or class together. To the extent that it exists, the unity of the labor movement, the business community, or the medical profession obviously rests to a significant degree on common ideological orientation; and the South would not be The South without the existence of popular symbols charged with the emotions of a pervasive social predicament. Finally, by the "advocatory explanation" is meant the action of ideologies (and ideologists) in articulating, however partially and indistinctly, the strains that impel them, thus forcing them into the public notice. "Ideologists state the problems for the larger society, take sides on the issues involved and 'present them in the court' of the ideological market place."[5] Although ideological advocates (not altogether unlike their legal counterparts) tend as much to obscure as to clarify the true nature of the problems involved, they at least call attention to their existence and, by polarizing issues, make continued neglect more difficult. Without Marxist attack, there would have been no labor reform; without Black Muslims, no deliberate speed.

It is here, however, in the investigation of the social and psychological roles of ideology, as distinct from its determinants, that strain theory itself begins to creak and its superior incisiveness, in comparison with interest theory, to evaporate. The increased precision in the location of the springs of ideological concern does not, somehow, carry over into the discrimination of its consequences, where the analysis becomes, on the contrary, slack and ambiguous. The consequences envisaged, no doubt genuine enough in themselves, seem almost adventitious, the accidental by-products of an essentially nonrational, nearly automatic expressive process initially pointed in another direction—as when a man stubbing his toe cries an involuntary "ouch!" and incidentally vents his anger, signals his distress, and consoles himself with the sound of his own voice; or as when, caught in a subway crush, he issues a spontaneous "damn!" of frustration and, hearing similar oaths from others, gains a certain perverse sense of kinship with fellow sufferers.

This defect, of course, can be found in much of the functional analysis in the social sciences: A pattern of behavior shaped by a certain set of forces turns out, by a plausible but nevertheless mysterious coincidence, to serve ends but tenuously related to those forces. A group of primitives sets out, in all honesty, to pray for rain and ends by strengthening its social solidarity; a ward politician sets out to get or remain near the trough and ends by mediating between unassimilated immigrant groups and an impersonal governmental bureaucracy; an ideologist sets out to air his grievances and finds himself contributing, through the diversionary power of his illusions, to the continued viability of the very system that grieves him.

The concept of latent function is usually invoked to paper over this anomalous state of affairs, but it rather names the phenomenon (whose reality is not in question) than explains it; and the net result is that functional analyses—and not only those of ideology—remain hopelessly equivocal. The petty bureaucrat's anti-Semitism may indeed give him something to do with the bottled anger generated in him by constant toadying to those he considers his intellectual inferiors and so drain some of it away; but it may also simply increase his anger by providing him with something else about which to be impotently bitter. The neglected artist may better bear his popular failure by invoking the classical canons of his art; but such an invocation may so dramatize for him the gap between the possibilities of his environment and the demands of his vision as to make the game seem unworth the candle. Commonality of ideological perception may link men together, but it may also provide them, as the history of Marxian sectarianism demonstrates, with a vocabulary by means of which to explore more exquisitely the differences among them. The clash of ideologists may bring a social problem to public attention, but it may also charge it with such passion that any possibility of dealing with it rationally is precluded. Of all these possibilities, strain theorists are, of course, very well aware. Indeed they tend to stress negative outcomes and possibilities rather more than the positive, and they but rarely think of ideology as more than a *faute de mieux* stop-gap—like nail-chewing. But the main point is that, for all its subtlety in ferreting out the motives of ideological concern, strain theory's analysis of the consequences of such concern remains crude, vacillatory, and evasive. Diagnostically it is convincing; functionally it is not.

The reason for this weakness is the virtual absence in strain theory (or in interest theory either) of anything more than the most rudimentary conception of the processes of symbolic formulation. There is a good deal of talk about emotions "finding a symbolic outlet" or "becoming attached to appropriate symbols"—but very little idea of how the trick is really done. The link between the causes of ideology and its effects seems adventitious because the connecting element—the autonomous process of symbolic formulation—is passed over in virtual silence. Both interest theory and strain theory go directly from source analysis to consequence analysis without ever seriously examining ideologies as systems of interacting symbols, as patterns of interworking meanings. Themes are outlined, of course; among the content analysts, they are even counted. But they are referred for elucidation, not to other themes nor to any sort of semantic theory, but either backward to the affect they presumably mirror or forward to the social reality they presumably distort. The problem of how, after all, ideologies transform sentiment into significance and so make it socially available is short-circuited by the crude device of placing particular symbols and particular strains (or interests) side by side in such a way that the fact that the first are derivatives of the second seems mere common sense—or at least post-Freudian, post-Marxian common sense. And so, if the analyst be deft enough, it does.[6] The connection is not thereby explained but merely educed. The nature of the relationship between the sociopsychological stresses that incite ideological attitudes and the elaborate symbolic structures through which those attitudes are given a public existence is much too complicated to be comprehended in terms of a vague and unexamined notion of emotive resonance. . . .

Asking the question that most students of ideology fail to ask—what, precisely, do we mean when we assert that sociopsychological strains are "expressed" in symbolic forms?—gets one, therefore, very quickly into quite deep water indeed; into, in fact, a somewhat untraditional and apparently paradoxical theory of the nature of human thought as a public and not, or at least not fundamentally, a private activity.[7] The details of such a theory cannot be pursued any distance here, nor can any significant amount of evidence be marshalled to support it. But at least its general outlines must be sketched if we are to find our way back from the elusive world of symbols and semantic process to the (apparently) solider one of sentiments and institutions, if we are to trace with some circumstantiality the modes of interpenetration of culture, personality, and social system.

[Geertz then goes on to explore how symbols are used as models of other systems.]

Thinking, conceptualization, formulation, comprehension, understanding, or what-have-you consists not of ghostly happening in the head but of a matching of the states and processes of symbolic models against the states and processes of the wider world: The extrinsic theory of thought is extendable to the affective side of human mentality as well.[8] As a road map transforms mere physical locations into "places," connected by numbered routes and separated by measured distances, and so enables us to find our way from where we are to where we want to go, so a poem like, for example, Hopkins's "Felix Randal" provides, through the evocative power of its charged language, a symbolic model of the emotional impact of premature death, which, if we are as impressed with its penetration as with the road map's, transforms physical sensations into sentiments and attitudes and enables us to react to such a tragedy not "blindly" but "intelligently." The central rituals of religion—a mass, a pilgrimage, a corroboree—are symbolic models (here more in the form of activities than of words) of a particular sense of the divine, a certain sort of devotional mood, which their continual re-enactment tends to produce in their participants. Of course, as most acts of what is usually called "cognition" are more on the level of identifying a rabbit than operating a wind tunnel, so most of what is usually called "expression" (the dichotomy is often overdrawn and almost universally misconstrued) is mediated more by models drawn from popular culture than from high art and formal religious ritual. But the point is that the development, maintenance, and dissolution of "moods," "attitudes," "sentiments," and so forth are no more "a ghostly process occurring in streams of consciousness we are debarred from visiting" than is the discrimination of objects, events, structures, processes, and so forth in our environment. Here, too, "we are describing the ways in which. . .people conduct parts of their predominantly public behavior."[9]

Whatever their other differences, both so-called "cognitive" and so-called "expressive" symbols or symbol-systems have, then, at least one thing in common: They are extrinsic sources of information in terms of which human life can be patterned—extrapersonal mechanisms for the perception, understanding, judgment, and manipulation of the world. Culture patterns—religious, philosophical, aesthetic, scientific, ideological—are "programs"; they provide a template or blueprint for the organization of social and psychological processes, much as genetic systems provide such a template for the organization of organic processes. . . .

The reason such symbolic templates are necessary is that, as has been often remarked, human behavior is inherently extremely plastic. Not strictly but only very broadly controlled by genetic programs or models—intrinsic sources of information—such behavior must, if it is to have any effective form at all, be controlled to a significant extent by extrinsic ones. Birds learn how to fly without wind tunnels, and whatever reactions lower animals have to death are in great part innate, physiologically preformed.[10] The extreme generality, diffuseness, and variability of man's innate response capacities mean that the particular pattern his behavior takes is guided predominantly by cultural rather than genetic templates, the latter setting the over-all psychophysical context within which precise activity sequences are organized by the former. The tool-making, laughing, or lying animal, man, is also the incomplete—or, more accurately, self-completing—animal. The agent of his own realization, he creates out of his general capacity for the construction of symbolic models the specific capabilities that define him. Or—to return at last to our subject—it is through the construction of ideologies, schematic images of social order, that man makes himself for better or worse a political animal.

Further, as the various sorts of cultural symbol-system are extrinsic sources of information, templates for the organization of social and psychological processes, they come most crucially into play in situations where the particular kind of information they contain is lacking, where institutionalized guides for behavior, thought, or feeling are weak or absent. It is in country unfamiliar emotionally or topographically that one needs poems and road maps.

So too with ideology. In polities firmly embedded in Edmund Burke's golden assemblage of "ancient opinions and rules of life," the role of ideology, in any explicit sense, is marginal. In such truly traditional political systems the participants act as (to use another Burkean phrase) men of untaught feelings; they are guided both emotionally and intellectually in their judgments and activities by unexamined prejudices, which do not leave them "hesitating in the moment of decision, sceptical, puzzled and unresolved." But when, as in the revolutionary France Burke was indicting and in fact in the shaken England from which, as perhaps his nation's greatest ideologue, he was indicting it, those hallowed opinions and rules of life come into question, the search for systematic ideological formulations, either to reinforce them or to replace them, flourishes. The function of ideology is to make an autonomous politics possible by providing the authoritative concepts that render it meaningful, the suasive images by means of which it can be sensibly grasped.[11]

It is, in fact, precisely at the point at which a political system begins to free itself from the immediate governance of received tradition, from the direct and detailed guidance of religious or philosophical canons on the one hand and from the unreflective precepts of conventional moralism on the other, that formal ideologies tend first to emerge and take hold.[12] The differentiation of an autonomous polity implies the differentiation, too, of a separate and distinct cultural model of political action, for the older, unspecialized models are either too comprehensive or too concrete to provide the sort of guidance such a political system demands. Either they trammel political behavior by encumbering it with transcendental significance, or they stifle political imagination by binding it to the blank realism of habitual judgment. It is when neither a society's most general cultural orientations nor its most down-to-earth, "pragmatic" ones suffice any longer to provide an adequate image of political process that ideologies begin to become crucial as sources of sociopolitical meanings and attitudes.

In one sense, this statement is but another way of saying that ideology is a response to strain. But now we are including *cultural* as well as social and psychological strain. It is a loss of orientation that most directly gives rise to ideological activity, an inability, for lack of usable models, to comprehend the universe of civic rights and responsibilities in which one finds oneself located. The development of a differentiated polity (or of greater internal differentiation within such a polity) may and commonly does bring with it severe social dislocation and psychological tension. But it also brings with it conceptual confusion, as the established images of political order fade into irrelevance or are driven into disrepute. The reason why the French Revolution was, at least up to its time, the greatest incubator of extremist ideologies, "progressive" and "reactionary" alike, in human history was not that either personal insecurity or social disequilibrium were deeper and more pervasive than at many earlier periods—though they were deep and pervasive enough—but because the central organizing principle of political life, the divine right of kings, was destroyed.[13] It is a confluence of sociopsychological strain and an absence of cultural resources by means of which to make (political, moral or economic) sense of that strain, each exacerbating the other, that sets the stage for the rise of systematic (political, moral, economic) ideologies.

And it is, in turn, the attempt of ideologies to render otherwise incomprehensible social situations meaningful, to so construe them as to make it possible to act purposefully within them, that accounts both for the ideologies' highly figurative nature and for the intensity with which, once accepted, they are held. As metaphor extends language by broadening its semantic range, enabling it to express meanings it cannot or at least cannot yet express literally, so the head-on clash of literal meanings in ideology—the irony, the hyperbole, the overdrawn antithesis—provides novel symbolic frames against which to match the myriad "unfamiliar somethings" that, like a journey to a strange country, are produced by a transformation in political life. Whatever else ideologies may be—projections of unacknowledged fears, disguises for ulterior motives, phatic expressions of group solidarity—they are, most distinctively, maps of problematic social reality and matrices for the creation of collective conscience. Whether, in any particular case, the map is accurate or the conscience creditable is a separate question, to which one can hardly give the same answer for Nazism and Zionism, for the nationalisms of McCarthy and of Churchill, for the defenders of segregation and its opponents.

NOTES

[1]F. X. Sutton, S. E. Harris, C. Kaysen, and J. Tobin, *The American Business Creed* (Cambridge, Mass., 1956), pp. 3–6.

[2]For the general schema, see T. Parsons, *The Social System* (New York, 1951), especially Chaps. I, VII. The fullest development of the strain theory is in Sutton, *et al., op. cit.,* especially Chap. XV.

[3]Sutton, *et al., op. cit.,* pp. 307–8.

[4]Talcott Parsons, "An Approach to Psychological Theory in Terms of the Theory of Action," in S. Koch, ed., *Psychology:* A Study of Science (New York, 1959).

[5]W. White, *Beyond Conformity* (New York, 1961), p. 204.

[6]Perhaps the most impressive *tour de force* in this paratactic genre is Nathan Leites's *A Study of Bolshevism* (New York, 1953).

[7]G. Ryle, *The Concept of Mind* (New York, 1949).

[8]S. Langer, *Feeling and Form* (New York, 1953).

[9]The quotations are from Ryle, *op. cit.,* p. 51.

[10]This point is perhaps somewhat too baldly put in light of recent analyses of animal learning; but the essential thesis—that there is a general trend toward a more diffuse, less determinate control of behavior by intrinsic (innate) parameters as one moves from lower to higher animals—seems well established. See [C. Geertz: "The Growth of Culture and the Evolution of the Mind" in J. Scher, ed., *Theories of the Mind* (New York) 1962.] where the whole argument, here strenuously compressed, is developed in full.

[11]Of course, there the are moral, economic, and even aesthetic ideologies, as well as specifically political ones, but as very few ideologies of any social prominence lack political implications, it is perhaps permissible to view the problem here in this somewhat narrowed focus. In any case, the arguments developed for political ideologies apply with equal force to nonpolitical ones. For an analysis of a moral ideology cast in terms very similar to those developed in this paper, see A. L. Green, "The Ideology of Anti-Fluoridation Leaders," *The Journal of Social Issues,* 17 (1961); 13–25.

[12]That such ideologies may call, as did Burke's or De Maistre's, for the reinvigoration of custom or the reimposition of religious hegemony is, of course, no contradiction. One constructs arguments for tradition only when its credentials have been questioned. To the degree that such appeals are successful they bring, not a return to naive traditionalism, but ideological retraditionalization—an altogether different matter. See Mannheim "Conservative Thought," in his *Essays on Sociology and Social Psychology* (New York, 1953), especially p. 94–8.

[13]It is important to remember, too, that the principle was destroyed long before the king; it was to the successor principle that he was, in fact, a ritual sacrifice: "When [Saint-Just] exclaims: 'To determine the principle in virtue of which the accused [Louis XVI] is perhaps to die, is to determine the principle by which the society that judges him lives,' he demonstrates that it is the philosophers who are going to kill the King: the King must die in the name of the social contract." A. Camus, *The Rebel* (New York, 1958). p. 114.

Free Enterprise in (Relatively Moral) Nation States [II]

M. Patricia Marchak

The strength of the liberal ideology lies in its apparent accommodation of diversity. All people are equal, all choices are legitimate, all alternatives are worthy. Good and evil are relative terms, and the latitude for personal action is wide. Life is a marketplace of competing claims for the attention of consumers. Having no apparent philosophical commitment to a hierarchy of values, the liberal must pose all problems as questions of strategy. Such questions are solved by the application of scientific research and the probing of the general will. For this reason, liberalism never appears to its adherents as an ideology. Marxism, Communism, Conservatism—but not Liberalism. Liberalism appears to them as simply a common-sense approach to life. After all, it is their common sense. The "end of ideology," heralded by the American writer, Daniel Bell, in a book by that title, seems an appropriate title for the liberal age—to the liberal.[1]

Yet when each man can choose his own moral obligations, there are no guarantees that a variety of social demands will be met. No lord is responsible for the poor, no employers for the unemployed, no upper class for the lower class. The young are not obliged to care for the old, the healthy for the sick, the educated for the ignorant. The moral obligations of manufacturers to consumers, corporations to employees, universities to the public, the mass media to viewers and readers, and governments to voters are all extremely vague.

From M. Patricia Marchak, *Ideological Perspectives on Canada* (Toronto: McGraw-Hill Ryerson, 1975), pp. 52–53. Reprinted by permission.

To answer that the solutions are matters of strategy is to assume that without moral obligation, and in spite of the ideology of achievement, individualism, material profit, and personal success, people and institutions will somehow ignore their private interests and act on behalf of the society as a whole whenever the two pose different requirements. Strategies are worked out after values and goals are chosen; they are means to desired ends. Desires are translated into action to the extent that people are able to make this translation.

In a society where wealth is of utmost importance, those with wealth can translate more desires into actions than those without wealth. There is no reason to expect them to put the desires of others above their own, and it is not surprising if they assume that their own desires are congruent with the social good.

The thesis of moral relativity provides a view of society as a collection of individuals whose interaction requires a coordinating body to ensure fair play. The question for the liberal is: when is intervention justified? When is protection required? Mill was famous for his defence of the principle that another man's liberty stopped short of this one's nose, but the room for abuse is far in excess of physical force. Is one's liberty impaired by polluted water, by political parties financed through organized corporations and international unions, by noise, by expropriation rights of governments acting in defence of other property interests, by tax spending on military defence, by control of industries by non-nationals, by the concentration of wealth and power? Whose liberty is impaired when corporate directors make decisions in the interests of the corporation which are not in the interests of their workers or the communities in which they operate? The liberal can have no philosophical answer to such questions, since liberty itself is defined in relative terms. Social good becomes whatever the will of the majority defines it to be, should the majority find a way of entering its competing claims, and subject to the decisions already made within the economic sphere not by the governments at all but by non-elected directors whose liberty is unimpaired by democratic procedures.

Notes

[1]Daniel Bell, *The End of Ideology* (Glencoe, Ill.: Free Press, 1960).

Ideologies and Policies

David Donnison

The incrementalists and their opponents each claim to explain how policies evolve and how decision-makers choose between alternative courses of action. But both are puzzlingly vague about the origins of these alternatives. While they debate whether alternative courses of action should be evaluated for their efficiency in attaining predetermined goals or for their effectiveness in accommodating immediate demands and pressures, neither tells us where the alternatives come from in the first place. . . .

Where Do Policy Options Come From?

These questions are important because they take us back to the seed-bed of ideologies in which new ideas germinate and are cultivated. The answers to them are, in detail, enormously complex and varied (historians devote their lives to discovering them) but in general they are not so mysterious. Well-tried formulae and new innovations are both alike generated within relevant professional, political and administrative groups. These groups have their own gradually evolving "climates of opinion" which reflect and help to shape the culture of the interest groups and the wider society surrounding them.[1] The groups that form and the ideas they generate depend to a great extent on administrative and political systems, the demands they make and the opportunities they afford. The way in which policy options are formulated can be glimpsed in two sharply contrasting examples.

From *Journal of Social Policy* (1971–2): 103–6, by permission of the Cambridge University Press and the author. Footnotes have been renumbered and given at the end. Another part of this paper follows chapter 7 and another section follows this one.

The plans for the new town of Milton Keynes, approved in May 1971 by the Secretary of State for the Environment after the usual public inquiries, were the outcome of an unusually determined attempt at rational, comprehensive, long-range planning. (Milton Keynes is even hoping to introduce PPBS.) These plans were prepared, with the help of consultants and much advice from interested bodies, by a Development Corporation, appointed by the central government, consisting of representatives of the areas exporting and receiving population and others with relevant experience from the industrial, commercial and academic worlds. They did their best to formulate their goals for the new town:

(i) Opportunity and freedom of choice
(ii) Easy movement and access, and good communication
(iii) Balance and variety
(iv) An attractive city
(v) Public awareness
(vi) Efficiency and imaginative use of resources.

These goals were elaborated throughout the plan. To secure "balance and variety", "the Corporation is determined to achieve a wider spread of social, age and racial groups, than has hitherto been achieved and also to attract to live in Milton Keynes people with a wide range of incomes."[2] The implications of this policy for employment, housing, education and other aspects of the project were fairly fully explored.

The plan, as I read it, expressed a rather clear philosophy, amounting to a sort of ideology, about new towns. It roughly indicated (rather than showing in detail) how the processes of economic and social growth which create a town—its industry, commerce, housing, education and health services—were to be set going and related to each other. It envisaged no final state, no "completion" of Milton Keynes. It tried to show how the town and its activities would be related to other towns and activities in the surrounding region. The Corporation's aim was not to design Milton Keynes in concrete detail or even to lay down a comprehensive map of land uses, but to build a framework of roads, drains, power supplies, schools, shops and other services that will over the years enable people to create their own town in response to opportunities and constraints not yet foreseeable. The plan proposed procedures for monitoring the town's development to help the Corporation respond to the unforeseen when it happens.

All this, the cynics will point out, is merely the rhetoric of urban planning, to be superseded by the normal improvisations and confusions as soon as building begins. It is too early to be sure, but my observation of events so far justifies no confident repudiation of that view. I am not arguing that Milton Keynes has found the secret of rational planning: the points I want to make are different.

The rhetoric is important, and the institutions which formulate it (committee meetings, seminars, master plans, public inquiries, opinion polls . . . etc. etc.) are more important still. They have already served as a vehicle on which to mobilize the commitments of many people whose help will be needed in building the town. These groups and the ideology they have generated provide a seed-bed from which more policy-options will grow when they are needed—or, to be less figurative, the initial planning process has recruited a loose-knit team of people (extending well beyond those on the Corporation's payroll), trained them to work productively together, and given them some shared aims and a language in which to communicate with each other.

Now consider an entirely different case: a town which prides itself on being as nearly as possible unplanned. There are many examples but Houston, Texas (no mean city, with its population of 1,200,000) is the best documented one I can find.[3] No ideologies here, you might think: no goals, no synoptic analyses, no PPBS—just market forces and a bit of healthy incremental politics. That, roughly, is the view of Bernard Siegan, upon whose account I mainly rely.

Yet Houston's growth reflects clear and distinctive aims and assumptions about urban development: a sort of ideology, in fact. Land-use controls are imposed by developers through restrictive covenants which "will remain in force for long periods. They may be as effective as zoning (by planners) in maintaining single-family homogeneity" (i.e. in keeping out apartment blocks and the poorer households who subdivide houses). In "deluxe" subdivisions catering to the wealthy . . . covenants have provided an exclusivity that the most restrictive zoning code could not achieve. . . . Lest property owners and their legal advisers become careless about their rights, the city administration is itself prepared "to enforce residential restrictive covenants" and, in effect, to extend them beyond their normal terminal date. The administration also imposes minimum sizes on residential lots—"5000 square feet where sewer and water services are available and 7000 where they are not"—along with other standards which together must go far to determine, through their prices who has an opportunity of getting a new house. Siegan commends this system because it is less restrictive than the usual zoning regulations and therefore encourages more "non-home construction"—possibly $11 million more in 1968, which would produce over $175,000 annually in taxes. "Non-home construction," Siegan points out, "is even more profitable for schools, since it results in considerably less children per tax dollar received than results from homes." He urges all cities to adopt similar arrangements.

I do not want the political overtones of this account to confuse the argument. My intention is neither to condemn nor to applaud the government of Houston or its apologists, but to show that they express a pattern of aims and assumptions about the "good" city, its development and administration, which are about as ideological as Milton Keynes'. Central to this ideology are the individual property owner's rights to secure for himself as much, or as little, as he can buy, his right to exclude citizens with less money or different life styles from his neighbourhood, and the community's obligation to promote investment which generates more revenue than expenditure. The city fathers of Houston do not lack goals, or ideologies, although they probably do lack Milton Keynes' procedures for making such ideas explicit and exposing them to the criticism of neighbouring authorities, higher levels of government and the public at large. Houston may therefore be in less danger of bureaucratic paralysis, but in greater danger of error: certainly it has no better evidence to justify its determination to preserve economic, social (and therefore racial) segregation than Milton Keynes has for following the opposite policies.

Whether one system is "better" than the other is not the point I wish to make. My conclusion is that the governments of both cities rely upon ideologies which are derived largely (not wholly) from their knowledge, resources and powers. A new town's Development Corporation, representing exporting and importing communities and holding the powers and resources conferred on such bodies by Parliament, naturally adopts different aims, and plans a different sort of community, from those to be expected of the authorities governing cities like Houston. Thus planners must treat the institutions of government as being themselves "plannable." Likewise, political science must play a central part in the study of social administration.

Notes

[1]Some evidence for these assertions can be found in a set of studies of innovations in social policy at the local or urban scale; D. V. Donnison, Valerie Chapman et al., *Social Policy and Administration* (London: Allen and Unwin, 1965).

[2]"The Plan for Milton Keynes," vol. 1, pp. 13, 15; Milton Keynes Development Corporation, 1970.

[3]See John Delafons, *Land-Use Controls in the United States* (Boston, Mass.: MIT Press, 1969), particularly chapter 5; and Bernard H. Siegan, "The Houston Solution: The Case for Removing Public Land-Use Controls," *Land-Use Controls Quarterly* 4 (Summer 1970).

Social Issues [II]

David Donnison

GROWTH AND DISTRIBUTION: THE CENTRAL THEMES

In this and many other countries debates about social questions deal almost obsessively with two themes: the growth and the distribution of resources. After the post-war years of reform and reconstruction and their first glimpse of affluence in the 1950's, the British came to realize how slow was their rate of economic growth by comparison with other countries', and how destructive were their recurring economic setbacks. Growth has since become so continuous a theme of political and academic debate that to document it would be superfluous. (I do not thereby imply that we are willing to do much about it.)

The second, more diverse, set of concerns arises partly from growing public recognition of the government's powers to regulate the distribution of rewards and opportunities, partly from pressures to raise minimum standards in education, health, housing and other fields, and partly from more general egalitarian demands. Education is a classic field in which to observe this trend. In 1938 the Spens Committee was dourly determinist: "Intellectual development during childhood appears to progress as if it were governed by a single, central factor, usually known as 'general intelligence,' which may be broadly descibed as innate all-round intellectual ability."[1] In

---

From David Donnison, "Ideologies and Policies," *Journal of Social Policy* vol. 1 no. 2 (1972):107–110. Footnotes have been renumbered and placed at the end.

Much of this section has already been printed in *The Three Banks Review* (no. 88, Dec. 1970, pp. 3–23), where some further discussion of its themes may be found. It is repeated here at the invitation of the editor of this journal and with the kind permission of the editors of *The Three Banks Review*.

1959 the Crowther Committee was cautiously hopeful: "It may well be that there is a pool of ability that imposes an upper limit on what can be done by education at any given time. But. . .the limit has not been reached. . . ."[2] In 1963 the Newsom Committee was confident: "Intellectual talent is not a fixed quantity with which we have to work but a variable that can be modified by social policy and educational approaches. . . ."[3] But for the Public Schools Commission in 1970 the question had changed. Whatever the human capacities available, ". . .our whole educational endeavour must be to get more and more children to take their education to a point that enables them to go on learning and adapting throughout their lives."[4] In the housing field similar things are happening.[5]

These are not the only problems we debate, but many of the others—unemployment, inflation, pollution, going into Europe. . .—are so entangled with the questions of growth and distribution that they can almost be treated as special aspects of them. In the rest of this paper I want to discuss the relationship between these two themes.

Growth, like motherhood, is something nearly everyone approves—provided neither interferes too much with our private lives—but it is much harder to find where people stand on distribution. Since inequalities persist in every corner of society most of us must approve, or at least tolerate, inequality. But it would no longer be polite to say so. Our Victorian forebears delighted in debating great moral issues of that sort, but in this more prudish age even the most resolute defenders of hierarchy feel compelled to assume an egalitarian guise: they argue, for example, that the direct grant grammar schools should be preserved because they "offer a valuable opportunity to clever boys and girls from poor or culturally deprived homes"[6]—despite the fact that the same publication clearly shows that poor children are almost wholly excluded from these schools.

The Conventional Wisdom

Politicians, whose job it is to unite even the most unlikely supporters, are not good at clarifying divisive issues. On this subject, therefore, it is no good consulting their manifestoes. But in society at large two contrasting standpoints can be approximately identified. The first, which might be called the standpoint of the tough-minded, economically oriented Right, goes something like this:

1. When policies are to be decided, top priority should normally be given to economic growth.
2. Economic growth means growth in the goods and services produced by private enterprise.

3. The fruits of growth should reach people in the form of money because it is healthier, both for the individual and for the country, if people buy what they want rather than getting things free though the social services.
4. To succour the casualties growth leaves in its wake there must be some redistribution of incomes. This is brought about through the social services which confer most of their benefits on poorer people, at the cost of taxes levied mainly on richer people.
5. So far as the poor are concerned, our aim must be to raise their living standards to an adequate minimum from which they should be encouraged to make further advances by their own efforts.
6. The growth of the social services must wait on the growth of the private sector of the economy for it is only from the surplus generated in this sector the resources for their expansion can be found.
7. Greater equality of incomes may be morally desirable, but it tends to be economically self-defeating because it is inflationary (the poor having low marginal propensities to save) and because it penalizes the most productive, rewards the idle and thus frustrates growth itself.
8. The success or failure of individuals is largely due to their psychological inheritance, cultivated by will and character. It is thus impossible to create a much more equal society than the one we now have.

The standpoint of the tender-minded, socially oriented Left goes somewhat as follows:

1. When policies are to be decided, top priority should normally be given to the equalization of incomes and living standards. That should be achieved by raising the standards of the poorest.
2. Equality is valued for essentially moral reasons: the more equal we become, the more civilized and compassionate will be our relationships with our fellow citizens.
3. Poverty does not mean failure to attain a fixed minimum, but exclusion from the continually rising standards of the country's middle income groups. Thus the problem of poverty can only be resolved by movement towards greater equality of rewards and living conditions.
4. The main instruments for redistribution are the social services (here the tender-minded broadly agree with the fourth point in the tough-minded set of propositions).
5. Economic growth, which is valuable if it enables the country to move towards greater equality, consists partly of the growth of the social services.
6. It is healthier, both for the individual and for the country, to distribute many of the basic essentials of life according to need and preferably without payment, rather than through the market.

7. The success or failure of individuals is largely due to environmental influences, many of which society is capable of modifying.

In real life, people do not divide as neatly as these formulae suggest. At least three different dimensions of attitude are involved—from tough to tender-minded, from economically to socially oriented, and from Right to Left—and the correlations between them are not very high. Nevertheless patterns of belief much like these go far to shape British discussions of growth and distributional questions. And that is alarming because so much in both sets of propositions is false.

Some social services confer most of their benefits on poorer people, but many do not; indeed, some of the most expensive of them—the education and health services for instance—were never intended to. The taxes which finance them are not levied mainly on richer people;[7] all forms of taxation together take remarkably similar proportions of the incomes of rich and poor. The social services are not merely parasitic upon the private sector of the economy; some of them furnish an important part of the national income, some instigate growth in the private sector, and some are an essential part of the social infrastructure required for a thriving economy. A more equal distribution of income and wealth does not necessarily frustrate economic growth; it is in the wealthiest and most highly industrialized countries that the pre-tax distributions of earnings tend to be most equal.[8] The wealthier countries also tend to spend the largest proportions of their national incomes on social services.[9] The big steps towards equalization of incomes, wealth and living standards have generally been taken in wartime, without disrupting economies which were then working at full blast. Many of the centrally planned East European economies, along with others describing themselves as socialist, have moved a good deal further towards equalization than the market economies. Their rates of economic growth—sometimes dramatic (as in Yugoslavia and the Soviet Union), sometimes disastrous (as in Cuba and Burma)—appear to depend not at all on the distribution of personal incomes; more important are their rates of investment in productive equipment and in education.[10]

Notes

[1]Secondary Education with Special Reference to Grammar Schools and Technical High Schools (the Spens Report) (London: HMSO, 1938), p. 185.
[2]15 to 18 (the Crowther Report) (London: HMSO, 1959), p. 206.
[3]Half our Future (the Newsom Report) (London: HMSO, 1963), p. 6.
[4]Second Report of the Public Schools Commission (London: HMSO, 1970), p. 109.
[5]First Report of the Working Party on "Homelessness in London," Dept. of Health and Social Security, May 1971, p. 10.
[6]Second Report of the Public Schools Commission, Points of Disagreement, vol. 1, p. 120 (London: HMSO, 1970).

[7]See The Incidence of Taxes and Social Service Benefits in 1969, *Economic Trends,* no. 208, February 1971 (London: HMSO). Alan Peacock and Robin Shannon ("The Welfare State and the Redistribution of Income," *Westminster Bank Review,* August 1968) argue that the evidence does not justify so simple a conclusion, but give no support to the conventional assumptions outlined in my text.

[8]See Harold Lydall, *The Structure of Earnings* (Oxford: 1968).

[9]See J. Frederic Dewhurst et al., *Europe's Needs and Resources* (London: Macmillan, 1961).

[10]Sir Arthur Lewis, "Socialism and Economic Growth," The London School of Economics and Political Science, 1971 p. 15.

9 Health Policy Making: The Fundamental Issues

The policy issues which have begun to present themselves are:

1. How can health policy contribute to a better social order?
2. What impersonal or general programmes of services should be developed as a matter of right through regulation and redistribution for groups in a particular society needing health care and for specific at-risk groups needing particular help, such as the disabled? How can these programmes be delivered without differentiating between claimants with similar needs? How can these be directed to those in need rather than those who demand them or who are more interesting to the suppliers of service?
3. To what extent can personalized services by health professionals continue to be delivered as a matter of professional caring and as a matter of individual justice?
4. What relationship should public programmes have with the existing privately developed institutions, programmes and personnel in the system of care?
5. How can individual consumers be made more self-reliant, less dependent on medical services for all kinds of counselling?
6. How best can prerogatives or rights be distributed among health service providers?

Defining Health

In deciding what are the fundamental issues, the definition of health is all important. If health is defined, as it is by the World Health Organization, as a complete state of physical, mental and social well-being and not merely the absence of disease or disability, then this concept takes the policy maker into broad realms of economic and social policy making—into examining questions about the ordering of society. Questions of individual physical well-being are determined (as McKeown (1975) and the Lalonde Report (Canada, 1974) pointed out) by life style, environment and biological factors. Questions of mental well-being are a matter of personal adjustment, but some psychiatrists have asked adjustment to what? Is there a myth of mental illness because it is socially defined? (Szasz, 1961). Questions of social well-being are certainly socially defined by communities which develop their own social contracts, their own patterns of relationships and norms of behaviour.

McKeown has provided a summary of the factors which have been important for promoting community health since mankind established itself upon earth: changes in reproductive practices (including the ending of infanticide); the prevention of starvation and the improvement of nutrition; the control of infectious diseases and of other physical hazards of the environment. It will be noted that he has not included the development of medical technology in its modern form and that, in his discussion, he minimizes the effects of biological malfunctioning in a society.

It is, of course, much easier to measure disease than health and to try to correct medical deficiencies. There have been established, through biomedical science, clear concepts of biological malfunctioning. But if we have clear ideas about biological malfunctioning we are not so clear about the concept of social malfunctioning. Since nations are normative forms of social organization, individuals' deviance from the norms may signal positive developments for society as well as negative ones, especially since western societies are continually questioning whether some of the established norms need to be reconsidered. As well, the physical and social environments to which individuals are exposed may need to be challenged. They may cause physical damage and psychological stress.

Nations are interested in the physical, mental and social well-being of their citizens because their citizens are the nation. But how greatly should governments be concerned to intervene to promote health? Are some citizens to be given more health resources than others through government intervention because they are more valuable to the nation? Or because they can exert more pressure on society? Or because they are vulnerable? Or should health be left to the individual's responsibility?

Wildavsky (1977) has commented on the displacement from health objectives in American society to other social objectives—first to health care and then to access to health care. Others have questioned why so much emphasis has come to be placed upon the development of medical technology. And others, why it was necessary for Lalonde to restate the Health Field Concept to remind Canada in 1974 (and other countries which were watching) that health policy is about far more than medical services.

Health: End or Means?

Individual Decisions

Health may be regarded as an end in itself or a means to an end both by individuals and by society. When individuals regard health as an end, they do pay attention to life style, and, as McKeown has suggested, try to relate their lives in a modern society to mankind's long history of hunting and gathering—eating and drinking moderately and taking enough exercise to keep fit.

Individuals who want to be healthy in order to live the lives they choose often regard health as a means, but they may not choose a healthy life style if it conflicts with their chosen pattern of daily living. They may seek repairs in case of breakdown rather than doing preventive maintenance. Societies have condoned this choice because the reasons for contracting particular diseases are still being explored. Causes of disease cannot all be easily linked to unhealthy lifestyles or environments although steady progress is being made in doing so. Similarly, the ethic of caring for the sick is so well established that the principle of withholding help from anyone, however blameworthy, is not well tolerated.

Society's Decisions

When society regards health as an end, the nation takes steps to consider its health promotion and illness prevention policies and its environmental conservation and development policies. As Titmuss (1950) pointed out, reviews of national health policies tend to come in the aftermath of war, depressions or other crises when a nation as an entity feels under attack, when its solidarity is visibly important to it. But western liberal democratic societies tend to act only as completely solidary organizations when exposed to external threats of war or internal threats of large scale economic disaster, otherwise they are more likely to behave as a series of groups or individuals making their own choices.

Promoting the health of citizens has certainly been regarded as a means by national governments, which, from time to time, have developed social policies to promote health of groups important to defence (members of the armed forces), or production (industrial workers) or population replacement (mothers and children).

Privileged Groups' Decisions

A number of American sociologists or writers on health care, fired by the inefficiencies of the U.S. system, have identified various privileged groups as the decision makers. McKinlay (1977) has discussed the domination of the capitalist health industry, Freidson (1970), the dominant medical profession. Klein (1974) has argued in favour of an intellectual elite who are interested enough to be concerned about the future of the British health service. Perhaps these groups are less interested in health than health care provision. Obviously the American groups are concerned with health as a means, whilst the elite British decision makers have been struggling to promote health as an end (Holland and Gilderdale, 1977).

Health, Health Care or the Preservation of Life?

In discussing displacement of objectives, Wildavsky remarked on the demand for access to health care, but this is the means to the end of preserving life through technological intervention.

The prizing of life itself, however poor its quality, rather than healthy living, is not a new problem for individuals, but it is a new problem for nations. They are not quite sure what health policies they should adopt. In the past they were struggling with basic health problems of early mortality, starvation, infection control. Now that McKeown has claimed that these problems are nearly solved, where should they go? The problems of health as an end are those of lack of quality of life or morbidity, the costs of health care and the allocation and rationing of scarce resources—who shall be treated? Who shall live? Who shall do the treating—individuals themselves taking more responsibility or health professionals?

As Crossman (1972) pointed out, voters are vague about what health policies they want, governments are not given clear instructions about what they are expected to do. And the interest intermediary groups move into the negotiations. How it all works out depends upon the strength of the ideologies of each of the negotiating groups, whether they have clear plans of action and how willing they are to trade off at the time of decision making.

In an attempt to bring more rationality into this situation, the supporters of the Social Indicators movement have attempted to measure how quality of life is experienced (Bauer, 1966; Abrams, 1972) as well as measuring social trends in demography, economic status, etc. However, it is clear that the concepts of individual, group and social well-being are not well understood or well shared, and that interpretations have varied since the Protestant ethic was introduced into western societies.

The Changing Context of Social Well-Being

We have attempted to explore the social policy issues which have emerged in four English-speaking liberal democratic societies in the last three centuries. With the more rapid development of resources after the rise of capitalism, these societies were gradually able to move out of subsistence living into affluence. However, this change was not brought about without great social stress. Whilst it is accepted that societies must change and develop, what seems to be of the greatest importance to all but dedicated revolutionaries is the preservation of the social order—evolution from the situation now into a better form of social organization, a renegotiated order. The methods of making change which have evolved in western democracies are designed to legitimate new ideas and to find feasible means of bringing them into operation. Thus new values are promoted and negotiated into the system and new structures and processes emerge to give substance to these new values.

As we have seen, the value "social well-being" is not an absolute but a relative matter; each society has to try to balance the components in its national armoury of resources to the best advantage of its citizens. In a negotiated order, societies have to proceed from earlier positions by slow degrees to make changes and so there are clear differences between the four countries of the study in their development of the concept of liberalism, which has been the dominant political ideology in all of them.

Reestablishing Social Reciprocities in Mass Societies

In simpler rural societies the social reciprocities were relatively clear. In the feudal system the lord protected his men and their families in return for their service and, when the feudal system broke down, the traditions continued. When reciprocities could not be worked out on a voluntary philanthropic or mutual aid basis, there was the common law to fall back on. It is still used to settle the majority of non-negotiable disputes in English-speaking societies. With the development of the common law, citizens were given some protection against unjust treatment by the ruling class—no arbitrary imprisonment, or other undue punishment—and protection against others' torts. Lowi's (1964) division of government activities into distributive, regulative and redistributive provides a helpful frame of inference for understanding the direction of change since the seventeenth century. The men who took power and governed in earlier times were concerned about distributing wealth to those who could give them reciprocal services. Later the liberals wanted regulative power to be exerted by government, for authority to be delegated to particular groups to carry out tasks for society. Government was to be the body which held the ring but did not interfere with business and professional activities carried out according to the regulations. Finally, the redistribution of resources was essentially a socialist idea. However, this idea has often been borrowed by the liberals when they have felt it to be necessary to meet challenges to the social order from the poor and discontented. Liberalism is pragmatic, it is about strategies, said Marchak (1975).

Britain has had to clear away more of its European heritage of monarchy and nobility, but it has also been more affected by European socialist ideas and by European wars. The other three countries seem to have retained a greater faith in liberalism. They had different experiences of colonization, of industrialization and the melting pots of immigration. As well, they have more natural resources still to be exploited. And the great distances between communities resulted in the setting up of different patterns of social reciprocity from those of the old country—patterns now breaking down as they too have become mass societies.

The reestablishment of social reciprocities in mass societies is a matter of reconsidering social justice. What rights should be guaranteed? What differences in social statuses are acceptable or unacceptable? Traditionalists, liberals and socialists have different views of what is right and proper, but all accept that social change should be negotiated. As their experiences differed, so each country made different choices in economic and social policy and developed different interpretations of social justice.

The Development of Health Policies

The foundations of the health policies of the four countries were laid down in the period 1840–1940 before the explosion of medical technology. All were concerned with infection control through a public health service, control of violent individuals who were mentally disordered, regulation of charities and provision for the sick poor who could not get other help, and regulation of the medical profession.

However, as Abel-Smith (see Chap. 3) has shown, the services which were developed in the U.S.A. and Britain were quite different in their approaches, for the British health services have evolved out of charity, Poor Law provision and the scientific training of doctors; whilst the American health services were initially aimed at the middle classes who were expected to pay for what they got. From the early nineteenth century, then, these services had different targets and although, on the surface, the structures may look fairly similar now, they have come through different routes to that point of similarity.

Public Health Policies

Britain pioneered the development of a public health service in the second half of the nineteenth century which, from the start, had two concerns—the first, infection control through improving sewage systems, water supplies and other environmental hazards, and the second, the behaviour of the poor who had no conception of how to manage their lives in a healthy manner.

The other countries used this model, too, but the U.S. and Australia did not develop it as far as the British, who, influenced by rival European states, built upon the pioneers' foundations in the early twentieth century to remedy weaknesses in working men's health identified during the Boer War. They used the structures of the public health service to bring health education to high-risk groups of working class people and to identify those in need of referral for treatment of disease.

It was during the Second World War that the public health service was extended to all social classes, for they seemed to be exposed to the same health problems and accepting the same risks in times of food rationing, bombing, etc.

Whilst the other three countries adopted the sanitarians and the first model of health education of the poor, Canada also adopted this second model of universal promotion of health and developed a strong public health service (Canada, 1966).

Mental Health Services

The mental health services show similarities in development in all four countries. Again, Britain, as the old country, pioneered many of the changes.

On the one hand changes tended to follow improvements in labelling. The development of a taxonomy of mental disorder was a long slow process culminating in reenactment of legislation to reclassify labels in most jurisdictions around 1960. The classification process was, in part, concerned with distinguishing organic from functional features of mental disorder, and there were many improvements in organic diagnosis. Scientists' work on inheritance, on intelligence and on disease processes led to much greater precision in categorizing patients. So far as functional diagnosis was concerned, in the mid-nineteenth century the distinction between responsible and irresponsible behavior was explored—what was a crime or a mental disturbance? And in the mid-twentieth century the distinction between a crime, a mental disturbance and a sin were considered when prostitution and homosexuality were examined as matters for social policy reconsideration.

On the other hand, changes followed the reorganization of institutions. There was a development in attitudes to the caring for or treatment of patients. From incarceration in Bedlam or its equivalent snake pits, there were moves in the second half of the nineteenth century towards moral treatment or kindly custodial care and employment within closed institutions, and later towards outpatient care and voluntary admissions in the 1930s. The retarded were also regrouped and new training programs developed. Forensic psychiatry was reviewed.

By the end of World War II, psychiatry was becoming well established as a specialty and with the advent of the new tranquillizer drug therapies in the 1950s, this group of physicians felt able to offer their services to transform mental hospitals from custodial to treatment institutions and to move many patients back into their communities.

Different countries have accepted the same general changes, but have developed different programs for each of these groups depending on their general approach to social policy and their attitudes to deviants. References are given in the bibliography.

Medical Education

With the advent of scientific medicine, which paralleled the economic and social developments of the protestant era, doctors began to want workshops in which to practice their skills. In Britain they found these in the charity institutions which promoted custodial care for the sick poor. The leaders of the scientific movement set up as teachers and enrolled students who walked the wards behind them. This was a very different pattern of teaching from that of the rest of Europe where professors taught in their classrooms and patients were seldom seen.

British standards were known to be high. The custodial charity hospitals were first changed into treatment hospitals for working people and, later, for the middle classes, as the doctors learnt how to control infection and cure morbid conditions (Abel-Smith, 1964).

In America, at first, the standards of the medical schools were variable and, in many cases, dubious, so that ultimately an investigation was called for and a report published by Flexner in 1910. American and Canadian medical schools started thereafter exhibited differences in their behavior. Funkenstein (1969) suggested that they tried to respond more to public concerns of the day, namely: better training of practitioners (1910–1935), better training of specialists (1935–1969) and more concern for community medicine (1969–). To a large extent founders' intentions have persisted in each school because new members of faculty are chosen by current faculty who tend to perpetuate their kind. The first orientation after Flexner (better training of general practitioners) incremented into the second (better training of specialists) and it is only the very newest schools which have been trying to make a break with the past which look at health rather than medical care.

In Britain, the nineteenth-century traditions were continued until 1968 (with some minor adjustments). A Royal Commission on Medical Education then suggested some changes in selection methods, curriculum design and continuing education.

The organization of the medical profession in Britain had separated the specialists who practised in teaching and municipal hospitals from the general practitioners who practised out of their own homes after they had finished training. Some of these had access to cottage hospitals in rural areas, but these were in the minority (Stevens, 1966). Thus the explosion of medical technology after World War II had a different impact on practising British and American doctors, for the British general practitioners were isolated from the centres of development. The Royal Commission deplored the separation of specialists and general practitioners in Britain and the exclusion of the latter from continuing education in advances of medical technology.

In Australia, where the medical schools had been modelled on the British, some changes were also introduced in the seventies.

The Hospitals

Because of the reputation which they had gained as centres of medical expertise, the middle classes strongly demanded treatment in established British hospitals. Private hospitals and nursing homes never really got off the ground before the government took over the hospitals in 1948.

The American medical profession had, from the start, aimed its services at the middle classes as an entrepreneurial activity (Stevens, 1971). Unlike the British hospitals which have now been taken over by the government, the American hospitals have many different sponsors—private enterprise groups of doctors or businessman or both, consumer groups, religious organizations, educational authorities, or, as a gap filling measure, governments.

It is customary for all American practitioners to seek hospital privileges and to use the hospital as their centre of professional activity; thus, they are all caught up in the development of new medical technology in a way that the British general practitioners have not been. There are, of course, advantages and disadvantages for both. American critics have pointed to the increase in iatrogenic disease caused by unfortunate and possibly unnecessary medical treatments since medical technology has advanced.

In Canada, the hospitals have been developed mainly since 1949 when a federal-provincial cost-sharing construction program was initiated. The early hospitals in the large cities of the east were usually charitable organizations; elsewhere the municipalities moved in to make provision. But there was a small scattered population in the country up till the end of the Second World War (1867, 3 million, 1941, 11 million, 1961, 22 million). One province, Saskatchewan, pioneered hospital development as a joint municipal activity from 1916 onwards and the Catholic church provided care in most of the larger centres of population and in the mission stations. Other churches also provided care to indigenous peoples (Agnew, 1974). The Canadians pride themselves on their community hospitals which do not discriminate against those on welfare. As in the U.S.A., doctors sought hospital privileges and used the hospitals as their centres of communication, but money shortages prevented the development of advanced technology to the same levels except in a few university centres.

In Australia, the model adopted for hospital development was the British charity hospital subsidized by governments from early on, and the history of Australian hospitals chronicles similar struggles by the doctors to change them into professionally controlled workshops. In the twentieth century the Australian States have developed a comprehensive if unevenly distributed hospital and specialist service. In order to bring greater rationality into the distribution of services, some States have established Health Commissions but, as in Canada, the hospitals have delegated authority and carry out their own policies within budgetary constraints.

Regulation of Charities

By the mid-nineteenth century there began to develop some concern about the administration of charities in England. Who was tapping these resources? Were they the proper people to be helped? Who was collecting subscriptions? Were they trustworthy? How far should governments intervene to regulate this activity? To fill gaps? To take over responsibility for redistribution in the community?

Much, of course, depended upon the visibility of the poor and the community's interest in their condition as to whether this seemed an important aspect of policy. Different decisions were taken in the different countries.

The role of nongovernmental agencies in the development of social policy has been of great importance in all four countries. One of the issues today is the question of their interrelationship with government. See chapter 13 for a further discussion of this topic.

Regulation of the Medical Profession

The emergence of a new consortium of physicians, surgeons and apothecaries in the early nineteenth century was discussed in chapter 6. In all four countries these new professional groups persuaded the governments to permit them to become self-regulating in the third quarter of the nineteenth century. This enabled them to battle against patronage and to become, in due course, self-controlling organizations setting their own terms. Having attained this status, they have not been anxious to move into the next stage of development outlined by Johnson (1972)—to accept governments as mediators, redistributing resources though they have been less concerned about mediation by capitalists financing the health industry. Yet, at the same time, the development of medical technology has been so rapid and so expensive that, even in the richest country in the world, the U.S.A., strong pressures have developed to bring in governments not just as ring holders and gap fillers (which have been their roles during the self-regulatory period) but as coordinators and integrators of health services.

Integrative Policies

The British Welfare State. In the 1930s an independent review body (PEP, 1937) published a report on gaps in the state supported health care system of England and Wales. This was followed five years later by the postwar reconstruction report (Beveridge, 1942) which advocated *inter alia* the organizing of a national health service in order to improve the social security of the British people. Beveridge proposed the restructuring of social welfare schemes in order to provide a safety net for all who were exposed to social risks, the development of a floor of supportive social services for all who needed them, services both of cash and kind. During the late nineteenth and early twentieth centuries a beginning had been made in providing health and social services to particular groups as the needs to support them were identified. Now it was proposed to make the welfare state services universal (a matter of right) not specific (i.e., a matter of dealing with poverty or, alternatively, high-risk groups). These new social services were to be organized to fit into existing structures (so far as this was possible) and were to be nondiscriminatory. Minor variations in public health programs and welfare services could be made by local government authorities which were required to contribute local tax funds but, in general, national standards were to prevail. The middle classes had to be persuaded to go into this total social security system to make it viable, but they were in strong support of the British National Health Service. It seems that they were afraid that the rising costs of medical technology would prevent them from being able to get care when they needed it at a price they could pay.

There is a long history of social investigation in Britain where researchers began to collect empirical data on living and working conditions of the population following Chadwick's example in the 1830s and 1840s (Finer, 1952). Social statistics began to be published in the early nineteenth century becoming more extensive and detailed as time went on. Interest in social environments has continued to be of intense concern since Chadwick's day, for if individuals were to be expected to adjust to social norms, then it became obvious that more information was needed about the individuals who were expected to adjust, and the norms of society that they were expected to move towards and whether these norms differed between social strata in a community and between different communities. It was known that, as a result of the division of labour and the stratification of society, individual members of society were not exposed to the same environments and behavioural choices with regard to reproductive activity, nutrition and physical hazards, but it could not be proven. The struggle to understand and relate to the problem of poverty that haunted many middle class people continued.

Beveridge proposed that British people should be provided with minimal social security, a baseline of equality of condition. This required government involvement in planning for prevention of environmental stress through provision of social security payments, health care, education, housing and town planning schemes, and employment policies each related to the other and integrated within each sector.

*The Canadian Policy.*The Canadian federal government was strongly influenced by the Beveridge Report and the Burns Report on the American New Deal policies of the 1930s (U.S., 1942). A postwar reconstruction plan for social security, including social insurance (Marsh, 1943) and health insurance (Heagarty, 1943), was commissioned and gradually implemented (Canada Year Book, 1978–9). In 1964 the Royal Commission on Health Services, reviewing the developments, spelt out a Health Charter for Canadians.

> The achievement of the highest possible health standards for all our people must become a primary objective of national policy and a cohesive factor contributing to national unity, involving individual and community responsibilities and actions. This objective can best be achieved through a comprehensive, universal, Health Service Programme for the Canadian people. [P. 11]

Is the Canadian health insurance programme together with the national social security programme, a binding factor in nationalism? It may well be, because Canada needs to have an independent social policy (as it is subject to colonializing treatment in economic policy) and health care is an acceptable social policy for a liberal country to adopt (whereas social welfare is still stigmatized).

Social and health insurance programmes have led to considerable redistribution of wealth across the country through cash benefits for those experiencing need and through business contracts and employment benefits for employees in the health services and social security offices. The contrasts with the U.S. and Australia which are not under such pressures to develop an identifiably different social policy emphasizing national identity are interesting and lead to speculation.

Technological Change

The basic health issues were settled in the four countries in the 1940s with cultural lags in poverty groups, indigenous groups and immigrant groups. Infant and maternal mortality decreased, starvation was prevented and infectious diseases brought under control. As well, progress has been made in meeting the first set of displaced health objectives, namely health care and access to health care, either through government schemes of provision for all citizens or private prepayment schemes backed up by social welfare programs.

Developments in medical technology which prolong life raise new and difficult questions. The equality questions posed about health and more readily dodged by resource development policies are now being posed about the right to life (and the right to death)—far more difficult ethically, (McLachlan, 1972) for it is easier to ignore ill health than mortality.

Whatever may have been the original rationales for developing national health policies—improvement of national strength or providing equal rights for citizens—health services today may be less about national health outcomes than about providing medical care to provide more comfortable and/or longer lives for individual members of a community. Governments which have been mediators in the situation are being faced with new questions, for as medical technology has found the way to prolong life, it has become so expensive that individuals cannot readily afford to pay (Campbell, 1978).

Life Policies or Health Policies?

Crossman spoke about the dilemmas of the British government faced with an insatiable demand for health care. Despite changes of the party in power, British health policies have been quite consistent since they were reviewed in the 1960s. The objective has been to update outmoded institutions and to limit the amount spent on advanced technology, to improve the community care services, to redistribute the budget to those regions in which indicators show that there is more ill health and to decentralize decision making. (Policy statements are listed in the references.) It is recognized that progress will be slow despite major structural reorganization of the NHS in 1973. The reasons for adopting these policies are the commitment to welfare, equality and cost limitations. In the U.S.A. the primary commitment of the society is to liberty rather than to equality, and such commitment to equality as exists is to equality of opportunity rather than equality of condition. Nevertheless, along with other developed countries, the U.S. has set up a social security scheme and has taken a number of categories out of its residual welfare group. Particularly noteworthy is the Medicare program for the elderly, who were finding that escalating costs were ruining themselves and their families, and Medicaid for the indigent (Wilson and Neuhauser, 1976).

The U.S. government has been under pressure for some years to introduce a national health insurance scheme so that those who are not now insured or assisted can be provided for, but what is the rationale for such scheme, overt or covert? Is it for health care or for life care? In the past decade much publicity has been given to Health Maintenance Organizations as the proper model for health service delivery (Easton, 1965; Gumbiner, 1975; U.S.H.E.W., 1978). These are integrated health schemes with a focus on prevention of inpatient admissions. However, most Americans are cared for in more traditional ways.

If we are to believe that Alford's model of planning in New York (1972) holds good for the rest of America, then the picture is one of drifting along from crisis to crisis without any clear direction in policy. He has identified three groups struggling for control—the pluralist or market group, the bureaucratic reform group and the group with institutional or class perspectives. In the 1960s, the last group, which is concerned with greater consumer involvement, made a considerable impact on the federal government, and money was made available for experiments in consumer control of health services. In the 1970s the bureaucratic reform group has made progress because of the apparent need to control costs. However, in general, Americans have not been convinced of the need to end entrepreneurialism in the provision of health services and to make it a matter of government's concern that services should be differently distributed.

Equally, in Australia, the citizens are of a divided mind about what health policies they want. When the federal Labour party has tried to introduce greater equalization policies, the medical profession has resisted and adjustments have been made by succeeding right wing governments such as the modification of the pharmaceutical subsidy scheme in the 1940s and the withdrawal of the Medibank scheme in the 1970s. At the same time, the need for rationalization has been recognized and State governments have been setting up Health Commissions to bring hospital costs under control and to locate unmet need for care. So far they seem to have had little success in stemming the demand for advanced technological equipment or redistributing professional services, but at least problems of unequal distribution have been identified and discussed. There is no consumer movement in Australia so the battling takes place between entrepreneurs and planners who are trying to bring some order into the system, though what should be the rationale, other than cost control, seems to be unclear (Dewdney, 1972).

In Canada, on the other hand, health policy has been used for purposes other than providing health care alone—as a means to national integration, as a key social policy (shown by the quotation from the Royal Commission Report above). Whilst it may have been a successful policy for economic development, thus keeping the country together in the immediate postwar years, it is not likely to be able to resolve the problems of provincial separatism. In the 1970s, after bringing in a series of health insurance programs, the federal government has let go the reins and handed decision making back to the provincial governments. They are busy restructuring their health departments and programs away from the acute care emphasis towards more outpatient care. A series of investigations has established new guidelines for action or has revealed that some actions cannot be taken because of strong resistances. A list of these reports is given in the references (see Canada).

Whilst Canadian governments may be responsible for health services to a much greater extent than the American or even the Australian governments (which control hospital expenditures but do not control the medical insurance programs), their present roles are, in no way, so clear as those of the British government. There is no general commitment to welfare—to equality of condition. It is not certain whether the emphasis is to be on health or life, though Canadian governments have jumped on to the Lalonde bandwagon which emphasizes health as the appropriate policy. Since they are in control of hospital funding, they have been able to restrict the excessive purchasing of advanced technological equipment. And there are ambiguities about the doctors' positions. Are they subsidized entrepreneurs or professionals paid fees by governments? This relationship of doctors to governments has never been clearly spelt out, and, in some provinces, the professional group is presently challenging the government to increase its subsidy payments or risk fight or flight.

Some Unforeseen Difficulties

What Beveridge and the British government of 1946 which enacted the NHS legislation failed to recognize was that by extending welfare state services as a right to all social classes, the demand for professional personal care service would not be equal, nor would the response be equal. Quite apart from any middle class demands for health through choice (paying more for more service) (Lees, 1961)—an open way of discriminating between socioeconomic groups—differential medical care would be provided through the individual collaboration of professional providers with middle-class consumers—a more subtle way of rationing scarce resources. Not only would the minimum or floor level of service be provided, the professional ethic of doing the best for each patient would be used to exert pressure on the state to increase funds so that the country's NHS could be compared with the best in the world. This is fine whilst a service is growing, but when it is being cut back there are some very difficult problems to solve.

The middle classes began to apply the concept of equality of opportunity to this service which was conceived in other terms, namely, equality of condition. And as Hirsch (1976) has shown, the extension of policies of equality of opportunity are likely to result in struggles for positional advantage among those who are most able to seize the opportunities.

Nevertheless as Rein (1976) and others have demonstrated, the NHS did enable the lower socioeconomic groups to get access to health services and use them to improve their health, since even in the postwar period, they were still disadvantaged. Social indicators show that in affluent America, Australia and (until Medical Care was introduced after 1968) Canada, some members of the lower socioeconomic groups have been unable to get access to the basic minimal level of care implied by the concept equality of condition until they had rights to a free service. It is for this reason that pressures continue to be exerted for a national health insurance scheme where it does not exist now.

The Fundamental Issues

From this very superficial review of health services some of the main issues and responses can be identified. As we have seen, if health policy is used as a means rather than an end, quite different issues emerge—issues of national solidarity, productivity, population development at the political level, and issues of liberty, equality, justice at the philosophical level. If health policy is used as an end, other issues emerge—whether health promotion or life preservation should be stressed.

One of the problems faced by all governments is the impact of ideas from other countries and the migration of professional manpower so that no health system is self-contained as a national health system.

The next part of the book will be concerned with structures and processes of policy making, how the general will is expressed and how scientists and technologists affect the issues. As Titmuss (1971) has pointed out in *The Gift Relationship,* interpretations of liberty, equality or justice get built into structures which, in turn, affect the thinking about the direction of future changes.

Discussion of Readings and References

In this chapter many issues raised earlier are reviewed again but from somewhat different angles. What is health? Is health an end in itself or a means to an end? Is this an individual or a social concern?

1. Some new information about the measurement of social well-being may

be gained by reading publications on Social Indicators listed in the bibliography, e.g., Bauer (1966), Gross (1969), Abrams (1972), de Neufville (1975), Andrews (1976). Judith de Neufville's *Social Indicators and Public Policy* is recommended as a useful overview of this approach to fact finding about societies.

2. But what is to be done to take action on this information? The reading from Theodore Marmor's *Politics and Medicare* attached to chapter 3 presents an analytic framework for considering what kinds of factual data are important for policy development, when these data are likely to be reconsidered in relation to existing structures, and when negotiations on implementation will take place.

In *The Gift Relationship,* R. M. Titmuss developed the idea that the institutional structures which had emerged in the different countries were a reflection of their ideologies and policies. In turn, because they existed, they affected the next round in the development of policies. This is recommended reading to supplement Marmor's concept about the effect of structures on limiting policy development.

The great importance of the concept of society as a negotiated order was brought out in chapters 7 and 8 and will not be pursued further here.

3. In this summarizing chapter, only one reading is attached—a part of R. H. S. Crossman's retrospective review of his problems as British Minister of Health and Social Security. In this he has discussed the problem of governments today in deciding where to go next in providing health services.

Rudolf Klein's *Policy Problems and Policy Perceptions in the N. H. S.,* part of which was attached to chapter 3, is concerned with making an objective analysis of the same period and may be contrasted with Crossman's subjective view.

Whilst Crossman was concerned about the confused messages coming from consumers, Klein was attempting to apply middle-range analytic paradigms to increase our understanding of health policy making in the late 1960s and early 1970s in Britain. Like Marmor, Klein was searching for different ways to view issues which might illuminate stages of the process or levels of policy making.

A Politician's View of Health Service Planning

R. H. S. Crossman

. . . Which are we more interested in, prolonging life in desperate cases or enabling healthy people to do their work by removing minor things which go wrong with them before they get serious? At present all the priority is on the first and not the second, and this is because we haven't really faced up to the question, "what is the Health Service for?" If you don't face up to the question and if you leave the consultants in a very powerful position, the Health Service's exclusive object will be to prolong life with more and more expensive medicines and more and more major operations. Because that's in the interest of medicine, that's what medicine is all about. . . . Are we going to plan the Health Services and allocate its scarce resources in money and skilled manpower so that for example, Spina Bifida children may live many years in special hospitals with special care and special nursing? I am not saying that I know the answer to this. I am only saying that until the public can face these problems the decision will be muffled, and hidden. Because of course, it is decided, either a man is given a renal dialysis or he is not. If he's not, he dies. There will always be a shortage so there will always be a choice of those condemned to death, just as there will be a choice between the health preservation services outside and the life preservation services inside. . . .

From Crossman, R. H. S. *A Politician's View of Health Service Planning.* 13th Maurice Bloch Lecture (Glasgow: University of Glasgow, 1972). Reprinted by permission of the Deputy Secretary of the Court.

Part IV

Policies into Practice

10 The General Will

Liberal democratic societies are guided in their decision making by science and the general will, said Marchak (1975), describing liberal ideologies. Before going on to explore scientific inputs, it may now be useful to examine how the general will finds expression in the four countries.

Maintenance and Change

It is usually the general will in liberal democracies that change should take place through evolution not revolution. A flow chart developed by Easton (1974) (fig. 10-1) explained his vision of the inputs, structures, processes and outputs of the political system and its feedback mechanisms. This paradigm was used by Hall et al. (1975) to structure their thinking about British social policy developments. Drawing on case studies of British social policy changes, they suggested that it was important to consider the movement of issues in two stages—the attaining of legitimacy and the organizing of feasibility. For both, support was required.

It was useful, said the authors, to think about different levels of legitimacy and the processes of working through these stages to its attainment.

Levels of Legitimacy

The methods by which new initiatives may be introduced were explored to some extent in chapter 4. Etzioni and Etzioni-Halevy (1973) provided five examples of the way initiatives are introduced—through incrementalism or laissez-faire, through planned change, by socialization, through activities of social movements or by revolutionary change. But this classification does

FIGURE 10–1

A DYNAMIC RESPONSE MODEL OF A POLITICAL SYSTEM

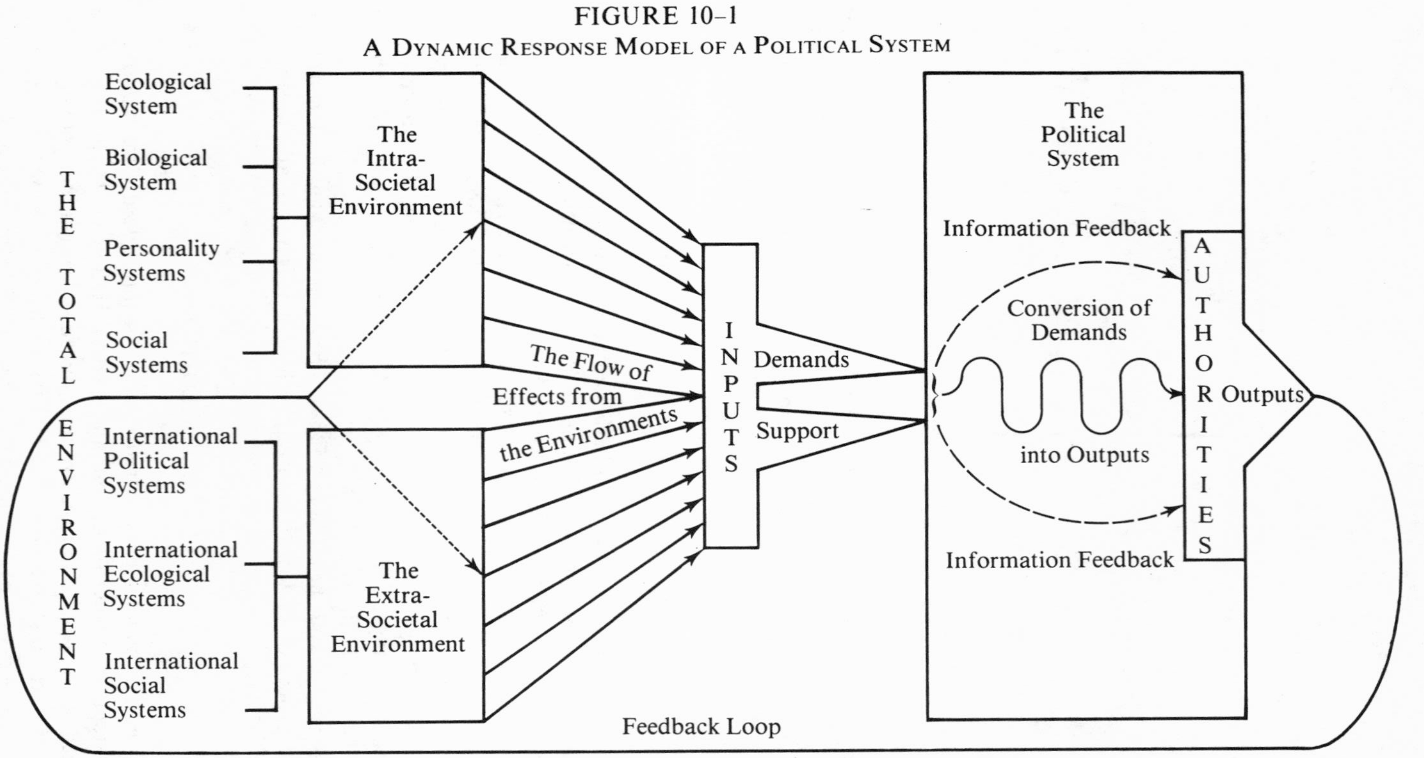

From "A Systems Analysis of Political Life" by D. Easton, New York: John Wiley and Sons 1964. Reprinted by permission of the author.

not distinguish between those climates which are suitable for change and those climates which are not. However, Smith's (1976) analysis indicates that events must form part of a process and a trend.

Support for Value Changes

Because they recognized the importance of climates of change—processes and trends—Hall et al. paid considerable attention to the concept of support for emergent policy issues, for, without support, initiatives will never become events; they will never move through the levels of legitimacy to become accepted policies. The establishment of legitimacy is often quiet and unobtrusive, climates change and new policies are needed and enacted. However, the basic ideological differences in those sectors of the community which are specially interested in health policy developments create many obvious instances of struggles to establish legitimacy of new policies. The twentieth century has seen governments' principal concern move from distributive and regulative policies towards implementing redistributive policies (Lowi, 1964). Redistributive proposals usually pose a threat to established ideologies of regulated entrepreneurialism and so its adherents express resistance.

Schmitter (1977) identified pluralist, corporatist and syndicalist interest groups. Such groups are allowed to pursue their own ends through the general will which is more concerned to preserve this liberty than to impose equality, even in the most convinced welfare state (see Donnison, 1972, chapter 7).

As Lukes (1974) has pointed out, interest groups may prevent new issues from being brought to public notice. And they may try to influence governments or to influence one another to resist changes.

There are many examples of resistance to change by medical professional groups threatened by redistribution policies and their consequences, namely state mediative controls. There were showdowns when the British government introduced National Health Insurance in 1911 (Gilbert, 1966), and when it introduced the National Health Service Act in 1946 (Eckstein, 1960). There were doctors' strikes in Canada when, first, the provincial government of Saskatchewan introduced Medical Care legislation in 1962 (Badgley and Wolfe, 1967; Taylor, 1978) and, later, when the Quebec government brought it into that province (Taylor). There have been continuing challenges in Australia from the medical profession whenever the government has introduced new legislation proposing that it act as third party in any professional payment schemes (Dewdney, 1972; Palmer, 1974). In every case, the profession was resisting a move towards the establishment of welfare state programs. Doctors have taken up the classical liberal position described by Marchak (see chapter 8) in which government is tolerated only as a regulating organization permitting the professionals to provide the services they deem appropriate.

Badgley and Wolfe as well as Taylor each assume that the legitimacy question is settled when legislation has been passed. However, this may not be so. When legislation is passed without working through the consent issues, there may have to be strategic withdrawals from legal commitments which cannot be implemented because of resistances from groups whose support is needed but was not obtained beforehand. The government of Quebec and the Australian federal government have often been more precipitate in legislating than other governments in the four countries. They have not made sure that there is adequate support for their legislative programs to the same degree as other governments. Because Quebec is determined to pursue the ordinary French speaking peoples' interests without further delay from other interest groups, they have, on occasion, had to make strategic retreats. The Hospital Act, 1971, which was passed, together with other health legislation, in an attempt to make a total change in approach to health care as part of the Quiet Revolution, has had to be modified because of the nurses' hostility to its provisions (Blain, 1978).

The Australian Labour Party has never been well prepared to take office when elected. The last health care programs that the Whitlam government enacted after 1972 were conceived by two small groups of intellectuals, rapidly adopted by the party when elected and (understandably) attacked by those groups who had not had time to attack it earlier. The medical profession has forced the Fraser government to reverse the Medibank legislation of its predecessors.

Rhodes (1975), reviewing the work of Royal Commissions and Departmental Committees in England and Wales from 1958–68 found proportionately more committees concerned with examining health service issues than any other matter. This would seem to indicate that there is more negotiation about health care than about other sectors of government activity, more trials of strength about prerogatives and rights at all levels of the system. Certainly, there is more open, more public contention. But whereas in England there has been a willingness to reach compromises, in Australia there has not, at least so far.

Government Involvement as an Issue

As Marchak has pointed out, liberals mistrust government interventions. The first question in any liberal democratic country, then, is: Should this be a matter for government at all? Is not the capitalist system able to provide adequate services through the market?

But some aspects of health care were taken out of the medical marketplace and put under government control over a century ago, and since then there have been consumer pressures (differing from country to country) for gap filling or the assumption of complete responsibility by governments for caring for the health and preserving the lives of citizens.

Evans (1975) has argued that all health care is "Beyond the Medical Marketplace" and that government intervention is necessary. The question, then, is how much? Can the government of a right wing liberal country persuade its health industry to recognize its mediative role? Much depends upon what that role is conceived to be and how the liberty of the service providers is curtailed. For, as discussed above, the legitimacy of government enactments can be undermined by a determined opposition which has veto power.

Feasibility of Introducing New Policies

Health service structures vary in complexity. In some, historically, the only feasible system of facilitating their operation has been to enact government regulations to permit complete delegation to municipalities, charities or private enterprise. In recent years governments have often been asked by the public to move in to take financial control and improve the services, but it has not been easy for them to get consent to do so from the providers. However, in some places, compromises have been worked out whereby practising clinicians who are financed by governments do not have to report directly to government but to some intermediate structural mechanism controlled by peers (or at least a majority of peers). (See Abel-Smith, Chap. 3).

Legitimating Feasibility

Hall et al. argued that it was useful to make the distinction between the attainment of adequate levels of legitimation and determination of feasibility in implementation. But the two are interlinked. Unless all groups who have veto power are involved in the legitimation process, they may decide to undermine the feasibility of the project. There is a process of legitimating the feasibility which is particularly important in the health care field.

The distinction between legitimacy and feasibility clarifies the division between political policy making and administrative policy making. Feasibility is a matter of logistics, of ensuring that structures and processes have been established and funding provided.

Marmor's analysis (1973) of the introduction of Medicare into the U.S. is of interest because he has recounted how the doctors recognized when the legitimacy negotiations were over and the feasibility negotiations had begun. At that point they changed their stance and began a different kind of negotiation (about remuneration). A similar shift in behavior has taken place in Canada whenever a provincial Medical Care Act has passed a certain point in the negotiations.

Powell (1975) noted with some regret that when, as British Minister of Health, he had met with representatives of the doctors' associations, they were unable to act except as negotiators demanding more resources. Their roles seemed to be restricted to dealing with group interest questions and they were unable to explore broader issues of experimentation and organizational development. They had become part of the bureaucratic structure they so disliked, confined within one structured set of relationships.

Discipline or Cooptation?

The Ehrenreichs (1975) have suggested that doctors use the mechanisms of disciplining or coopting their patients when they meet in a service relationship. Since there is strong resistance to any disciplinary control, the only alternative left to governments is to coopt or be coopted.

A classic account of the cooptation process and an exposition of the theory can be found in Selznick's analysis of the introduction of a new program of social development in America in the 1930s: *TVA and the Grass Roots* (1966). Unfortunately, the cooptation of health service providers is more difficult than the cooptation of Tennessee farmers, for the former are very resistant to change and are themselves experts in coopting others.

Service Delivery: Policies into Practice

The importance of attaining open agreements about legitimacy and feasibility can be seen when we come to examine implementation. In redistributing income across a nation it is not unduly difficult to build into the rules specifications for egalitarian, ascribed, universal and impersonal treatment, but in redistributing personal services, the problems are manifold.

Questions like these arise: Are patients entitled to equality of care? If so, what does this mean—equal treatment? Equitable treatment? Equality of access? If an individual wants to earn more and spend his money on health care, should he be denied this privilege? (Or is it his right?)

Can universal impersonal service be provided (such as tends to be given in hospital casualty departments) when doctors are used not only as technicians of medical care but as gatekeepers for society, advisers on normative behaviour, preventers of deviance? Is it sensible to try to provide an equal service when patients' wants are not equal and when services are organized unequally to make the best use of available technology?

As has already been discussed, personal service professionals are not only diagnosticians of technical problems but also of social dislocation; they are also therapists who show society's care for those members who feel the need to drop out of demanding normative roles and/or positions for a while. They can prescribe further diagnostic procedures, counselling or institutional care for therapy or custody in their roles as allocators and rationers of services on behalf of society.

It can readily be seen that if there are ideological differences about legitimacy or great gaps between the concept and the feasible reality of service delivery, then the implementers of policy will feel constrained to deliver services in their idiosyncratic way. Personal service professionals will follow their own conceptions of what should be provided to their clients, they will use their own discretion and their own uncoordinated ideas of justice will prevail, not a universal approach to citizens' rights. This may be of little consequence if there is an adequate minimum amount of service for all and if the concept of building in addition to the idea of equality of condition is accepted. But the controversies about private wing treatment in Britain and elective surgery in North America seem to indicate that resolution of the issue of distribution of professional services is not so easy.

For it is not altogether certain whether the implementers of policy are really aware of the fundamental policy issues. Have the doctors in Canada really faced up to the ideological questions about legitimate authority in the recent Medical Care disputes. Articles in the Toronto Globe and Mail (May 7–9, 1979) would seem to indicate that they are uncertain about their contracts with governments and how they should be interpreted. A Health Services Review '79 was set up to examine these issues. And the growing amount of litigation in the U.S.A. is another demonstration of the gap between profession and clients.

It is not only the medical profession which has to make these decisions about personal service delivery. Parker (1967) discussed the techniques used by social workers to manage their work, methods of rationing which protect the workers but which may create inequalities among client groups. Judge (1978) has made a useful distinction between financial and service rationing.

The social workers' strike of 1978 in Britain was an expression of discontent about the responsibility of adjusting the ideal of complete care to the reality, but the strikers were quite unable to articulate the reasons for their industrial action. Their behavior and others' comments (e.g., *Manchester Guardian*, 1979) indicated the absence of a clear perception that their positions are made up of a whole series of roles which might conflict with one another—the caring roles with the social control roles and the allocation and rationing of services roles.

Similarly, doctors who are expected to care, to do the utmost they can for individual patients—patients who may die—are also expected to share the resources of the health system among all the potential patients of the system. Their own economic self-interest is not necessarily the only reward involved in doing more for individual patients (as some economists would have us believe). Their psychosocial interests—the personal rewards in saving people from death or suffering, and in treating grateful patients, hardly accessible rewards when impersonal decisions are made about bed ratios, preventive care and so on—are also served.

The strains of this position and the ideological defences created to cope with them were discussed in chapter 8 (Blishen, 1969; Geertz, 1964).

Generating General Support for Changes in Policy

It may be useful now to consider how general public support for new policies is generated.

Figure 10–2 is an attempt to show: (a) different levels in policy making from social philosophy to service delivery, and (b) to demonstrate the parallel entrepreneurial and government systems with feedback mechanisms.

Party Politics

Figure 10–3 presents a paradigm of political policy development in a western democracy. It is customary for democratic governments to be formed by political parties who have sought public support for their proposed policies in elections conducted at intervals prescribed in the constitution or by established custom. Thus, the U.S. parties seek a mandate from the voters every two years whilst the parliamentary governments must go to the people not less frequently than every five years and the period is usually much shorter than that.

In order to gain a nomination as a candidate for election, a party member must accept the party's ideology and agree to promote it. But there is usually quite a lot of room for variations in interpretation and the parties of the centre seem to be more pragmatic than those at either end of the spectrum. The different ideologies of the political parties in the four countries were discussed in chapter 8 and references provided for further reading.

Whilst, on the one hand, the party member who becomes a nominated candidate must convince his constituency party that he is ideologically sound, he has usually to start his political career by seeking to be elected in a marginal constituency. To get enough support there he will have to emphasize those aspects of the party's platform which have appeal for the uncommitted voters, and to adopt an easy style which is not threatening to them in putting across his message. But since elections get national coverage, the

FIGURE 10–2
Paradigm Showing Stages in the Process of Translating Social Philosophies into Social Services

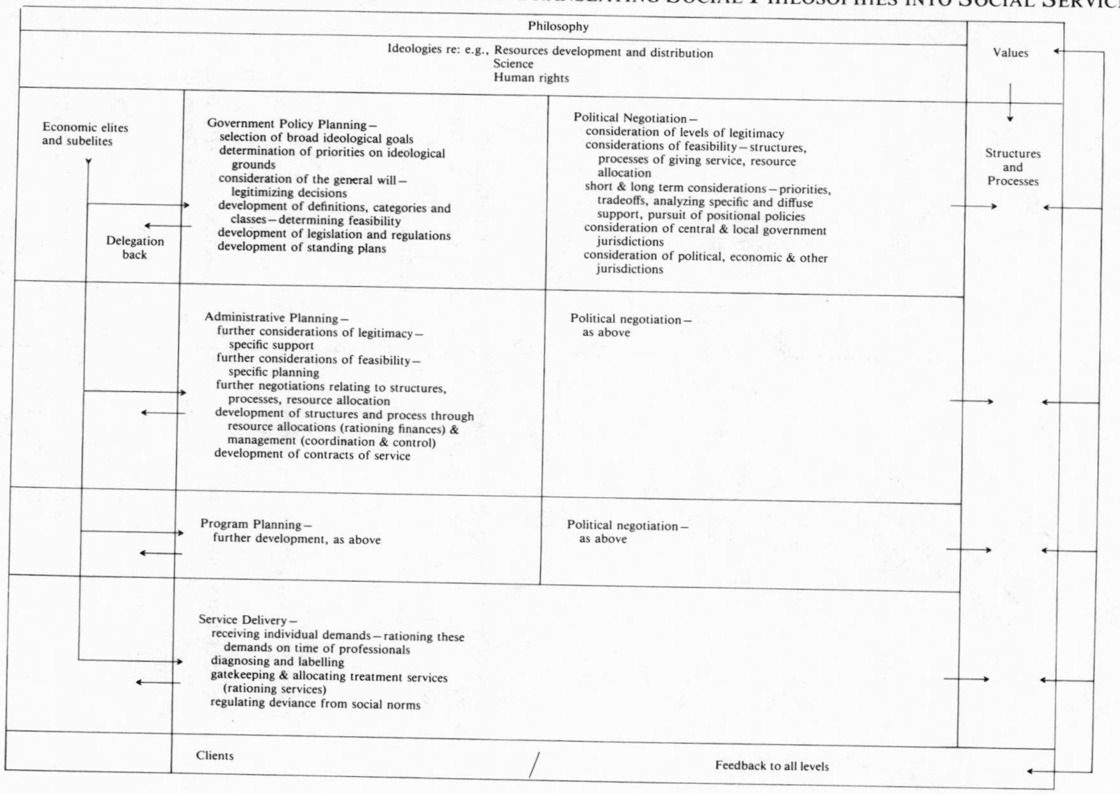

Philosophy

Ideologies re: e.g., Resources development and distribution
Science
Human rights

Values

Economic elites
and subelites

Delegation
back

Government Policy Planning –
selection of broad ideological goals
determination of priorities on ideological grounds
consideration of the general will – legitimizing decisions
development of definitions, categories and classes – determining feasibility
development of legislation and regulations
development of standing plans

Political Negotiation –
consideration of levels of legitimacy
considerations of feasibility – structures, processes of giving service, resource allocation
short & long term considerations – priorities, tradeoffs, analyzing specific and diffuse support, pursuit of positional policies
consideration of central & local government jurisdictions
consideration of political, economic & other jurisdictions

Structures
and
Processes

Administrative Planning –
further considerations of legitimacy – specific support
further considerations of feasibility – specific planning
further negotiations relating to structures, processes, resource allocation
development of structures and process through resource allocations (rationing finances) & management (coordination & control)
development of contracts of service

Political negotiation –
as above

Program Planning –
further development, as above

Political negotiation –
as above

Service Delivery –
receiving individual demands – rationing these demands on time of professionals
diagnosing and labelling
gatekeeping & allocating treatment services (rationing services)
regulating deviance from social norms

Clients

Feedback to all levels

FIGURE 10–3
STAGES IN POLITICAL POLICY DEVELOPMENT IN A DEMOCRACY
(Time is not shown to scale)

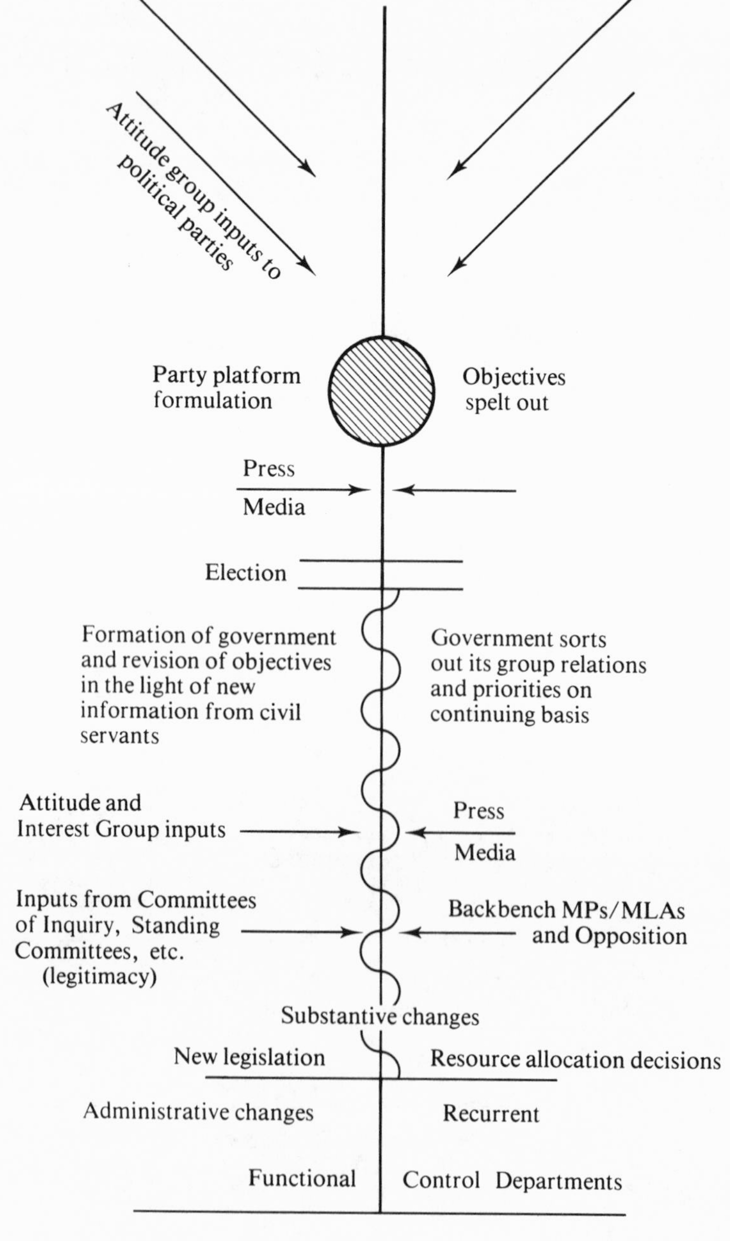

parties, generally, modify their platforms at this time, picking out those planks which have the greatest appeal to the man in the street.

The concept of a party platform is to draw up a list of possible initiatives, set them before party members first and, when somewhat modified, present them to the public at election times. These party platforms are built up from resolutions thrown up at constituency party meetings or thought up by the party executive and organized into a program for the party conference (held annually or in preparation for an election). Socialist parties tend to be much more ardent in discussion than conservatives, to have greater problems in dealing with minor ideological differences. And liberal parties are pragmatic, interested in strategies rather than ideological purity.

Whilst most issues in the sphere of government can be dealt with through the party political organization (which has other mechanisms for dealing with urgent initiatives between elections), there are some social problems which seem to need more thorough investigation than political parties can give them, or which do not fall neatly into political party ideological territories, such as changes in sexual relations, in attitudes to crime and punishment or in use of drugs and alcohol—issues which may require new legislation to legitimate what are now to be regarded as acceptable behaviours and deviations from the normal. But how is a government to know what is tolerable—can be legitimated—before attempting to change legislation?

It can be seen then, that the first process in legitimation of change is to promote wide public discussion of issues and to observe how support is developing. It is necessary for governments to monitor press and other media reports and to act when sufficient support has been engendered. But what is sufficient? Klein (1974a) has argued that the great mass of people do not understand, nor can they be expected to understand, all the details of policy making and what is good timing for the introduction of new policy; consequently, a case can be made out for elite decision making.

Use of the Media

Apart from day to day discussion of policy developments, the media may be used to dramatize incidents. Promotion of scandals is a tactic of some supporters of change. They blow up reports of critical incidents in the hope of creating more awareness of social issues. Thus, in England in the late 1960s, a whole series of incidents of maltreatment of patients in long-stay institutions was reported and built up into a demand for better care in such institutions. (There were similar reports of cases in the eastern U.S. and Canada.) Some action was taken by the Ministry, but not much, said Klein (1974b), because the response was constrained by incrementalism and the Minister's inability to move the rest of the established system to accommodate the new demands.

Committees of Inquiry

A method of discovering what values are currently held in a society is to set up an independent commission of inquiry to examine the evidence and report to the constituency concerned. Such commissions may fail to reach agreement (the LeDain Commission on Non-Medical Use of Drugs in Canada, 1973, was an example of this, where three out of five commissioners wrote minority reports) or, if they reach agreement, the government in power may decide to table the report for some years till public opinion catches up with the commissioners' views (as for the Royal Commission on Marriage and Divorce in Britain in 1912. Legislation followed in 1937). It has also been suggested that the establishment of commissions may be used to defer action by governments under pressure and the use of commissions in the health field certainly seems to bear this out. The Royal Commission on the National Health Service in Britain, 1976–9, has given the government breathing space to try out the reorganization of the service introduced in 1973 (Levitt, 1976). How are commissioners selected to ascertain the general will? This is discussed by a number of writers on Committees of Inquiry (e.g. Rhodes, 1974; Merton, 1975).

Consumer Participation Mechanisms at Grass Roots Level

It may be, however, that the masses are not involved because there is a lack of mechanisms or a lack of suitable mechanisms to encourage their involvement at the point of delivery. Whilst the concept of community hospital boards, acting as trustees for the institution, has been an acceptable and adaptable mechanism in North America (Weeks, 1976), other community health boards have had less success in finding their niche. Considerable efforts were made to develop Community Health Centres with advisory boards or management committees in the decade 1965–75 in the U.S. and Canada, but for various reasons these seem to have been less than successful (Anderson et al., 1976; Wildavsky, 1977; Hastings et al., 1972; Mott et al., 1973). They were constrained by established patterns of health service continuing to exist alongside. The forces of conservatism are strong and it seems to be impossible for consumer groups to make great changes in the health care system largely because of the way in which technological skills are prized and because of the power this gives to the possessors of these skills who are consulted about and expected to give support to proposals for change before they are brought in.

Consumer Advisory Councils for the Health Service, which were set up in Britain from 1973 onwards, and of which little was expected, seem, on the other hand, to be beginning to have greater impact. They are not management bodies but a statutory opposition set up to watch management and offer critical comment (Klein and Lewis, 1976). Further references on consumer participation are cited in chapter 12.

Specific Support and Diffuse Support

Hall et al. discussed issues which have specific support and those which can be carried through by governments on diffuse support when governments have been given authority to govern for a period of time. Much depends on the credit of the government, its decisions on what risks it can take in introducing new legislation or changing resource allocation and what tradeoffs can be negotiated. Thus the Labour government in Britain in 1945, which had a landslide majority, felt strong enough to go through with the welfare state legislation which was quite threatening to many interest intermediary groups. Similarly, the Quebec governments of the 1960s and 1970s are pursuing francophone interests wholeheartedly. Other governments, with less support, have taken the chance, whilst being in office, to bring in legislation which appeals to the mass of people but lacks specific support from interest groups. They are prepared to risk political defeat for a partial achievement of goals, knowing that if their legislation is challenged later, it is unlikely to be nullified completely and partial success may be regarded as being better than no movement forward at all. Thus the 1970s socialist governments of Australia, British Columbia and Manitoba, to take only three examples, have been prepared to introduce legislative changes in health and social welfare for the extension of citizens' rights without having specific support, and, though much of their development work has been undone, some has survived and the level of legitimacy of the issues has been raised considerably (Australian Hospital Commission, 1974–6; Talbot, 1978; Manitoba White Paper, 1972).

There are, of course, daily transactions which occur, in which politicians with diffuse interests exchange specific promises of support with others who need their help to achieve their ends. Political scientists have been interested in studying temporary coalitions between groups for the purposes of bringing about social change.

Discussion of Charts, Readings and References

1. The chart developed by David Easton to explain political systems provides a useful overview.
2. The four countries have developed different political structures and processes over time. It is regarded as important that health policy analysts should thoroughly understand these structures and processes although it is

impossible to discuss them here. A list of readings is attached to this chapter.
3. This chapter has been concerned with the democratic process of discovering and realizing the general will. As has been suggested in earlier chapters, social philosophies are translated into ideologies which are developed into policies. Policies are guidelines for realization of objectives. Vague ideas must be operationalized through legislation, program development, allocation of existing resources or development of new resources.

Figures 10–2 and 10–3 indicate some of the stages in the movement of an issue into the political process beginning with some pressure groups' concern for change. From the adoption of the issue into a party platform, it may move on to become government policy, an administrative plan, a specific program and in due course, available for service delivery.
4. There is only one reading attached to this chapter, that is part of the chapter on "Propositions Emerging" developed by Phoebe Hall and her colleagues from a series of case studies of British social policy. Unfortunately, for reasons of space, the whole chapter could not be included and the second part on issue characteristics which has had to be omitted should be regarded as essential reading.

The propositions which this team of analysts has drawn out of the case studies score an immediate hit with anyone who has worked on policy development. To distinguish legitimacy issues from feasibility issues is of great importance in liberal societies where values are often kept ambiguously vague for the purposes of making political tradeoffs between groups with ideological differences, groups who need to cooperate with one another in order to survive. Failure to distinguish these conflicts in values may not be vitally important at the time of making the tradeoffs, but may have long-term implications for the survival of the partnership and the service provided. Thus in Canada, the Hall Commission (1979–80) is having to sort out the questions left unclear at the time of bringing in Medicare Legislation in 1967. Are the doctors subsidized entrepreneurs or in contract with governments to provide services? This legitimacy issue was never settled when Medicare was introduced because the negotiators avoided that question at that time. It has now surfaced because of the doctors' demand to be allowed to bill patients for additional amounts beyond those from Medicare funds.

Enoch Powell's review of his experience as British Minister of Health in the early 1960s is of interest here because it begins by reviewing the terms of his relationship with the medical profession. He was always anxious to discuss broad health system legitimacy issues, but the doctors who came to meet him as Minister behaved as negotiators interested solely in questions of the feasibility of getting more money. The discussion by Hall et al. of differing levels of legitimacy is also helpful. In the part of the chapter which is not reprinted, they consider what are the factors which may increase the attention given to an issue—association and scope, crises, trend expectation and prevention, origin, information, ideology. This analysis has practical value for the policy maker attempting to understand where particular issues stand in the levels of priority and may suggest ways of raising them to new levels. These emerging propositions are worth careful consideration as a rich source of ideas.

Elsewhere in their book, Hall et al. have examined one particularly relevant case—the development of British health centres. This case was written up using the framework of analysis described in the emerging propositions. It is of interest to see the analytic framework applied to the process of policy development of a new health service structure.

5. It is suggested that some reports of Committees of Inquiry be examined in relation to their timing, their terms of reference, the committees' composition, their recommendations and ultimate outcomes. Questions have been raised about the purposes of these committees for managing legitimacy, feasibility and support problems. Australia, which does not seem to use this mechanism much, has more frequent open clashes between governments and the medical profession. Gerald Rhodes' study of British Committees of Inquiry of the 1960s may suggest why these are important institutions.

Are Committees of Inquiry one method used to coopt interest groups? For further information about the concept of cooptation, read Philip Selznick's introduction and conclusion to his case study, *TVA and the Grass Roots.* In this, he considered the way in which a social policy developed by central government was introduced into the region most affected by it, and how positive attitudes towards its acceptance were developed.

Further References on Policy-Making Structures and Processes

Great Britain

Jenkins, W. I. and Roberts, G. K. *The Policy Perspective*. London: Fontana, 1976.

Brown, R. G. S. *The Administrative Process in Britain*. London: Methuen, 1970.

——. *The Management of Welfare*. London: Fontana, 1975.

Smith, B. and Stanyer, J. *Administering Britain*. London: Fontana, 1976.

Self, P. *Governmental Planning*. London: Fontana, 1976.

United States

Wildavsky, A. *The Presidency*. Boston: Little, Brown and Co., 1969.

Gawthrop, J. F. *Bureaucratic Behavior in the Executive Branch*. New York: Free Press, 1969.

Scheiner, E. V., ed. *Policy Making in American Government*. New York: Basic Books, 1969.

Ripley, Randall B. and Franklin, Grace A., eds. *Policy Making in the Federal Executive Branch*. New York: Free Press, 1975.

White, M. J. et al. *Management and Policy Science in American Government*. Lexington: D.C. Heath, 1975.

Meltsner, Arnold J. *Policy Analysts in the Bureaucracy*. Berkeley: University of California Press, 1976.

Sundquist, J. L. *Making Federalism Work*. Washington, D.C.: Brookings Institution, 1969.

Canada

Doern, G. B. and Aucoin, P. *The Structures of Policy Making in Canada*. Toronto: Macmillan of Canada, 1971.

Kernaghan, W. D. K. *Bureaucracy in Canadian Government*. 2nd ed. Toronto: Methuen, 1973.

White, W. H. and Strick, J. C. *Policy, Politics and the Bureaucracy in Canadian Government*. Don Mills: Science Research Associates, 1970.

Khaulak, O. M. et al., eds. *The Canadian Political Process*. Toronto: Holt, Rinehart and Winston, 1973.

Fox, Paul, ed. *Politics: Canada*. 3rd ed. Tornoto: McGraw-Hill, 1970.

Meekison, Peter, ed. *Canadian Federalism: Myth or Reality*. 2nd ed. Toronto: Methuen, 1971.

Australia

Crisp, L. F. *Australian National Government*. 3rd ed. Hawthorn, Victoria: Longman, 1975.

Mayer, J. and Nelson, H., eds. *Australian Politics: A Third Reader*. Melbourne: Cheshire, 1973.

Spann, R. N. *Public Administration in Australia*. 3rd ed. Canberra: Government Printer, 1973.

Hughes, Colin A. *Readings in Australian Government*. St. Lucia: University of Queensland Press, 1968.

Wilshire, Kenneth W. *Administrative Federalism*. St. Lucia: University of Queensland Press, 1977.

Greenwood, Gordon. *The Future of Australian Federalism*. 2nd ed. St. Lucia: University of Queensland Press, 1976.

Mathews, Russell, ed. *Making Federalism Work*. Canberra: Australian National University, 1976.

Change, Choice and Conflict in Social Policy: Propositions Emerging from Case Studies on Social Policy

Phoebe Hall
Hilary Land
Roy Parker
Adrian Webb

Summary

If we regard an issue[1] as having a natural history[2] then, at any particular time, certain levels of legitimacy, feasibility and support will be ascribed to it by authorities having the power to settle its priority. However, this will rarely be enough to explain its progress to or from that point. In order to account for such movements at least one of three further considerations must be added.

(i) Since many issues with broadly similar claims compete for priority, even when they are well to the fore in our hypothetical queue, progress depends upon *comparative* strengths. A clear example of what we have in mind is the way in which certain issues are set aside at the outbreak of war in preference to others which, in the changed circumstances, take on a special urgency.[3]

(ii) The characteristics of an issue may change, or be believed to have

---

From Phoebe Hall, Hilary Land, Roy Parker and Adrian Webb, *Change, Choice and Conflict in Social Policy* (London: Heinemann, 1975), pp. 507–9 and selections from pp. 476–486 by permission of Heinemann Educational Books, Ltd. and authors. Footnotes have been renumbered and placed at the end.

changed, in ways which enhance or lessen its legitimacy, feasibility or support. It may, for instance, become associated with a new set of other issues. It may reach "crisis proportions" or threaten to do so. It may accord with a refashioned party programme or it may, perhaps, capture the interest of a Minister or a senior civil servant.

(iii) The criteria of legitimacy, feasibility or support are not fixed. Changes in their interpretation will bring changes in the pattern of issue priorities. An ideological shift on the part of the authorities may well alter conceptions of legitimacy. In a similar fashion a change of party in power will alter the relevance of certain kinds of support.

Change in an issue's priority is, therefore, either the outcome of alterations in its comparative strength, in its characteristics, or in the basic criteria against which it is judged. Sometimes it involves a combination of all these things. The aim of partisans is usually to modify the image of the issue in which they have an interest so that it satisfies the three main criteria more or less well. What they actually do depends upon whether they wish to advance or retard its progress. Either way this, and any counter moves by authorities, constitute the tactics of social policy politics. The strategy, on the other hand, seeks to secure shifts (or a firmer consolidation) in what are considered to be the legitimate spheres of government, in how feasibility is assessed and in the broad structure of support.

Our case studies cover certain periods in the natural histories of the issues with which they deal. The stories could begin earlier and could continue beyond the point at which we bring them to a close. Each period does, however, contain a recognizable policy change which needs to be explained. In order to do so it may be helpful to think in terms of the issue obtaining a score on the scales of legitimacy, feasibility and support at the "beginning" and then to ask how this was subsequently improved by the "end." More specifically, it is helpful to consider which of the three component scores was raised in particular and as a result of which changes. Were the criteria redefined? Was the image of the issue recast by changes in its characteristics and, if so, in which ones and how did this happen?

None of our cases involve fundamental redefinitions of the general criteria. The changes they recount are primarily the result of alterations over time in the characteristics of specific issues. It would be hard to say which of the six characteristics that we discussed in the last section was most important. All, in our view, were noteworthy because, once they were seen to change, they began to modify the orientation of influential groups, not least government itself, towards the issues concerned. . . .

The General Criteria

Legitimacy

To determine legitimacy we must ask: is this an issue with which government considers it should be concerned? At the most general level, how this question is answered will reflect assumptions about the proper role and sphere of government action. More specifically it is likely to vary with the ideology of the party in power and with its suppositions about what "public opinion" or important interest groups consider the limits of State action to be. The precise nature of these limitations is rarely clear cut but it is possible and useful to think in terms of prevailing *levels* of legitimacy. At the one extreme there are those issues to which government must traditionally respond if it is to retain credibility; for example, disorder on the streets. At the other end of the scale there are those which do not even get into the hypothetical queue competing for its attention; for instance, the selection of marriage partners.

As our case studies are concerned with identifiable changes in social policy all the issues attained or were ascribed a measure of legitimacy. However, in some of them,. . .there was a comparatively low level of legitimacy early on which was only later improved by other changes. War in particular alters widespread assumptions about the legitimate spheres of government. But part of the tactical skill in strengthening the position of an issue may be in persuading government that it is indeed a legitimate (or more legitimate) candidate for attention. Conversely, of course, those wishing to play down an issue may aim to show that it is not a proper concern of government and hence, in effect, not an issue at all. . . .

The importance of so-called "temporary" measures in times of exceptional circumstances, the initiation of experiments, or the introduction of State intervention in 'special cases' can all contribute important precedents in this matter of legitimacy. . . .

It may also prove difficult to limit State intervention to "special areas or cases when circumstances change in ways which challenge the grounds for distinguishing between the special and the general or which serve to make this distinction an issue in itself. . . .

What is or is not considered to be a legitimate concern of government is not immutable and not everything which is legitimate gains priority. Consequently it is sometimes difficult to be sure when this factor significantly contributes to an explanation of the priority which an issue obtains. It can probably best be recognized when the opposition is conducted as a dispute about the proper limits of government. . . .

Our discussion of the concept of legitimacy should not lead to the conclusion that where it is useful in explaining the progress or retardation of an issue other considerations do not underlie it. All we wish to suggest is that issues with low levels of legitimacy can be more readily opposed or resisted (for whatever reason) and that those where legitimacy is not in question do not have to overcome this particular hurdle. They are, therefore, more firmly placed in our hypothetical queue: indeed, without a modicum of legitimacy they do not enter it. These may be pertinent considerations in certain circumstances. We now discuss what these are.

Earlier we classified the changes with which our case studies were concerned as *initiation* (policies which are new departures); *development* (policies for changing the scale of an activity which already exists); and *reform* (the recasting of policies in existing spheres of involvement). We suggest that questions of legitimacy will be important when the recognition of an issue is likely to require government action in quite new areas or in radically different ways; that is, where the changes fall into our first category above. Furthermore, we suggest that this will be especially the case when the origins of the issue are extra-governmental or when the basis of opposition to it mainly rests upon questions of legitimacy. Usually, when the issue is about administrative reform or the development of existing government responsibilities this factor plays no substantial part. . . .

However, we must note that these propositions may also be applicable to issues involving termination rather than initiation. It is possible that if the present functions of the "welfare state" are increasingly challenged, the question of legitimacy will emerge again in spheres where it has not seriously been contested for several decades. Our case studies do not provide any instances of such situations but there are several contemporary examples which illustrate the point. Changes in policy have occurred which appear to reflect an influential view that the control of certain behaviour and relationships is no longer the legitimate concern of government: the regulation of homosexual behaviour is one. The Wootton committee struggled with another: the smoking of cannabis. It may be, therefore, that levels of legitimacy are a particularly relevant consideration in understanding the introduction or termination of policies which are concerned directly with altering existing patterns of individual freedom or responsibility. This formulation accepts that an issue may gain priority by the *reduction* of its assumed legitimacy, in which case the solution or change will involve the termination of policies rather than their initiation.

Legitimacy is a central and longstanding subject of political philosophy and it arises in all realms of government activity. However, historical accounts of the growth of the "welfare state" are much occupied with the relationship between these developments and the establishment and enlargement of the legitimate role of government. Good reasons for this may be found in the fact that social policies are concerned with more than the regulation of social relationships. The supply of goods and services is also involved, and on an increasingly large scale. Although regulation can only be achieved in most instances through the collective action of the State, welfare goods and services may be (and are) supplied by other systems. There are alternatives—principally the family, the market, employers, and voluntary or philanthropic bodies. It is by no means immediately apparent what, in any particular area of supply, the balance between these systems should be. Unlike matters of defence or foreign policy, in the sphere of the social services the legitimacy of State intervention has had to be established, as it were, against the claims of these other systems.

Feasibility

The concept of feasibility can be elusive. It is, nevertheless, important because the possibility (or the assumed possibility) of taking steps to deal with a problem may well determine its chances of gaining attention. Considerations of feasibility are also likely to influence the choice between several alternative solutions; and hence it can probably help us answer the question of why one remedy is introduced rather than another. There are several different elements in the notion of a "feasible policy" which must be identified.

First, feasibility is, in its broadest sense, determined by the prevailing structure and distribution of theoretical and technical knowledge. Developments in these fields may alter quite radically the possibility of dealing with a problem which was previously considered to be an inevitable or unresolvable state of affairs. But it is important to note that neither the theory nor its application necessarily has to be correct; merely that they are generally believed to be so. There are also areas in which theoretical knowledge outstrips the ability to apply it to practical problems or where it waits upon adequate and convincing validation. As well as these aspects, new theory or growing knowledge may serve to redefine a problem in such a way that certain solutions take on a fresh relevance.

However, the general state of knowledge, understanding or technology only set the boundaries to the concept of feasibility. Our second point is more specific: it is that feasibility is not entirely independent of who does the judging. Particular ideologies, interests, prejudices and information will affect the kinds of conclusions which are drawn about the feasibility of different alternatives. In particular, actors in the policy-making process are likely to assess feasibility differently to the extent that they are aware of and are influenced by different sets of constraints. Thus there may well be several competing views about feasibility; and the progress of a proposal can be affected by how this competition is resolved.

The third noteworthy feature about feasibility is that it is rarely immediately apparent. As we pointed out earlier, much of the work undertaken by the civil service is concerned with assessing the feasibility of various courses of action or inaction. Consequences will be estimated and modifications made. We argued that this was a key phase in the progress of an issue, where considerable regulation was likely to occur. The personal accounts of both Ministers and senior civil servants bear witness to the importance of this "testing for feasibility."[4] Certain aspects tend to reappear in the calculations. Three in particular must be noted. They are: concern about resources, collaboration and administrative capacity.

The feasibility of a particular change in policy (or of continuing a policy unchanged) will be assessed against the resources available and those required (or released) by the change. There are various kinds of resources—money, manpower, parliamentary time, or capital equipment. Let us take the first two as examples. Money is always scarce and different items of public expenditure compete with each other. Therefore, solutions involving less rather than more expenditure will usually commend themselves and those which distribute additional costs in ways which do not concentrate them on the Exchequer will be preferred. In testing financial feasibility, however, the calculation is usually more complicated than this suggests. It is not only a matter of more or less but especially of just how much is involved now and in the future. For example, some solutions are very difficult to cost, whether in terms of the economics they achieve or the extra costs they impose. They may be open-ended either because no accurate figure can be put on the financial implications or because the emerging expenditures are not controllable by central government. To take some specific examples, we may note that the introduction of family allowances could be accurately costed and estimates of the costs in subsequent years could be made with some confidence—at least in the short-term. In any case the control of costs was firmly in the hands of central government from year to year. In contrast, the Open University could not be costed accurately. Once in operation, however, costs were broadly controllable; similarly with health centres. No government is likely to sign what amounts to a blank cheque.

The distribution of the financial costs and benefits is also likely to be pertinent when the feasibility of a scheme is being tested. For example, in the clean air study the cost of introducing control could be, and was, arranged in such a way that it was borne by the local authorities, householders, and industry as well as by the Exchequer. In the case of the health centre developments costs were, to some extent, also spread. But the health centre programme was related to the encouragement of community care and to a shift away from the increasingly expensive hospitals. On balance, therefore, additional expenditure on health centres could be offset against the assumed savings to be made by reducing institutional care.

What financial feasibility actually amounts to is difficult to say. It varies over time, between governments and probably between departments; but the key questions will be about amount, distribution, and longer-term implications. The importance of each of these questions is sharpened by the fact that the radical reallocation of public spending on a massive scale is, at least in the short run, itself unlikely to be judged feasible. Changes in the level and in the pattern of expenditure will occur most often at the margin.

Manpower resources are another aspect of feasibility which is likely to be assessed. Raising the school leaving age, extending the social work services, improving the take-up of supplementary benefits by seeking out potential claimants or opening more detention centres, all require more staff or their transfer from one sector to another. Just as there are limitations upon relocating the fixed capital equipment of the social services, so too there are certain restrictions upon the movement of staff. Questions about the feasibility of recruitment and training are, therefore, likely to be involved and will be especially relevant if government has undertaken, as an election promise for instance, to reduce the number of civil servants. . . .

Certain changes in social policy not only require extra resources but also new patterns of collaboration and new levels of commitment on the part of those individuals and organizations upon whom successful implementation depends. The likelihood of obtaining the right kind and amount of collaboration will form part of the calculation of feasibility. Commonly it is the local authorities that government relies upon for putting new policies into practice. They in their turn may respond to central government proposals on the basis of their own estimations of local feasibility. The health centre study shows the extent to which both central and local government assessed feasibility against the expected and known attitudes of doctors towards working in the centres. Little progress could be made where few general practitioners were willing to participate. . . .

The processes of "sounding out" and of "informal approaches" are part of the exploration which is often needed in order to determine the reactions of vital collaborators in the operation of a new policy.

Tests of administrative feasibility will also be applied to proposals. Can particular schemes be implemented? Does adequate administrative capacity exist, or can it be created? . . . Two kinds of question appear to be involved in estimations of administrative feasibility. First, there are issues about authority. Certain policies may be judged not feasible because they are unenforceable. With hindsight, prohibition in the United States might so have been judged. Second, there are questions about the availability of administrative means. Does a suitable administrative organization exist? Can one be adapted? Will it become overloaded? Is the necessary up-dating, recording, selecting or identifying possible? . . .

We do not suggest that considerations such as these about resources, collaboration, or administrative practicalities are the overriding determinants of whether it is judged feasible to embark upon new or changed social policies. Although some things are not possible before the advent of certain technical developments . . . one suspects that issues rarely emerge until there is at least the *prospect* of practical action. The process of testing for feasibility is more often a testing for the costs of converting those prospects into reality. For example, the prevention of air pollution by cement dust is not possible without an adverse effect upon the output and price of cement, and thus upon the housing programme and the balance of payments. Authorities assess feasibility as they see it and usually within a restricted time span. In the long-run almost anything could become possible (and indeed legitimate) but, typically, feasibility is being considered as between now and, say, the election after next. Or it is bounded by the planning periods to which authorities become accustomed: in universities it would probably be the quinquennium after next.

Support

[Earlier] we introduced the concept of "support" and considered how and why authorities strove to secure its regulation. We argued, following Easton, that "diffuse support" enabled governments to act in ways which were, in any case, damaging to the interests of some individuals, groups or classes. As Gamson explains, in discussing the similar notion of "political trust," when "the supply in the reservoir is high, the authorities are able to make new commitments on the basis of it and, if successful, increase such support even more. When it is low and declining, authorities may find it difficult to meet existing commitments and govern effectively."[5] The concept of diffuse support concerns what, in everyday language, are referred to as the "stock" or the "credit" of a government. It locates the prevailing boundary of tolerable discontent.

None of these concepts can be applied in a precise fashion or set out in a tidy equation but authorities do make assessments of this kind. Questions about the expected acquisition or erosion of support are posed and the answers or uncertainties taken into account in drawing conclusions about political feasibility. Because policy change alters, or is thought to alter, some features of an existing distribution of power, influence, benefits, status or values, inevitably it will create some satisfaction and some discontent. The notion of the political feasibility of an issue is closely connected with its implications for this balance. Two considerations determine how it is estimated by authorities. The first is *whose* discontents and *whose* satisfactions are involved and the second is the general state of the reservoir of support.

The question of whose reactions are involved is answered in both general and specific terms, and we shall discuss each in turn. Measures which attract extensive approval will, obviously, improve a government's stock of general support. Conversely, widely unpopular policies will reduce it. However, the amount of active support or opposition rarely indicates their full extent. Gamson, especially, has pointed out that potential partisans (those who are affected by a policy decision) greatly outnumber the actual partisans who deliberately seek to affect its outcome. The extent of the support enjoyed, or likely to be enjoyed, by different policies cannot readily be assessed except occasionally by such means as opinion polls or referenda, and these are crude and subject to error. The degree of support that alternative governments attract is only practically tested in the elections. Despite all these difficulties estimations are made of the state, or likely reaction, of public opinion to different issues and endeavours are made to modify it. Although what "public" feeling actually is about an issue can rarely be determined empirically, what it is *thought* to be by authorities is more important in the short-term.

In spite of the elusiveness of the notion of public opinion it does serve as a means of applying one test of support. Since all governments must pay some attention to the likely effect of their actions upon general levels of support or acquiescence some such concept is needed. This is not to say that all issues are examined against this yardstick or that only those which are thought not to jeopardize general support gain prominence. But, hypothetically, some kind of ledger has to be kept by government in order that the overall or cumulative effect of many different decisions can be estimated . . . .

Assumptions about the pervasiveness of certain public values and beliefs are moulded by the values and beliefs of those who do the judging, as well as by the sources from which they obtain their information. Furthermore, the attitudes of their significant constituencies are likely to be generalized to the population as a whole.

So far, we have looked at the question of whose satisfactions and discontents enter into the calculus of support only in connection with a broadly conceived public opinion or response. But the sensitivity of an electoral group's support for a project may depend not so much on whether it likes it, or the government, as on the marginality of the issue and the group. Will they change sides at the election—and on this issue? Indeed, the language of electoral analysis includes frequent reference to marginal voters and marginal constituencies.

Electoral support is, of course, rarely the only consideration. Particular sets of interests and interest groups are involved in specific policy proposals or changes. They may include other departments, backbenchers, industrial organizations, the trade unions, local authorities, promotional groups and so on. How much a group's support is assumed to matter will vary with the issue as well as with the general level of support accorded by that group to the relevant authority. How seriously these consequences are regarded will depend upon the extent to which the future or continuing collaboration of the body in question is felt to be necessary in general or for the operation of particular policies. The generalized discontent of groups which control certain key resources will be avoided where possible. The level of a government's standing with such bodies will affect how far it is prepared to antagonize them on any one issue and whether, in turn, they mobilize and exercise their potential influence in Opposition.

Since the case studies are all concerned with actual changes in social policies, they satisfied, as it were, the criterion of support. Nonetheless, as we have already suggested, in some of them an initial absence of progress can be related to assumptions about the implications of action (or inaction) for support. Considerations of general support also appear to influence the kind of solution adopted in response to a particular problem . . .

A shift in the attitude of important partisan groups towards certain issues may alter the support implication of related policy decisions. Evidence about such changes is likely to be influential. In the health centres case the commitment of central government to the development followed the local demonstrations that there were general practitioners willing to collaborate.

At the beginning of this section we maintained that two considerations affected a government's evaluation of the support implications of any courses of action. We have, so far, discussed only one of these; namely, the question of whose discontents and whose satisfactions are involved. The other consideration concerns the assumed general state of a government's support or credit. This will vary over time. It will ebb and flow, be consumed and be replenished. Its particular level and trend will create somewhat different constraints and opportunities. Broadly, issues which authorities feel will affect support adversely are better placed at times when this support is high or rising and weakly placed when it is low or falling. These considerations will apply with especial force when general elections are impending, since only then is this level actually tested . . .

Our contention that the criterion of support is, explicitly or implicitly, applied to all issues in the process of determining their priority should not obscure the fact that issues do advance despite scoring low, or even negatively, on this scale. Capital punishment was abolished; homosexual law reformed and health service charges introduced. In almost all circumstances government finds itself in a position in which its actions have mixed consequences for support. There are some potential gains and some losses: trade-offs are assessed and the effects of cancelling out taken into account. Perhaps we should refer to the net implications for support of a government promoting or ignoring an issue. We should also consider the comparatively short time perspective within which such calculations seem to be made. But in whichever way reference to the support criterion is qualified we contend that it constitutes a permanent and initial hurdle for all issues.

NOTES

[1]No word is entirely satisfactory in describing the variety of claims, bids, proposals, demands, suggestions or exhortations that "something must be done." We have chosen the term "issue" to refer to all these things. It covers demands that particular problems be attended to as well as demands that particular solutions or remedies be applied.

[2]See S. Becker, *Social Problems*, 4th ed. (New York: Wiley and Sons, 1966), pp. 11-23.

[3]The pre-war Criminal Justice Bill is a good example. Having been introduced in 1939, war halted further progress. It was not until 1948 that it was reintroduced.

[4]See, for example, Lord Bridges, "The Treasury as the most Political of Departments," in C. J. Friedrich and S. E. Harris, eds., *Public Policy* 12 (1963).

[5]W.A. Gamson, *Power and Discontent* (New York: Dorsey, 1968), pp. 45–6.

11 Science and Policy Making

Western civilization has sought to increase the rationality of its decision making since the ancient Greek philosophers demonstrated the existence of scientific laws and the power of reasoning. However, as we have seen, mankind is not always rational in its planning for society as a whole. Individuals and groups seek to realize their particular interests resulting in multiple levels of rationality in a society. What may be good for an individual or a group or a neighbourhood may conflict with the interests of society, and whether society or the individual group or neighbourhood interest should prevail is a matter of negotiation between the groups concerned. Yet, despite this "pulling and hauling" as Allison (1969) described it—the recognition that there are different interests and different rationales in social policy making—there are strong pressures to seek scientific answers to policy problems, whether these answers are in the areas of natural or social science, as well as relying upon the general will.

Development of Science Policies

When the Greek legacy was taken over and renewed in the period of the Renaissance, it was not conceived narrowly. The Renaissance Man, typified by Leonardo da Vinci, was interested in arts and sciences, in expressions of emotion and reason. The classical education of elite European men, which developed out of this legacy, was expected to produce a generalist, a well-rounded individual who could see wholes rather than parts, and who could take up the duties of ruling in any society whenever called upon to do so.

This adaptation of the Greek tradition fitted well into the ideology of the mercantilist and developing industrial societies of the eighteenth and nineteenth centuries. This classical education socialized self-reliant leaders who were not afraid of risk taking. Gradually, however, it came to be recognized that a classical education was not quite the same thing as a scientific education. The one kind of education began to diverge from the other, but not quickly.

Science as an Ideology

In the confusions of the eighteenth century, scientific answers seemed to provide better guidance for development than traditional religious or classical ways of thinking. The empirical method of scientific inquiry became well established and distinct from philosophical speculations. As empirical inquiry began to reveal more and more about the universe, so scientific careers began to have more appeal as western societies realized that discoveries in fundamental science were rewarding and that science applied could enable entrepreneurs to uncover and exploit the hidden resources in the world. Science seemed to offer a method of countering the strains of development. It is now an accepted part of western ideology that science can help men to master the world, to climb out of hard, primitive lives into more comfortable existences.

Science and Nationalism

Scientific knowledge became more and more important to competitive societies as the demand for applied science rose, particularly during wars.

It was not until scientists had already devised their own international network of communication and their own international patterns of migration that nations recognized their need to plan their science policies for resource development and for shaping their task and manpower systems. It was not until after the middle of the twentieth century that the four English-speaking nations really began to take stock of their national science policies. A crisis was recognized to exist when, in the early 1950s, American and British nuclear scientists were caught giving away hard won defence secrets to the enemy, Russia. Treason trials of the early fifties revealed the issues at stake—national defence vs. freedom of exchange of scientific information. And the crisis of confidence in free exchange deepened when Russia was first to launch the Sputnik space probe in 1956, for the English-speaking countries had prided themselves on their preeminent scientific ability (thought to be challenged only by the German scientists who were then recovering from the war).

British Problems

The relationship between the physical scientists and the rest of society became a matter of great concern. In Britain, the crisis led to numerous investigations of educational policy. Was there too much emphasis on the traditional classical education, (which had produced effective colonial civil servants in the days of empire but for whom there was now no demand)? Was the German technical education system not a better model for an industrial country without natural resources other than manpower? The top fundamental British scientists were good, none better, but the rest of the task and manpower system, as it was organized in the early 1950s, failed to back them up. How could the British education system be changed in order to increase the supply of fundamental scientists and better technologists, technicians and better craftsmen? How could young people be encouraged to select scientific careers rather than the traditional ones devoted to leadership? How could industry be reorganized to provide scientific opportunities? And after reorganization, how could these scientists be kept in touch with society's other cultural developments in the humanities and the arts so that their loyalties were not only to the scientific world but to their nation of birth or adoption? For to the rest of society the single-minded natural scientists of the period seemed politically naive, lacking in the well-rounded education of the earlier elite groups of citizens whilst holding elite positions in society (Snow, 1959).

As well as thinking about developments in natural sciences, Britain had noted the lack of well-trained social scientists for assisting in postwar reconstruction activities. Funds were made available in 1949 to develop University departments of social science. At first this funding was used to increase the scope of departments training economists and political scientists, and to develop social administrators and social workers for the expanding welfare state, but gradually the need for sociologists and social policy analysts was identified, and more departments employing them were established in the 1960s.

American Problems

In America the task and manpower system had been geared to different objectives, not to colonial administration but to industrial expansion and natural resource exploitation. The need for applied scientists was well recognized and the school system had responded. The growth of interest in science was such that Apter (1964) suggested that America in the 1950s was becoming increasingly discontented. Science was leading to greater recognition of social inequalities, for scientists expected to join the privileged

FIGURE 11-1
THE GAP BETWEEN THOSE WITH SCIENTIFIC TRAINING AND THE REST OF SOCIETY

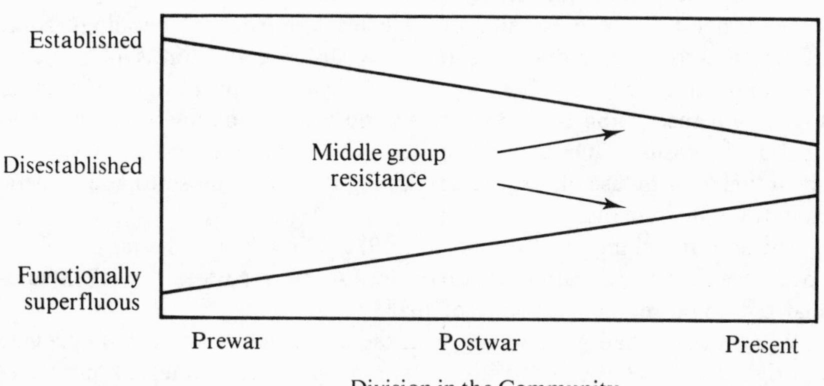

Reprinted with the publishers' permission. From IDEOLOGY AND DISCONTENT, edited by David E. Apter, Published by The Free Press, a division of Macmillan Publishing Co., Inc., New York, 1964, p. 33.

classes. The gap between those with scientific training and those without was now recognized to exist and resented by the have nots.

In addition to a large supply of natural scientists, America had developed more social scientists—economists, political scientists, and sociologists—whose contribution seemed particularly necessary after the depression of the 1930s. Sociology was a popular subject of study because American society was a melting pot and many non-Anglo-Saxon immigrants had been more questioning of their changed social situation than those in the English tradition.

In America, the pace of technological development increased geometrically after World War II. Berliner (1970) noted that American investment in biomedical research had increased by 5000 percent in the previous twenty years. Other research effort was also increased hugely during this period.

By 1969, America had become a questioning society wondering why such great investment in science was failing to bring victory in Vietnam or to solve the country's social problems. Among other expressions of discontent there was some measure of revolt against the ever increasing discoveries of biomedical technology without giving similar attention to their social applications. How far were the discoveries about the rehabilitation of heart, cancer and stroke victims being spread out to the mass of Americans? This was the period when experiments in heart transplant were going on and it was clear that these could never fit a person for return to normal living, nor could transplants be provided for more than the very few. Could science not be used to investigate health care issues rather than increasing such esoteric discoveries? Was the solidarity of society (recognized in response to war) not more important than the saving of a few individual lives?

Other questions were raised about the developments in technology, some of which were explored in chapter 5. What were the limits of resource development which were best for society? Was the juggernaut of technological advance going to destroy the world through competitive wars and nuclear explosions? Or through exhaustion of natural resources such as fossil fuels? Or by use of insecticides, killing the birds and setting up genetic mutations in humans?

The soul searching went on into the 1970s. Now it was the failure of the social sciences which came under review. A *Time* editorial of 1973 summarized some of the questions of that period.

What, in fact, had gone wrong with the belief that science could provide the right answers? Social scientists began to spell out the facts about value-laden applications of natural science (Willer, 1972) and value premises underlying all social science investigations (Rein, 1976).

Development of Science Policies in Canada and Australia

In lieu of the elite informal networks which had existed before, Canada and Australia developed formal national science policies in the 1960s modelled on British and American ones. They recognized the inevitability of internationalism in exchange of ideas and personnel and the predominance of U.S. resources. Like Britain and the U.S.A., they accepted the concept of professional peer review as the mechanism for ensuring innovation in research and the preservation of scientific independence. Yet the necessity of providing government funding was recognized. Whilst independent research was one key issue, the second was how best to link scientific findings into national needs through the commissioning process or the establishment of special agencies; the third was how best to use science for the illumination of answers to social problems.

Communication of Ideas

Although it is regarded as necessary for all children in western democracies to learn about rational thinking and scientific investigation in high school and, for those who proceed to University, there too, this does little to ensure that rational thinking and scientific evidence is applied to all aspects of decision making about society. For as technology has advanced, scientists have had to become more and more specialized, working hard in narrow fields of endeavour. Their problems are not unlike those of the policy makers but are somewhat different. Whilst they are developing their professional expertise they are unlikely to find time to become generalists, to take a broad view of their place in society. Nor do they find it easy to communicate their ideas to others than their peers. Social scientists who are working on societies' problems are accused of concealing their ideas behind jargon.

The problems of communication and political control of science have not been solved as was clearly demonstrated by the Vietnam war, where scientific solutions were applied to means without questioning ends—American society had not communicated about legitimacy to the scientists, only about feasibility. Similarly, the communication by scientists to society continues to be a problem.

To communicate ideas from scientists to others outside their peer group requires another set of motivations and a new range of skills as Lees and Shaw (1974) pointed out in writing up the findings of a conference of British social scientists concerned with studying disabilities. In their opinion the scientists did not even begin to acknowledge that if their findings were to be implemented they would have to be taken into the political arena. It was more comfortable to exchange ideas with other scientists.

Merton (1975) discussed the relationship between social scientists in the arena who had been appointed by Presidential Commissions of Inquiry in the U.S.A. and the members of these commissions. Communication was poor and scientific information did not get through the barriers into the political system.

The scientists who are most successful, politically—those who are able to communicate with their sponsors or with the public, who are able to convince existing funding bodies that they should be supported or get new funding bodies set up to finance them—are often the scientists working on defence and biomedical problems. They have been particularly good at this because they can appeal to the individual's clearly understood feelings of about life and death. Despite all the questionings about the overdevelopment of medical technology which took place in the late 1960s, the biomedical scientists have shown considerable energy and great political success in getting funding maintained or increased all through the 1970s when other research fundings had been cut back more ruthlessly. Fox and Swazey (1974) have described the high-profile biomedical scientists who have been working on organ transplants, and the fascination of their work for the public can clearly be seen.

In 1970, Barry, a political scientist addressing the question of the very limited impact of the social sciences on politics reviewed the work of those he deemed to be leaders in the field of economic and sociological theory—namely Downs and Olson (economists) and Parsons (sociologist). He said

> The most striking fact, to me at least is how primitive is the stage things still are in. By this I mean that the theoretical literature of both "economic" and "sociological" approaches is surprisingly sparse, in spite of the new books on politics that appear each year. [P. 182]

One of the problems which Barry identified is the different ideological bases from which economists and sociologists start. He has speculated on the possibility of recombining the elements of the two packages so that political science could advance beyond its present primitive state by drawing more fruitfully on these two sources of analysis of social problems.

In 1972, Carrier and Kendall considered why British social policy makers seldom applied sociology to their decision making. They were critical of the constructs being used by the policy makers and of the analytical data and interpretations offered by the sociologists. They argued in favour of applying phenomenological sociology instead "which attaches importance to comprehending the actors' view of reality" (p. 210). (c.f. Glaser and Strauss, 1967). But there are almost as many views of the failure of social sciences to have impact as there are social scientists.

Some Problems of Applying Science to Social Policy Analysis

Neither Barry nor Carrier and Kendall really got to grips with the fundamental issues of analysing societies and their problems and communicating the analysis to the decision makers.

In chapters 2 and 3 consideration was given to two of the major difficulties of applying science to policy analysis. Chapter 2 reviewed the question *What Is Policy*? and it was necessary to agree with Marshall (1970) that existing definitions of policy have customarily been chosen because they are convenient or conventional. In chapter 9 the complexity of policy choices was explored in a discussion of *The Fundamental Issues*. Earlier, the concept of bounded rationality was discussed as well as De Miguel's (1975) suggestion that the macro questions are too difficult to submit to scientific analysis and the micro questions are too limited. But there are some macro-micro areas in between. A study of these may produce some useful answers to limited questions. A large number of investigators are advocating the uses of middle-range theory rather than grand designs. (Merton, 1957; Holt and Richardson, 1970; Pinder and Moore, 1978).

In chapter 3 the *Practical Policy Frameworks* selected by policy analysts and their various uses were considered, e.g., for examining causes,considering consequences, or clarifying structures and processes. In this chapter the issue of value-free and value-laden science was also discussed. It is not difficult to agree with Barry's conclusions that science as applied to social problems is still in a primitive state.

The concept of paradigms for analysis being developed was raised in chapter 3 and is discussed at length in chapter 14.

International Migration

Scientists who became members of the international community found that their skills were readily transferable to other countries. The problem of loyalties of natural scientists was discussed above, but despite treason trials, America continued to recruit across frontiers in order to man its ever-growing research centres. It was not only the scientists but also those personal service professionals whose training was mainly scientific who became migrants. The brain drain from the developing to the more highly developed (or at least the resource rich) countries began to be studied in the late 1950s (Gish, 1971; Dublin, 1972; Abel-Smith and Gales, 1963; Abel-Smith, 1976).

One of the problems of migrating natural and social scientists and personal service professionals is to recognize the normative differences in their environments. This is especially important for professionals moving into social investigation and social control roles.

Borrowing of Ideas Across International Boundaries

Heidenheimer et al. (1976) have discussed international borrowings of social policy concepts, but they are sceptical about the transferability of ideas from one culture to another unless the timing is right and the ground has been prepared. It is obvious that some concepts are able to make the transition without difficulty—natural science and biomedical technology have little trouble in crossing frontiers. But they may do so at the expense of social development in a nation or may distort the social policies that a nation might wish to choose by their appeal to selfish instincts of individuals and groups rather than the nation as a society.

Social Science Policies

Despite or because of the international borrowings of ideas about how to establish national science policies, these social policies are no less confused than most other liberal social policies. They exhibit in microcosm the same struggles for the development of resources for the sake of discovery, the same demands for privilege, the same issues of the recognition of human rights and of applying findings to peoples' needs rather than their demands.

Because of international rivalries, scientific, technical and professional manpower has been wooed for the last half century and scientists and professionals have been powerful interest groups in any society. With the ending of the Vietnam war and the recession beginning the the 1970s, new questions are beginning to be asked about their contribution. But the acceptance of science as an ideology is now so strong that it would seem that the prerogatives of this group will not easily be forfeited, though their activities may be brought more under control by politicians and the bureaucracy.

Discussion of Readings and References

1. The successful application of science to the solution of problems in World War II and in the period of social reconstruction which followed it led to great expectations of the scientific community and vastly increased investment in scientific investigation in the postwar years, particularly in America. However, it soon became clear that there were value problems relating to the behaviour of scientists and, later in the Vietnam war period, to the applications of science without sufficient consideration of context. C. P. Snow's Rede Lecture on *The Two Cultures* was an important statement about the need for change in socialization of scientists through curriculum development. Rachel Carson's *Silent Spring* was an indictment of their failure to consider long-term consequences.
2. Not only was there disappointment with physical scientists' activities, social scientists also failed to meet the expectations of society that they could provide answers to questions of social disorganization. Alvin Gouldner (1970) reviewed the achievements and failures of sociology.
3. One of the problems is the failure of communication between the different scientific disciplines, a problem discussed by Brian Barry, a political scientist who considered the contributions of three theory-building social scientists in the liberal tradition—Parsons, Olsen and Downs—and the lack of relationship between their analytic frameworks and these frameworks to practical politics in liberal societies: in *Sociologists, Economists and Democracy*.
4. It is not only the theory builders who are not communicating with the practical policy makers. Dennis Lees and Stella Shaw reported on a conference of scientists—biomedical and social scientists—working on disability research in England. An excerpt from their report on the conference is attached to this chapter. Whilst they were concerned about the lack of communication between the different disciplinary groups doing research, they were even more disturbed about the scientists' lack of interest in the political processes of implementing their findings. Robert Merton was asked to review the activity of social scientists working with United States committees inquiring into social problems. Again he reported failures in com-

munication between them and the members of the committees appointed to ascertain the general will. He discussed the problems of social scientists asked to provide research evidence to committees set up by governments wanting immediate answers, whilst good scientific research needed a different time frame.

5. Others, such as sociologists taking the phenomenological approach, are critical of existing theoretical approaches. Particularly important for health policy researchers has been the discussion of *The Discovery of Grounded Theory* by Barney Glaser and Anselm Strauss which proposed that analysis should follow collection of empirical data rather than that data should be collected according to a prearranged schedule, for generation rather than verification of ideas.

6. Whilst there are no ready answers, most applied disciplines (political science or business administration or health care planning to take examples) seem to be convinced that the whole range of scientific approaches can provide helpful answers to practical decision makers, but the need is for the development of better middle-range paradigms. This point of view was expressed in relation to health research by De Miguel (1975).

7. There follows a listing of books concerned with social research and policy making. Applications of science to health policy are listed after chapter 13.

8. Chapter 14 is a discussion of production, organization and storage, distribution and uses of knowledge. It considers how individuals and societies structure their thinking and how changes are negotiated into social systems.

Further Refernces on Social Research and Policy Making

Cherns, A.B. et al. *Social Science and Government.* London: Tavistock, 1972.

Freeman, H. E. and Sherwood, C. C. *Social Research and Social Policy.* Englewood Cliffs, N.J.: Prentice-Hall, 1970.

Harris, Fred R., ed. *Social Science and National Policy.* Chicago: Transaction Books (Aldine), 1970.

Goodwin, L. *Can Social Science Help Resolve National Problems?* New York: The Free Press, 1973.

Ritchie, Ronald S. *An Institute for Research on Public Policy.* Ottawa: Information Canada, 1971.

Doern, G. Bruce. *Science and Politics in Canada.* Montreal: McGill-Queen's University Press, 1972.

Breton, Raymond. *The Canadian Condition: A Guide to Research on Public Policy.* Montreal: Institute for Research on Public Policy, 1977.

Brownlea, Arthur. *A Report on the Interaction between Policy Makers and Researchers in the Health Services Field in Canada with Some Australian Comparisons.* Toronto: University of Toronto, Department of Preventive Medicine and Biostatistics, 1979. Mimeo.

Impairment, Disability and Handicap: Report on a Conference of Research Workers

Dennis Lees
Stella Shaw

This paper was written as [a] contribution to a small working conference sponsored by the Social Science Research Council to discuss "The Cost of Human Impairment."[1] The decision to hold such a meeting was in itself an interesting and rather surprising one, since although the subject is one in which a great many people express interest, it is also one which inspires little actual research or participation in serious public discussion. Understandably, most are made wary by the considerable challenges posed at many levels, including philosophical and methodological, by attempts to place money values on human impairment, disability and suffering.

Rationale for the Conference

Nevertheless, those people who have engaged in studies of social policy and those who actually have to take responsibility for resource allocation, invariably find themselves facing the problems inherent in a situation of finite resources for which there is almost infinite demand; how much to allocate, and to what purposes, in order to achieve maximum results, and

From Dennis Lees and Stella Shaw, *Impairment, Disability and Handicap* (London: Heinemann Educational Books, Ltd., 1974), pp. 1–14. Reprinted by permission of the publisher. Notes have been placed at the end.

what criteria to use as the basis for these decisions? The identification and measurement of the costs of impairment are at the hub of these problems.

Apart from the general delicacy surrounding the subject matter of this meeting, there was, and still is to a large extent, a further barrier to progress in this field. This is the divergence of interests of people who actually have daily contact with impairment and disability—doctors, lawyers, social workers, employers, families, the individuals themselves—whose practical approaches have in turn to be reconciled to the more academic ones of economists, medical and legal research workers, sociologists, psychologists and social administrators. This is, of course, a common problem for much research in the social sciences, but it appears in an acute form in this context, where divergency may amount to clash of interests, due to the frequently differing objectives of each of these groups. . . .

The Decision Process

By the end of our two days of discussion it had become apparent that the one factor which had not been tackled openly was the political one. Little mention was made of the political context within which the choices and decisions concerning impairment and disability are made, or, indeed, of who takes these decisions. To some extent this was predetermined by the need to focus the conference on a relatively limited topic, but the general reluctance to discuss the political realities was nevertheless surprising, in view of the enormous sums of money which change hands in the process of the prevention, treatment, alleviation and compensation of disablement, with which many of the people present were actively concerned. For example community care is currently a fashionable concept, and there is a lot of pressure for home care and treatment of various kinds of long-term illness. This appears to be the result of administrative decisions, taken on the basis of crude cost calculations without taking into account the kinds of considerations already discussed above. Little political debate has taken place, and the switch in emphasis from hospital to home care has taken place without provoking public discussion of the kind generated by so many recent changes in, for example, the educational system. No political party has embraced these issues with the fervour which surrounded debates on the introduction of comprehensive education or the abandonment of free milk. Education is, of course, an area where politicians are subject to powerful lobbying from the consumers—or rather, their parents—and, although no politician wishes to appear sufficiently illiberal as to cast doubt on the generally held notion that the disabled must be cared for, few wish to actually challenge any move aimed directly at cutting these costs—not even to the extent of examining them closely. Other factors at work include the general layman's reluctance to question decisions which appear to be based on the clinical judgment of the medical profession.

At present the small but highly active pressure groups which have grown up to press the case for greater financial support for disabled people seem generally content to agitate for an overall increase in funds allocated to the purpose, rather than for any fundamental re-examination of the thinking behind the spending. This is, again, easily understood, since they are breaking new ground so far as disablement is concerned and their priorities lie with getting a larger cake rather than worrying about the recipe and ingredients.

Only one area of the cost of human impairment is currently under public review, that of compensation for physical damage due to accident, and even here it appears that the attention of the Royal Commission will be confined largely to the appropriateness of tort as a basis for deciding whether or not compensation is due. It will not, for example, consider whether such compensation should be extended to severe congenital abnormalities. The decision to mount such a Royal Commission was a political one as was the definition of its terms of reference, and was the outcome of a single accident with a new drug rather than of any deliberate recognition that the present system might be inefficient, unjust and outmoded.

It may well be that this apparent lack of a public interest in and debate over the most desirable measures for coping with problems arising from serious impairment and disability is an expression of the fundamental conflict between two major factors which policy must take into account. These are the need to minimize the overall cost of impairment, and the wish to distribute those costs equally among the population. The first consideration derives from hard-headed financial and economic considerations, and the second from the implicit social judgment that the troubles of those who have been treated "unfairly" by circumstances should, as far as possible, be shared by the community.

The clash between the value judgment and the economic issues manifests itself in several ways. Economics demands that we minimize costs by encouraging measures by both individuals and the community that will prevent impairment and disability; that we limit their extent where prevention is unavoidable; and that we minimize the consequences of disability and the suffering it causes, partly through offering incentives to people to achieve the maximum independence their physical condition will allow, and partly by providing support through financial compensation and services.

These measures are, in fact, at odds with the principle of equity, which implies that all sufferers should receive full compensation for their disabilities, without acknowledging that such compensation might actually have a disincentive effect at both the collective and individual levels.

It seems highly likely that we will continue to muddle along in our policies, swayed first by economic considerations and then by our values, unless these issues are made explicit and subjected to public scrutiny.

Although of course it may be that the protagonists in the debates which do take place are fully aware of this dilemma, and prefer it to remain hidden and unresolved rather than risk a possible change in public attitudes which could be unfavourable to their own approach.

Notes

[1]Held at Rutland Hall, University of Nottingham, on 21–23 March 1973. For list of participants see Appendix B (of the Report).

12 Policy, Planning and Administration

Policy Research, Planning and Administrative Processes

Yarmolinsky's (1971) list of the policy researchers' activities (which some might regard as planning)—trend analysis, advising on policy choice, program development, troubleshooting and evaluation—match quite closely Stewart's (1963) list of managerial roles—emissaries, discussers, troubleshooters and backroom specialists. So perhaps it is useful to consider policy programmatic research and planning as kinds of management forecasting activity—the cliché "forward planning" should perhaps read forward management.

Classifying Types of Planning

Friedmann and Hudson (1974) have reviewed and categorized the development of planning theory up to 1974. The Great Debate of the 1950s on capitalist freedom versus communist-type planning continues, but many nations have accepted the need for planning in order to survive and prosper. Schonfield (1965) has discussed the alternative forms of planning developed by the capitalist nations of western Europe (chapter 5). Despite Milton Friedmann's efforts to encourage Americans to return to the marketplace, it seems that some government planning is here to stay.

Among planners, one of the main distinctions can be made between incremental planners—problem solvers—and those who are developmental planners. The incremental model might be described as troubleshooting. It identifies a problem, evaluates it, coordinates the responses and endeavours to control the situation; the developmental model begins by researching the issues, selecting from alternative choices, making and taking decisions, operationalizing the changes, evaluating and feeding back results. Without using the terms incremental and developmental, Confrey (1975) has described and contrasted the two approaches as used in U.S. planning.

Glennerster (1975) has contrasted incrementalist, managerial and pluralist planning. (This is not quite the same as incrementalist and developmental.) On a different wavelength, John Friedmann (1967) proposed a conceptual model of planning which distinguishes between allocative, innovative, developmental and adaptive planning. And there are other classifications which may be useful in considering planning activities (Faludi, 1973).

It is clear that planners, like policy analysts, have no clearly agreed framework but a whole series of frameworks which vary from setting to setting and person to person.

The Uses of Rationality

For all kinds of planning, however, what is needed is a good data base, otherwise decisions will be founded upon opinions only without adequate factual evidence. The measurement of health through the development of health and social indicators is improving. Health indicators, as distinct from general social indicators, are particularly good in Canada where government data banks have been rationalized since the early 1970s after the introduction of the Medical Care schemes. Using the Ontario data base, Culyer (1978) a health economist, has discussed some of the practical problems of measurement.

Although it would seem that there can be no confident promise of finding the right scientific answers, there is no doubt that scientific evidence has helped to clear up many social problems, (although perhaps, at times, creating others as unintended consequences, e.g., population growth following disease control). But the questions about how and when to use rational scientific knowledge are still poorly worked out.

When can rational evidence best be applied to policy making? It seems clear from the reports of Marmor (1973), Eckstein (1956) and others, that rational thinking can sensibly be used to assemble information about possible directions of change.

How much causal background should be included is a matter of confidence in the social order's ability to absorb change, a confidence which has obviously been much greater in the new lands. Britain seems to be much more concerned with the analysis of causes of social disorganization than the other three countries. It has a longer history, and so its history may seem to be more important to understand, but the emphasis upon research into causes as against research into impacts of new policy is so noticeably different that there have to be other reasons, some of which have been explored. These appear to be ideological and structural. In its social policies, Britain has been less concerned about promoting individual liberty to achieve individual equality of opportunity than liberating individuals from poverty (equality of condition) (Donnison, 1972). And structurally, it is a more centralized state than the other three federations.

Bounded Rationality

Eckstein discussed the bounded rationality of planning. The rational information presented in order to promote a policy is expected to establish facts but it cannot be comprehensive.

There is a case to be made for using professional planners, usually academics, bureaucrats or consultants for support of the many nonprofessional planners/policy makers/managers in the health care field. These part-time planners may, for example, be developing health programs for a political party, or, as cabinet members, deciding on resource allocations for health services, or, as a group of teachers, planning curriculum development, or, as clinicians, considering new uses of CT scanners, but on the whole, their rationality is very tightly bounded by their own special concerns. Professional planners can provide more information and widen these boundaries.

Although Eckstein concluded that, "planners face important and potentially ineradicable obstacles in pursuit of a well-planned and fully-effective health service," in his opinion this did not make bounded planning any less useful as a basis for action. He argued that the devlopment of a bounded plan for the N. H. S. still resulted in getting better value for money. Abel-Smith (1976) supported this view.

The Success or Failure of Planning

When is planning successful and when does it fail? One reason for lack of impact is poor communication. A chart developed by Wilensky (1967) is helpful for analyzing failures in communication. Confrey and Coleman (1975) have argued that techniques of analyzing effective policy impacts are not yet well developed. Another reason is given by Heidenheimer et al. (1976). Ideas must be timely and fit in with the climate which exists. The policy of Community Care, accepted as necesary in Britain in the early 1960s, made little progress until the reorganization of National Health Service structures in the 1970s and the introduction of a new system of resource allocation. However, Eckstein made the most important comment on the planning process when he said that, however imperfect the techniques, it is the will to plan that matters. The first step is to achieve enough consensus among the negotiating interest groups that they will sit down together to work on problems. Without that agreement planning will fail.

The assembling of facts may have no impact unless researchers and planners are willing to consider how to communicate scientific findings or find someone else to do so for them and that there is a group of action-oriented policy makers who are willing to receive the information and use it. As Alford (1975) suggested, the collection and sifting of information by Commissions may also be used as a stalling tactic "*not* because they lead to significant policy innovations but because they serve to convince the public that action is being taken. . . ."

Values and Evidence

Alford has raised this question in another form—for what purposes would rational evidence be used? In New York the three interest groups involved in planning the hospital services held three different ideological positions and so they wished different kinds of policies to be adopted and cited different evidence in support of their views.

Evidence, then, is usually collected by interest groups to serve their purposes (and one of the principal interest groups may be governments themselves).

In a discussion of *The Functions of Social Conflict,* Coser (1956) distinguished between conflicts about values (legitimacy) and conflicts about structures. If the values of those in conflict were too far apart, he said, the conflicts would be destructive, whereas when values were agreed upon, conflicts about structures (feasibility) might lead to invention and positive gains.

It may be that all that can be achieved by Alford's New York planners is to preserve the status quo. For Alford's theoretical section examined irreconcilable rifts between the most important structural interests in the health field.

The differing values of interest groups involved in providing health care and life care were explored in chapter 9, but they are summarized again here because they are of crucial importance to planners.

Values and Planners

Clearly, different kinds of planning agency require different kinds of briefs to be developed. It may be that the only obvious biases are those of advocacy planning agencies. In theory, academic planners are independent and unbiased unless they have accepted contract work with prescribed limitations. Eversley (1973) was concerned that the planner employed by government should continue to maintain professional values despite the pressures put upon him. He should have a social awareness, a consciousness of his duty to the public.

> What matters is consciousness of one's values, one's belief, one's directions and preferences—an evaluation of the extent to which one is able to carry one's ideology to its logical conclusion. For one man it will be silence and craven compromise, for another it will mean public dissent, dismissal, suffering, or a reduction of income and status in order to join the community which he feels to be disadvantaged as a result of his activities, against his former colleagues.
>
> All these positions are tenable. What is probably untenable (prevalent as it is) is a total ethical vacuum. . . . [P. 321]

Johnson (1972) argued that there are three positions in which a professional might find himself today, viz. selfemployed, responding to patronage, or employee. In the last two positions a planner has to be responsive to his patron/employer, but he may be in a better position to achieve results than the academic back room planner because he is nearer to the action.

Value Differences

Government Involvement. By the mid-nineteenth century the industrializing societies started to recognize that patronage was inefficient. What were the alternatives? Entrepreneurialism and professionalism on the one hand, bureaucracy on the other; but taken to extreme, all of these have their faults. Is it possible to combine them efficiently? Here the first conflict of values becomes evident. Many entrepreneurs and professionals mistrust government as a distributive, regulative or redistributive agency, except in the most noninterventionist way possible.

Science Policy. Should the scientists alone determine what is to be the subject of their research through peer group decision, emphasizing validity and reliability of their projects and deciding for themselves what is relevant, or should relevance be decided by the funding bodies (public or private) and tenders invited? The formulation of questions by scientists or for scientists to try to answer is a major issue which has emerged in science policy.

It is not a simple single issue for it is related to the whole question of independence and political control of ideas—the role of the universities, the freedom of academic professionals to extend knowledge, and by association and freedom of clinical professionals to choose how to practice their skills.

Health-Promotion or Life-Preservation Policies. Which of the roles of health professionals should be given the most weight? Should their roles as technologists be emphasized even more, so that they become more competent life preservers? Or should their roles as gatekeepers for society be made more obvious—the social controller and allocator and rationer roles? Psychiatrists have demonstrated that doctors can be very sucessful in taking over even more of the social controller roles but medical involvement in allocator and rationer roles are another matter. Clinicians are reluctant to become managers.

As discussed in chapter 9, there are great value conflicts between the different ways in which resources can be allocated, particularly between the physician's private patient and all other patients, and between acute hospital care, care for the impaired and health promotion. All of these have their advocates and all are right as far as individuals are concerned. But what of society's needs? Scribner and his associates made a bold move when they attempted to sort out criteria for admitting the candidates to renal dialysis programs in the early days, to bring into the open the content of corridor consultations and negotiations which go on about who shall live (Fox and Swazey). But with the development of more resources in home dialysis, the general issue has been hidden again and decision making returned to individual nephrologists. The issue will not go away, however hopeful some may be that it can be resolved as a matter of patients' choosing to pay more for health care as vacationers may choose to do for their holidays. For the resources are not infinite, the availability of health services is limited in a way that spending in holiday resorts is not.

So whose decisions should prevail—the individual physicians', the health institutions' (supporting hospital accreditation or other quality-control policies), the governments' as redistributive bodies, or the persons who can pay most? Where the government has taken over the financing of the system as in Britain and Canada, the pressures upon doctors to deal with these questions of limiting quality or quantity of care openly are mounting.

If planning is left entirely to interest groups it may become sterile (as Alford has indicated), an exercise in futility and failure. If planning is taken over entirely by government it may also become sterile if the interest groups are able to resist the legitimation of implementation of policies. However, the chances are that governments will be more successful than voluntary planning groups because they can usually command more authority than consortia where representatives are expected to report back to their membership groups and have primary loyalties to them.

The Context of Planning

After studying British and American approaches to planning, Glennerster concluded that governments with highly centralized power tended to do more managerial (bureaucratic) planning and that governments based on pluralist power had to use other techniques: more technical planning (which may take the form of after-the-event evaluation and feedback) and more advocacy planning. He decided that England planned but did not evaluate policies and programs whilst the U.S. evaluated programs but did not plan. He put this down to the different political structures which had evolved in the two countries. England, with its highly centralized government, was able to make different kinds of decisions from those made in the U.S., with its separation of powers in the central decision-making machinery, its federal states with their multilevels of government, and with much authority delegated to voluntary organizations. By evaluating programs, information could be provided to the decision makers and, if they could receive and act on it, corrections made. Of course, to make this extreme distinction between the two countries is to exaggerate, but it contains elements of truth.

There are policy analysts and planners working for the governments of both countries, sifting evidence and preparing briefs so that new legislation can be enacted or new administrative decisions taken, but much depends upon the acceptance of governments' powers in the community.

Governments are required to plan; consequently, politicians in office must necessarily assume planning functions, become temporary professional planners. In addition, there are those who have chosen to become full-time planners. Gilbert and Specht (1974) have suggested that there are three different contexts of professional planning which create different bounded rationalities. They have proposed a scheme which distributes planners' roles along a continuum:

1) the planner as a technocrat accountable primarily to the profession and operating with a view of the public interest derived from the special skills and knowledge in his possession;
2) the planner as a bureaucrat accountable primarily to the political and administrative hierarchy and operating with a view of the public interest derived from institutional leadership; and finally,
3) the planner as an advocate accountable primarily to the consumer group that purchases his services and operating with a view of the public interest derived from consumer group preferences.

Politicians in Office as Policy Planners

Figure 12–1 indicates that there is an overlap between political and administration policy making in government. Much depends upon the way in which the politicians decide to play their roles and the structures in which they operate. As well, much depends upon the way in which politicians are prepared to continue to accept established policies and to develop them or whether they intend to disrupt the continuity and to introduce their own party's different program when they get into office. It is seldom possible to bring in many rapid changes and remain in office.

FIGURE 12–1
STAGES IN ADMINISTRATIVE POLICY DEVELOPMENT

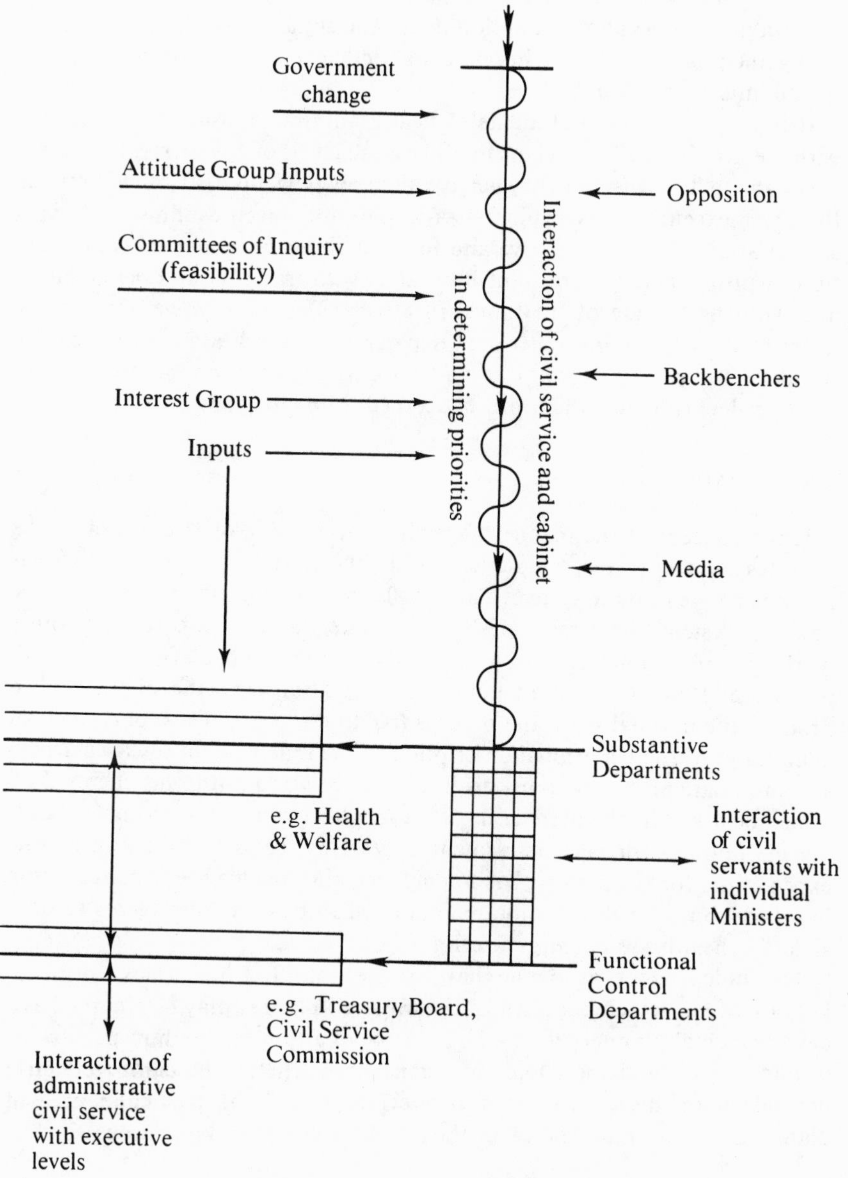

Much depends upon the interrelationship of voters, politicians and civil service as to how planning is carried out. How much are politicians prepared to delegate? This depends upon the competence of the civil service to give good advice and to handle difficult questions when the choices are to be operationalized. Politicians are, by temperament, troubleshooters, whilst civil servants who see governments come and go may be more ready to undertake long-term policy development. And sometimes, politicians, recognizing their own and their bureaucrats' deficiencies, may bring in special consultants to develop policies.

It is suggested that if students of health administration are not familiar with the activities of politicians in office at all levels of government, then it is necessary to discover how they behave and how power is distributed between the chief executive, his cabinet-as-a-whole, and specific ministers (giving special attention to substantive and functional departments). This distribution of power is not a constant but varies with tradition and personalities and with the climate of the times. In a recession, more power tends to be given to the controlling functional departments, which are concerned with the development of regulations and allocations; in a boom, to the substantive departments which are concerned with programs.

Technocratic Planning

Is the concept of the planner as technocrat a viable one? Certainly, if he operates as a specialist employed within the health care system and has proper linkage into the system. Can the planner operate independently of the ongoing system? Anderson (1976) has made out the case for a planner working from a unit based in a university setting. He has argued that both planner and patron have an independent relationship—the one is free to produce the optimal plan, the other is free to reject it. This is, of course, an adaptation of the traditional description of the independent researcher who seeks to relate primarily to his professional peers and not to his clients. Yet, it may be asked, is the planner in the same position as a researcher, presenting his findings for peer assessment only? This seems to be an unrealistic expectation, for the planner has to convince not only his peers (as Anderson has done) but also those who are appointed to be executive agents responsible for health system organization.

The independent academic has his freedom but may lack influence because of his detachment, whilst the involved planner may be regarded as a developmental planner "with a high degree of autonomy with respect to the setting of ends and the choice of means," but whether he can be effective depends upon his control over the technology of the particular area of planning and its importance in the whole decision-making process.

In an overview of the planning process, Reinke and Williams (1972) have discussed the skills which one might expect to find in technocratic health planners—demographic, epidemiologic and economic and with expertise in the more applied areas of physical planning, manpower planning, information collection and analysis and policy planning.

The contribution of demographers to health planning has long been recognized. They focus upon health status inputs and outcomes, as do epidemiologists, but it is only relatively recently that epidemiologists have begun to make clear statements about their contribution to health planning. In order to do this, they have had to modify their views about the range of activities in which they are prepared to engage. Cochrane (1972) stated the traditional position (which is somewhat difficult to implement) which favours randomized controlled trials for assessing efficiency and effectiveness, whilst others have taken a much more open position about methods of evaluation (Henderson, 1976). References are attached to chapter 13.

The summary of the proceedings of a conference on health economics (Hauser, 1972) provides some indication of the concerns of this group of specialists. (A further list of reading suggestions follows chapter 13.) Economists have helped to focus upon system objectives and the most efficient methods of reaching these.

Reinke and Williams have not included four groups of social scientists in their listing of health planners—but historians, philosophers, sociologists and social psychologists have contributed more to the understanding of causal factors and to analyses of processes and structures of health services than the technologists they have included, probably because causal analysis is less immediately appealing to those policy makers who are concerned with measuring outcomes—program impacts—but it has its uses.

One area in which causal analysts have made considerable contribution is in analysing the operationalization of policy concepts by suggesting the need to consider underlying concepts in the categorizing of beneficiaries (Warham, 1974; Mercer, 1973). They have helped to distinguish between the use of diagnostic classifications, institutional classifications, vocational rehabilitation potential classifications and others as bases for program development of health services.

However, many scientists have had problems relating research to planning. Lees and Shaw (1974) considered why the important topic of the cost of human impairment had not yet become a political issue in England. They concluded that the researchers on disability were not yet on the political wavelength—they seemed to be unwilling to get involved in political discussions about a well-recognized problem area. Reinke may well have identified the groups which have made this transition from the ivory tower to the marketplace.

Bureaucratic Planning (Governmental Planning Activities)

What, then, are the skills required by bureaucratic planners? They should try to introduce rationality, said Eckstein, but not perfectionism. What they will be able to accomplish will be limited because of the pressures which are brought to bear upon them and to which they will react. Eckstein identified three such pressures: logical difficulties, psychological pressures, and data pressures arising from a lack of control over a multitude of factors crucial to adequate calculation. How, then, can they cope with these? The experienced politicians and the experienced civil servants have their defence mechanisms, said Eckstein. "The principal adjustment they made involved the reduction of the area of rational decision making and in some cases the manifest abdication of rational decision making" (p. 55). The defences he has listed are those which have given bureaucracy a bad name—using routine formulae and stereotyped rules, elaborating procedures, exhibiting rigidity and inertia through allowing temporary arrangements to become permanent, permitting unsatisfactory decisions to remain unchanged, postponing action for further inquiries, allowing political decisions to replace rational decisions and centralizing administrative powers.

The importance of the civil service, not only as the executive arm of government, but as its advisory and planning arm, has been given recognition by many countries in the postwar years. Investigations have been conducted to establish whether there are sufficient skills in the civil service and that these are properly deployed. The concept of the civil servant as the well-rounded, well-educated generalist administrator has been challenged in a world seeming to become even more complex. The importance of getting more inputs from technically well-qualified policy planners has been the concern of most democratic governments, but how best to organize this input has been uncertain. (A list of reports is given in the references.)

Balancing the inputs from substantive departments, e.g., health, against those of the functional departments, such as treasury board and civil service commission, has led some governments to establish special planning groups within their cabinet offices in order to assist in the determination of priorities. And this has encouraged the departments themselves to improve their planning and sort out their priorities. It seems to be somewhat easier to do this at the higher levels of government than lower down where there may be much greater involvement of civil servants in operational activities. At this level planning is almost always incremental unless a special effort is made to counter the forces of incrementalism, for the middle ranks of the civil service tend to be concerned with maintenance activities, whilst the higher ranks are being pressured to look at change. Incrementalist planning is the easy way out—it means adding or subtracting at the margin without thoroughly investigating those services which are already established.

Particularly in advanced bureaucracies there has been concern to link substantive planning into the techniques of control developed by the functional departments. Spiers (1975) has described British techniques of planning in some detail and Brown (1975) has shown how the British NHS ties into this planning cycle. Glennerster has compared the methods employed by the U.S. federal government.

The activities of the civil service may be divided into regulative, allocative and operational control functions. It is clear that the developmental model of planning is a more appropriate response to regulative planning—if laws are to be changed, then they should be considered broadly, though frequently this does not happen. So far as allocative planning is concerned, incrementalism seems to have been the rule for many governments, with an occasional major change (about once every generation) in the structures and processes of allocation.

Whilst at national levels of government, in interaction with the civil service, the planning function has long been recognized, this may not be so true at the lower levels (e.g., state or municipal government) where politicians may still make the decisions without much input from the bureaucrats. The lack of skilled administrators/planners at provincial levels was particularly noticeable in Canada when, in 1949, it was decided to introduce matching grants for hospital construction. The federal government, using the American Hill-Burton Act as a model, made it a condition of grant aid to the provinces that they should prepare plans for the siting and use of proposed hospitals, but few of the provinces had public servants capable of this review (Saskatchewan being a notable exception [Taylor, 1949]). When consultants were brought in to amend the lack, there were no strong departments which could follow through their recommendations to the conclusions they had proposed. Consequently, Canada was forced into politically responsive and unplanned incrementalism (Tropman's policy making as surprise [1976]) for the next generation. And even now, well-developed health planning in many provinces is conspicuously absent.

The amount of bureaucratic planning can easily be determined by the documentary evidence of published reports, rules and regulations for the operating of the health care system. Judged by this measure, Great Britain is by far the most advanced country in bureaucratic planning, and, of course, this output leads to criticism about overdoing it.

Marmor's analysis of the development of the Medicare legislation was presented in chapter 3. It will be recalled that he emphasized frames of inference, that is, the contexts in which issues are reviewed and the inferences which follow from the structuring of the situation. Bureaucratic planners have to be very much concerned about establishing the frames of inference for their work. This may be the reason for their great concern about terms of reference and structures and processes of action rather than substantive outcomes, for it seems to be the only way to cope with the hostile world around them.

Whilst it is possible for innovative planners to function within bureaucracies, they may find it difficult to do so unless their intention is to make economies and unless they can be accommodated in functional departments such as treasury boards or personnel departments where they can get departmental backing. Innovative planners in substantive departments who desire to change the established way of doing things will find this is not easy since the allocative planners will prefer incrementalism to fundamental change. It is for this reason that some governments prefer to use consultants or academics to propose plans for change so that they can discover whether they can get support for the new proposals without greatly disturbing the ongoing allocative planning mechanisms. It is easier for consultants or academics to be disowned if their plans seem inappropriate. They may even be able openly to admit that they have misjudged a situation in a way that a bureaucrat cannot—some consultants to the English Department of Health and Social Security on reorganization seem to have had second thoughts about their recommendations at a later stage.

However, bureaucrats may be able to make innovative contributions to substantive policy development if they can find a way to break through (Laframboise, 1973; see chapter 13 reading), but whilst a successful shift in the substantive frame of inference may be made, this does not necessarily mean that it is accompanied by a similar shift in the functional frame. The British decision to focus more attention on the elderly and the handicapped became a legitimated substantive policy in the early 1960s, but it was not easy to alter the thrust of the service towards increasingly expensive acute care, despitescandals about neglect of impaired groups. It seemed necessary to make a break in the continuity of incrementalism through a major reorganization of functional structures for new allocative policies to become feasible. Following structural reorganization in 1974, two major policy statements werepublished in 1976, *Priorities for Health and Personal Social Services in England* and *Sharing Resources for Health in England*—the first substantive, the second functional. Whilst the first is called a consultative document and gives advice from the minister to the regional boards, the second carried the real message through its resource allocation proposals, which will force greater compliance than there has been in the past.

The interaction between functional and substantive planning is not always clearly understood. Thus, Powell (1975), recounting his experiences as British Minister of Health, has described how disappointed he was with the relationship he had with the doctors. He expected them to help him to innovate, but all they seemed to want was assurance about income security.

Their frames of inference were different and the doctors were able to impose their frame on his because they had technical power.

Advocacy Planning

Technical planning, or health research, may be out of touch, but advocacy planners must be closely in tune with public or interest group feelings. That is the justification for their existence. Unless an advocate understands timing and appropriateness of his input, he will be ineffective. One example of misjudgment of an opportunity was the Foulkes Report on *Health Security for British Columbians* (1973). Foulkes had been a strong supporter of the New Democratic Party in opposition, and when it came into office as a provincial government in 1972, he was commissioned to prepare a consultant's plan for health care for the province. When his report was published after the government had been in office for sixteen months, it was couched in inappropriate terms—a statement of social philosophy suitable to the preelection stage, but not to the administrative implementation state which had then been reached. The Minister was obliged to put some distance between himself and this document, terming it a Green Paper or Advisory Report, for by then the government had become involved in negotiating compromises with the groups on which it was dependent for service (such as the physicians, the employees of the mental health service, etc.)—groups which were attacked by Foulkes. Foulkes had not recognized the different context in which he was operating since the government had attained power, that it was now necessary for the Minister to be concerned with adaptive rather than developmental planning, with bureaucratic rather than advocacy planning, and with resource allocation rather than innovation.

Figures 10–3 and 12–1 have attempted to show where different kinds of inputs are made into the political process. From these it is possible to identify where advocacy planning is likely to occur at different stages of the political process. Perhaps the most well-documented advocacy planning is in the attitude group or party platform statements. These statements may take different forms such as appeals for funds for cardiac or cancer research or proposals for reforming the health care delivery system as a whole or in part (e.g., Owen, 1968).

Advocacy planning is obviously more important where there appear to be greater opportunities of influencing the system. Consequently, its advantages can readily be seen at the preelection period when the situation is more open to change, but this is not the only time when advocacy may be used. When a government is in office the opposition may seek to find embarassing incidents in its record of administration. Scandals may be developed out of the mishandling of one case, but a mishandled case is unlikely to become a scandal unless a climate of opinion and an advocate exist ready to receive and respond to the incident, to publicize it and to use it to justify reform proposals. There is also maintenance advocacy.

Klein (1974) has discussed one successful case of advocacy planning in which a series of scandals were used to raise public consciousness of the need for change. But Klein makes it very clear that the amount of change which can be expected through incrementalism even in crises is very slight, because of ongoing commitments. Hall et al. (1975) also discuss crises.

A British ex-Minister of Health, Crossman (1972), has expressed his concern that the advocacy system of planning does not result in clear guidance to politicians, for the public's desire for more health care than a nation can afford requires decisions about priorities to be taken. Since this nation is not prepared to leave health care to market forces, most decisions are taken in the political arena and it is usually adaptive bureaucratic planners who determine the course of action in Britain.

Advocacy planning is obviously more acceptable where there are greater opportunities for pluralist decision making, where there is a philosophy of the separation of powers (as in the U.S.A.) or a philosophy of decentralization (a concept which seems to be growing in popularity in the second half of the twentieth century).

The advocacy planner needs to be well aware of the context in which he seeks to function and to relate to the traditional structures of democratic societies, whether he decides to choose a consensus model or a confrontation model as his frame of inference, recognizing the perils of either course (Cox et al., eds., 1974a, 1974b). It is for this reason that many advocacy planners have been trained in community development and concentrate on improving the political skills of their constituents (Draper, 1971). It was recognized that the difficulties in establishing Neighbourhood Health Centres in the U.S. under the Office of Economic Opportunity program were often related to lack of committees' skills in promotion (Haughton, 1974).

Discussion of Readings and References

If the previous chapter seemed to express many negative sentiments about the prospect of applying research to policy making, this chapter should have corrected that impression.

1. Adam Yarmolinsky's paper on "The Policy Researcher" was mentioned in chapter 3 and is again recommended for its review of the disciplinary and interdisciplinary approaches of different kinds of policy researchers. The interdisciplinary approach moves away from strictly controlled scientific models towards a planning orientation.
2. Attached to this chapter is part of a paper by James Coleman on policy

impact research which takes an interdisciplinary approach. This paper has been shortened and the examples chosen to illustrate his principles have been omitted, but he has argued in favour of timely information which is relatively accurate rather than research which is scientifically impeccable but out of touch with social demand for data. Easton's chart (10–1) is useful for distinguishing causal from impact or consequential issues.

3. At the end of his paper Coleman has considered the difference between research focussing upon inputs/outputs and social audits.

The second reading chosen is a part of Avedis Donabedian's article on "Evaluating the Quality of Medical Care" in which he spells out the importance of evaluating all the steps in a systems model—inputs, structures, process, outputs—in order to achieve a proper understanding of what is happening. Reading Donabedian in conjunction with Coleman is useful because it answers some of the questions raised at the end of Coleman's paper.

4. Since research seems to mean anything from tightly controlled experiments to Yarmolinsky's trend analysis, advising on policy choice, program development, trouble shooting and evaluation (which might also be regarded as planning) how does planning differ from research? Neil Gilbert and Harry Specht have argued that there are three types of planners: technocrats, bureaucrats and advocates. Clearly Yarmolinsky's policy researchers' activities overlap with those of the first two categories of planners.

But what is planning according to the planners? There are many definitions. For those who are interested in the development of planning concepts, an article by Friedmann and Hudson (1974) reviewed the activities of planning theorists up to that date. Andreas Faludi's *A Reader in Planning Theory* provides a more detailed exposition of a range of planners' views and includes a chapter which describes a conceptual model developed by Friedmann which distinguishes between allocative, innovative, developmental and adaptive planning.

5. However, here we continued to use Gilbert and Specht's framework.

Technocratic health planning is reviewed more comprehensively in the next chapter and references are listed there. Eckstein (1956) examined bureaucratic planning in the Ministry of Health in London. He found that planners' behaviour followed the stereotype of bureaucratic behaviour but considered this to be excusable as a defensive measure. He assessed their contribution positively in getting value for money for taxpayers. For further information about the development of government bureaucracies and their planning activities a list of readings is attached to this chapter.

Some references to advocacy planning and community development were given on the last page of this chapter immediately before this discussion of readings. They may be followed up in the bibliography. The development of nongovernmental voluntary organizations is to be reviewed in chapter 13.

6. Robert Alford, who studied planning for health services in New York, saw planning activity in that context as a destructive stalling tactic. A reading from Alford is attached describing his view of dynamics without change.
7. In his book *Organizational Intelligence,* Harold L. Wilensky has developed a chart for analyzing failures in communication. This chart is helpful in diagnosing planning failures.

Further References on Civil Service Functioning

Great Britain

Great Britain. (Fulton) Report of the Committee on the Civil Service, 1966–8. London: H. M. S. O., 1968.

Brown, R. G. S. *The Administrative Process in Britain.* London: Methuen, 1970.

United States

Macy, John W., Jr. *Public Service.* New York: Harper and Row, 1971.

Canada

Canada. (Glassco) Report of the Royal Commission on Government Organization. Ottawa: Queen's Printer, 1963.

Saskatchewan. Report of the Royal Commission on Government Organization. Regina: Queen's Printer, 1965.

Australia

Australia. (Coombs) Report of the Royal Commission on Australian Government Administration. Canberra: Australian Government Publishing Service, 1976.

Australia. (Campbell) Royal Commission on Australian Government Administration. Report of the Health and Welfare Task Force. Canberra: Australian Government Publishing Service, 1975.

Australia. (Gross) Royal Commission on Australian Government Administration. Towards Rational Administrative Structures for Health and Welfare Services in Australia. Canberra: Australian Government Publishing Service, 1975.

Australia. (Bailey) Report of the Task Force on Coordination in Welfare and Health. Canberra: Australian Government Publishing Service, 1976.

Further References on Budgetary Structures and Processes

Great Britain

Heclo, H. and Wildavsky, A. *The Private Government of Public Money.* Berkeley: University of California Press, 1974.

Spiers, Maurice. *Techniques and Public Administration.* London: Fontana, 1975.

United States

Wildavsky, Aaron. *The Politics of the Budgetary Process.* Boston: Little, Brown and Co., 1964.

Niskanen, William A. *Bureaucracy and Representative Government.* Chicago: Aldine, 1971.

Brundrage, P. F. *The Bureau of the Budget.* New York: Praeger, 1970.

Pechman, J. A., ed. *Setting National Priorities: The 1978 Budget.* Washington, D.C.: Brookings Institution, 1977 (and annually).

Canada

Breton, Albert. *The Economic Theory of Representative Government.* Chicago: Aldine, 1974.

Hartle, Douglas. *A Theory of the Expenditure Budgetary Process.* Toronto: Ontario Economic Council, 1976.

Australia

Knight, Kenneth W. and Wiltshire, Kenneth W. *Formulating Government Budgets.* St. Lucia: University of Queensland Press, 1977 (compares Australia, Canada and U.S.).

Maxwell, James A. *Commonwealth-State Financial Relations in Australia.* Melbourne: University Press, 1967.

Mathews, R. L. and Jay, W. R. C. *Intergovernmental Financial Relations in Australia since Federation.* Canberra: Australian National University, 1976.

Problems of Conceptualization and Measurement in Studying Policy Impacts

James S. Coleman

In this paper, I have attempted to do two things: first, to show how a fundamentally different methodological foundation is needed for policy research than exists for discipline research; and second, to show some of the elements that such a methodology should have. It is clear that the ideas for such a methodology are still in the formative state; but what is important, even at this early stage, is to recognize that policy research requires methodological development of its own, beginning at the most fundamental philosophical or conceptual level.

The Properties of Methods for Policy Analysis

It is important at the very outset to sharply distinguish a methodology that has as its philosophic base the testing and development of theories from a methodology that has as its philosophic base a guide to action. This is not to say that the methods developed as an aid in theory construction cannot be used as components of a methodology that constitutes guides to action. It is rather to say that, at the most fundamental philosophical level, a difference exists: the goal is not to further develop theory about an area of activity, but

---

Reprinted from *Public Policy Evaluation,* Sage Yearbooks in Politics and Public Policy, vol. 2, ed. Kenneth M. Dolbeare, copyright 1975, pp. 21–40 by permission of the publisher, Sage Publications, Inc. (Beverly Hills/London).

to provide an information basis for social action. Cronbach and Suppes (1969) have expressed the difference in a pair of terms that they use to describe research in education: The first is "conclusion-oriented research," in which the aim is to arrive at certain conclusions about what is, descriptively, the state of affairs. This research is designed to contribute to knowledge in a substantive area, and directly or indirectly to contribute to theory. The second is "decision-oriented research," in which the aim is to provide information that is important for policy decisions that must be made. Here I will not use these terms, but will call that research which is designed to advance knowledge in a scientific discipline "discipline research," and will call that research designed as a guide to social action "policy research."

When we adjust our ideas in this way, and explore the implications of a change in the philosophical base from research for the discipline to research for social policy, a number of differences emerge. I will not present an exhaustive catalog here, because no such exhaustive catalog exists. What I will do is to urge that serious attention be devoted to discovering and examining these differences.

[Coleman then goes on to discuss the six principles which should be applied in policy research which he summarized as follows:]

For policy research,

- *partial information available at the time an action must be taken is better than complete information after that time. . . .*
- *the ultimate product is not a "contribution to existing knowledge" in the literature, but a social policy modified by the research results. . . .*
- *results that are with high certainty approximately correct are more valuable than results which are more elegantly derived but possibly grossly incorrect. . . .*
- *it is necessary to treat differently policy variables which are subject to policy manipulation, and situational variables which are not. . . .*
- *the research problem enters from outside any academic discipline, and must be carefully translated from the real world of policy or the conceptual world of a client without loss of meaning. . . .*
- *the existence of competing or conflicting interests should be reflected in the commissioning of more than one research group, under the auspices of different interested parties where possible. Even in the absence of explicitly conflicting interests, two or more research projects should be commissioned to study a given policy problem. . . .*

The principles listed above give some indication of the kinds of points that a methodology for policy research should include. Their principal aim here is to show that important differences between policy research and discipline research do exist, and that it is possible to develop a methodological foundation for policy research.

Apart from these principles, there are some points, both technical and nontechnical, which are especially important in one or another kind of policy research. Campbell . . . (1971) . . . has begun to develop a number of these. I will mention below a few others, without any suggestion of being exhaustive, comprehensive, or even systematic. These points are those which have arisen in my experience, which appear to have general relevance. I suspect that in the development of a policy research methodology, it will for some time be necessary merely to collect such points before putting them in any systematic and coherent order.

Methodological Points for Policy Research

Analysis of Policies as an Aid to Methods for Policy Research

Although, as I have indicated, theory must play a distinctly secondary role in policy research, this does not imply that certain theoretical efforts may not be extremely useful. Certainly the existence of confirmed theory about an area of activity is quite valuable in the design and analysis of policies and research when the policy implementation is accompanied by research. That should be trivially evident. There is another matter, however, that may not be so evident. This is the importance of developing a theory about policies, in the sense of an understanding of important differences between types of policies. For example, there are policies that involve resource distribution (such as a Head Start program) versus policies that do not (such as the Supreme Court decision in 1954 outlawing a racially dual school system). Those policies that involve resource distribution allow, for example, research designs that trace the resources as they flow through a system (say a school system, or a housing program) and reach their final destination (or are diverted on the way). . . . Nonresource distribution policies do not allow such a research design. Thus to make such a distinction immediately gives an indication of the kind of research that can be carried out.

As another distinction, policies can be distinguished according to the relation between the direct receptor of policy and the locus of its ultimate intended impact. If the ultimate impact desired is upon children in school, and there are funds allocated to (or directives given to) a school system, then there is a long organization path which mediates impact of the policy on its ultimate intended recipients. The research design can, and probably should, include some examination of this path. In contrast, if the ultimate desired impact is on children, and resources are given directly to them or their families . . . the types of research designs that may be fruitfully used are different.

It is not my intention to develop systematically the relation between types of policies and types of research designs, but only to indicate that this can be done, and that it should be done as part of the development of a methodology for policy research. As that task is done, then knowledge of the type of policy to be investigated immediately brings into play a certain set of possible research designs, and excludes others. It is this kind of linkage that is important in the movement of policy research from an art to a science.

Two Types of Research: Inputs and Outputs Versus Social Audits

I want to describe here two types of research that may be used to study the same problem, to draw sharply the contrast between them, and then to come out strongly in favor of one of them. The type of policies to which these designs are relevant are policies involving resource distribution. In studies of resource distribution where the aim is to examine the effectiveness of these resources, the usual kind of research design has involved measurement of resource inputs, measurement of policy-relevant outcomes, and establishment of a relation between them (either through research design, as in experimental design, or in ex-post statistical controls, as in analysis of the impact of an ongoing program . . .).

I want to contrast this general research design with another that might be called a social audit. In a social audit, resource inputs initiated by policy are traced from the point at which they are disbursed to the point at which they are experienced by the ultimate intended recipient of those resources. It is, then, those resources as experienced that are related to the outcomes in the research, rather than the resources as disbursed. For there are two possible causes of the ineffectiveness of resources: the resources as experienced may be ineffective in bringing about any change; or the resources as disbursed never reach the ultimate intended recipient and are instead lost somewhere on the path between point of initial disbursement and point of experience by the ultimate recipient. In research that does not trace the resources along this path, it is impossible to distinguish these two causes of ineffectiveness, and the assumption is ordinarily made that resources as experienced are the same as resources as disbursed. But this may not be true at all . . . .

Research which is designed to trace such resource loss might be described as a "social audit." Just as with a financial audit, the flows of resources are examined to discover the paths that resources take and the possible loss of these resources through diversion. As in a financial audit, proper use of resources does not insure the ultimate effectiveness of the resources; but it does tell whether the resources are available at point of use, and if they are not, where and how they got lost. A social audit is not a substitute for a study of the effectiveness of resources which have reached their destination. It should be accompanied by such an examination. But the crucial value of the social audit as compared to research which relates inputs to outputs is that it simply gives much more information for policy. Research that relates input resources stemming from social policy to various possible outcomes of policy can tell only the levels of effectiveness and kinds of effectiveness. If it shows little or no effectiveness of certain resources, as much recent policy research in education has shown, there is little more that can be learned. It is not possible to learn from this research design whether ineffectiveness was due to intermediate resource loss or due to ineffectiveness of resources, and if the former, to see just where and how resources got diverted.

The methods for social audits have not been developed, and obviously they would differ according to the kind of institutional structure through which resources flow. The development of such methods would, however, constitute an important development in methods for policy research. Social audits would be appropriate only to certain kinds of policies, those involving resource allocation; but for those policies, they would constitute, I believe, a far superior research method than those which concentrate on relating inputs as disbursed to final outputs.

This kind of design would constitute an important change for policy research generally. For it applies to a very wide range of "evaluation research" such as that called for in much current social legislation in the United States. Most evaluation research is now carried out largely according to some "inputs versus outputs" design, without any kind of tracing of resource flow. Change to a social audit design would give much greater insight into what kind of modifications are needed for effective policies.

References

Campbell, D.T. 1971. "Methods for the experimenting society." Northwestern University, Department of Psychology. Mimeo.

Cicarelli, V. et al. 1969. The Impact of Head Start: An Evaluation of the Effects of Head Start on Children's Cognitive and Affective Development. Washington, D.C.: Government Printing Office. Distributed by Clearinghouse for Federal Scientific and Technical Information.

Coleman, J.S. 1968. "The concept of equality of educational opportunity." *Harvard Educational Review* 38 (Winter):7–22.

______, E. Heau, R. Peabody and L. Rigsby 1964. "Computers and election analysis: The New York Times project." *Public Opinion Quarterly* 28 (Fall):418–446.

Coleman, J.S., E.Q. Campbell, C.J. Hobson, J. McPartland, A.M. Mood, F.D. Weinfeld and R.L. York 1966. Equality of Educational Opportunity. Washington, D.C.: Government Printing Office.

Cronbach, L.J. and P. Suppes, eds. 1969. Research for Tomorrow's Schools. New York: Macmillan.
Hanushek, E.A. and J.F. Kain 1972. "On the value of equality of educational opportunity as a guide to public policy," in F. Mosteller and D.P. Moynihan, eds. *On Equality of Educational Opportunity.* New York: Random House.
Haworth, L. 1960. "The experimenting society: Dewey and Jordan." *Ethics* 71 (October): 27–40.

Evaluating the Quality of Medical Care

Avedis Donabedian

Many advantages are gained by using outcome as the criterion of quality in medical care. The validity of outcome as a dimension of quality is seldom questioned. Nor does any doubt exist as to the stability and validity of the values of recovery, restoration and survival in most situations and in most cultures, though perhaps not in all. Moreover, outcomes tend to be fairly concrete and, as such, seemingly amenable to more precise measurement.

However, a number of considerations limit the use of outcomes as measures of the quality of care. The first of these is whether the outcome of care is, in fact, the relevant measure. This is because outcomes reflect both the power of medical science to achieve certain results under any given set of conditions, and the degree to which "scientific medicine," as currently conceived, has been applied in the instances under study. But the object may be precisely to separate these two effects. Sometimes a particular outcome may be irrelevant, as when survival is chosen as a criterion of success in a situation which is not fatal but is likely to produce suboptimal health or crippling.[1]

Even in situations where outcomes are relevant, and the relevant outcome has been chosen as a criterion, limitations must be reckoned with. Many factors other than medical care may influence outcome, and precautions must be taken to hold all significant factors other than medical care constant if valid conclusions are to be drawn. In some cases long periods of time,

---

From Avedis Donabedian, "Evaluating the Quality of Medical Care," *Milbank Memorial Fund Quarterly,* July 1966, Vol. 44, part 2, pp. 168–170. Reprinted by permission. Footnotes have been renumbered and placed at the end.

perhaps decades, must elapse before relevant outcomes are manifest. In such cases the results are not available when they are needed for appraisal and the problems of maintaining comparability are greatly magnified. Also, medical technology is not fully effective and the measure of success that can be expected in a particular situation is often not precisely known. For this reason comparative studies of outcome, under controlled situations, must be used.

Although some outcomes are generally unmistakable and easy to measure (death, for example) other outcomes, not so clearly defined, can be difficult to measure. These include patient attitudes and satisfactions, social restoration and physical disability and rehabilitation.[2] Even the face validity that outcomes generally have as criteria of success or failure, is not absolute. One may debate, for example, whether the prolongation of life under certain circumstances is evidence of good medical care. McDermott, *et al.*, have shown that, although fixing a congenitally dislocated hip joint in a given position is considered good medicine for the white man, it can prove crippling for the Navajo Indian who spends much time seated on the floor or in the saddle.[3] Finally, although outcomes might indicate good or bad care in the aggregate, they do not give an insight into the nature and location of the deficiences or strengths to which the outcome might be attributed.

All these limitations to the use of outcomes as criteria of medical care are presented not to demonstrate that outcomes are inappropriate indicators of quality but to emphasize that they must be used with discrimination. Outcomes, by and large, remain the ultimate validators of the effectiveness and quality of medical care.

Another approach to assessment is to examine the process of care itself rather than its outcomes. This is justified by the assumption that one is interested not in the power of medical technology to achieve results, but in whether what is now known to be "good" medical care has been applied. Judgments are based on considerations such as the appropriateness, completeness and redundancy of information obtained through clinical history, physical examination and diagnostic tests; justification of diagnosis and therapy; technical competence in the performance of diagnostic and therapeutic procedures, including surgery; evidence of preventive management in health and illness; coordination and continuity of care; acceptability of care to the recipient and so on. This approach requires that a great deal of attention be given to specifying the relevant dimensions, values and standards to be used in assessment. The estimates of quality that one obtains are less stable and less final than those that derive from the measurement of outcomes. They may, however, be more relevant to the question at hand: whether medicine is properly practiced.

This discussion of process and outcome may seem to imply a simple separation between means and ends. Perhaps more correctly, one may think of an unbroken chain of antecedent means followed by intermediate ends which are themselves the means to still further ends.[4] Health itself may be a means to a further objective. Several authors have pointed out that this formulation provides a useful approach to evaluation.[5] [6] It may be designated as the measurement of procedural end points and included under the general heading of "process" because it rests on similar considerations with respect to values, standards and validation.

A third approach to assessment is to study not the process of care itself, but the settings in which it takes place and the instrumentalities of which it is the product. This may be roughly designated as the assessment of structure, although it may include administrative and related processes that support and direct the provision of care. It is concerned with such things as the adequacy of facilities and equipment; the qualifications of medical staff and their organization; the administrative structure and operations of programs and institutions providing care; fiscal organization and the like.[7] [8] The assumption is made that given the proper settings and instrumentalities, good medical care will follow. This approach offers the advantage of dealing, at least in part, with fairly concrete and accessible information. It has the major limitation that the relationship between structure and process or structure and outcome, is often not well established.

Notes

[1]P. A. Lembcke, "Medical Auditing by Scientific Methods," *JAMA* 162 (1956) 646–655. (Appendixes A and B supplied by the author.)

[2]H. R. Kelman and A. Willner. "Problems in Measurement and Evaluation of Rehabilitation," *Archives of Physical Medicine and Rehabilitation* 43 (April, 1962): 172–181.

[3]W. McDermott *et al.*, "Introducing Modern Medicine in a Navajo Comunity," *Science* 131 January 22 and 29, 1960: 197–205 and 280–287.

[4]H. A. Simon, *Administrative Behavior* (New York: The Macmillan Company, 1961), pp. 62–66.

[5]G. B. Hutchinson, "Evaluation of Preventive Services," *Journal of Chronic Diseases* 11 May, 1960: 497–508.

[6]G. James, *Evaluation of Public Health*, Report of the Second National Conference on Evaluation in Public Health, Ann Arbor, The University of Michigan, School of Public Health, 1960: pp. 7–17.

[7]E. R. Weinerman, "Appraisal of Medical Care Programs," *American Journal of Public Health* 40 September, 1950: 1129–34.

[8]F. Goldmann and E. A. Graham, *The Quality of Medical Care Provided at the Labor Health Institute, St. Louis, Missouri* (St. Louis: The Labor Health Institute, 1954). This is a good example of an approach to evaluation based on structural characteristics. In this instance, these included the layout and equipment of physical facilities, the competence and stability of medical staff, provisions made for continuity of service centering around a family physician, the scheduling and duration of clinic visits, the content of the initial examination, the degree of emphasis on preventive medicine and the adequacy of the medical records.

The Political Economy of Health Care: Dynamics Without Change

Robert R. Alford

. . . The overwhelming fact about the various reforms of the health system that have been implemented or proposed—more money, more subsidy of insurance, more manpower, more demonstration projects, more clinics—is that they are absorbed into a system which is enormously resistant to change. The reforms which are suggested are sponsored by different elements in the health system and advantage one or another element, but they do not seriously damage any interests. This pluralistic balancing of costs and benefits successfully shields the funding, powers, and resources of the producing institutions from any basic structural change.

This situation might well be described as one of "dynamics without change." This paper argues that both the expansion of the health care industry and the apparent absence of change are due to a struggle between different major interest groups operating within the context of a market society–professional monopolists controlling the major health resources, corporate rationalizers challenging their power, and the community population seeking better health care.

Although the paper generalizes from the scholarly literature as well as from documents and from interviews which took place in New York City, it should be regarded as a set of "outrageous hypotheses," in the spirit of Robert S. Lynd's classic *Knowledge for What?*[1] rather than as a theory inferred from reliable empirical findings.

Selections from pp. 128–9, 132–3, 138–9, 140, 161–4 by permission of *Politics and Society* and Robert R. Alford. Winter, 1972.

Market Versus Bureaucratic Reform

Pressures for change come largely from three types of reformers, of which the first two are most important. The first, whom I shall call the "market reformers," would expand the diversity of facilities available, the number of physicians, the competition between health facilities, and the quantity and quality of private insurance. Their assumptions are that the public sector should underwrite medical bills for the poor and that patients should be free to choose among various health care providers. The community population is regarded as consumers of health care like other commodities and is assumed to be able to evaluate the quality of service received. Market pressures will thus drive out the incompetent, excessively high priced or duplicated service, and the inaccessible physician, clinic, or hospital. The market reformers wish to preserve the control of the individual physician over his practice, over the hospital, and over his fees, and they simply wish to open up the medical schools to meet the demand for doctors, to give patients more choice among doctors, clinics, and hospitals, and to make that choice a real one by providing public subsidies for medical bills.

These assumptions are questioned by the "bureaucratic reformers." They stress the importance of the hospital as the key location and organizer of health services and wish to put individual doctors under the control of hospital medical boards and administrators. The bureaucratic reformers are principally concerned with coordinating fragmented services, instituting planning, and extending public funding. Their assumption is that the technology of modern health care requires a complex and coordinated division of labor between ambulatory and in-hospital care, primary practitioners and specialists, and personalized care and advanced chemical and electronic treatment. The community population is regarded as an external constituency of the health providers to be organized to represent its interests if necessary to maintain the equilibrium of the system. . . .

Major Interest Groups

Strategies of reform based on either "bureaucratic" or "market" models are unlikely to work. Each type of reform stresses certain core functions in the health system and regards others as secondary. But both neglect the way in which the groups representing these functions come to develop vital interests which sustain the present system and vitiate attempts at reform.

For the market reformers, supplying trained physicians, innovating through biomedical and technological research, and maintaining competition between diverse health care producers are the main functions to be maintained. They view the hospitals, medical schools, and public health agencies as only the organizational framework which sustains the primary functions of professional health care and biomedical research. However, these types of work become buttressed through institutional mechanisms which guarantee professional control, and come to constitute powerful interest groups which I shall call the "professional monopolists." Because these interest groups are at present the dominant ones, with their powers and resources safely embedded in law, custom, professional legitimacy, and the practices of many public and private organizations, they do not need to be as visibly active nor as cohesively organized as those groups seeking change.

For the bureaucratic reformers, the hospitals, medical schools, and public health agencies at all governmental levels perform the core functions of organizing, financing, and distributing health care. Hospitals are seen ideally as the center of networks of associated clinics and neighborhood health centers, providing comprehensive care to an entire local population. The bureaucratic reformers view physicians and medical researchers as performing crucial work, but properly as subordinated and differentiated parts of a complex delivery system, coordinated by bureaucrats, notably hospital administrators. However, these large-scale organizations also become powerful interest groups, which I shall call the "corporate rationalizers." These interest groups are at present the major challengers of the power of the professional monopolists, and they constitute the bulk of the membership of the various commissions of investigation and inquiry into the health care "crisis."

A third type of reformer is relatively unimportant in the American context as yet: the "equal-health advocates," who seek free, accessible, high-quality health care which equalizes the treatment available to the well-to-do and to the poor. They stress the importance of community control over the supply and deployment of health facilities, because they base their strategies upon a third set of interest groups: the local population or community affected by the availability and character of health personnel and facilities. The community population is not as powerful or as organized as the other two sets of interest groups, but has equally as great a stake in the outcomes of the operations of health institutions.

Each of these three major interest groups is internally heterogeneous. The professional monopolists include biomedical researchers, physicians in private or group practice, salaried physicians, and other health occupations seeking professional privileges and status, who differ among themselves in their relationships to each other, as well as to hospitals, medical schools, insurance plans, and government agencies, and thus their interests are affected differently by various programs of reform. But they share an interest in maintaining professional autonomy and control over the conditions of their work, and thus will—when that autonomy is challenged—act together in defense of that interest.

The corporate rationalizers include medical school officials, public health officials, insurance companies, and hospital administrators, whose organizational interests often require that they compete with each other for powers and resources. Therefore, they differ in the priority they attach to various reform proposals. But they share an interest in maintaining and extending the control of their organizations over the conditions of work of the professionals (and other employees) whose activities are key to the achievement of organizational goals.

The community population constitutes a set of interest groups which are internally heterogeneous with respect to their health needs, ability to pay, and ability to organize their needs into effective demands, but they share an interest in maximizing the responsiveness of health professionals and organizations to their concerns for accessible, high-quality health care for which they have the ability to pay. . . .

Investigations of the Health System

. . . Using the words of the 1967 National Advisory Commission on Health Manpower, the report summarizes the state of affairs: "Medical care in the United States is more a collection of bits and pieces (with overlapping, duplication, great gaps, high costs and wasted effort) than an integrated system in which needs and efforts are closely related." But, according to the Rockefeller committee, "The situation is more acute than four years ago, and deteriorating rapidly."[2]

This picture is restated in every diagnosis of the "crisis" of the health system. The figures portray dynamics without change: a rapid increase in almost every index of growth—dollars, manpower, programs—except those pertaining to quality, distribution, accessibility, and reasonable cost to the consumer.

It should be noted that the empirical criteria and basis for the judgments of quality and the adequacy of quantity and distribution are not given in this report, nor are the basic data available which would be necessary to evaluate either a specific health service or the character of coordination of diverse health institutions. The reasons for this absence of information will be discussed later in a more theoretical context, but the point is that the many critiques of the health "system" are not cumulative nor based on solid research, and thus have an ideological character, rooted in images and theories about the proper way to reorganize and coordinate the "system" . . .

What is the likely course of change? Given the central interests of each set of groups and the ease with which the equal-health advocates can be coopted, change is extremely difficult.

Crisis and the Political Economy of Health

Periodic crises, notably those in the last ten years in New York City, have been precipitated by the corporate rationalizers in an attempt to arouse support for their goals, although media exposure which defines a crisis usually has nothing to do with any change in the basic performance of the health system. The series of investigations in New York City by private, city, and state agencies from 1950 to 1971 stress the fragmentation and lack of coordination of the system, a sure sign of the ideology of corporate rationalization—as are the various reorganizations of the hospitals carried out in the last decade. But none of the reforms has touched the basic power of the private sector and its institutions.

A few crises have been precipitated by equal-health advocates moving outside the established framework of representation and influence to take disruptive, militant action. These have produced specific responses, usually in the form of new programs or still more "representation," taking the forms already described[3] . . . .

An explanation of the deep-rooted character of the dynamics without change must thus ultimately go back to the dominance of the private sector and the upper middle class. As Ginzberg also says, "The industry remains dominated by the private sector–consumers, private practitioners, voluntary hospitals."[4] Thus, a major characteristic of the public sector is that it does not have the power to challenge the domination of the private sector. Given this domination, it seems a reasonable assumption that major characteristics of the health system are due to private control. Government policy is not fundamentally important, except insofar as the policy is *not* to interfere with the private sector, or only to come forth with financial subsidies for the private sector. . . .

Given a system which cannot provide decent care for all because of the domination by the private sector, and thus a continuing "crisis," there is increasing pressure upon government to step in. But, again, because of the dominance of the private sector, government cannot act in a way which could change the system without altering the basic principle of private control over the major resources of the society. Thus, the health system exhibits a continuous contradiction between the expectations of the people for decent health care, the impossibility of the private sector to provide decent and *equal* health care for all, and the impossibility of the public sector to compensate for the inadequacies of the private sector. . . .

. . . Change is not likely without the presence of a social and political movement which rejects the legitimacy of the economic and social base of pluralist politics.

NOTES

[1] Robert S. Lynd, *Knowledge for What?* (Princeton: Princeton University Press, 1939).

[2]See the "Preliminary Report of the Governor's Steering Committee on Social Problems on Health and Hospital Services and Costs," April 15, 1971, henceforth referred to as "Preliminary Report." p. 41.

[3]See Barbara Ehrenreich and John Ehrenrich, *The American Health Empire: Power, Profits and Politics* (New York: Vintage Books, 1971), a publication of the activist New York group Health-PAC, for a similar perspective, although the authors are more optimistic about the prospects for and consequences of militant community action isolated from broader movements than my argument would lead me to be. Michael Halberstam, "Liberal Thought, Radical Theory, and Medical Practice," *The New England Journal of Medicine* 284 (27 May 1971): 1180-1185, criticizes the "radical" position on health care for essentially accepting the position I have called "bureaucratic reform." Interestingly, this criticism would apply also to the proposals advanced by Robb Burlage, one of the founders of Health-PAC. (See his *New York City's Municipal Hospitals: A Policy Review* [Washington, D.C.: Institute for Policy Studies, 1967].) Halberstam, an M.D. himself, stresses the importance of reducing alienation and depersonalization and believes that only committed individual responsibility to a patient by a health professional can provide such personalized care. In this respect the "radical" position exhibits a curious schizophrenia between a faith in the potential rationality of large-scale organization and a faith in the redeeming power of community control. Perhaps the two can be reconciled, but there have been few serious efforts to think through this problem.

[4]Eli Ginzberg et al., *Urban Health Services* (New York: Columbia University Press, 1971), p. 226.

13 Policy Development and Planning by Health Agencies

So far, we have been considering policy making by governments, but in countries where national ideologies support market solutions rather than bureaucratic ones, most policies are developed in the private sector by profit and nonprofit organizations. Even where national policies now support governmental solutions, there may still be a large group of professional and voluntary organizations, often grant-aided by government, which are responsible for service delivery. The separation of government policy making from local policy making (of administrative from executive activity) helps to avoid centralized policy making based on hard cases which make bad law. It can deal with general principles at some distance, whilst allowing sufficient discretionary authority at the executive level to permit an institution to satisfy local needs within a broad framework of policy rulings.

The rulings presented by government to executive levels may be of two kinds: the first relating to legitimation of the activity (regulation), the second relating to funding. Many countries are in a transitional position between total free enterprise and total state regulation and control of funding (Crichton, 1976); consequently, there are many profit and nonprofit organizations providing health and social services which were started before state takeovers, or which have moved in to fill gaps in state services. Naturally, there is some tension arising out of interorganizational relationships—between governments and service providers and between the providers themselves.

When governments first started to become involved in standard setting in the mid-nineteenth century, they delegated power to professional groups to control entry to membership and to take responsibility for members' professional conduct. Thus, strong professional associations developed with their own corporate policies. Gradually, as medical technology has changed and individual professionals can no longer offer a complete service on their own, there has had to be some modification of their mid-nineteenth century position. Some control over professionals is now exerted by the institutions in which they work, hospitals or other large scale organizations such as public health departments, group practices, etc., as well as by their internalized professional standards learnt while in training (Vollmer and Mills, 1966).

Controlling Standards of Practice

The medical student, the nursing trainee or the health administration resident learn during professional training years to model themselves upon established practitioners. In earlier days, ideal models were clear and unambiguous, but this is less true today—questions are continually being raised about the roles of general practitioners or nurses. And hospital administrators, who arrived late on the scene (Wilensky, 1962), are not even certain whether they are or want to be allied health professionals or business managers or something in between.

In the past, the job of the general practitioner was relatively static. He learned what was known about diagnosis and treatment of disease and how to relate ethically to his patients and his peers whilst he was studying for his degree. His general education was better than that of most people in the community and so, when he went into practice, his leadership was sought in community affairs. The specialists continued even longer with their education and role modelling. Abel-Smith (1964) has described how they often had to wait for very long periods of time to get to the top of their profession and to head up a teaching hospital department. Control was exerted by the Hippocratic Oath taken on graduation, by the power of public opinion in the community and, in the last resort, by the professional association's legal right to remove offenders' names from the medical register if they were demonstrated to be unethical.

Apart from peer reviews which were, traditionally, concerned with professional ethics only, there were some other methods used to control young professionals—those still in training, though qualified, were responsible to their teachers. Writing in 1958, Hughes also drew attention to the way in which nurses and pharmacists working alongside were expected to catch doctors' mistakes (thus teamwork is not a new concept).

But technology has developed so fast that no doctor can rely only on what he or she was taught during professional training. As well, the doctor is no longer one of the very few well-educated people in a community. Other people have been well-educated and are unwilling to be dependent on professionals' leadership. It has become clear that professional associations wishing to maintain regulatory control must be concerned with (a) maintenance of competence, (b) concern over economic exploitation and (c) involvement of the public in examination of complaints.

Professional Associations' Controls

Professional associations have a problem in standard setting because of the lack of absolutes. What is meant by competence, ethical behavior, economic exploitation, clients' rights? In addition to enforcing initial entry standards and the traditional ethical codes which were set up to protect the individual doctor-patient encounter, the associations have had to consider how to make sure that professionals keep up to date with technical information through continuing education. They have had to modify the ethical code to fit more with the times, to appoint lay representatives to their boards and to consider how to control economic exploitation. It is clear that they have been more successful in some countries than in others. Roemer (1970) has reviewed the systems of regulation internationally because it was clear that professional regulation was not working satisfactorily in the U.S., judging by the number of court cases brought against doctors. Johnson (1972) has discussed the changing position of professions today.

Different countries have sought different solutions to the new problems of control. Some have laid great emphasis on compulsory continuing education requirements, others have explored the complaints mechanisms and introduced change in judges, representation and procedures, whilst in those countries in which government is involved in funding services, there has been some scrutiny of patterns of practice. In general, since it is difficult to establish absolutes (except to set minimal standards in examinations), there has been pressure towards establishing norms of practice so that, at least, there can be comparative measurement of activity and those who are deviant may be asked to account for this deviance to their peers (McLachlan, 1976).

Obviously, control over unethical, incompetent or exploitative activities rests upon knowledge of these activities and there has been a good deal of resistance to computer control over professionals. Checks on ethics, quality and quantity of work are not much further advanced than they were in the early twentieth century, except where computerized records are kept, analysed and opened up to public view. But at least the problems are now recognized, if they are not yet being dealt with to the satisfaction of the public. The reason for the failure to advance from individual complaints to general surveillance will be obvious—for the public is dependent upon the technical expertise of the professionals who are not yet willing to accept this general surveillance as legitimate and they still have the power to resist interventions into their affairs.

It is still relatively easy for professional associations to remain in power as the regulatory bodies where there is a market situation for health care, but as soon as government starts to become the third party, involved in paying for services, then confrontations take place. The medical profession is concerned that governments will start to intervene in their discretionary areas (which are ill-defined), for governments are expected to be accountable to the taxpayers for funds spent. Just what controls will be introduced when government starts to pay? Two interesting accounts of professional resistance to government involvement in third-party payment schemes are those of Eckstein (1960) and Badgley and Wolfe (1967). Fight or flight have been two responses of individuals to the introduction of government payment schemes whilst some have been determined to work through to solutions. Badgley and Wolfe have stressed the importance of separating the regulatory from the economic bargaining functions of professional associations, but the two become difficult to disentangle when government becomes responsible both for quality and quantity of care.

Hospital Controls

Whilst the hierarchical controls over young qualified professionals have been associated with continuation of training in Europe, these are also institutional controls because postgraduate training is given in service institutions. Whilst a pyramid of authority continues to be tolerated where teaching is a major objective, hospital professional hierarchies are not very acceptable to physicians where there is no teaching. Thus, England has had to abandon the concept of the Medical Superintendent, though such a post continues to be built into the Scottish and Australian non-teaching hospitals. Hierarchies are still accepted in Eastern Europe.

The Australians, however, are moving towards the American concept of peer review based on hospital records which was introduced as part of the hospital accreditation quality control scheme in the second decade of the twentieth century (Egdahl et al., 1976). Whilst this scheme has been extremely important in its time and has been revised and updated, nevertheless, like the early professional regulatory schemes, it is not linked across to controls over efficiency, patient satisfaction or continuing education, but is concerned only with minimal standards. In England, there is great hope that consensus management will result in better control over quality and cost (Great Britain, 1972).

Group Practice Controls

There seems to be general agreement that group practice is better than solo practice for stimulating exchange of information, establishing a sound base of support and ensuring that the community physician can get some leisure (Great Britain, 1963; Field, 1976).

At the present time, controls over the standards of primary care are weak. By promoting new group practice organizations, it is thought that standards will rise. Doctors will help one another more and patients will get better care. However, there have been problems associated with the development of groups as partnerships, for many doctors are individualists who find it hard to work with others—to reach and continue agreement on sharing of expenses and profits. In consequence, the emergence of group practices has been uneven and their survival uncertain. The importance of developing better standards in primary health care is well-recognized, but the organization of structures for delivery of high standard care has been difficult to achieve. The eastern bloc has been able to build this first tier into the hierarchy more effectively than the western democracies.

Different countries have tackled this issue differently, but all have encountered certain problems: (1) the legal status of groups: should they be encouraged to incorporate rather than retain professional partnership status? (2) what are to be the organizational interrelationships between such groups and other institutions delivering services such as public health departments, hospitals, etc. In England, better linkages between public health departments and primary care physicians have been encouraged through financial incentives, whilst in North America, hospitals have begun to move into ambulatory care. The H. M. O. movement in the U.S. has been greatly encouraged because of its emphasis on prevention and on continuity of care—the linkage of surveillance and treatment programs. But in Canada and Australia there have been great difficulties in finding what incentives can be used to stimulate new and better structures for delivering primary health care. There has been great resistance to the (community) health centre movement in Britain (Hall et al., 1975), Canada (Canada, 1972), and Australia (Sax, 1972), again on grounds of possible loss of autonomy by doctors who think they may have to account to lay boards, to work in teams with other health professionals, to become salaried.

Controlling Costs

The basic ideologies of different countries have had important effects upon the development of funding policies, as Abel-Smith (1972) has pointed out.

The American ideology of free enterprise and residual welfare has resulted in a scarcely modified market system for supply of health services. Northern European nations, on the other hand, are divided between state-controlled and welfare state countries, whilst Canada and Australia respond in different ways to their colonial heritages.

The first move towards modification of the rigours of the market system was charity and the hospital systems of many countries are affected by their charitable origins. Abel-Smith (1964) has described the difficulties of British hospitals which began as custodial charitable institutions but became medical teaching centres of excellence whose services were sought by those who could pay. Australian hospitals have had some of the same problems of deciding how to manage their funding problems arising out of using the British model of voluntary charity hospitals when the model was not really appropriate in that setting.

The second move was towards the introduction of prepayment systems in Europe in the mid-nineteenth century (Abel-Smith, chapter 3), whereby those in the artisan group set up sick clubs to ensure that they could get medical care when in need of it. These sick clubs might contract with a doctor for services, but doctors greatly resented the need to make such contracts which they saw as too restrictive upon their autonomy. The taking over of such arrangements by governments later led to the inheritance of many negative feelings on the part of the professionals towards state prepayment schemes.

What is important today about health insurance schemes are the legacies they have been left which can hinder or promote the development of better interorganizational linkages. British general practitioners have been wary since before the introduction of National Health Insurance in 1911, and, despite two major reorganizations of health services since then, have continued to bargain for a certain independence from bureaucratic control (Levitt, 1976). Negative feeling toward the NHS, which was reciprocated, resulted in their initial exclusion from hospitals from 1948–1973 and neglect of their continuing education for over twenty years (Great Britain, 1968). Efforts are now being made to rectify these exclusions, but general practitioners are still anxious to maintain their distance and have bargained for a different form of remuneration from all other health service employees. This sets them apart.

Doctors in continental Europe much more readily accepted prepayment schemes because the sick funds were allowed to continue to handle the payments to them, thus providing a buffering mechanism.

In North America, prepayment schemes came in much later and had different origins from those of Europe. They were not bred out of the desperations of avoiding pauperism, but out of middle class providence. The main development of these schemes came after the Second World War and this has had important consequences for the future of health services, since as in nineteenth century Europe the first priority was to ensure that hospital expenses were paid. This led to development at first of hospital services rather than improved primary care services. It was not until the sixties that ambulatory care began to be stressed (see discussion of Neighborhood Health Centers and HMO's in Wildavsky reprint, chapter 5). (Somers and Somers, 1961).

In Canada and Australia, doctors, many of whom were British immigrants, have been reluctant to support state-subsidized medical care programs because of the perceived threat to their autonomy and have sought extensive safeguards before joining any insurance plan. Negative attitudes towards Medicare and Medibank have carried over into other sectors of health service organization, such as the development of community health centres mentioned above.

The main criticisms of unsubsidized insurance schemes are that they are inegalitarian, that they result in badly distributed professional and institutional services, they neglect the poor in favor of the middle classes and emphasize treatment rather than prevention. However, their advantages are that they enable the thrifty investor to provide for himself and his family a much wider range of service than most governments would be willing to organize as a matter of tax redistribution. They provide for choice—what many citizens want in liberal democratic countries.

Insurance programs still survive even in Britain with its state-supported health service, or because of it. The middle classes found that insurance through a provident association enabled them to beat the queue and to schedule elective treatments when they wanted them, rather than when they were summoned. However, in 1975–76, there was an open battle between the unionized hospital employees and the doctors remunerated through provident association schemes, a battle resolved by the Minister of Health agreeing to phase out private beds. (This decision was reversed in 1979 by a change in government.) Insurance schemes are, in that country, challenged by those who believe they interfere with attempts to develop egalitarian policies.

In North America, on the other hand, health insurance programs are reaching out into wider and wider fields—dental and pharmaceutical services, appliances, home nursing may now be covered by extended insurance programs. Whilst individuals seem to want this additional unsubsidized coverage (often part of a collective bargaining agreement for fringe benefits), governments are beginning to become very concerned at the amount of national income being diverted to this activity because it does not seem to be buying better health status for the people generally. The growth of medical technology and third-party health insurance, particularly since World War II, have resulted in improvements to, and demand for, diagnostic and treatment services, but little change in health outcomes.

The demand from patients for services increases when services become available; the demand by doctors for services increases as more technology becomes available, and it has become hard to exert control over demand except by restricting availability of treatment beds or diagnostic facilities.

As the rising costs of health care are recognized to be a major element in inflation, all governments are having to take direct or indirect action to control these costs whether they are in welfare state or free enterprise societies.

Medical Costs

As one can examine standards in professional practice and standards in institutional practice, so one can separate medical care costs and institutional costs, although there is some overlap.

Glaser (1970) and Marmor and Thomas (1971) have explored the effect of different payment systems for physicians upon the kind of work they do. Salaries, capitation payments and fee-for-service each have advantages and disadvantages. The greatest difference between the first two and the last is that in inflationary times doctors may be able to increase volume of services in order to retain real income levels. Naturally, this poses problems for countries like Canada and Australia which are committed to national health programs with fee-for-service remuneration for doctors within a limited budget. In the U.S., third-party insurance schemes may also obscure the real costs from buyers and sellers in a market situation.

Ideological attitudes have (up till now) determined how governments would establish policies relating to medical costs. Some governments decided many years ago that there should be equal opportunities for citizens to seek medical care—and this does not mean equal access, which is another question altogether (see Aday and Andersen, 1975). Other governments focused upon the access question and made special provision for the old or the poor who might otherwise have had difficulty paying for services. The opposite of these were rationing policies attempting to prevent overuse of services where equal eligibility had earlier been introduced but had begun to be abused.

A nation's medical care costs are affected by citizens' knowledge about how to use health services: eligibility, access and rationing policies; methods of remunerating providers and distribution of provider resources. Since it is difficult for governments to control these other aspects of policy (because they must seek consents), much attention has recently been paid to manpower distribution policies. The world market for medical manpower is now being brought under greater control through better planning of training and immigration policies. Despite some challenges by medical professional groups at local levels, governments have been able to start bringing some order into this market. This may enable smaller and poorer countries to retain those in whom they have invested capital.

Hospital Costs

Again, as in deciding how to deal with medical costs, ideological approaches will determine attitudes towards hospital costs. Knowledge by the public about how to use services; entitlement, access and deterrence policies; distribution of resources and methods of hospital financing will again be important features. In an earlier chapter, it was pointed out that hospitals are perceived to be more than medical treatment institutions—they are important centres of employment, they encourage business in the town, they are symbols of achievement and they may be important training centres.

With this range of objectives, then, policy making is complicated. One of hospitals' major problems is to decide on the locus of control, because hospital costs, apart from salaries and hotel services, are generated largely by medical staff. Whether to opt for hierarchical authority or consensus management is a matter of judgment which may have strong implications for costs.

It is clear that hospitals' objectives are not static—they vary in relation to stages of internal development and in relation to interorganizational pressures. Perrow (1965) traced three stages in the life of a community hospital in which power passed from the trustees to the medical staff and to the administrators, but Feldman (1973) has suggested that policies develop out of shifting combinations of power groups to meet those needs which are identified to be important at a particular time. Strauss et al. (1963) have also discussed the hospital's negotiated order.

Feldman's explanation of the sources of organizational power are helpful for understanding how organizations function. It will be recognized that the composition of leadership groups in small rural hospitals differs from that of large metropolitan hospitals and that their relationship to the local community, to other organizations and to governments also differs. Consequently, one can understand that different interpretations will be put upon the functioning of the hospital. Is it primarily seen as a source of employment, of tender loving care for patients or of technical excellence in diagnosis and medical treatment? Is it principally focused upon service to patients now, or teaching of students and maintenance and development of medical expertise, which have implications for future service?

Given that there is an uneven distribution of medical and administrative skill, it seems to be important to recognize that different answers will be given to the question, what is an appropriate hospital policy? And cost policies cannot be developed separately from policies about standards of service, training responsibilities, employee responsibilities and interorganizational relationships (Thompson, 1968).

THE CONTRIBUTION OF VOLUNTARY ORGANIZATIONS

In most countries voluntary organizations have pioneered new types of service provision. They often fill gaps in countries which have attempted to provide a full-scale national health service. One of the problems most nations have is the difficulty in deciding what is sickness and what is handicap or impairment and who should be responsible for the latter—health or welfare agencies?

With moves towards greater government involvement in the provision of health and welfare services, the respective functions of health and social service departments and of voluntary organizations have come into question and there has been major reconsideration (new regulation) and reorganization of charitable activities. These developments have been reviewed in the different western countries where the changes have taken place. Beveridge (1948) examined the responsibilities of voluntary bodies in Britain immediately after the introduction of the major welfare-state legislation which removed service functions across to government. He concluded that they still had an important role to play which professional workers could not fill—they had time, compassion and could experiment. Similarly, the Canadian consortium of voluntary agencies which reported on the problem of dealing with the needs of One Million Children with emotional and learning disabilities (Commission on Emotional and Learning Disorders in Children, 1970) argued that professional psychiatrists could not possibly hope to cope with such a load; it would be necessary to recruit all the potential identifiers of need and those willing to help in the community to provide the necessary services to these children.

Because they have been dependent upon subscriptions, donations or legacies, voluntary health and welfare organizations have often been very cost-conscious and have pioneered in moneysaving activities, such as outpatient care for surveillance of long-term conditions. It is the voluntary organizations which have pioneered in interorganization linkage in North America. The problem of rationalizing moneyraising and determining a more effective way to redistribute funds led American voluntary organizations in the postwar years to band together into Community Chests (later United Funds) and subsequently to set up research departments to evaluate the distribution of funds and establish priorities among the member agencies. This process and the subsequent moves into urban social planning have been reviewed by Manser (1976) in the U.S. and Carter (1974) in Canada.

Similarly, consortia of voluntary health organizations attempted to rationalize their activities and to determine priorities in joint discussions. However, like the voluntary welfare organizations, they met with difficulties because members were often unwilling to sink their individuality in the group and reserved the right to act in their own best interests. It is only very recently that nations have begun to recognize that, for a complete health care service, single hospitals are inadequate—there have to be organized linkages between hospitals and between hospital, community care and personal care programs. However, hospitals as entities are not always able to accept these ideas. Consequently, when the going became rough, the large organizations in voluntary consortia (such as the teaching hospitals) would pull out to negotiate directly and leave the smaller hospitals to cope with their own problems. It is clear that rather than being effective interest groups organized to stand up for an agreed policy, consortia of voluntary organizations have often given way to internal strains. This does not mean that they have been entirely ineffective. They have been able to channel communications—to coordinate information for members, to receive and sometimes to give agreed messages to government, and to act as buffer groups between government and hospitals.

Corporate Policies

The term corporate implies that an organization is incorporated, that it has a constitution and clearly understood terms of reference in relation to its shareholders, members, or, in the case of a municipality, its citizens. Its workforce is not part of this corporate agreement, but may have negotiated separate relationships under by-laws or contracts under current industrial relations regulations. (We have used the term loosely in this chapter to include professional associations and group practices, as well as hospitals and voluntary organizations. Not many are, in fact, incorporated.)

A profit-making organization has a clear duty to its shareholders, whilst a nonprofit institution is accountable to its voting members or appointed board. Naturally, the composition of the board will be of the greatest importance in determining how the objectives are established and worked through, but it is clear (from Perrow's study) that hospitals are further along the path towards bureaucratic management than are many governments—that is, that authority has been vested in the chief executive to develop policies and administer programs. Organizations at the operational level of the health system can be viewed in much the same way as governments for the purposes of considering policy-making processes. They need to sort out party platforms (or their equivalent) so that ideologies are clearly understood and accepted by the members, they need to be concerned about board elections and the performance of trustees (Weeks, 1976) and they need to be particularly aware of the special problems of managing organizations as complex as health service institutions both singly and linked into a system.

As in group practices/community health centres, there seem to be two main ideological issues in hospitals related to:

1. The Board's conception of its functions—should it confine itself to the business management of the hospital (representing taxpayers' interests or those of the money-raising community); or should it be specially concerned to respond to the demands of patients or potential consumers of services?
2. The concept of management styles—should there be strong hierarchical management or greater spread of responsibility through consensus management, teamwork or matrix management?

Whilst in the U.S. there now appears to be a stronger emphasis on what are called corporate managerial policies (which are equated with greater control through hierarchical authority), in the U.K. the newly reorganized NHS has gone the other way, assuming that doctors and nurses have to be brought into equally powerful management positions with the administrator so that they will begin to recognize each individual professional's responsibility for controlling costs in his clinical work.

The U.S. position is a response to the closer control over financing by the consumer and his representatives on the board, the U.K. position is a recognition that, in third-party financing, the professionals have to exert controls over spending.

Whilst there may be insufficient clarification of ideologies and a need to spell these out better, there would also appear to be need to consider making more appropriate use of scientific methods in policy development: to explore causes and measure consequences of actions, though sometimes even by describing a situation as a detached observer the participants in that situation may be able to see themselves differently and can take remedial action.

A report on a recent survey of chief executive officers' activities in American hospitals and group health plans (Kuhl, 1977) lists four major areas of responsibility: internal management (in which there are six main areas of work: organizational design, personnel management, financial management, logistical management, service delivery and legal work); organization development; external relations (in which they have responsiblity for community relations, organization relations and government relations) and environmental surveillance (or market research).

Clearly, given the scope of this reader, it is not possible to look at any of these areas in detail. It is assumed that students of health services administration/planning/research will also be studying organization theory and management practice and so no further references are given.

This chapter has been concerned with identifying some difficult issues of effectiveness and efficiency in the professional association, group practice, or hospital. It has attempted to clarify that the problems of standards and costs cannot be solved without interorganizational cooperation at the service delivery level, although much can be done within corporate organizations to improve management efficiency by developing clear policies to deal with the multiplicity of objectives which have to be met. Much more is known about internal management theory than about interorganizational theory (Mechanic, 1976) but the need for greater understanding both of theory and practice has come to be recognized.

Discussion of Readings and References

For planning at the institutional level of the health care system there is much practical advice available, so much that it has been impossible to select readings to match all the topics raised.

Only one reading has been chosen:

1. Herbert L. Laframboise's account of "Moving a Proposal to a Positive Decision" (reprinted in part) is, in fact, about bureaucratic planning but since it discusses general principles of effective policy implementation in the health field, it seems to be appropriate to put forward as a final reading in this book.

2. A useful review of methods of quality control in health services is available in *A Question of Quality*? edited by Gordon McLachlan which includes papers by British and American experts.

Control of standards through licencing of practitioners has had to be reconsidered in recent years, particularly since new occupational groups of health professionals have been emerging. Ruth Roemer began by studying regulations in the United States and has since made a series of international investigations. These are listed in the bibliography.

3. If control of quality (effectiveness) has been one concern, control of costs (efficiency) has been another. A broad review of this territory can be found in Brian Abel-Smith's, *Value for Money in Health Services* (which takes an international approach).

4. Elliot A. Krause has discussed "Health Planning as a Managerial Ideology" in the *International Journal of Health Services* 3 (1973) pages 445–62.

5. Three lists of references are attached to this chapter: the first is concerned with epidemiologists' contribution to health planning, the second with work of health economists, the third lists some publications of health manpower planners. A general review of *Health Planning in the U.S.*, which discussed the contributions of the various disciplines to practical problem solving, edited by W. A. Reinke and K. N. Williams was published in 1972. More recent publications are those of H. H. Hyman (1975).

6. Since then, centralized planning agencies in the United Kingdom and the United States have developed manuals for guidance for the use of local health planning agencies (e.g., Great Britain D. H. S. S. 1976, U. S. H. E. W., 1963, 1976) and forecasts have begun to emerge from these agencies. Forecasts of bed needs and manpower resources required are now being calculated. Examples of these forecasting documents can be obtained locally from planning departments.

7. Finally, students may be interested in the continuing contribution of voluntary agencies to social service planning. The reviews by Wolfenden (1978), Manser (1976), Carter (1974), and Australian Council of Social Service (1977) will provide information about this sector of activity in the four countries.

Further References on Epidemiology and Its Applications

General Texts

Friedman, G. D. *Primer of Epidemiology.* Toronto: McGraw-Hill, 1974.

MacMahon, B. and Pugh, T. F. *Epidemiology: Principles and Methods.* Boston: Little, Brown and Co., 1970.

Morris, J. N. *Uses of Epidemiology.* New York: Churchill Livingstone, 1975.

White, K. L. and Henderson, M., eds. *Epidemiology as a Fundamental Science.* New York: Oxford University Press, 1976.

Hetzel, Basil S. *Health and Australian Society.* Harmondsworth, Middlesex: Penguin, 1974.

Epidemiology and Planning

White, K. L. and Henderson, M., eds. *Epidemiology as a Fundamental Science.* New York: Oxford University Press, 1976.

Holland, Walter and Gilderdale, Susie, eds. *Epidemiology and Health.* London: Henry Kimpton, 1977.

Knox, G., ed. *Epidemiology: Uses in Health Care Planning.* I. E. A. and WHO Handbooks. London: Oxford University Press, 1979.

Cochrane, A. L. *Effectiveness and Efficiency.* London: The Nuffield Provincial Hospitals Trust, 1972.

Health Commission of New South Wales, Division of Health Research. *Health Care Survey 1975.* Sydney: H. C. N. S. W., 1978.

Hyman, H. H., *Health Planning: A Systematic Approach.* Germantown, Md.: Aspen Systems Corp., 1975.

MacStravic, R. E., *Determining Health Needs.* Ann Arbor: Health Administration Press, 1978.

Epidemiology and Management

Bunker, John; Barnes, Benjamin; Mosteller, Frederick. *Costs, Risks and Benefits of Surgery.* New York: Oxford Univeristy Press, 1977.

Schoenbaum, Steven et al. "Benefit Cost Analysis of Rubella Vaccination Policy." *New England Journal of Medicine* 294 (1976): 306–10.

Weinstein, Milton and Stason, William. *Hypertension: A Policy Perspective.* Cambridge: Harvard University Press, 1977.

Neuhauser, Duncan and Lewicki, Ann. "National Health Insurance and the Sixth Stool Guaiac." *Policy Analysis* 2, (Spring 1976): 175–96.

Jonsson, Egon and Mark, Lars-Ake. "CAT Scanners: The Swedish Experience." *Health Care Management Review* 2 (Spring 1977): 37–53.

Epidemiology and Program Evaluation

Rutman, L., ed. *Evaluation Research Methods: A Basic Guide.* Beverly Hills: Sage Publications, 1977.

Schulberg, H. C.; Sheldon, A. and Baker, F., eds. *Program Evaluation in the Health Fields.* New York: Human Sciences Press, 1977.

Suchman, E. A. *Evaluative Research.* New York: Russell Sage Foundation, 1967.

Weiss, Carol H. *Evaluation Research.* Englewood Cliffs, New Jersey: Prentice-Hall, 1972.

Brook, R. H. and Appel, Francis A. "Quality-of-Care Assessment: Choosing a Method of Peer Review." *New England Journal of Medicine* 288 (June 21, 1973): 1323–29.

Deniston, O. L. and Rosenstock, I. M. "The Validity of Non-Experimental Design in Research." *Health Services Reports* 88 (1971): 153–64.

Donabedian, A. "Evaluating the Quality of Medical Care." *Milbank Memorial Fund Quarterly* 44, part 2 (July 1966) 166–206.

Enterline, P. E. et al. "Effects of Free Medical Care on Medical Practice—The Quebec Experience." *New England Journal of Medicine* 288 (31, May 1973): 1152–55.

Greenberg, D. S. "X-Ray Mammography: Background to a Decision." *New England Journal of Medicine* 295 (1976): 739–40.

Greenberg, D. S. "X-Ray Mammography: Silent Treatment for a Troublesome Report." *New England Journal of Medicine* 296 (1976): 1015–16.

Hulka, B. S. "Epidemiological Applications to Health Services Research." *Journal of Community Health* 4 (1978): 140–49.

Ipsen, J. "Epidemiology and Planning." *International Journal of Health Services* 1 (1971): 149–53.

Kessner, D. M.; Kalk, C. and Singer, J. "Assessing Health Quality: The Case for Tracers." *New England Journal of Medicine* 288 (June 1973): 189–94.

Mather, H. E.; Pearson, N. G.; Read, K. L. Q. et al. "Acute Myocardial Infarction: Home and Hospital Treatment." *British Medical Journal* 3 (1971): 334–38.

Meredith, J. "Program Evaluation Techniques in the Health Services." *American Journal of Public Health* 66 (1976): 1069–73.

Porter, A. C. and Chibucos, T. R. "Common Problems of Design and Analysis in Evaluative Research." *Sociological Methods in Research* 3 (Feb. 1975): 235–37.

Roghman, K. J. et al. "Rochester Child Health Surveys I: Objectives, Organization and Methods." *Medical Care* 8 (Jan.-Feb. 1970): 47–59.

Roos, N. "Evaluating Health Programs, Where Do We Find the Data?" *Journal of Community Health* 1 (Fall 1975): 39–51.

Shapiro, C. et al. "Periodic Breast Cancer Screening in Reducing Mortality from Breast Cancer." *Journal of the American Medical Association* 215 (1971): 1777–85.

Schoolman, H. M. et al. "Statistics in Medical Research: Principles vs. Practices." *Journal of Laboratory and Clinical Medicine* 71 (March 1968): 357–67.

Winkelstein, W., Jr. "Epidemiological Considerations Underlying the Allocation of Health and Disease Care Resources." *International Journal of Epidemiology* 1 (1972): 69.

Further References on Economics of Health Care

Hauser, M. M., ed. *The Economics of Medical Care.* London: George Allen and Unwin, 1972.

Cooper, Michael H. and Culyer, Anthony J., eds. *Health Economics.* Harmondsworth, Middlesex: Penguin, 1973.

Abel-Smith, Brian. *Value for Money in Health Services.* London: Heinemann, 1976.

Culyer, A. J. *Need and the National Health Service.* London: Martin Robertson, 1976.

Cooper, Michael H. *Rationing Health Care.* London: Croom Helm, 1975.

McKinlay, John B., ed. *Economic Aspects of Health Care.* New York: Prodist, 1973.

Fuchs, Victor R. *Who Shall Live?* New York: Basic Books, 1974.

Harris, Seymour E. *The Economics of Health Care.* Berkeley: McCutcheon, 1975.

Judge, Ken. *Rationing Social Services.* London: Heinemann, 1978.

Migue, J.-L. and Belanger, G. *The Price of Health.* Toronto: Macmillan, 1975.

Evans, Robert G. "Economic Perspective." In *National Health Insurance: Can the U.S. Learn from Canada*?, ed. Spyros Andreopoulos. New York: John Wiley and Sons, 1975.

Seldon, A.; Culyer, A. J. and Lindsay, C. *The Price of Health.* Melbourne: Office of Health Care Finance, 1969.

Scotton, Richard B. *Medical Care in Australia: An Economic Diagnosis.* Melbourne: Sun Books, 1974.

Further References on Health Manpower Planning

Abel-Smith, Brian and Gales, Kathleen. *British Doctors at Home and Abroad.* London: Occasional Papers in Social Administration, no. 8, Bell, 1963.

Gish, Oscar. *Doctor Migration and World Health.* London: Occasional Papers in Social Administration, no. 43, Bell, 1971.

Abel-Smith, Brian. *Value for Money in Health Services.* London: Heinemann, 1976.

Dublin, T. D. "The Migration of Physicians to the U.S. *New England Journal of Medicine*, 20 April, 1972, p.1.

Hall, Thomas L. "Estimating Requirements and Supply: Where do We Stand?" First Pan-American Conference on Health Manpower Planning, Washington, D.C.: P.A.H.O. and W.H.O., 1974, pp.58–66.

Kreisberg, Harriet M.; Wu, John; Hollander, Edward D. and Bow, Joan. *Methodological Approaches for Determining Health Manpower Supply & Requirements.* Vols. I and II. Washington, D.C.: DHEW Publications nos. (HRFA) 76–14511/2, 1976.

Roemer, Ruth and Roemer, Milton I. *Health Manpower Policies under Five National Health Care Systems.* Washington, D.C.: DHEW, 1977.

Roemer, Ruth and Roemer, Milton I. *Health Manpower under National Health Insurance—the Canadian Experience.* Washington, D.C. D.H.E.W.

Roemer, Ruth and Roemer, Milton I. *Health Manpower in the Changing Australian Health Services Scene.* Washington, D.C.: U.S. Dept. of HEW, (HRA) 76–58, 1976.

Moving a Proposal to a Positive Decision: A Case History of the Invisible Process

Hubert L. Laframboise

The Throne Speech of January 4, 1973 contained the following statement:

"In response to the increasing importance of fitness for the well-being and health of Canadians, and the need for greater opportunities for people to participate in sports activities, it is proposed over the next three fiscal years to more than double the current level of expenditures under the fitness and amateur sport program.

"Plans for a greatly expanded and a strengthened program will be announced."

The foregoing announcement, which reflected a proposed increase from 8.8 to 17.5 million dollars over the next 3 years, was the culmination of a process of ten months' duration. The process had two aspects, i.e. the "visible" aspect which consisted of personalities and attitudes, of timing, of the inevitable role of luck or good fortune, of contacts and discussions outside of channels, and of public opinion.

The mechanical or procedural steps by which a proposal is moved up the decision-making ladder are no secret. Whatever the bureaucracy, these steps are formalized and are available in one book of rules or another. In the federal service there are two principal routes, one via the budget process leading, through a Minister, to the Treasury Board, and the other, by Cabinet submission, again through a Minister, to the Privy Council Office, to a cabinet committee and to the Cabinet itself. A knowledge of these

---

From Hubert L. Laframboise, "Moving A Proposal to a Positive Decision: A Case History of the Invisible Process", reprinted from *Optimum,* vol. 4, no. 3, 1973, Bureau of Management Consulting, DSS, Ottawa, Ontario K1A 0T5.

processes in mechanical terms is the stock in trade of every senior official and needs no elaboration here.

What is not known, in a conceptual way, are the conditions, events and steps outside the formal process which are often decisive in the outcome of a proposal. This "invisible" process is an arcane field to most planners and innovators, who are at a loss to understand why some perfectly sound proposals lie stillborn and dusty in a file drawer while other, apparently less worthy, proposals are accepted and implemented . . . .

Run a Horse Not Outclassed by the Field

"There is a law of limited numbers which applies to ideas in good currency just as it applies to ladies' fashions—that is to say there can only be so many operative at one time."[1]

What are "ideas in good currency"? They are the ideas or problems, relatively few in number at any given time, which occupy public and political attention. It follows that proposals developed within the framework of current ideas or current problems have a much greater chance of success than those developed in areas where there is no widespread awareness, sensitivity, or feeling of the need for forward thrust. . . .

In the case of Fitness and Amateur Sport, the proposal developed in the Department of National Health and Welfare to drastically augment the program touched on two concerns: the quality of life, including particularly the use of leisure time, and the rising costs of health care, much of which could be attributed to the lack of fitness of the general population. Coupled with these was the prospect of the 1976 Olympic Summer Games in Montreal, and a surge of public interest, particularly in Ottawa, in cycling, jogging, weight reduction and ice skating. These conditions are all positive and reflect the kind of indicators that should be used in selecting an area for policy development.

The first lesson to be learned from this case history of the Fitness and Amateur Sport decision, therefore, is that it is important to select areas for policy development that fall within current concerns, and that affect as many of these current concerns as possible. Proposals so chosen might not win the race but they will, at least, not be outclassed by the field.

Personalities Count

In the early spring of 1972, Philippe de Gaspé Beaubien, President of the National Advisory Council on Fitness and Amateur Sport, decided that the time was ripe to make a plea for a greatly expanded federal program for physical recreation and sport. He knew that the Prime Minister was not only a strong believer in physical recreation and fitness but that he also pursued a lifestyle in which exercise and sport played an important part.

Sharing the Prime Minister's interest, particularly in the field of sports excellence, was the then Minister of National Health and Welfare, the Honourable John Munro. The major sports activities launched by Mr. Munro during his tenure are legion including the Canada Winter and Summer Games, the Olympic trials, the Canada Fitness Awards and the Arctic Games. His keen interest and support were critical in the staging of the historic Russia-Canada hockey series of 1972. He was instrumental in the establishment of the National Sports Administration Centre in Ottawa.

It is a truism that ideas move forward among sympathetic partisans who share the decision-making power and that they stall when the partisans are unsympathetic. Sympathetic partisans look at proposals with rose-coloured glasses; they accept some exaggeration as justification and overlook potential drawbacks. Unsympathetic partisans, on the other hand, magnify drawbacks and see the slightest error in fact as grounds for discrediting all the evidence.

The besetting sin of the "rational" planner is that he assumes that his case hinges on the evidence he presents with too little consideration for the personalities and attitudes of the "jury." In the case of the Fitness and Amateur Sport decision the "jury" was sympathetic indeed.

Always Do Your Homework

Proposals that are trite and supported only by shoddy or transparent arguments are offensive to intelligent people even when the proposals are made in an area of current concern and the decision-makers are initially sympathetic. It follows that good solid staff work is needed even when circumstances are otherwise favourable.

After conversations with the Minister of National Health and Welfare, and the Deputy Minister of National Welfare, Philippe Beaubien identified a consensus in favour of a comprehensive ten-year Master Plan for a greatly-augmented federal Fitness and Amateur Sport Program. Such a document, prepared for consideration by the National Advisory Council on Fitness and Amateur Sport, and submitted by the Council to the Minister of National Health and Welfare, would carry the added weight of the Council, made up of twenty-eight citizens influential in, and representative of, physical recreation and sports interests in Canada.

The following strategy was adopted for preparing the ten-year Master Plan. An official was chosen to coordinate the preparation of the document; an advisory committee was formed of knowledgeable senior officials; discussions were held to present and review ideas; Directors of Recreation from several provinces were invited to come to Ottawa and express their views; a Dean of Physical Education accepted an invitation to present his ideas; and interviews were held by the coordinating official with individual senior program managers including some on the Health Side of the Department.

All this was done with very tight deadlines that were designed to have a polished document ready for submission to the National Advisory Council at its meeting in June, 1972. Started in April the report was finished on time to be circulated in French or English to all Council members prior to the June meeting. Also prior to the meeting a committee was chosen from among Council members to give particular attention to revising the Report.

The Report eventually submitted to Council proposed two sets of activities, one to focus on mass physical recreation, the other to focus on the pursuit of sports excellence. A number of key activities were identified, proposed and costed within each of the two areas and these costs were calculated for every year in the ten-year plan. The activities chosen to make up the proposal were the most attractive and sensible from among the dozens that had been suggested during the fact-finding and review process. The product of this phase was a 21-page report, written in the plainest possible language but covering all the major issues that related to the subject.

And Add a Little Pizzaz

The inclination of some federal bureaucrats to think of innovation as simply doing more of the same, and their inclination to couch their reports in excessively sober and cautious terms is well-known. To counteract these tendencies a contract was entered into with a consultant in marketing whose task was to work closely with the coordinating official and the advisory committee to ensure that both the content and the form of the Master Plan Report conformed with the best marketing principles. In capsule form these principles require the right product, with the right promotion, put in the right place at the right price.

The consultant, who had a deep background in advertising and marketing, provided the yeast for what could otherwise have been an unleavened mass of fact and argument. He contributed during the preparation of the report to the Fitness and Amateur Sport Council and made the revisions which Council proposed before giving the final approval.

The lesson to be learned from the successful participation of the outside consultant is that it pays to have a contribution by someone who is skilled in advocacy, who is sensitive to the shape and presentation of a good product, and who is untainted by the conservatism of career bureaucrats.

Find a Prophet from Another Country

In no milieu is the quotation "A prophet is not without honour, save in his own country and in his own house," more apt than in the federal public service. The worth of recommendations from insiders tends to be discounted while the value of those from outsiders tends to be inflated. The significance of this phenomenon is well understood in business circles where outside management consultants often wield a lot of influence even where the solutions eventually proposed by the consultants have been suggested to them by regular staffers of the firm under examination.

In the case of the Master Plan, the report was written at the request of the National Advisory Council on Fitness and Amateur Sport by insiders with the advice of the marketing consultant on contract, reviewed by the advisory committee and offered for consideration to the National Advisory Council which was, in this case, the outside authority. At its June 1972 meeting, the Council considered the proposals for much-expanded activities and decided on some modifications. These were recorded by the marketing consultant who was charged with whipping the Master Plan Report into its final form. The report was then circulated to all members of the Council who gave their approval.

The extent of the lobbying by individual Council members, who come from every province in Canada, is not known. . . .

On June 30, 1972, the Report was submitted to the Minister of National Health and Welfare by the National Council, and received by him with enthusiasm as a document which he could use in support of augmenting the activities and the funding of recreation and sports programs. With the imprimatur of the National Council, the Report carried the weight of the outside authority, and the Council, in effect, had performed the role of the "prophet from another country."

Timing, Timing, Timing!

The summer of 1972 was a period during which political parties were busy putting together platforms for the forthcoming federal election. In the case of the party in power, the preelection period is a time for reviewing all the proposals in hand to determine which ones can be presented to the people during the campaign. It was under these circumstances that the Master Plan Report was no doubt discussed.

A decision was taken to propose a greatly-increased Fitness and Amateur Sport program as part of the platform of the Liberal Party. . . .

There is no doubt that the timing of the Master Plan Report, coming as it did just prior to an election campaign, was superb even though this was not necessarily planned in advance. Nor is it suggested that all proposals be held back until just before an election, which would be patently ridiculous.

At the same time, the officials involved in preparing the Report were not unconscious of the timing element. Deadlines were scrupulously observed to ensure that the Report from Council was received in ample time for consideration prior to the election. If, for instance, the deadlines had been slipped, and if the Report, as a consequence, had not been ready till October 1, it could easily have fallen on barren ground in the sense that the election platform of the party in power would have already been formed.

The timing factor is critical in other ways. The budget cycle, for instance, has deadlines for various stages which limit the periods during which proposals can be included. If a critical deadline is missed, a whole year can be lost, and the proposal can be dusty and dog-eared by the time it is resurrected. There are avenues, of course, by which proposals can be acted upon outside the regular budget cycle such as by Cabinet submission and supplementary estimates, but this route can be fraught with obstacles.

On the other hand, for the real gamblers, there may be an advantage in putting proposals forward outside the budget cycle, particularly if they involve large sums of money. The rationale for doing this is that a proposal may be lost in the ruck of all other budget proposals while it is sure of separate consideration if it is dealt with outside the cycle.

In the case of the Fitness and Amateur Sport Program, the proposal for a much-increased scale of activity was actually dealt with outside the budget cycle, i.e. by Cabinet submission and supplementary estimates, but this was not done by choice. The decision announced in the Throne Speech on January 4 was itself out of phase with the cycle and separate handling was therefore necessary.

Marshall the Troops and Strike Up the Band

The collaboration of Health Side and Welfare Side officials during the preparation of the Master Plan Report led to the idea that both the medical profession and the physical educators had critical contributions to make to fitness programs. It was also noted that cooperation between the two professions in the fitness field left much to be desired.

From this conclusion it was decided to look into the holding of a National Conference on Fitness and Health to which leaders in medicine, recreology and physical education would be invited. Initial enquiries made it abundantly evident that such a Conference had a broad base of enthusiasm on which to build.

Accordingly it was decided to hold a National Conference in Ottawa, and to invite about 150 participants from the interested professions. An invitation list was compiled on the basis of a 75 per cent acceptance rate and a tentative program of talks and workshops was drawn up.

As it turned out the enthusiasm was much underestimated. Not only did practically every invitee accept but the telephone lines were clogged by calls from professionals who were irate at having been overlooked in the initial round of invitations. . . .

In preparing the program, the organizers went after the very best speakers and the highest-ranking dignitaries.

The Conference was a resounding success and the enthusiasm of the participants was communicated to the new Minister of National Health and Welfare, the Honourable Marc Lalonde, who underwent the exercise and fitness tests which were demonstrated as part of the conference proceedings. At the principal dinner, Mr. Lalonde spoke glowingly of the federal interest in recreation and sports.

It is a matter of luck that the Conference was held at the same time as decisions were being made on what to include in the Speech from the Throne. It was at this time that the actual decision to implement the proposal for a much-expanded program was taken. The decision was announced in the Throne Speech of January 4, 1973. Approval had at last been obtained after a process of ten months' duration.

There is no doubt that the National Conference, which "marshalled the troops and struck up the band" was an important factor in assuring federal authorities of the widespread support for an expanded program.

Conclusion

Many of the events and circumstances of the "invisible process" leading to a favourable decision on the Fitness and Amateur Sport proposal were sheer luck, and some of the actions taken, such as the holding of the National Conference on Fitness and Health, were not part of any overall strategy.

In these respects, this case history is an exercise in hindsight. At the same time the story has some lessons to teach which could usefully become part of the strategy to move proposals up to a point of favourable decision.

To paraphrase T. S. Eliot—

Between the idea and the action
Between the conception and the creation
Between the emotion and the response
Falls the Shadow.

With the rate and scale of change in our society, and the need to create or alter policy to meet that change, the "invisible process" can be ignored only at great peril if the Shadow is to be removed and plans translated into action.

NOTES

[1]Donald Schon, "Change and Industrial Society," The 1970 Reith Lectures, British Broadcasting Corporation.

14 The Use of Paradigms in Policy Analysis

Structuring Thinking

This book has tried to bring together many people's ways of looking at policy and trying to make sense of it.

The volume begins with a discussion of the concept policy, which is, in general, well understood to be guidelines for action. However, the boundaries of policy are not well established. Policy analysts and policy makers tend to include discussions of whatever is convenient to them, because these interpreters of reality cannot cope with more than a middle-range level of thinking. It is not practical to try to include all the variables when developing guidelines for action because of the impossibility of identifying what they are and how they relate to one another.

Individuals develop mental maps of the society which surrounds them. Some have more extensive and more detailed mental maps than others. The maps are all unique, having been developed out of the individuals' experiences of living. Yet, much is shared by those living in the same cultural milieux—no map may be the same as any other, but neither will the maps of those who live in close proximity and share similar beliefs be altogether different.

Paradigms

The main purpose of this book has been an attempt to identify paradigms which policy analysts and policy makers might be able to use to structure their thinking. It may be stretching the term to call the propositions analysed in this book paradigms, but I have found no better word to explain the relationship of these propositions to that slice of reality which is the subject of analysis here—namely, policy making.

According to Horowitz (1961), it was Merton (1945) who developed the idea of using paradigms as instruments of scientific analysis:

> The paradigm which began as a formal schematization of a set of hypotheses or theories pertaining to a particular field of investigation, has now grown into a methodological device for the reduction of problems to a logically consistent model. . . . The purposes of the paradigm are to offer a classificatory system that can account for all the aspects of a given frame of reference, an inventory of extant findings, an indication of the consistency of results achieved and the conceptual apparatus used, and also to assess the nature and quality of the evidence brought into play. The paradigm is thus not so much a method of investigation as a formal mode of investigating the investigators. . . . A significant use of the paradigm has been the blocking out of unsystematic work into a systematic form. This enables the investigator to get at the logical core of a position, if indeed the core is found to be logical.

Horowitz was careful to point out that paradigms have their limitations: "While it may often be the case that the inability to place the study in paradigm form is evidence that such a study is illogical or vaporous, such an inability may also be due to the complexities of issues under consideration." [Pp. 117–19]

The concept of paradigms was developed further by Kuhn (1962) when he was reviewing the history of scientific revolutions. "These I take to be universally recognized scientific achievements that for a time provide model problems and solutions to a community of practitioners." [P. x] Kuhn distinguished between rules ("the particular loci of commitment" at a period of time), paradigms ("a set of recurrent and quasi-standard illustrations of various theories in their conceptual, observational and instrumental applications" [p. 43]), and normal science ("research firmly based upon one or more past scientific achievements, achievements that some particular scientific community acknowledges for a time as supplying a foundation for its further practice" [p. 10]). A community's paradigms, he said, "are revealed in its textbooks, lectures and laboratory exercises," and, despite occasional ambiguities, "the paradigms of a mature scientific community can be determined with relative ease (p. 43)."

Kuhn pointed out that the scientific approach to problem definition and problem solving is not universal. It occurs only in those countries where the Greek heritage was accepted. In the ideology of science is the concept of progress:

> Scientific progress is not different from progress made in other fields but the absence at most times of competing schools that question each other's aims

> and standards makes the progress of a normal scientific community far easier to see. Reception of a common paradigm has freed the scientific community from the need to reexamine the first principles, [so that] the members of that community can concentrate exclusively upon the subtlest and most esoteric of the phenomena that concern it. [Pp. 161–62]

Kuhn also recognized that there were some analogies between the development of knowledge in scientific communities and other communities of interest such as the arts or theology.

> No creative school recognizes a category of work that is, on the one hand a creative success, but is not, on the other, an addition to the collective achievement of the group. If we doubt, as many do, that non-scientific fields make progress, that cannot be because individual schools make none. Rather it must be because there are always competing schools, each of which constantly questions the very foundations of the others. . . . [P. 162]

There are, of course, more competing schools of thought in the social sciences than in the natural sciences, so these make the value context more obvious.

Policy making may be regarded as an art rather than a science, though policy analysis appears to be becoming more scientific. Is it reasonable to consider applying the concept of paradigms to policy development?

In a recently published *Dictionary of the Social Sciences* (Reading, 1977), the definition of a paradigm is much looser than either Merton's or Kuhn's definitions: it is defined as "1. case employed as example, 2. framework of basic *concepts* and *postulates* within which research proceeds (Kuhn)." This book has considered case studies and postulates rather than concepts. The lack of a generally agreed framework of concepts for viewing health policy development was the theme of a recent issue of the *Journal of Health Politics, Policy and Law* (1:2 [1976]: 196–213).

Yet, it would seem that some order has begun to emerge, that the cases and postulates can be linked together so as to make some sort of pattern in thinking. One way of linking the postulates is to set them within a framework of knowledge and its uses, the other to set them within a political context. The two are not separate but overlapping. The former emphasizes content—methods of analysis of reality, findings, communication of ideas—the latter emphasizes process—the movement of issues through the political system.

Knowledge and Its Uses

Stark (1958) developed a paradigm to explain the elements involved in the process of cognition:

The subject and his approach	The categorical layer of the mind (time, space and causality)
	The physical apparatus of perception
	The axiological layer of the mind ("established truths")
The objective world	The objects of knowledge The materials of knowledge

> The apprehension of meaning will be an act of the *whole* personality including the specifically social sector of the mind. . . . In matters social at any rate, valuation—valuation of a specific kind, entirely unlike what is commonly called prejudice— does not follow upon but must *precede* the act of cognition. Out of the welter and boundless variety of social facts we only study—indeed we only notice—those which have significance according to the system of values with which we approach them. . . . [p. 108]

Willer (1971) has explained how different societies rely upon different approaches to social analysis—magical, mystical, religious, and scientific. Scientific approaches have greater power because this kind of thinking combines rationalism, empiricism, and abstraction, but since scientific thinking is more complex, there has been no society in which science has predominated in determining thought.

> Sciences have, instead, formed subcultures separated by their distinctive mode of thought from simple empiricism and/or rationalism in other sectors of society. . . . [P. 105] Magical empirical power, whether political or economic, has been able to control most scientific work in Western societies. . . . [P. 136]
>
> Science is not working for its own goals but is subordinated to empirical goals of worldly power. . . . The lopsided development of science in favour of physical, chemical and biological science over the social sciences is not due to the complexity of data of the social sciences or any of the other excuses that are bandied about—all data are complex until subsumed under a rational system of explanation. . . . If social science were to develop scientifically, it is probable that its scientific power would replace the present magical power in these societies and the whole basis of the present power structures. It is doubtful, however, that this development would be popular in the present power circles; the economic and political structures as long as they are based on magical power will continue to reserve support for physical sciences and for empirical work only in the social sciences. [P. 131]

It will be recalled that Lukes (1974) developed a concept of the three dimensions of social power: 1) open discussion of social issues in democratic societies, with 2) concealment of important relevant information by elites and 3) failure to recognize issues because of cultural limits to knowledge. Holzner and Marx (1979) have examined how knowledge is disseminated through a society whilst other sociologists, such as Fay (1975), have taken more of an action orientation in order to consider how change in use of knowledge is brought about.

For Holzner and Marx,

> The knowledge system can be seen as social arrangements clustering around the processes of knowledge production, organization and storage, distribution and use. . . . E. C. Hughes (1958) distinguished among three occupational models: science, professions and business. Science is concerned with the discovery and systematization of knowledge; the professions represent the giving of esoteric services to clients who, as laymen, cannot be expected to handle highly technical problems by themselves. The clients are further perceived as incapable of evaluating the work of the professionals, whose practice is based on some body of applied theory. . . . [Pp. 12–13] Business, the formation of policy, social and political movements, all are among the users of organized knowledge. . . . The idea of a postmodern society is that of a relatively self-conscious, reflective social system, which some view as an object capable of deliberate change through the systematic use of organized knowledge. . . . The expectation that organized knowledge in the sciences and technical and professional fields is to be a major factor in production, policy forming and indeed in the quality of life experienced by citizens is virtually taken for granted today. [Pp. 14–15]

Since business, policy formulators, and social and political movements are users of organized knowledge produced by others, it may be best to start by looking at the processes of knowledge production first.

The Production of Knowledge about Society

Berger and Luckmann (1966) have explained three different approaches to the structuring of thinking:

> The man in the street does not ordinarily trouble himself about what is "real" to him and about what he "knows" unless he is stopped short by some sort of problem. He takes his "reality" and his "knowledge" for granted. The sociologist cannot do this if only because of his systematic awareness of the fact that men in the street take quite different "realities" for granted as between one society and another. The sociologist is forced by the very logic of this discipline to ask, if nothing else, whether the difference between the two "realities" may not be understood in relation to various differences between the two societies. The philosopher, on the other hand, is professionally obligated to take nothing for granted and to obtain maximal clarity as to the ultimate status of what the man in the street believes to be "reality" and "knowledge". Put differently, the philosopher is driven . . . to differentiate between valid and invalid assertions about the world. . . . [P. 2]

But all of these, the man in the street, the sociologist, and the philosopher, develop their social constructions of reality within a social context which has ideologizing influences. Mannheim (1936), who made a major contribution to understanding the sociology of knowledge,

> believed that ideologizing influences, while they could not be eradicated completely, could be mitigated by systematic analysis of as many as possible of the varying socially grounded positions. In other words, the object of thought becomes progressively clearer with this accumulation of different perspectives

> on it. . . . Mannheim believed that different social groups vary greatly in their capacity . . . to transcend their own narrow social position [and he] stressed the power of "utopian" thought which (like ideology) produces a distorted image of social reality but (unlike ideology) has the dynamism to transform that reality into its image of it. . . . [P. 9]

There is usually a closer identification between the philosopher and sociologist than between the sociologist and the man in the street, because the sociologist is exposed to philosophical learning when he is being trained in methodology. Benton (1977) and other philosophers have discussed the philosophical foundations of the different social scientific approaches, and a reader that was developed by Emmet and MacIntyre (1971) has compared and contrasted philosophers' and sociologists' ways of thinking about society. Within sociology there are a number of schools of thought which have been explained by such sociologists as Smelzner (1976) and Turner (1977). Horowitz described the instruments used by social scientists to assemble and analyze data:

> We can subdivide the instruments employed by the sociology of knowledge . . . into six types, often used in conjunction with one another, and sometimes used separately. They are 1) mathematical and statistical analysis 2) functionalist theory 3) paradigms and linguistic typologies 4) field theories 5) ideal typologies 6) historical models. What is inextricably involved in the sound use of any of these kinds of approaches is a distortion-free description of a slice of reality. The very ability to distinguish bias elements from truth elements indicates that a core of useful results are possible, whatever the social position of the investigator. [P. 47]

Horowitz argued that, by using these different methods of investigation, "alternative explanations of the same phenomenon are possible and, indeed, can facilitate a complete understanding of any given problem." [P. 47] Additionally, he drew attention to different levels of thinking:

> At the first level [the sociology of knowledge] separates factual, logical and normative statements. At the second level it provides an analysis of the social basis of mental production as well as well as the deviants in thought. At the third level, [it] separates the various ideological and non-ideological elements in the formation of any given science. [P. 70]

There has been much discussion about value-free and value-laden social science. Benn and Peters (1957), among others, thought that there was a considerable difference between the achievements of the natural sciences and those of the social sciences. They took the position that Benton has called the "humanist" position, on the ground that, in the natural sciences, the laws seem to be more absolute, or less relative, than in the social sciences, which are concerned with examining social organizations—the creations of men, not of nature. But Benton, Kuhn, and others are less certain about this easy distinction. Scientific revolutions in natural science occur when scientists are able to reinterpret the same findings differently, often in a new context, or to make new findings which change the context of scientific thinking. They stress that natural science is also practised in a value context.

Organization, Storage, and Distribution of Knowledge about Societies and Their Problems

Freidson (1970) pointed out that modern societies have an unusual diversity of role statuses and of institutions for organizing, distributing, and storing knowledge. He raised questions about how the information that is produced "gets established as recognized knowledge and how its development and utilization become organized, evaluated and controlled" (p. 80). Freidson was writing at a time when the authority of experts, scientists, professionals, and academics in the United States was under extreme challenge. Individual professionals, occupational groups, and interdisciplinary aggregates of experts were seen to be failing to cope with social problem solving, and they appeared to have little accountability to the public.

Holzner and Marx have demonstrated that much of the information about organization, storage, and distribution of knowledge is to be found in the literature about professions. The scholarly and learned professions create and elaborate the formal knowledge of a civilization, whilst the practising or consulting professions apply that knowledge in everyday life (Freidson, Ben David, 1964).

From time to time, societies become concerned about the way in which knowledge is being developed, organized, stored, and distributed, for knowledge is power.

> . . . [S]urfeits of information, differentiated rationales, and decision criteria used by experts, and sensory overload do, in fact, erode the confidence and certainty a practical person may have in the common stock of his traditional knowledge. It may at any moment be superseded by either new knowledge or new fashions. [P. 19]

At the time of the Vietnam War, American citizens did feel let down by their experts and this led to their challenge by social movements—large-scale mobilizations for social change.

> Political parties, military organizations or revolutionary cadres were and are the prototype of this pattern. Movements dealing with grievances against institutional patterns, the distribution of power or economic reward and the like persist in vitality. But the older form is being supplemented by cultural movements. Contemporary movements may be thought of as media contexts, channels and mechanisms for the ideological reconstruction of models of identity. They become legitimate contexts for intentional adult resocialization. One may speak of movements for identity transformation and reconstruction. [Holzner and Marx, p. 19; c.f. Smith, 1976; Wilson, 1973]

In his examination of the way in which social theory is linked to political practice, Fay discussed the way in which positivist, interpretive, and critical social science approaches are structured. The positivist or "modern empiricist philosophy of science" is associated with technological problem solving; interpretive social science stresses the need to examine "the meanings of particular types of actions but does not investigate those causal factors which give rise to and support the continuing existence of these meanings." The "critical" social scientist is concerned with consciousness raising in order to create "a transformation which will increase [the actors'] autonomy by making it possible for them to determine collectively the conditions under which they will live." [P. 109]

The Use of Organized Knowledge

Societies develop the common sense of their traditions into a cultural system (Geertz, 1973), said Holzner and Marx, but the redefinition of the concept of

> "common sense" in this kind of highly differentiated, self reflective, knowledge oriented society [results in] a form that is different. . . . The common sense of a modern, knowledge based society requires acceptance of varied, differentiated frames of reference and confidence that rules exist or can be discovered for their translation into each other. . . . [It] rests on the assumption that differentiated, specialized bodies of knowledge are in principle accessible and usable by anyone who is willing to undergo the necessary training to grasp them. Furthermore, [it] makes specialized knowledge and expertise accessible by defining general routes for knowledge search and conditions for use. Finally it provides a code for responsible conduct in which the use of expertise and knowledge plays a specialized role. [Pp. 19–20]

Given this definition of "common sense," what we have been concerned to discover in this book are what we might call "the general routes for knowledge search and conditions for use" of knowledge in policy formulation and implementation.

Policy Formulation and Knowledge

"The notion of reflective incrementalism, in which a continuous cycle between decision, action and assessment through research plays an important role, has recently become particularly prominent as an explicit value in democratic policy conduct." [Holzner and Marx, pp. 287-88] The range of knowledge which seems to be needed to take a comprehensive view of society and its problems is too great for the decision maker to cope with in the short term. Even for the academic health care researcher with a longer time span for thinking, De Miguel (1975) has recommended a middle-range stance, since he finds that studies at both ends of the spectrum (micro and macro) are not very useful.

In order to bridge the communication gap between philosophers or socio-

FIGURE 14–1

Knowledge and Its Applications

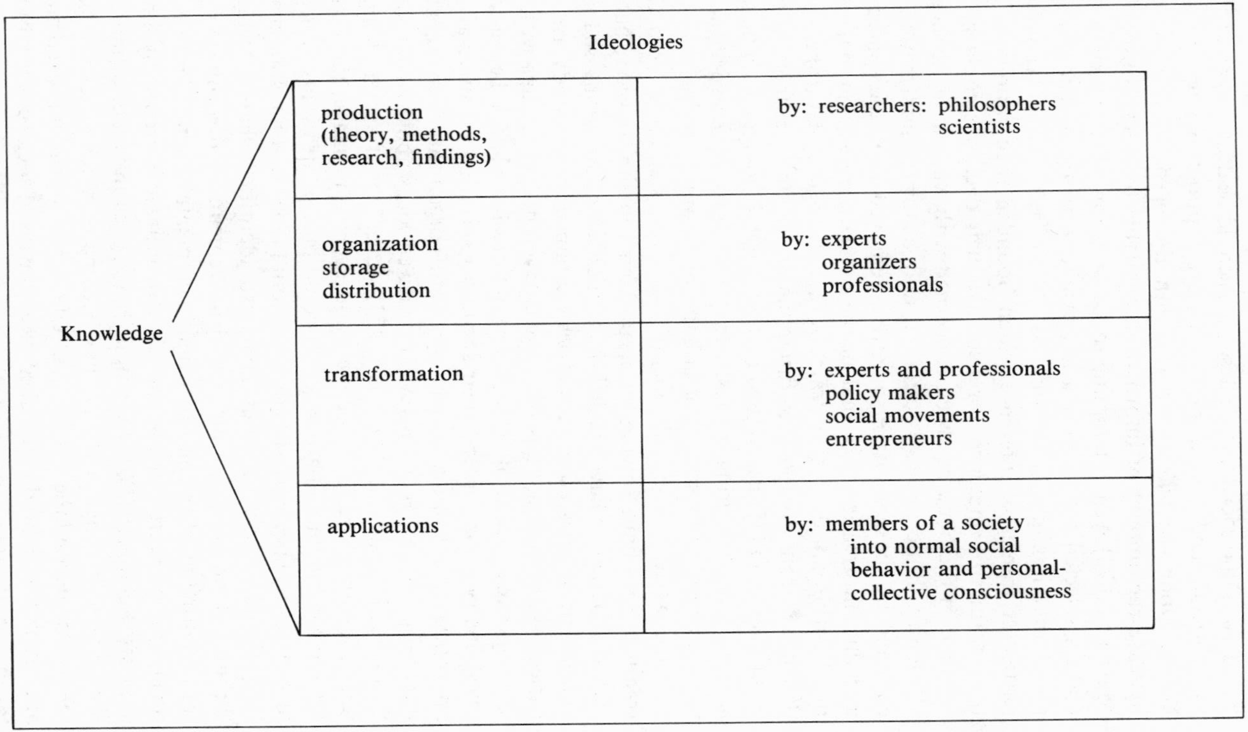

Ideologies

Knowledge

production (theory, methods, research, findings)	by: researchers: philosophers, scientists
organization storage distribution	by: experts organizers professionals
transformation	by: experts and professionals policy makers social movements entrepreneurs
applications	by: members of a society into normal social behavior and personal-collective consciousness

logists and decision makers, Donnison (1971) argued the need to prepare standing plans which were well thought through in terms of ideology and based on sound social facts. These plans could be drawn upon at short notice by politicians and administrators who are required to make quick decisions. Whilst Donnison was concerned with the need for decision makers to increase the amount of information available to them, Allison (1969) and Marmor (1973) were attempting to explain how different kinds of decision makers selected from information available to them. These analysts proposed that it might be possible to identify why particular groups set up particular frames of inference which bounded their rationality, and what these frames of inference were, so that their decisions could be predicted.

Much of the book has been concerned with eludicating ideologies within ideologies. Philosophical, scientific, and historical information is usually collected by those who are somewhat removed from the sphere of action, and this information, like that of the immediate decision makers, is structured within an ideological framework. The ideological frameworks differ, of course, from discipline to discipline and from level to level of involvement. Geertz (1975) has argued that although ideologies may be interpreted as a way of structuring interests, they may also be regarded (and perhaps more usefully) as a means of countering strain.

Thus, western liberal democratic societies stemming from the British tradition set about solving many problems in similar ways, but their historical experiences have pushed them in different directions, so that the four national ideologies of the countries examined in our study are now quite varied. Within the nations there have developed subgroups with their own ideologies (e.g., the professions). The nations have had to be concerned with questions of social order—their social organization for survival—and with appropriate ways of making changes in this organization under external and internal pressures. Watkins (1975) reviewed ideas about social control, and Smith (1976) and the Etzionis (1973), ideas about social change. Whilst Smith identified trends, processes, and events in change, the Etzionis considered the human initiatives which could precipitate events or become part of processes. They agreed with Lindblom (1959) that much of change came through incrementalism, but they also identified change brought about through planning, education, social movements, and revolution. The need for accepting mechanisms other than incrementalism in order to bring about social change more quickly and less disruptively is argued by a number of analysts. Schon (1971), for example, has argued in favour of more planning now that technological change has become so much faster and has moved the world "beyond the stable state." Of course, education, social movements, and revolution are old established mechanisms of social change, but each has fallen out of favour, or at least come under criticism, in recent years. The difficulties of using education as a social change mechanism have been discussed by Young (1958) in *The Rise of the Meritocracy* and by Hirsch (1976) in *Social Limits to Growth*, whilst from Wilson (1973) we learn that social movements depend upon the climate of the times for getting their legitimacy established, and they may or may not succeed in their mission to develop feasible programs. Revolutions are risky affairs for those who take part in them.

To many analysts, planning seems to be more likely to provide the alternative to unthinking (or surprised) incrementalism, but such group decision making is a challenge to the "protestant ethic" of individual freedom to exploit resources. To a large extent, this book is concerned with the struggle between entrepreneurs and planners, at both the conceptual and the practical levels.

In addition to the ideological conflict between entrepreneurs and planners, there is, as Alford (1975) pointed out, a division among those committed to planning—between the experts (or corporate planners) and community/consumer groups. As Glennerster (1975) indicated, this might result in a different way of developing planning inputs. In Britain, where government was centralized and had power to act, planning could be undertaken by the experts without much consultation, whereas in the United States, where there was more decentralization and more opportunity for receiving members' inputs, the experts had to proceed by evaluating and feeding back information into the system—to try to convince people that it was their general will to amend policies or, more often, programs. Alford has argued that in health planning in New York City this has resulted in "dynamics without change," a show of planning without any reality, for none of the groups involved has been able to convince the other groups of the necessity to move.

Selznick (1966), on the other hand, describing the technological planning of the Tennessee Valley Authority in the thirties, identified a process which is often used in democratic societies—cooptation, whereby groups who should have been or were consulted were rendered powerless to do anything else but agree, whether through ignorance or through having been manipulated into a powerless position. Here we can use Lukes' analysis again. He took the trite phrase "knowledge is power" and turned it around, showing how power groups manipulate others through withholding knowledge, so that the open expression of the general will may be restricted to some of the less important decisions of society. In order to counter this, various tactics have been adopted, such as the effort of the Whitlam government in Australia to develop more consumer involvement through the Australia Assistance Plan, or the consciousness raising activities of black groups, women's groups, and so on in the United States. Britain and Canada have set up more buffering mechanisms, such as Royal Commissions and Committees of Inquiry, but these could be perceived as looking after the interests of the elite groups, as much cooptative mechanisms as being collectors of public opinions.

Whilst Weller's chart (1974) was concerned with setting out political structures, it was also concerned with differentiating the power of the various groups in the Canadian health care system. French and Raven (1959) distinguished five types of social power which can be used singly or in combination: power to reward, power to punish, formal power, expert power, and referent (or status) power. Other analysts (e.g., Dubin, 1959) have made similar classifications. Thus, whilst health service deliverers are individuals making lower level organizational decisions than policy makers in government or bureaucracies, they have great discretion to make individual clinical decisions (with implications for organization of services) because they are able to combine most of the types of social power so as to maintain their professional freedom to choose courses of action on behalf of their clients, and in so doing they can embarrass the governments by challenging the organizational decisions made at higher levels.

There is a volume of literature about the social control roles of professionals. The views of the Ehrenreichs (1973) and of Watkins were quoted. The former distinguished between the Parsonian concept of discipline and Freidson's concept of cooptation as control mechanisms. It is assumed that readers, if not already familiar with Parsons' ideas about "the sick role," will wish to become more aware of this concept and the critiques which have recently been made of it (Levine and Kozloff, 1978; Bynder and New, 1976; Gallagher, 1976, etc.). The views of McKinlay (1977) on the American medical profession's ideologies and Blishen (1969) on the Canadian's provide useful comparisons and contrasts. They set the profession in its national social context, one ideology enclosed within another.

The Movement of Issues through Political Systems

The diagram of political processes developed by Easton (1964) was reproduced in Chapter 10. This diagram can assist the student to understand when the analysis of causes and the analysis of consequences is useful. It explains, for example, where Abel-Smith's (1972) and McKeown's (1975) historical reviews of health service developments fit in with the approaches of the American policy analysts described by Yarmolinsky (1971) and Coleman (1975). The first two can be seen as analyzing inputs at the left-hand side of the chart, whilst the latter are concerned with predicting impacts on the right-hand side of the chart. Yarmolinsky distinguished the different stance of the academic analysts interested in history from that of the bureaucratic interdisciplinary policy analysts further along the spectrum who are expected to respond to demands for information about feasible schemes which might be introduced, whilst Coleman also discussed the modifications in the approach of the policy analyst who was more concerned about policy impacts than about historical causation. Under the pressure of time constraints, these action-oriented analysts may have to make compromises about the extent of their research efforts and may need to use available rather than complete evidence. It is clear that British analysts have a much greater concern with the past than those from the ex-colonial territories, who seem to have futuristic orientations (judging by the volume of evidence). This, of course, stems from the different problems that a very old established country thinks it has with the management of social change without the loss of social control—maintaining the social order of the community whilst moving into new times. The new countries have also had highly stratified societies (Tumin, 1967), but their citizens have been persuaded that there is a significant amount of opportunity for advancement, and they have been less obsessed by poverty (social insecurity), except during the depression of the thirties; for there are resources still to be developed and distributed and with the increase in resources more rights can be realized (Benn and Peters, 1959). The problems are not those of "want, disease, ignorance, squalor, and idleness" (Beveridge, 1942) so much as "positional advantage" (as described by Hirsch). The effect of the Vietnam War upon the United States was to stimulate the social indicators movement (Boulding, 1967; Gil, 1970) to endeavour to evaluate the quality of life in the society generally, so that information could be fed back into the system and, possibly, corrections made. Questions were already being raised about the social order and the need for change (Piven and Cloward, 1971; Marris and Rein, 1967).

Many of the paradigms which were discussed in earlier chapters fall within the boundaries of Easton's larger box. The propositions of Hall et al. (1975) about the movement of issues—the development of legitimacy, the attainment of feasibility, and questions of support fit here. So also do the concepts of Allison and Marmor, who have suggested that there are different stages at which different kinds of informational inputs are appropriate—the stage of presenting rational argument in favor of an issue gives way to structural considerations, and that gives way to negotiation of agreements. Powell (1975), as a practising politician in Britain, noticed that medical professionals' behaviour changed after they were admitted to the N.H.S. so that they could only see themselves in a negotiating framework when they met the minister for discussions (see also Johnson, 1972).

A more fully developed view of negotiating processes was put forward by Strauss (1970), who analyzed these processes in considerable detail. His explanation can be used to explore broad negotiations such as those about privileges and rights or to examine detailed accounts of the bureaucratic process such as that described by Laframboise (1973).

Easton's diagram does not clearly indicate how many of the political processes of decision making are in government's hands and how many are carried on outside the electoral system. His ultimate box is labelled "the authorities." The question of elites was raised in the discussion earlier, together with Lukes' development of that idea into three dimensions of power: the democratic process of discussion, the use of power by elite groups to conceal their purposes, and the failure by a society to recognize that issues may exist. Marchak (1975) added to this analysis by discussing the limits of governments' power in western liberal democracies. Weller, further developing this theme, has usefully distinguished the structural interests in the health sector of policy making. He divided the "withinputs" of politicians and bureaucrats from the "inputs" of entrepreneurs, professionals, nongovernmental voluntary agencies, and so on. "Inputs" into the health system were divided by him into those made by established groups and those made by challenging groups—that is, those with the power to withhold their consent to new developments—authorities in the sector. Klein (1974) also referred to the way in which the powerful medical profession could hold back change in the N.H.S.

Another contribution by Lowi (1964) to our understanding of governments' power cannot easily be identified on Easton's diagram, but should be considered together with it. It will be recalled that Lowi suggested that governments move from concern with distribution to regulation and then to redistribution. Johnson's (1972) model of professional power fits with this paradigm.

Students may well be able to fit other analytic schemes discussed earlier in the book into these paradigms of the political process.

Envoi

It takes time and effort to become familiar with the paradigms, to learn the new "common sense," how to fit them to the analysis of actual situations or to case studies of planning, administration, or professional behaviour. However, those students who try to use them to widen their views of policy analysis and policy making can become quite adept at employing them to diagnose situations, to begin to sort out why some activities are more successful than others. There are always unintended consequences of taking action—consequences which cannot be foreseen—but using paradigms for analysis may help to improve ways of approaching intended actions and may increase effectiveness of personal contributions to policy making.

However, it must be recognized that paradigmatic analysis of policy making is at an early stage. As Klein pointed out, all the paradigms which are presently in use seem to explain something; none of them explains everything. Policy analysis is like playing a multidimensional game of chess.

Bibliography

(Where author is a country, reports are given in order of publication date.)

Abel-Smith, Brian. "The History of Medical Care." In *Comparative Development in Social Welfare,* ed. E. W. Martin. London: George Allen and Unwin, 1972.

______. *A History of the Nursing Profession.* London: Heinemann, 1960.

______. *The Hospitals 1800–1948.* London: Heinemann, 1964.

______. *Value for Money in Health Services.* London: Heinemann, 1976.

Abel-Smith, Brian, and Gales, Kathleen. *British Doctors at Home and Abroad.* London: Occasional Papers in Social Administration, no. 8, Bell, 1963.

Abel-Smith, B., and Townsend, P. *The Poor and the Poorest.* London: Bell, 1965.

Abrams, Mark. "Social Indicators and Social Equity." *New Society,* no. 529 (1972), pp. 454-55.

Aday, Lu Ann, and Andersen, Ronald. *Access to Medical Care.* Ann Arbor: Health Administration Press, 1975.

Agnew, G. Harvey. *Canadian Hospitals 1920-70.* Toronto: University of Toronto Press, 1974.

Albrecht, G. L. "Social Policy and the Management of Human Resources." In *The Sociology of Physical Disability and Rehabilitation,* ed. G. L. Albrecht, pp. 251–85. Pittsburgh: Pittsburgh University Press, 1976.

Alford, Robert R. *Health Care Politics.* Chicago: University of Chicago Press, 1975.

______. "The Political Economy of Health Care: Dynamics without Change." *Politics and Society,* Winter 1972, pp. 127–64.

Allentuck, A. *Who Speaks for the Patient?* Don Mills, Ontario: Burns and McEachern Ltd., 1978.

Allison, Graham T. "Conceptual Models and the Cuban Missile Crisis." *Political Science Review* 63 (Sept. 1969): 689–718.

Altenstetter, Christa. *Health Policy-Making and Administration in West Germany and the United States.* Beverly Hills: Sage Publications, 1974.

Anderson, Donald O. "Canada: Epidemiology in the Planning Process in British Columbia: Description of an Experience with a New Model." In *Epidemiology as a Fundamental Science,* eds. Kerr L. White and Maureen M. Henderson. New York: Oxford University Press, 1976.

Anderson, D. O., and Crichton, A. O. J. *What Price Group Practice?* Vancouver: University of British Columbia, 1973.

Anderson, E. J.; Judd, L. R.; May, J. T., and New, P. K. M. *The Neighbourhood*

Health Center Program—Its Growth and Problems: An Introduction. Washington, D. C.: National Association of Neighbourhood Health Centers, Inc., 1976.

Andreopoulos, S., ed. *National Health Insurance: Can We Learn from Canada?* New York: John Wiley (and Sons), 1975.

Andrews, Frank M., and Withey, Stephen B. *Social Indicators of Well-Being. Americans' Perceptions of Life Quality.* New York: Plenum Press, 1976.

Apter, David E. *Ideology and Discontent.* New York: The Free Press, 1964.

Atkins, R., and Graycar, A. *Governing Australia.* Sydney: John Wiley and Sons Australasia Pty. Ltd., 1972.

Australia. (Baikie) Report of the Multiphasic Screening Services Committee. Canberra: National Health and Medical Research Council, 1972.

———. (Bailey) Report of the Task Force on Coordination in Welfare and Health. Canberra: Australian Government Publishing Service, 1976.

———. (Woodhouse-Meares) Report of the National Committee of Inquiry into Compensation and Rehabilitation in Australia. Canberra: Australian Government Publishing Service, 1974.

———. Hospital and Health Service Commission Reports. Canberra: Australian Government Publishing Service, 1974-6.

———. (Henderson) Commission of Inquiry into Poverty. Canberra: Australian Government Publishing Service, 1974.

———. (Campbell) Royal Commission on Australian Government Administration. Report of the Health and Welfare Task Force. Canberra: Australian Government Publishing Service, 1975.

———. (Gross) Towards Rational Administrative Structures for Health and Welfare Services in Australia. Royal Commission on Australian Government Administration. Canberra: Australian Government Publishing Service, 1975.

———. (Bailey) Report of the Task Force on Coordination in Welfare and Health. Canberra: Australian Government Publishing Service, 1976.

———. (Coombs) Report of the Royal Commission on Australian Government Administration. Canberra: Australian Government Publishing Service, 1976.

———. (Martin) *Social Medical Aspects of Poverty in Australia,* 3rd Main Report. Commonwealth Government Commission of Inquiry into Poverty. Canberra: Australian Government Publishing Service, 1976.

Australian Council of Social Service. *Real Reform or Sideways Shuffle? The Bailey Report. Federalism and Welfare Health Services.* Sydney: ACOSS, April 1977.

Badgley, Robin F., ed. "Social Science and Health in Canada." *Milbank Memorial Fund Quarterly* 49 (April 1971): Part I.

Badgley R. F., and Wolfe, S. *Doctors' Strike.* Toronto: Macmillan, 1967.

(Baikie) Australia. Report of the Multiphasic Screening Services Committee. Canberra: National Health and Medical Research Council, 1972.

(Bailey) Australia. Report of the Task Force on Coordination in Welfare and Health. Canberra: Australian Government Publishing Service, 1976.

Bailey, Joe. *Social Theory for Planning.* London: Routledge and Kegan Paul, 1975.

Bales, R. F. *Group Interaction Process Analysis.* Reading, Mass.: Addison Wesley, 1950.

Barry, Brian. *Political Argument.* New York: The Humanities Press, 1965.

_____. *Sociologists, Economists and Democracy*. London: Collier Macmillan, Ltd., 1970.

Bates, F. L. "Position, Role and Status: A reformulation of concepts." *Social Forces* 34 (1956): 313–21.

Battistella, R. M., and Rundall, T. G., eds. *Health Care Policy in a Changing Environment*. Berkeley, Calif.: McCutcheon Pub. Co., 1978.

Battistella, Roger M., and Weil, Thomas. *Medical Care Organization Bibliography*. Washington, D. C.: Association of University Programs in Health Administration, 1968.

Bauer, Raymond A., ed. *Social Indicators*. Cambridge, Mass.: The M. I. T. Press, 1966.

Bean, J. J., and Laliberty, Rene. *Understanding Hospital Labor Relations*. Don Mills, Ontario: Addison-Wesley Publishing Co., 1977.

Beck, R. Glen. "Economic Class and Access to Physicians' Services under Public Medical Care Insurance." *International Journal of Health Services* 3 (1973): 341–55.

Becker, Ernest. *Revolution in Psychiatry*. New York: The Free Press, 1964.

Beckhard, Richard. "Organizational Issues in the Team Delivery of Comprehensive Health Care." *Milbank Memorial Fund Quarterly,* (July 1972), pp. 287–316.

Bell, Daniel. *The End of Ideology*. Glencoe: Free Press, 1960.

Ben-David, Joseph. "Professions in the Class System of Present Day Society." *Current Sociology* 12: (1964) 247–330.

Benn, S. I., and Peters, R. S. *Social Principles and the Democratic State*. London: George Allen and Unwin, 1959.

Bennis, Warren G.; Benne, Kenneth D., and Chin, Robert. *The Planning of Change*. New York: Holt Rinehart and Winston, 1961.

Bentham, Jeremy. *An Introduction to the Principles of Morals and Legislation*. 1789.

Benton, Ted. *Philosophical Foundations of the Three Sociologies*. London: Routledge, 1977.

Berger, Peter L., and Luckmann, Thomas. *The Social Construction of Reality*. Garden City, N. Y.: Doubleday and Co., 1966.

Berliner, R. W. "The Relevance of Medical Science to Medical Care." *Archives of International Medicine* 125 (March 1970): 509-11.

Beveridge, Lord. *Voluntary Action*. London: Allen and Unwin, 1948.

(Beveridge) Great Britain. *Social Insurance and Allied Services*. London: H. M. S. O., 1942.

Biddle, Bruce, and Thomas, Edwin J., eds. *Role Theory: Concepts and Research*. New York: John Wiley and Sons, 1966.

Birrell, Derek, and Murie, Alan. "Ideology, Conflict and Social Policy." *Journal of Social Policy* 4 (1974–75); 245–58.

Blackstone, Tessa. *Social Policy and Administration in Britain* (a bibliography). London: Frances Pinter Ltd., 1975.

Blackstone, Sir William. *Commentaries on the Laws of England*. 1665–69.

Blain, Gilbert. *Essais sur la Gestion des Services de Santé*. Montreal: Université de Montréal, 1978.

Blishen, Bernard. *Doctors and Doctrines.* Toronto: University of Toronto Press, 1969.

Blum, Henrik, and Bellavita, Christopher. *Policy Studies Reading List.* Berkeley: University of California. Western Network Program. Mimeo. 1979.

Borson, John M., ed. *John Stuart Mill: A Selection of His Works.* Toronto: Macmillan, 1966.

Bottomore, T. B. *Elites and Society.* London: Watts, 1966.

(Boudreau) Canada. Department of National Health and Welfare. Report of the Committee on Nurse Practitioners. Ottawa: Information Canada, 1973.

Boulding, Kenneth. "The Boundaries of Social Policy." *Social Work* 12 (Jan. 1967): 11–21.

Boyer, John M.; Westerhaus, Carl L., and Coggleshall, John H. *Employee Relations and Collective Bargaining in Health Care Facilities.* 2nd ed. St. Louis: C. V. Mosby Co., 1975.

Breton, Albert. *The Economic Theory of Representative Government.* Chicago: Aldine, 1974.

Breton, Raymond. *The Canadian Condition: A Guide to Research on Public Policy.* Montreal: Institute for Research on Public Policy, 1977.

Briggs, Asa. "Public Health: The Sanitary Idea." *New Society* 11 (1968): 229–31.

———. "The Health of the Nation." *New Society* 11 (1968): 267–70.

Brook, R. H., and Appel, Francis A. "Quality-of-Care Assessment: Choosing a Method of Peer Review." *New England Journal of Medicine* 288 (June 21, 1973): 1323–29.

Brown, J. C. *A Hit and Miss Affair.* Ottawa: Canadian Council on Social Development, 1977.

Brown, R. G. S. *The Administrative Process in Britain.* London: Methuen, 1970.

———. *The Management of Welfare.* London: Fontana, 1975.

Brownlea, Arthur. *A Report on the Interaction between Policy Makers and Researchers in the Health Services Field in Canada with Some Australian Comparisons.* Toronto: University of Toronto, Dept. of Preventive Medicine and Biostatistics, 1979. Mimeo.

Brundrage, P. F. *The Bureau of the Budget.* New York: Praeger, 1970.

Brunet, Michel, and Vinet, Alain. *Les Professions: Un Obstacle au Changement Social?* Quebec: Université Laval, 1978. Mimeo.

Bunker, John; Barnes, Benjamin, and Mosteller, Frederick. *Costs, Risks and Benefits of Surgery.* New York: Oxford University Press, 1977.

Burnham, James. *The Managerial Revolution.* New York: The John Day Co., 1941.

(Burns) United States. National Resources Planning Board. *Security, Work and Relief Policies.* Washington, D. C.: U. S. Government Printing Office, 1942.

Bynder, H., and New, P. K. "Time for a Change: From Micro to Macro Social Concepts in Disability Research." *Journal of Health and Human Behavior,* 17: 45–52, 1976.

Campbell, Alastair V. *Medicine, Health and Justice: The Problem of Priorities.* Edinburgh: Churchill Livingstone, 1978.

(Campbell) Australia. Royal Commission on Australian Government Administration. Report of the Health and Welfare Task Force. Canberra: Australian Government Publishing Service, 1975.

Canada. (Heagerty) *Health Insurance.* Report of the Advisory Committee on Health Insurance. Ottawa: King's Printer, 1943.

______. (Marsh) *Social Security for Canada.* Report of the Advisory Committee on Reconstruction. Ottawa: King's Printer, 1943.

______. (Glassco) Report of the Royal Commission on Government Organization. Ottawa: Queen's Printer, 1963.

______. (Hall) Royal Commission on Health Services. Ottawa: Queen's Printer, 1964.

______. (Hastings and Mosley) Royal Commission on Health Services. *Organized Community Health Services.* Ottawa: Queen's Printer, 1966.

______. (Kohn) Royal Commission on Health Services. *The Health of the Canadian People.* Ottawa: Queen's Printer, 1967.

______. Department of National Health and Welfare. Task Force on the Costs of Health Care. Ottawa: Queen's Printer, 1969.

______. (Paltiel et al.) Department of National Health and Welfare. *Legislation, Organization and Administration of Rehabilitation Services for the Disabled in Canada.* Ottawa: Queen's Printer, 1971.

______. (Hastings) Department of National Health and Welfare. *The Community Health Centre in Canada.* 3 vols. Ottawa: Information Canada, 1972–73.

______. (Boudreau) Department of National Health and Welfare. Report of the Committee on Nurse Practitioners. Ottawa: Information Canada, 1973.

______. (Le Dain) Final Report of the Commission of Inquiry into the Non-Medical Use of Drugs. Ottawa: Information Canada, 1973.

______. (Lalonde) Department of National Health and Welfare. *A New Perspective on the Health of Canadians.* Ottawa: Information Canada, 1974.

______. Year Book 1978–79. Ottawa: Information Canada, 1979.

Canadian Mental Health Association. *More for the Mind.* Toronto: Canadian Mental Health Association, 1963.

Carrier, John and Kendall, Ian. "Social Policy and Social Change." *Journal of Social Policy* 2 (1972–73): 209–24.

Carr-Saunders, Sir Alexander M., and Wilson, P. M. *The Professions.* London: Oxford University Press, 1933.

Carson, Rachel. *Silent Spring.* New York: Houghton Mifflin, 1962.

Carter, Novia. *Trends in Voluntary Support for Non-Governmental Social Service Agencies.* Ottawa: Canadian Council on Social Development, 1974.

Caskie, Donald. *Canadian Fact Book on Poverty.* Ottawa: Canadian Council on Social Development, 1979.

Chaney, W. H., and Beech. T. R. *The Union Epidemic.* Germantown, Md.: Aspen Systems Corporation, 1976.

Cherns, A. B., et al. *Social Science and Government.* London: Tavistock, 1972.

Christian, William, and Campbell, Colin. *Political Parties and Ideologies in Canada: liberals, conservatives, socialists, nationalists.* Toronto: McGraw-Hill Ryerson, 1974.

Clark, C. L. *An Annotated Bibliography on Long Term Care Administration.* Washington, D. C.: Association of University Programs in Health Administration, 1976.

Cochrane, A. L. *Effectiveness and Efficiency.* London: The Nuffield Provincial Hospitals Trust, 1972.

Coleman, James S. "Problems of Conceptualization and Measurement in Studying Policy Impact." In *Public Policy Evaluation,* ed. Kenneth M. Dolbeare, pp. 19–40. Beverly Hills: Sage, 1975.

Commission on Emotional and Learning Disorders in Children. *One Million Children.* Toronto: Leonard Crainford, 1970.

Confrey, Eugene A. *The Process of Articulating Goals and Standards.* Washington, D. C.: U. S. Department of Health, Education and Welfare. Health Resources Administration, 1975. Mimeo.

Cook, Thomas J., and Scioli, Frank P., Jr. "Impact Analysis in Public Policy Research." In *Public Policy Evaluation,* ed. Kenneth M. Dolbeare, Beverly Hills: Sage, 1975, pp. 95–117.

(Coombs) Australia. Report of the Royal Commission on Australian Government Administration. Canberra: Australian Government Publishing Service, 1976.

Cooper, Michael H. *Rationing Health Care.* London: Croom Helm, 1975.

Cooper, Michael H., and Culyer, Anthony J., eds. *Health Economics.* Harmondsworth, Middlesex: Penguin, 1973.

Coser, Lewis. *The Functions of Social Conflict.* London: Routledge and Kegan Paul, 1956.

Cox, Fred M., et al., eds. *Community—Action, Planning Development.* Itasca, Ill.: F. E. Peacock, 1974.

———. *Strategies of Community Organization.* 2nd ed. Itasca, Ill.: F. E. Peacock, 1974.

Crichton, Anne. "A Comparison of Programs for the Delivery of Rehabilitation Services in Australia, Canada and Britain." *Social Science and Medicine,* Vol. 14A, No.4, June 1980, pp. 287–296.

———. ed. *Epidemiology and Health Administration.* Unpublished paper.

———. "From Entrepreneurial to Political Power in the Canadian Health System." *Social Science and Medicine,* January 1976, pp. 59–67.

Crisp, L. F. *Australian National Government.* 3rd. ed. Hawthorn, Victoria: Longman, 1965.

Crossman, R. H. S. *Diaries of a Cabinet Minister.* 2 vols. London: Hamish Hamilton, 1975–76.

———, ed. *New Fabian Essays.* London: Turnstile Press, 1962.

———. "A Politician's View of Health Service Planning." 13th Maurice Bloch Lecture. University of Glasgow, 1972.

Culyer, A. J. *Measuring Health: Lessons for Ontario.* Toronto: Ontario Economic Council, 1978.

———. *Need and the National Health Service.* London: Martin Robertson, 1976.

Dahrendorf, Rolf. "Social Stratification in Britain." *Manchester Guardian Weekly,* 21 July, 1979, p. 12.

Davies, A. F. *Australian Democracy.* Melbourne: Longmans, 1964.

De Miguel, Jesus M. "A Framework for the Study of National Health Systems." *Inquiry,* supplement to 12, no. 2 (1975), pp. 10–24.

Deniston, O. L., and Rosenstock, I. M. "The Validity of Non-Experimental Design in Research." *Health Services Reports* 88 (1971): 153–64.

De Neufville, Judith Innes. *Social Indicators and Public Policy.* New York: Elsevier Scientific Publishing Co., 1975.

de Schweinitz, Karl. *England's Road to Social Security.* New York: A. S. Barnes and Co., 1961.

Dewdney, J. C. H. *Australian Health Services.* Sydney: John Wiley and Sons Australasia Pty. Ltd., 1972.

Dewdney, J. C. H., and Weil, T. P. *Australian Health Care Organization Bibliography.* Kensington, N. S. W.: University of New South Wales. 1969.

Doern, G. Bruce. *Science and Politics in Canada.* Montreal: McGill-Queen's University Press, 1972.

Doern, G. Bruce, and Aucoin, Peter, eds. *The Structures of Policy Making in Canada.* Toronto: Macmillan of Canada, 1971.

Dolbeare, Kenneth M., and Dolbeare, Patricia, with Jane A. Hadley. *American Ideologies.* 2nd ed. Chicago: Rand McNally, 1973.

Donabedian, Avedis. *Aspects of Medical Care Administration: Specifying Requirements for Health Care.* Cambridge, Mass.: Harvard University Press, 1973.

______. "Evaluating the Quality of Medical Care." *Milbank Memorial Fund Quarterly* 45 part 2 (July 1966): 166–206.

Donnison, David. "Ideologies and Policies." *Journal of Social Policy* 1 (1972):97–117.

Draper, James A., ed. *Citizen Participation: Canada.* Toronto: New Press, 1971.

Dubin, Robert. *The World of Work.* Englewood Cliffs, N. J.: Prentice-Hall, 1958.

Dublin, T. D. "The Migration of Physicians to the U. S." *New England Journal of Medicine,* 20 April 1972, p. 870–77.

Easton, Allan, ed. *The Design of a Health Maintenance Organization.* Hampstead, New York: Hofstra University Yearbook of Business, series 9, vol. 3, 1973.

Easton, David. *A Systems Analysis of Political Life.* New York: John Wiley and Sons, 1965.

Eckstein, Harry. "Planning: A Case Study." *Political Studies* 4 (1956); 46–60.

______. *Pressure Group Politics: The Case of the British Medical Association.* London: Allen and Unwin, 1960.

Editorial. "Control of Spending: the Suspension of the Lambeth, Southwark and Lewisham Area Health Authority." *Lancet* (N. H. S.), 11 August 1979, pp. 313–14.

______. *Manchester Guardian Weekly,* Jan. 7, 1979, p. 1.

______. *Time Magazine,* April 2, 1973, p. 79.

Egdahl, Richard H. and Gertman, Paul M. *Quality Assurance in Health Care.* Germantown, Md.: Aspen, 1976.

Ehrenreich, Barbara and Ehrenreich, John. "Health Care and Social Control." *Social Policy* 5 (May–June 1974): 26–40.

______. "Medicine and Social Control." In *Welfare in America: Controlling the 'Dangerous Classes,'* ed. Betty Reid Mandell. Englewood Cliffs, N. J.: Prentice-Hall, 1975.

Ehrenreich, Barbara, and English, Deirdre. *Complaints and Disorders.* Old

Westbury, New York: S.U.N.Y., The Feminist Press, 1973.

Emerson, Richard M. "Social Exchange Theory." *Annual Review of Sociology* 2 (1976): 335–62.

Emmet, D., and MacIntyre, A. *Sociological Theory and Philosophical Analysis.* London: Macmillan, 1970.

Encel, S. *Equality and Authority: A Study of Class Status and Power in Australia.* Melbourne: Cheshire, 1970.

Engelmann, Frederick C., and Schwartz, Mildred A. *Canadian Political Parties: Origin, Character, Impact.* Scarborough, Ontario: Prentice-Hall of Canada, 1975.

Enterline, P. E., et al. "Effects of Free Medical Care on Medical Practice: The Quebec Experience." *New England Journal of Medicine* 288 (31 May 1973): 1152–55.

Etzioni, Amitai. *The Active Society.* New York: The Free Press, 1968.

———. *A Comparative Analysis of Complex Organizations.* Glencoe, Ill.: The Free Press, 1961.

———, ed. *The Semi-Professions and Their Organization: Teachers, Nurses, Social Workers.* New York: The Free Press, 1969.

Etzioni, A., and Etzioni-Halevy, eds. "Human Initiative in Social Change." In *Social Change: Sources, Patterns, and Consequences.* New York: Basic Books, 1973, pp. 488–92.

Evans, R. G. "Beyond the Medical Marketplace." In *National Health Insurance: Can the U. S. Learn from Canada?,* ed. Spyros Andrepoulos, pp. 129–79. New York: John Wiley and Sons, 1975.

Evans, R. G., and Williamson, M. F. *Extending Canadian Health Insurance: Options for Pharmacare and Denticare.* Toronto: Ontario Economic Council Research Series, 1978.

Eversley, David. *The Planner in Society.* London: Faber and Faber, 1973.

Faludi, Andreas. *A Reader in Planning Theory.* Oxford: Pergamon Press, 1973.

Fay, Brian. *Social Theory and Political Practice.* London: Allen and Unwin, 1975.

Feldman, Saul, ed. *The Administration of Mental Health Services.* Springfield: Charles C. Thomas, 1973.

Field, John W. *Group Practice Development.* Germantown, Md.: Aspen, 1976.

Finer, Samuel. *Life and Times of Sir Edwin Chadwick.* London: Methuen, 1952.

Flexner, Abram. *Report on American Medical Colleges.* New York: Carnegie Foundation, 1910.

Foot, Michael. *Aneurin Bevin.* London: MacGibbon and Kee, Vol. 1, 1962; Vol. 2, 1973.

Forcese, Dennis. *The Canadian Class Structure.* Toronto: McGraw-Hill Ryerson Ltd., 1975.

Forsyth, Gordon. *Doctors and State Medicine.* 2nd ed. London: Pitman, 1973.

Foulkes, Richard B. *Health Security for British Columbians.* Victoria: Queen's Printer, 1973.

Fox, Paul W., ed. *Politics: Canada.* 3rd ed. Toronto: McGraw-Hill, 1970.

Fox, Renee C., and Swazey, Judith P. *The Courage to Fail.* Chicago: University of Chicago Press, 1974.

Freeman, H. E., and Sherwood, C. C. *Social Research and Social Policy.* Englewood Cliffs, N. J.: Prentice Hall, 1970.

Freeman, Howard E.; Levine, Sol, and Reeder, Leo G. *Handbook of Medical Sociology*. Englewood Cliffs, N. J.: Prentice-Hall, 1963.

Freidson, Eliot. *The Profession of Medicine*. New York: Dodd Mead, 1970.

______. *Professional Dominance*. New York: Atherton, 1970.

Fremont-Smith, Marion R. *Foundations and Government*. New York: Russell Sage, 1965.

French, John R. P., and Raven, Bertram. "The Bases of Social Power." In *Studies in Social Power,* ed. Dorwin Cartwright, pp. 150–67. Ann Arbor: The University of Michigan, 1959.

Friedman, G. D. *Primer of Epidemiology*. Toronto: McGraw-Hill, 1974.

Friedmann, John. "A Conceptual Model for the Analysis of Planning Behavior." *Administrative Science Quarterly* 12 (Sept. 1967): 225–52.

Friedmann, John, and Hudson, Barclay. "Knowledge and Action: A Guide to Planning Theory." *American Institute of Planning Journal,* January 1974, pp.2–16.

Friedmann, M. *Capitalism and Freedom*. Chicago: Chicago University Press, 1962.

Fuchs, Victor R. *Who Shall Live?* New York: Basic Books, 1974.

(Fulton) Great Britain. Report of the Committee on the Civil Service, 1966—68. London: H. M. S. O., 1968.

Funkenstein, D. A. Medical Students, Medical Schools and Society during Three Eras. Paper given at Bowman Gray School of Medicine, Winston Salem, N.C., June 25, 1969.

Galbraith, John K. *The Affluent Society*. Boston: Houghton Mifflin, 1966.

Gallagher, Eugene B. "Lines of Reconstruction and Extension in the Parsonian Sociology of Illness." *Social Science and Medicine* 10 (1976): 207–18.

Gawthrop, J. F. *Bureaucratic Behavior in the Executive Branch*. New York: The Free Press, 1969.

Geertz, Clifford. "Common Sense as a Cultural System." *Antioch Review* 33 (1975) :1.

______. "Ideology as a Cultural System." In *Ideology and Discontent,* ed. David E. Apter, pp. 47–76. New York: The Free Press, 1964.

Georgeopoulos, B. S. *Hospital Organization Research: A Resource Book*. Philadelphia: W. B. Saunders Co., 1975.

Gerth, Hans, and Mills, C. Wright. *From Max Weber*. London: Routledge and Kegan Paul, 1946.

Giddens, A. "Elites in the British Class Structure." In *Elites and Power in British Society,* eds. P. Stanworth and Anthony Giddens. London: Cambridge University Press, 1974.

Gil, David G. "A Systematic Approach to Social Policy Analysis." Waltham, Mass.: Brandeis University, Working Paper no. 1, Social Policy Study Program, 1970.

______. "A Systematic Approach to Social Policy Analysis." *The Social Service Review* 44 (Dec. 1970): 411–26.

______. *Unravelling Social Policy*. Cambridge, Mass.: Schenkman Publishing Co., 1973.

Gilbert, Bentley, B. *The Evolution of National Insurance in Great Britain: The Origins of the Welfare State*. London: Joseph, 1966.

Gilbert, Neil, and Specht, Harry. *Dimensions of Social Welfare Policy*. Englewood Cliffs, N. J.: Prentice-Hall, 1974.

Gin, John T. *A Guide to Doing Library Research on Health Policy and Politics* (U. S. A.). Iowa City: Graduate Program in Health Administration, University of Iowa, 1979. Mimeo.

Gish, Oscar. *Doctor Migration and World Health.* London: Occasional Papers in Social Administration, no. 43, Bell, 1971.

Glaser, B., and Strauss, A. *The Discovery of Grounded Theory.* Chicago: Aldine, 1967.

Glaser, William A. *Paying the Doctor.* Baltimore: Johns Hopkins Press, 1970.

———. *Social Settings and Medical Organization.* New York: Atherton Press, 1970.

(Glassco) Canada. Report of the Royal Commission on Government Organization. Ottawa: Queen's Printer, 1963.

Glennerster, Howard. *Social Service Budgets and Social Policy.* London: George Allen and Unwin, 1975.

Goffman, Irving. *Stigma.* Englewood Cliffs, N. J.: Prentice-Hall, 1963.

Goldthorpe, John H. *The Affluent Worker.* London: Cambridge University Press, 1968.

Goodman, Raymond D., ed. *Professional Standards Review Organization: An Educational Symposium.* Los Angeles: University of California, Los Angeles, 1975.

———. *Professional Standards Review Organization: A Selected Bibliography.* Rockville, Md.: Capital Systems Group, Inc., 1975 (prepared for U. S. Department of Health, Education, and Welfare).

Goodwin, L. *Can Social Science Help Resolve National Problems?* New York: The Free Press, 1973.

Gould, Julius, and Kolb, William L. *A Dictionary of the Social Sciences.* New York: The Free Press, 1964.

Gould, Peter, and White, Rodney. *Mental Maps.* Harmondsworth: Pelican, 1974.

Gouldner, Alvin, W. *The Coming Crisis of Western Sociology.* New York: Basic Books, 1970.

———. "Cosmopolitans and Locals: Toward an Analysis of Latent Social Roles." *Administrative Science Quarterly* 2 (Dec. 1957–March 1958): 281–306, 444–80.

———. *For Sociology.* London: Allen Lane, 1973.

———. "The Norm of Reciprocity: A Preliminary Statement." *American Sociological Review* 25 (April 1960): 161–78.

Govan, Elizabeth, S. L. *Voluntary Health Organizations in Canada.* Royal Commission on Health Services. Ottawa: Queen's Printer, 1966.

Gove, W. R., ed. *The Labelling of Deviance.* New York: John Wiley and Sons, 1975.

Great Britain. Report of the Royal Commission on Marriage and Divorce. London: H. M. S. O., 1912.

———. (Beveridge) *Social Insurance and Allied Services.* London: H. M. S. O., 1942.

———. Report of the Royal Commission on the Law Relating to Mental Illness and Mental Deficiency, 1954–57. London: H. M. S. O., 1957.

———. Ministry of Health. *The Field of Work of the Family Doctor.* London: H. M. S. O., 1963.

———. (Fulton) Report of the Committee on the Civil Service 1966–68. London: H. M. S. O., 1968.

______. (Todd) Report of the Royal Commission on Medical Education. London: H. M. S. O., 1968.

______. Department of Health and Social Security. *Management Arrangements for the Reorganized National Health Service.* London: H. M. S. O., 1972.

______. Department of Health and Social Security. *The N. H. S. Planning System.* London: D. H. S. S., 1976.

______. Department of Health and Social Security. *Priorities for Health and Social Services in England.* London: H. M. S. O., 1976.

______. Department of Health and Social Security. *Sharing Resources for Health and Social Services in England.* London: H. M. S. O., 1976 (Resource Allocation Working Party Document).

______. (Pearson) Royal Commission on Civil Liability and Compensation for Personal Injury. London: H. M. S. O., 1978.

______. (Merrison) Report of the Royal Commission on the National Health Service. London: H. M. S. O., 1979.

Greenberg, Daniel S. "X-Ray Mammography: Background to a Decision." *New England Journal of Medicine* 295 (1976): 739–40.

______. "X-Ray Mammography: Silent Treatment for a Troublesome Report." *New England Journal of Medicine* 296 (1976): 1015–16.

(Gross) Australia. *Towards Rational Administrative Structures for Health and Welfare Services in Australia.* Royal Commission on Australian Government Administration. Canberra: Australian Government Publishing Service, 1975.

Gross, Bertram M. *Social Intelligence for America's Future.* Boston: Allyn and Bacon, Inc., 1969.

Gumbiner, Robert. *HMOs: Putting it all together.* St. Louis: C. V. Mosby, 1975.

(Hall) Canada. Royal Commission on Health Services. Ottawa: Queen's Printer, 1964.

Hall, Phoebe. *Reforming the Welfare.* London: Heinemann, 1977.

Hall, Phoebe; Land, H.; Parker, R., and Webb, A. *Change, Choice and Conflict in Social Policy.* London: Heinemann, 1975.

Hall, Thomas L. "Estimating Requirements and Supply: Where do we Stand?" First Pan-American Conference on Health Manpower Planning, Washington, D.C.: P.A.H.O. and W.H.O., 1974, pp. 58–66.

Halmos, Paul. *The Faith of the Counsellors.* London: Constable & Company Ltd., 1965.

Harp, John, and Hofley, John R., eds. *Poverty in Canada.* Scarborough, Ontario: Prentice-Hall of Canada, 1971.

Harris, Fred R., ed. *Social Science and National Policy.* Chicago: Transaction Books (Aldine), 1970.

Harris, Seymour E. *The Economics of Health Care.* Berkeley: McCutcheon, 1975.

Hartle, Douglas. *A Theory of the Expenditure Budgetary Process.* Toronto: Ontario Economic Council, 1976.

(Hastings) Canada. Department of National Health and Welfare. *The Community Health Centre in Canada.* 3 vols. Ottawa: Information Canada, 1972–73.

(Hastings and Mosley) Canada. *Organized Community Health Services.* Royal Commission on Health Services. Ottawa: Queen's Printer, 1966.

Hastings, J. E. F.; Mott, F. D., Hewitt, D., and Barclay, A. "An Interim Report on the Sault Ste. Marie Study: A Comparison of Personal Health Services Utilization." *Canadian Journal of Public Health* 61 (1970): 289–96.

Haughton, James G. *Citizen Involvement in Health Planning.* Community Health Centres Papers. Ottawa: Canadian Public Health Association, 1974. Mimeo.

Hauser, M. M., ed. *The Economics of Medical Care.* London: George Allen and Unwin, 1972.

(Heagerty) Canada. *Health Insurance.* Report of the Advisory Committee on Health Insurance. Ottawa: King's Printer, 1943.

Health Commission of New South Wales. *Health Care Survey of Gosford, Wyong and Illawara, 1975.* Sydney: Division of Health Services Research, 1978.

Heclo, H. H. "Review Article: Policy Analysis." *British Journal of Political Science* 2 (1970): 83–108.

Heclo, H., and Wildavsky, A. *The Private Government of Public Money.* Berkeley: University of California Press, 1974.

Heidenheimer, A. J.; Heclo, H. and Teich Adams, C. *Comparative Public Policy.* London: The Macmillan Press Ltd., 1976.

(Henderson) Australia. Commission of Inquiry into Poverty. Canberra: Australian Government Publishing Service, 1974.

Henderson, Maureen. "The Engagement of Epidemiologists in Health Services Research." *American Journal of Epidemiology* 103 (Feb. 1975).

Hetzel, Basil S. *Health and Australian Society.* Harmondsworth, Middlesex: Penguin, 1974.

Hewitt, Margaret. *Wives and Mothers in Victorian Industry.* London: Rockliff, 1958.

Hilleboe, H. E.; Barkhus, A.; and Thomas, W. C. *Approaches to National Health Planning.* Geneva: WHO, 1972.

Hiller, Harry H. *Canadian Society.* Scarborough, Ontario: Prentice-Hall of Canada, 1976.

Hirsch, Fred. *Social Limits to Growth.* Cambridge, Mass.: Harvard University Press, 1976.

Hobbes, Thomas. *Leviathan, or The Matter, Form and Power of a Commonwealth Ecclesiastical and Civil.* 1651.

Hobhouse. J. T. *Elements of Social Justice.* 4th ed. London: Allen and Unwin, 1958.

Holland, Walter, and Gilderdale, Susie, eds. *Epidemiology and Health.* London: Henry Kimpton, 1977.

Hollingshead, A. B., and Redlich, F. C. *Social Class and Mental Illness.* New York: John Wiley and Sons, 1958.

Holt, Robert T., and Richardson, John M., Jr. "Competing Paradigms in Comparative Politics." In *The Methodology of Comparative Research,* eds. Robert T. Holt and John E. Turner. New York: The Free Press, 1970.

Holzner, Burkhart, and Marx, John H. *Knowledge Application.* Boston: Allyn and Bacon, 1979.

Horowitz, Irving Louis. *Philosophy, Science and the Society of Knowledge.* Springfield, Illinois: Thomas, 1961.

Hughes, E. C. *Men and Their Work.* New York: The Free Press, 1958.

Hulka, B. S. "Epidemiological Applications to Health Services Research." *Journal of Community Health* 4 (1978): 140–49.

Hume, David (1711–76) *Posthumous Works*, 1777.

Hunter, T. A. "Planning National Health Policy in Australia." *Public Administration* 84 (1966): 315–32.

Hyman, H. H. *Health Planning: A Systematic Approach.* Germantown, Md.: Aspen Systems Corp., 1975.

Illich, Ivan D. *Medical Nemesis.* London: Calder and Boyars, 1975.

Inglis, K. S. *Hospital and Community: A History of the Royal Melbourne Hospital.* Carlton: Melbourne University Press, 1958.

Ipsen, J. "Epidemiology and Planning." *International Journal of Health Services* 1 (1971): 149–53.

Jenkins, W. I., and Roberts, G. K. *The Policy Perspective.* London: Fontana, 1976.

Johnson, Terence J. *Professions and Power.* London: Macmillan, 1972.

Jones, Kathleen. *Mental Health and Social Policy 1845–1959* London: Routledge and Kegan Paul, 1960.

Jonsson, Egon, and Marke, Lars-Ake. "CAT Scanners: The Swedish Experience." *Health Care Management Review* 2 (Spring 1977): 37–53.

Judge, Ken. *Rationing Social Services.* London: Heinemann, 1978.

Kahn, Alfred J. "Formation of Policy, The Standing Plan." In *Theory and Practice of Social Planning* pp. 130–34, 61–62. New York: Russell Sage Foundation, 1969.

Kelsall, R. K., and Kelsall, Helen M. *Stratification*, London: Longman, 1974.

Kernaghan, W. D. K. *Bureaucracy in Canadian Government.* 2nd ed. Toronto: Methuen, 1973.

Kessner, D. M.; Kalk, C.; and Singer, J. "Assessing Health Quality: The Case for Tracers." *New England Journal of Medicine* 288 (June 1973): 189–94.

Kewley, T. H. *Social Security in Australia: 1900–72.* Sydney: University Press, 1973, 2nd ed.

Kruhlak, O. M., et al., eds. *The Canadian Political Process.* Toronto: Holt, Rinehart and Winston, 1973.

Kilbourn, William. *Canada: A Guide to the Peaceable Kingdom.* New York: St. Martin's Press, 1970.

Kleiber, Nancy, and Light, Linda. *Caring for Ourselves: An Alternative Structure for Health Care.* Vancouver: School of Nursing, University of British Columbia, April, 1978.

Klein, Rudolf. "The Case for Elitism: Public Opinion and Public Policy." *Political Quarterly* 45 (1974): 406–17.

______. "Policy Problems and Policy Perceptions in the National Health Service." *Policy and Politics* 2 (1974): 219–39.

Klein, R., and Lewis, J. *The Politics of Consumer Representation.* London: Centre for Studies in Social Policy, 1976.

Knight, Kenneth W., and Wiltshire, Kenneth W. *Formulating Government Budgets.* St. Lucia: University of Queensland Press, 1977.

Knox, E. G., ed. *Epidemiology: Uses in Health Care Planning.* London: International Epidemiological Association and WHO Handbooks, Oxford University Press, 1979.

Kohn, Robert. *The Health of the Canadian People.* Royal Commission on Health Services. Ottawa: Queen's Printer, 1967.

Kosa, John; Antonovsky, Aaron; and Zola, Irving Kenneth, eds. *Poverty and Health.* Cambridge, Mass.: Harvard University Press, 1969.

Krause, E. A. "Health Planning as a Managerial Ideology." *International Journal of Health Services* 3 (1973): 445–62.

———. *Power and Illness.* New York: Elsevier, 1977.

Kriesberg, Harriet M.; Wu, John; Hollander, Edward D.; and Bow, Joan. *Methodological Approaches for Determining Health Manpower Supply and Requirements.* 2 vols. Washington, D. C.: Department of Health, Education, and Welfare Publication nos. (HRFA) 76–14511/2, 1976.

Kuhl, Ingrid K. *The Executive Role in Health Service Delivery Organizations.* Washington, D. C.: Association of University Programs in Health Administration, 1977.

Kuhn, Thomas S. *The Structure of Scientific Revolutions.* Chicago: Chicago University Press, 1965.

Laframboise, Hubert L. "Moving a Proposal to a Positive Decision." *Optimum* 4 (1973): 31–41.

(Lalonde) Canada. Department of National Health and Welfare. *A New Perspective on the Health of Canadians.* Ottawa: Information Canada, 1974.

Lancet. (Editorial) *Control of Spending: The Suspension of the Lambeth, Southwark and Lewisham Area Health Authority* (N. H. S.), 11 August 1979, pp. 313–14.

Lang, Ronald W. *The Politics of Drugs.* Lexington, Mass.: Saxon House, 1974.

Lasswell, Harold. *Politics: Who Gets What, When, How.* New York: World Publishing, 1948.

Lawrence, R. J., ed. *Community Service.* Sydney: Australian Council of Social Service, 1966.

———. "A Social Transaction Model for the Analysis of Social Welfare Activities." *Australian Journal of Social Issues* 3 (1968): 51–72.

(Le Dain) Canada. Final Report of the Commission of Inquiry into the Non-Medical Use of Drugs. Ottawa: Information Canada, 1973.

Lee, Sidney S. *Quebec's Health System: A Decade of Change 1967–77.* Toronto: The Institute of Public Administration of Canada, Monographs on Canadian Public Administration no. 4, 1979.

Lees, Dennis S. *Health Through Choice.* London: Institute of Economic Affairs, 1961.

Lees, Dennis, and Shaw, Stella, eds. *Impairment, Disability and Handicap.* London: Heinemann, 1974.

Levine, Sol, and Kozloff, Martin A. "The Sick Role: Assessment and Overview." *Annual Review of Sociology*, 4 (1978): 317–43.

Levitt, Ruth. *The Reorganized National Health Service.* London: Croom Helm, 1976.

Lindblom, Charles E. "Rational Policy Through Mutual Adjustment." In *The Intelligence of Democracy: Decision Making through Mutual Adjustment.* New York: The Free Press, 1965.

———. "The Science of Muddling Through." *Public Administration Review,* Spring 1959, pp. 79–88.

Lipset, Seymour Martin. *The First New Nation.* New York: Basic Books, 1963.

Litman, Theodore J. *The Sociology of Medicine* (a research bibliography). San Francisco: Boyd and Fraser, 1976.

Lowi, Theodore J. "American Business, Public Policy, Case-Studies, and Political Theory." *World Politics* 16 (1964): 677–715.

Lukes, Steven. *Power: A Radical View.* London: MacMillan, 1974.

Macbeath, George. *Can Social Policies Be Rationally Tested?* London: Oxford University Press, 1957.

McCarthy, Lord. *Making Whitley Work: A Review of the National Health Service Whitley Council System.* London: H. M. S. O., 1976.

Mackenzie, Norman Ian, ed. *Conviction.* London: McGibbon and Kee, 1959.

McKeown, Thomas J. "The Determinants of Human Health: Behaviour, Environment and Therapy." In *Health Care Teaching and Research*, ed. William C. Gibson, pp. 58–77. Vancouver: Alumni Association and the Faculty of Medicine, University of British Columbia, 1975.

McKinlay, John B. "The Business of Good Doctoring or Doctoring as Good Business: Reflections on Freidson's Views of the Medicinal Game." *International Journal of Health Services* 7 (1977): 459–83.

———., ed. *Economic Aspects of Health Care.* New York: Prodist, 1973.

McLachlan, Gordon, ed. *Patient, Doctor, Society.* London: Oxford University Press, 1972.

———., ed. *A Question of Quality?* London: Nuffield Provincial Hospitals Trust, 1976.

MacMahon, B., and Pugh, T. F. *Epidemiology: Principles and Methods.* Boston: Little, Brown and Co., 1970.

MacStravic, Robin E. *Determining Health Needs.* Ann Arbor, Michigan: Health Administration Press, 1978.

Macy, John W., Jr. *Public Service.* New York: Harper and Row, 1971.

Maines, David R. "Mesostructure and Social Process." *Contemporary Sociology* 8 (July 1979): 524–27.

Manchester Guardian Weekly. Editorial. Jan. 7, 1979, p. 1.

———. "Social Stratification in Britain," Rolf Dahrendorf. 21 July 1979, p. 12.

Mandell, Betty Reid, ed. *Welfare in America: Controlling the 'Dangerous Classes.'* Englewood Cliffs, N. J.: Prentice-Hall, 1975.

Manitoba. Cabinet Committee on Health, Education and Social Policy. White Paper on Health Policy. Winnipeg: Government of Manitoba, 1972.

Mannheim, Karl. *Ideology and Utopia: An Introduction to the Sociology of Knowledge.* tr. Louis Wirth and Edward A. Shils. New York: Harcourt, Brace and World, 1936.

Manser, Gordon. *Giving in America: Toward a Stronger Voluntary Service.* New York: Family Service Association of America, 1976.

Marchak, M. Patricia. *Ideological Perspectives on Canada.* Toronto: McGraw-Hill Ryerson, 1975.

Marmor, T. R. *The Politics of Medicare.* Chicago: Aldine, 1970.

Marmor, T., and Thomas, D. "The Politics of Paying Physicians: The Determinants of Government Payment Methods in England, Sweden and the United States." *International Journal of Health Services* 1 (1971): 71–78.

Marris, Peter, and Rein, Martin. *Dilemmas of Social Reform.* New York: Atherton, 1967.

Marsh, David D. *The Future of the Welfare State.* Harmondsworth, Middlesex: Penguin Books, 1964.

(Marsh) Canada. *Social Security for Canada.* Report of the Advisory Committee on Reconstruction. Ottawa: King's Printer, 1943.

Marsh, Leonard. *Report on Social Security for Canada 1943.* Toronto: University of Toronto Press, 1975.

Marshall, T. H. *Social Policy.* 4th ed. London: Hutchinson University Library, 1970.

______. "Value Problems in Welfare Capitalism." *Journal of Social Policy* 1 (1972): 15–32.

(Martin) Australia. *Social Medical Aspects of Poverty in Australia*, 3rd Main Report. Commission of Inquiry into Poverty. Canberra: Australian Government Publishing Service, 1976.

Martins, J. M. *The Financing of Health Services in Australia.* Sydney: Health Commission of New South Wales, 1975.

Mather, H. E.; Pearson, N. G.; Read, K. L. Q., et al. "Acute Myocardial Infarction: Home and Hospital Treatment." *British Medical Journal* 3 (1971): 334–38.

Mathews, R. L., and Jay, W. R. C. *Intergovernmental Financial Relations in Australia since Federation.* Canberra: Australian National University, 1976.

Maxwell, James A. *Commonwealth-State Financial Relations in Australia.* Melbourne: University Press, 1967.

Maxwell, Robert. *Health Care: The Growing Dilemma.* New York: McKinsey and Co., Inc., 1974.

Mayer, Henry, and Nelson, Helen, eds. *Australian Politics: A Third Reader.* Melbourne: Cheshire, 1973.

Maynard, Alan. *Health Care in the European Community.* Pittsburgh: University of Pittsburgh Press, 1975.

Mechanic, David. "The Comparative Study of Health Care Delivery Systems." In *The Growth of Bureaucratic Medicine.* New York: John Wiley and Sons, 1976.

______. *Politics, Medicine and Social Science.* New York: John Wiley and Sons, 1974.

Meekison, Peter, ed. *Canadian Federalism: Myth or Reality.* 2nd ed. Toronto: Methuen, 1971.

Meilicke, C. A., and Storch, J. L., eds. *Perspectives on the Canadian Health and Social Services System: History and Emerging Trends.* Ann Arbor: Health Administration Press, 1980.

Meltsner, Arnold J. *Policy Analysts in the Bureaucracy.* Berkeley: University of of California Press, 1976.

Mencher, Samuel. *Poor Law to Poverty Program.* Pittsburgh: University of Pittsburgh Press, 1967.

Mercer, Jane R. *Labelling the Mentally Retarded.* Berkeley: University of California Press, 1973.

Meredith, J. "Program Evaluation Techniques in the Health Services." *American Journal of Public Health* 66 (1976): 1069–73.

(Merrison) Great Britain. Report of the Royal Commission on the National Health Service. London: H. M. S. O., 1979.

Merton, Robert K. "Social Knowledge and Public Policy." In *Sociology and Public Policy*, ed. Mirra Komarovsky, pp. 166–77. New York: Elsevier, 1975.

______. *Social Theory and Social Structure*. 2nd ed. Glencoe, Ill.: The Free Press, 1957.

______. "Sociology of Knowledge." In *Twentieth Century Sociology*, ed. G. Gurvitch and Wilbert E. Moore. New York: Philosophical Library, 1945.

Migue, J.-L., and Belanger, G. *The Price of Health*. Toronto: Macmillan, 1974.

Mill, John Stuart. *On Liberty*, 1859.

Mills, C. Wright. *The Power Elite*. New York: Oxford University Press, 1959.

Moore, Barrington, Jr. *Social Origins of Dictatorship and Democracy*. Harmondsworth, Middlesex: Penguin, 1973.

Moore, Peter J. *O'Dea's Industrial Relations in Australia*. 3rd ed. Sydney: West Publishing Corp. Pty. Ltd., 1974.

Morris, J. N. *Uses of Epidemiology*. New York: Churchill Livingstone, 1975.

Mott, F. D.; Hastings, J. E. F., and Barclay, A. T. "Prepaid Group Practice in Sault Ste. Marie, Ontario II." *Medical Care* 11 (May–June 1973): 173–88.

Murray, Robert. *The Split: Australian Labor in the Fifties*. Melbourne: Cheshire, 1970.

Navarro, Vicente. *Medicine Under Capitalism*. New York: Prodist, 1977.

______. "Social Class, Political Power and the State and Their Implications in Medicine." *Social Science and Medicine* 10 (1976): 437–57.

Neuhauser, Duncan, and Lewicki, Ann. "National Health Insurance and the Sixth Stool Guaiac." *Policy Analysis* 2 (Spring 1976): 175–96.

Newman, Peter C. *The Distemper of our Times*. Toronto: McClelland and Stewart, 1966.

New Zealand. (Woodhouse) Royal Commission of Inquiry. Report on Compensation for Personal Injury in New Zealand. Wellington: Government Printer, 1967.

Nightingale, Benedict. *Charities*. London: Allen Lane, 1973.

Niskanen, William A. *Bureaucracy and Representative Government*. Chicago: Aldine, 1971.

Oakeshott, M. *Rationalism in Politics*. London: Heinemann, 1962.

Owen, David. *English Philanthropy 1660–1960*. Harvard: Belknap Press, 1966.

Owen, David, ed. *A Unified Health Service*. Oxford: Pergamon Press, 1968.

Pack, Mary. *Never Surrender*. Vancouver: Mitchell Press, 1974.

Palmer, G. R. "Social and Political Determinants of Changes in Health Care Financing and Delivery." In *Searchlight, Medicine*, ed. P. Gross. Sydney: Australian and New Zealand Association for the Advancement of Science, 1974.

(Paltiel) Canada. Department of National Health and Welfare. *Legislation, Organization and Administration of Rehabiitation Services for the Disabled in Canada*. Ottawa: Queen's Printer, 1971.

Parker, R. A. "Social Administration and Scarcity: The Problem of Rationing." *Social Work* 24 (April 1967): 9–14.

Parkin, Frank. *Class, Inequality and Political Order*. London: McGibbon and Kee, 1971.

Parry, Noel, and Parry, Jose. *The Rise of the Medical Profession*. London: Croom

Helm, 1976.

Parsons, Talcott. "The Present Position and Prospects of Systematic Theory in Sociology." In *Essays in Sociological Theory*. New York: The Free Press, 1964.

———. *The Social System*. London: Tavistock Publications, 1952.

(Pearson) Great Britain. Royal Commission on Civil Liability and Compensation for Personal Injury. London: H. M. S. O., 1978.

Pechman, J. A., ed. *Setting National Priorities: The 1978 Budget*. Washington, D. C.: The Brookings Institution, 1977 (and annually).

P. E. P. (Political and Economic Planning). *The British Social Services*. London: P. E. P., 1937.

Perrow, Charles. "Hospitals: Technology, Structure and Goals." In *A Handbook of Organizations*, ed. James G. March. Chicago: Rand McNally, 1965.

Pickering, A. E. *Special Study Regarding the Medical Profession in Ontario*. Toronto: Ontario Medical Association, 1973.

Pinder, Craig C., and Moore, Larry F. *The Inevitability of Multiple Paradigms of Organizational Behavior*. Vancouver: Faculty of Commerce and Business Administration, University of British Columbia, 1978. Mimeo.

Pinel, Patricia N. *Comprehensive Bibliography on Health Maintenance Organizations, 1970–73*. Denver, Colorado: Medical Group Management Association, 1974.

Pinker, Robert. *Social Theory and Social Policy*. London: Heinemann, 1971.

Piven, Frances Fox, and Cloward, Richard A. *Regulating the Poor: The Functions of Public Welfare*. New York: Pantheon Books, 1971.

Pole, J. D. "Mass radiography: A cost/benefit approach." In *Problems and Progress in Medical Care*, ed. Gordon McLachlan. London: Nuffield Provincial Hospitals Trust, 1971.

Pondy, L. R. "Varieties of Organizational Conflict." *Administrative Science Quarterly* 14 (Dec. 1969): 449–506.

Porter, A. C., and Chibucos, T. R. "Common Problems of Design and Analysis in Evaluative Research." *Sociological Methods in Research* 3 (February 1975). 235–37.

Porter, John. *Canadian Social Structure*. Toronto: McClelland and Stewart, 1967.

———. *The Vertical Mosaic*. Toronto: University of Toronto Press, 1965.

Powell, J. Enoch. *Medicine and Politics: 1975 and After*. London: Pitman Medical Publishing, 1975.

Raphael, D. D. *Problems of Political Philosophy*. London: Pall Mall Press, 1970.

Rawls, John. *A Theory of Justice*. London: Oxford University Press, 1972.

Rein, Martin. *Social Science and Public Policy*. Harmondsworth, Middlesex: Penguin Books Ltd., 1976.

Reinke, W. A., and Williams, K. N., eds. *Health Planning: Qualitative Aspects and Quantitative Techniques*. Baltimore: The Johns Hopkins University School of Hygiene and Public Health, 1972.

Reissman, Leonard. *Inequality in American Society*. Glenview, Illinois: Scott, Foresman and Co., 1973.

Rhodes, G. *Royal Commissions and Committees of Inquiry 1959–69*. London: Royal Institute of Public Administration, 1975.

Ripley, Randall B., and Franklin, Grace A., eds. *Policy Making in the Federal*

Executive Branch. New York: The Free Press, 1975.

Ritchie, Ronald S. *An Institute for Research on Public Policy*. Ottawa: Information Canada, 1971.

Roberts, Leigh M.; Halleck, Seymour; and Loeb, Martin, eds. *Community Psychiatry*. Madison: University of Wisconsin Press, 1966.

Robin, Martin, ed. *Canadian Provincial Politics*. Scarborough, Ontario: Prentice-Hall, 1972.

Roe, Jill. *Social Policy in Australia: Some Perspectives, 1901 to 1975*. Sydney: Cassell, 1976.

Roemer, Ruth. *Licensing and Regulation of Medical and Medical Related Practitioners in Health Service Teams*. Los Angeles: Institute of Government, University of California, 1970.

Roemer, Ruth and Roemer, Milton I. *Health Manpower in the Changing Australian Health Services Scene*. Washington, D. C.: DHEW 1976.

______. *Health Manpower Policies under Five National Health Care Systems*. Washington, D. C.: DHEW, 1977.

______. *Health Manpower Policy under National Health Insurance—the Canadian Experience*. Washington, D. C.: DHEW, 1977.

Roghman, K. J., et al. "Rochester Child Health Surveys I: Objectives, Organization and Methods." *Medical Care* 8 (Jan–Feb. 1970): 47–59.

Roos, N. "Evaluating Health Programs, Where Do We Find the Data?" *Journal of Community Health* 1 (Fall 1975): 39–51.

Rousseau, Jean Jacques. *Du Contrat Social*, 1762.

Rubel, Maximilien; Meyer, Alfred G., and Bottomore, Tom. *International Encyclopaedia of the Social Sciences*, vol. 10 (on Karl Marx, Marxism and Marxist sociology).

Runciman, W. G. *Relative Deprivation and Social Justice*. London: Routledge and Kegan Paul, 1966.

Rutman, L., ed. *Evaluation Research Methods: A Basic Guide*. Beverly Hills: Sage Publications, 1977.

Sackett, D. L.; Spitzer, W. O.; Gent, M., et al. "The Burlington Randomized Trial of the Nurse Practitioner: Health Outcomes of Patients." *Annals of International Medicine* 80 (February 1974): 137-42.

Saskatchewan. Report of the Royal Commission on Government Organization. Regina: Queen's Printer, 1965.

______. *Definitions of Levels of Care in Hospitals and Nursing Homes*. Regina: Queen's Printer, 1969.

______. *Criteria for Levels of Care for the Province of Saskatchewan, June 1969, amended April 1972*. Regina: Queen's Printer, pp. 1–10.

Sawer, G. *Australian Government Today*, 10th ed. Melbourne: Melbourne University Press, 1964.

Sax, Sidney. *Medical Care in the Melting Pot*. Sydney: Angus and Robertson, 1972.

Scheff, Thomas J. *Mental Illness and Social Processes*. New York: Harper and Row, 1967.

Scheiner, E. V., ed. *Policy Making in American Government*. New York: Basic Books, 1969.

Schmitter, Philippe C. "Modes of Interest Intermediation and Models of Societal

Change in Western Europe." *Comparative Political Studies* 10 (April 1977): 7–37.

Schoenbaum, Steven, et al. "Benefit Cost Analysis of Rubella Vaccination Policy." *New England Journal of Medicine* 294 (1976): 306–10.

Schon, Donald A. *Beyond the Stable State.* New York: Random House, 1971.

Schoolman, M. H., et al. "Statistics in Medicine Research: Principles vs. Practices." *Journal of Laboratory and Clinical Medical* 71 (March 1968): 357–67.

Schulberg, H. C.; Sheldon, A.; and Baker, F., eds. *Program Evaluation in the Health Fields.* New York: Human Sciences Press, 1977.

Schumacher, E. F. *Small Is Beautiful.* London: Abacus, 1974.

Scotton, Richard B. *Medical Care in Australia: An Economic Diagnosis.* Melbourne: Sun Books, 1974.

———. and Ferber, Helen, *Public Expenditures and Social Policy in Australia,* Vols. I and II. Melbourne, Longmans, 1979.

Seldon, A.; Culyer, A. J., and Lindsay, C. *The Price of Health.* Melbourne: Office of Health Care Finance, 1969.

Self, P. *Governmental Planning.* London: Fontana, 1976.

Selznick, Philip. *T. V. A. and the Grass Roots.* New York: Harper and Row, 1966.

Shapiro, C., et al. "Periodic Breast Cancer Screening in Reducing Mortality from Breast Cancer." *Journal of the American Medical Association* 215 (1961): 1777–85.

Shaw, George Bernard. *The Doctor's Dilemma.* Harmondsworth, Middlesex: Penguin, 1946.

Shonfield, Andrew. *Modern Capitalism.* London: Oxford University Press, 1965.

Skipper, James K., and Leonard, Robert C. *Social Interaction and Patient Care.* Philadelphia: J. B. Lippincott, 1965.

Smelzner, Neil J., and Warner, R. Stephen. *Sociological Theory.* Morristown, N. J.: General Learning Press, 1976.

Smith, Anthony. *Social Change.* London: Longman, 1976.

Smith, B., and Stanyer, J. *Administering Britain.* London: Fontana, 1976.

Snow, C. P. *The Two Cultures and the Scientific Revolution.* London: Cambridge University Press, The Rede Lecture, 1959.

Soderstrom, Lee. *The Canadian Health System.* London: Croom Helm, 1978.

Somers, Anne. *Hospital Regulations: The Dilemma of Public Policy.* Princeton, N. J.: Princeton University Press, 1969.

Somers, H. M., and Somers, A. R. *Doctors, Patients and Health Insurance.* Washington, D. C.: The Brookings Institution, 1961.

Spann, R. N. *Public Administration in Australia.* 3rd ed. Canberra: Government Printer, 1973.

Spiers, Maurice. *Techniques and Public Administration.* London: Fontana, 1975.

Stark, W. *The Sociology of Knowledge.* London: Routledge and Kegan Paul, 1958.

Stevens, Rosemary. *American Medicine and the Public Interest.* New Haven: Yale University Press, 1971.

———. *Medical Practice in Modern England: The Impact of Specialization and State Medicine.* New Haven: Yale University Press, 1966.

Stewart, Rosemary. *The Reality of Management.* London: Heinemann, 1963.

Storch, Janet L., and Meilicke, Carl. *Health and Social Services Administration: An*

Annotated Bibliography. Ottawa: Foundation of the Canadian College of Health Service Executives, 1979.

Strauss, Anselm. *Negotiations*. San Francisco: Jossey-Bass, 1978.

______, ed. *Where Medicine Fails*. New York: Transaction Books, 1970.

Strauss, Anselm; Schatzman, Leonard; Ehrlich, Danuta; Bucher, Rue; and Sabshin, Melvin. "The Hospital and its Negotiated Order." Chapter 5 in *The Hospital in Modern Society*, ed. Eliot Freidson. New York: The Free Press, 1963.

Suchman, E. A. *Evaluative Research*. New York: Russell Sage Foundation, 1967.

Sundquist, J. L. *Making Federalism Work*. Washington, D. C.: The Brookings Institution, 1969.

Szasz, T. *The Myth of Mental Illness*. New York: Dell Publishing Co., 1961.

Talbot, John. *Community Human Resources and Health Centres: The British Columbia Situation*. Victoria: Department of Health Development Group, 1978. Mimeo.

Tawney, R. H. *Equality*. London: Unwin, 1931.

______. *Religion and the Rise of Capitalism*. Harmondsworth, Middlesex: Penguin, 1938.

Taylor, Malcolm G. *Health Insurance and Canadian Public Policy*. Montreal: McGill-Queen's, 1978.

______. "Quebec Medicare: Problem Formulation in Conflict and Crisis." *Canadian Public Administration* 15 (1972): 211–50.

______. *The Saskatchewan Hospital Services Plan*. Regina: Health Services Planning Commission, 1949.

Thompson, John D. "On Reasonable Costs of Hospital Services." *Milbank Memorial Fund Quarterly* 46 (January 1968): 33–51, part 2.

Thorburn, Hugh G., ed. *Party Politics in Canada*. 3rd ed. Scarborough, Ontario: Prentice-Hall of Canada, 1972.

Time Magazine. Editorial, April 2, 1973, p. 79.

Titmuss, Richard M. *Essays on the Welfare State*. London: George Allen and Unwin, 1956.

______. *The Gift Relationship*. London: George Allen and Unwin, 1971.

______. *Problems of Social Policy*. London: H. M. S. O., 1950.

______. *Social Policy*. London: George Allen and Unwin, 1974.

(Todd) Great Britain. Report of the Royal Commission on Medical Education. London: H. M. S. O., 1968.

Toren, Nina. "Bureaucracy and Professionalism." *Academy of Management Review* 1 (1976): 36–46.

Toronto Globe and Mail. Series on Medical Care in Canada. May 7–9. 1979.

Townsend, Peter. *The Concept of Poverty*. London: Heinemann, 1970.

______. *The Social Minority*. London: Allen Lane, 1973.

______. *Sociology and Social Policy*. London: Allen Lane, 1975.

Tropman, J. E. et al., eds. *Strategic Perspectives on Social Policy*. New York: Pergamon Press, 1976.

Tumin, Melvin M. *Social Stratification*. Englewood Cliffs, N. J.: Prentice-Hall, 1967.

Turner, Jonathon H. *The Structure of Sociological Theory*. Homewood, Illinois: Dorsey Press, 1974.

United Nations. *Universal Declaration of Human Rights,* 1948.

United States. (Burns) Natural Resources Planning Board. *Security, Work and Relief Policies.* Washington, D. C.: U. S. Government Printing Office, 1942.

———. Department of Health, Education, and Welfare. *Procedures for Area Wide Health Facility Planning.* Washington, D. C.: D. H. E. W., 1963.

———. Department of Health, Education, and Welfare. *The Process of Articulating Goals and Standards,* by Eugene A. Confrey. Washington, D. C.: D. H. E. W., Health Resources Administration, 1975. Mimeo.

———. Department of Health, Education, and Welfare. *Guide to Data for Health Service Planners.* Washington, D. C.: D. H. E. W., 1976.

———. Department of Health, Education, and Welfare. *Health Manpower Policy under National Health Insurance: the Canadian Experience* by Ruth Roemer and Milton I. Roemer. Washington, D. C.: D. H. E. W., Public Health Service, Bureau of Health Manpower, Division of Medicine, 1977.

———. Department of Health, Education, and Welfare. *A Student's Guide to Health Maintenance Organizations.* Washington, D. C.: D. H. E. W., 1978.

Viner, Jacob. "Bentham and J. S. Mill: The Utilitarian Background." *American Economic Review* 39 (1949): 360–83.

Vollmer, H. M., and Mills, D. L., eds. *Professionalization.* Englewood Cliffs, N. J.: Prentice-Hall, 1966.

Waitzkin, H. B., and Waterman, B. *The Exploitation of Illness in a Capitalist Society.* New York: Bobbs Merrill, 1974.

Warham, Joyce. *The Concept of Equality in Social Policy.* Vancouver: Department of Health Care and Epidemiology, University of British Columbia, 1974. Mimeo.

Watkins, C. Ken. *Social Control.* London: Longman, 1975.

Wedderburn, Dorothy. *Poverty, Inequality and Class Structure.* London: Cambridge University Press, 1974.

Weeks, Lewis E., ed. *Education of a Hospital Trustee.* Battle Creek, Michigan: Kellogg Foundation, 1976.

Weinstein, Milton, and Stason, William. *Hypertension: A Policy Perspective.* Cambridge, Mass.: Harvard University Press, 1977.

Weiss, Carol H. *Evaluation Research.* Englewood Cliffs, N. J.: Prentice-Hall, 1972.

Weller, G. R. "Health Care and Medicare Policy in Ontario." In *Issues in Canadian Public Policy,* ed. G. Bruce Doern and V. Seymour Watson. Toronto: MacMillan of Canada, 1974.

Wessen, A. F. "The Apparatus of Rehabilitation: An Organizational Analysis." In *Sociology and Rehabilitation,* ed. M. Sussman, pp. 148–78. Washington, D. C.: American Sociological Association, 1966.

White, K. L., and Henderson, M., eds. *Epidemiology as a Fundamental Science.* New York: Oxford University Press, 1976.

White, M. J., et al. *Management and Policy Science in American Government.* Lexington: D. C. Heath, 1975.

White, W. H., and Strick, J. C. *Policy, Politics and the Bureaucracy in Canadian Government.* Don Mills: Science Research Associates, 1970.

Wildavsky, Aaron. "Doing Better and Feeling Worse: The Political Pathology of Health Policy." In *Doing Better and Feeling Worse: Health in the United States,* ed. John H. Knowles, pp. 105–23. New York: W. W. Norton and Co., 1977.

______. *The Politics of the Budgetary Process.* Boston: Little, Brown and Co., 1964.

______. *The Presidency.* Boston: Little, Brown and Co., 1969.

Wilding, Paul, and George, Vic. "Social Values and Social Policy." *Journal of Social Policy* 4 (1974–75): 373–90.

Wilensky, H. L. "The Dynamics of Professionalism: The Case of Hospital Administration." *Hospital Administration,* Spring 1962, pp. 2–15.

______. *Organizational Intelligence.* New York: Basic Books, 1967.

______. "The Professionalization of Everyone?" *American Journal of Sociology* 70 (Sept. 1964): 137–58.

Willer, Judith. *The Social Determination of Knowledge.* Englewood Cliffs, N. J.: Prentice-Hall, 1971.

Wilson, F. A., and Neuhauser, D. *Health Services in the United States.* Cambridge, Mass.: Ballinger Publishing Co., 1976.

Wilson, John. *Equality.* New York: Harcourt, Brace and World, 1966.

______. *Introduction to Social Movements.* New York: Basic Books, 1973.

Winkelstein, W., Jr. "Epidemiological Considerations Underlying the Allocation of Health and Disease Care Resources." *International Journal of Epidemiology* 1 (1972): 69.

Report of the Wolfenden Committee. *The Future of Voluntary Organizations.* London: Croom Helm, 1978.

(Woodhouse) New Zealand. Royal Commission of Inquiry. Report on Compensation for Personal Injury in New Zealand. Wellington: Government Printer, 1967.

(Woodhouse-Meares) Australia. Report of the National Committee of Inquiry into Compensation and Rehabilitation in Australia. Canberra: Australian Government Publishing Service, 1974.

World Health Organization. *The First Ten Years of the World Health Organization.* Geneva: WHO, 1958.

______. Report of the Director-General. Geneva: WHO, 1979.

______. World Health Statistics. Geneva: WHO, Annual.

Yarmolinsky, A. "The Policy Researcher: His Habitat, Care and Feeding." In *The Use and Abuse of Social Science*, ed. I. Horowitz, pp. 196–211. New Brunswick, N. J.: Transaction Books, 1971.

Young, Michael. *The Rise of Meritocracy.* London: Thames and Hudson, 1958.

Young, Michael, and Willmott, Peter. *Family and Kinship in East London.* Harmondsworth, Middlesex: Penguin, 1957.

Zald, Mayer N. *Occupations and Organizations in American Society.* Chicago: Markham, 1971.

Index

Academic: authority, 375; freedom, 316; privileges, 159

Access: to health care, 128–29, 139, 146–57 passim, 223–24, 252–53, 254, 263, 342, 352. *See also* Choice; Equality

Administration: 140, 263, 292–93

Administrators: 152–54, 346, 355–56

—evaluation of, 323, 338. *See also* Bureaucracy; Civil Service; Hospitals; Management

—planning by, 318, 322–25

Affluence: 26, 81, 130, 137, 138–39, 195, 255, 266

Ageing: *See* Elderly

Bargaining: in bureaucratic politics, 65, 90, 94–96, 99–103; individual, 94. *See also* Buffer groups; Mediation; Negotiation; Trade unions

Behaviour: as determinant of health, 7–16, 18; government as modifier of, 21, 252; health, end or means, 253; Health field concept, 18; lifestyles, 18–21 passim, 253, 363

—affects costs, 223, 352, 353. *See also* Doctors: Consumers; Bargaining

—in organizations, 92–94

Buffer Groups: 350, 355, 379

Bureaucracy: definition of, 161–62

—development, general, 261; in occupations, 172; in health services, 212; in hospitals, 220, 355

—processes, 264, 339–44, 361–68, 381; Marmor's paradigm, 89–97, 98–106

—relationships with entrepreneurs, 162, 316; professionals, 99–103 passim, 154, 155, 162, 220, 224, 265, 277, 306, 316

Capitalism: 135–38, 206, 216–17, 255

—doctors, as tools of, 116–18 passim; mediate health care system, 182, 260–61, 348, 349

—and political rights, 194–95; changing balance of public and private power, 139

Caring: for sick, 73, 147, 155–56, 251, 253

Categorization: labelling, 62–64, 127, 257–58; and stigma, 166–67, 262

—categories identified: change, 118–19, 271–73; class structures, 113; clients, 62–64, 321; contributing factors in health problems, 21; environments, 18; frames of inference, 89–97; government's objectives, 255; lifestyle risks, 19; managerial activities, 312; mechanisms for dealing with strain, 233; medical care organization, 85–86; medical schools, 258; mental disorder, 257–58; negotiations, 164, 184–88; paradigms for analysing social policy, 369–82; payment schemes for health services, 352; planning, 139, 264, 312–13, 316, 317–18, 321, 323, 324, 325; policy, 287–93; power, 115, 255, 273, 380; professional power, 160, 162, 164, 178–83, 316, 340, 382; of professional roles, 277–78, 316–17, 417–30, 476–78, 492; pressure groups, 122, 219, 264, 322, 339–40; rehabilitation, 127, 354; social control mechanisms, 117, 126–31; social policy, 43–55; social policy issues, 287–97; social policy researchers' orientations, 312; socialism, 215

—required for equalization, 193

—ideologies affect, 76, 217, 231

—underlying principles for operationalizing social policy, 62, 63, 99, 321

—by professionals, 63; by types of service, 62

Change: categorization of, 119, 378

—in the social order, 111, 144, 237, 255, 256,

378, 381; ideologies counter strain, 231–39; in social processes, 29, 266, 368
—in health care system, 101–2, 340. *See* Professional associations and government; Maintenance
—policy change frameworks, 58; higher civil service concerned, 322
—trends, 57, 103, 111, 118–19, 121; by conquest, 111; cognitive dissonance, 101–2; through education, 40, 121, 163, 379; effect of pressure groups, 123; effect of wars, 118, 139, 381; events in, 95, 101, 111–19; evolutionary, 47, 111, 271; human initiative in, 119; incremental, 29, 121, 326, 376; marketing of, 21; *See also* Planning; processes of, 51, 111, 118–19, 211, 219, 255, 264, 293, 325, 339–43; resistance to, 111, 119, 131, 159, 222, 273, 274, 340, 348, 350; revolutionary, 111, 121, 214, 379; socialism and, 215; technology and, 263, 378
Choice: in health care, 83, 221, 223–24 passim. *See also* Payment schemes, Policy choices
Civil service: 99, 293, 322–25, 365
—in planning, 82, 86, 245, 262, 264, 268, 315–20, 322–25, 361–68
—as professional elite, 162; Canadian, 323. *See* Administration; Administrators; Bureaucracy
Collectivism: 45–55, 86, 138–40, 156, 165–170, 215–16, 225
Community health services; 75–76, 86, 104, 128, 263, 292, 309, 314
Complaints; 153, 347–48
Conflict: dilemmas, 38, 204; theory, 50. *See* Marxism; Radicals
—in processes of decision making, 25–26, 28
Consumers: complaints, 152, 347–48; demands, 151, 224, knowledge, 352–53, 373; powers, 178–83, 379; values, 223, 251; worries of, 153
—changing relationships with providers, 76, 150, 181–83, 220, 224, 265, 341
—and costs, 223, 352–53, 356; and payment, 76, 85, 87, 221. *See also* Government; Payment schemes; Insurance; Hospitals
—participation, 264, 282–83; on advisory councils, 43, 282–83; as advocates, 325–26, 341, 365; in neighborhood health centres, 154, 326; as patients, 150–51, 180, 221, 224–25, 340, 342; as pressure group members, 87, 219, 340–43
Cooptation: 129–32 passim, 154, 276, 342, 379
Corporate policy: 355–57
Cosmopolitan: 194
Costs: 155, 346–49 passim, 352–54. *See also* Choice; Payment schemes; Resources, allocation
—affected by ideology, 352; by consumer behaviour, 223, 352–53
—of health care, 22, 149, 151–57, 222, 226, 263–64, 309, 342, 353–54; of impairment, 308–11
—quality issues, 156; and benefits, 339; quantity issues, 224
—social costs, 136, 139
Crises: 288, 299; in health care provision, 146–57, 339–44; scandals, 99, 281, 326
Culture: 203. *See* International comparisons
—rests on economic foundations, 171, 181, 203; and ideologies, 87, 127, 218–19, 230–39 passim, 376

Decision making: distinguished from decision taking, 29
—by elites, 254, 281; by hospital employees, 222; pluralist, 326; by professionals, 100, 220; in science, 302, 304, 316. *See also* General will
—political processes of, 94–96, 224, 271, 309–11, 361–68, 376, 380–82; disjunctions, 64, 209; cycles of, 376; incremental, 67; multiple levels in, 317. *See also* Bargaining issues; Bureaucracy; Negotiations; Rationality
—for social goal attainment, 3–4, 225; analysis and evaluation of, 106, 139, 254, 378
Demands: of patients, 223–24, 251, 265, 352; of doctors, 159–61, 219–22, 349, 351. *See also* Access; Needs
Deviance: mental illness, 257–58; in social relationships, 49, 112; "the sick role," 112, 115. *See also* Social order; Norms
—labelling of, 49, 63, 257; as signal for positive development, 252; treatment of, 40
Dilemmas: re liberty; equality; fraternity, 206
—collective vs. individual interests, 135–41, 138, 156, 212, 225, 251–67; public vs. private sector provision, 15, 146–57, 182, 222, 251, 263–64, 274–75, 293, 343, 380
—re life and death, 138, 146–57, 263–65, 268, 311, 316–17. *See also* Conflict; Health, policy

—priorities in providing scarce services, 23, 146–57, 226, 263, 265, 316–17
Disability: definition, 63; as an economic issue, 311, 482; as a political issue, 146, 321; pressure groups, 310; research, 303, 308–11
—health policies, 251, 301, 310; outcomes, 337. *See also* Morbidity
Distribution. *See* Social order; Reciprocities; Stratification
—differs from redistribution, 224, 255–56, 382; government's part in, 138, 224, 273, 293, 316, 382; of expectations and income, 36, 148
—of professional services, 148, 220, 341
—of tasks. *See* Manpower; Labour
Doctors: roles of; as agents of capitalism, 116–18 passim; as caring persons, 147, 155; as controllers of standards, 346–49; as entrepreneurs, 265; general, 78, 220, 346; as general practitioners, 74, 78, 346, 349–50; as managers of services, 153–55, 222, 346–54, 356; as social controllers/gatekeepers, 115–18, 126–32; as specialists, 74, 78, 223, 533;
—behaviour, as pressure group, 79, 93, 99, 279; dominance, 99–100, 116; as strikers, 222
—hierarchies, 74, 346, 348
—ideologies, 116, 183, 212, 219–22, 233, 380; re autonomy, 160, 347, 349; re change, 119, 222, 293, 348, 350; re fellow workers, 72–88, 346–47, 351; re government, 99–103, 160, 162, 221, 265, 277, 316, 345, 350–51; to patients/consumers, 24, 77, 128–31, 150, 180, 220, 224–25, 341; re the poor, 128–29, 220–21; re prestige, 155
—neglect of continuing education, 350; hospitals centres of work, 259–60
—payment. *See* Payment schemes; Professionals; Professional associations
Drugs: in Australia, 221, 264; pharmaceutical benefits, 79. *See also* Insurance, health
—therapies, 258; non-medical use of, 282

Economic analysis: defined, 35; distinguished from social policy analysis, 3, 33, 46; limits, 303–4; in relation to health policy, 3, 62, 252, 321
—development, 39, 138, 152, 204, 207, 240–41, 246, 342; attitudes to growth, 36, 191, 246–50; exploitation and imperialism, 26, 246, 347
Education: and social solidarity, 195; and social change, 40, 121, 163, 378
—individual change through socialization, 115, 135–56, 193, 299, 301, 346, 347, 350
Elderly: neglected, 15, 99–103; population trends, 89, 103–4, 146; processes of aging, 17–18; social problems of, 92, 352; as social responsibility, 89–97, 240; and social security, 151–52, 221, 351. *See also* Poverty; Medicare; Social security
Elite: 65, 99, 113–14, 155, 174, 194; as decision makers, 89, 123, 154–58, 254, 281, 372, 382
—education of, 298; civil servants as, 100, 162; professionals as, 100
Ends and means: 225–26, 253–54. *See also* Goals
Entrepreneurs: emergence of, 159; exploiters of labour, 130, 214; ideology of, 38, 143, 214, 273; and privileges, 143, 211
—in health care provision, 72, 82, 117, 146–57, 182, 221, 251, 259, 263–65, 274, 316, 343; in health planning, 244, 264, 340, 379
Environment: 3–4, 18–21, 27, 151, 252. *See* Food; Public health; Social order; Society; Starvation
Epidemiology: 62, 321
Equality: definitions: of condition, 142–45, 193, 217, 262–63, 265; of consideration, 193; before the law, 217; general, 53, 192–93, 203–10, 266; justice, 192–93, 203; of opportunity, 142–45, 174, 176, 193, 208, 215, 217, 247, 263, 266, 314; of shares (equity, fairness), 193, 310
—implication issues: income distribution, 249. *See also* Poverty; life chances, 216, 263; science identifies inequalities, 301; unequal distribution of services, 116, 146–57, 209, 265, 276–78, 341–42. *See also* Access; Entitlements
—and liberty, 191, 206, 215; political ideologies, 45, 191–92, 206–10, 214–15, 240–41, 263–64, 314; Declaration of Human Rights, 190; of women, 131. *See also* International comparisons
—and the social order, tolerance, 163–64, 171–77, 247. *See also* Stratification; Elite
Experts: 24, 375; doctors as, 100, 155; planners, 379

Feasibility: definition of, 66, 275
—of introducing or maintaining issues/

policies, 91, 119, 154, 216, 222, 271, 275, 287–97, 315, 481; in administration 293
—of using science, 303
Frameworks: of knowledge, 371–83
—for analysis: academic approaches, 33–44, 56–62 passim, 192; comparative, 57; descriptive vs. schematic, 58; health policy analysis, 3–5, 17–22, 253, 262; policy analysis, 3–5, 23–27, 45–55, 65, 189–97, 304; systems analysis, 4–5, 17–22, 89–97, 126, 371
—of inference, 30, 45, 66, 89–97, 378, 381, 323–26
—of legislation, 142–43, 224, 246, 320, 345
—for action, 58, 362; for identifying deviance, 49. *See also* Health services organization; for negotiation, 184–88
Fraternity: 190, 203–10 passim

Goals. *See* Social order; the American Dream, 27, 67, 126–27, 215; capitalist, 137–38; of equality, 46, 192, 203, 214, 263–64, 314; of fraternity, 203; humanitarian, 214–15, 225; ideologies direct thrust towards goals, 215–16; of individualism, 136, 139–41, 144–45, 215. *See also* Collectivism; Nations; liberal, 140, 143–45, 206–10, 214, 218, 240–41, 255, 271, 274, 298; of liberty, 192, 214; socialist, 330; utilitarian, 144, 204–5, 214–15, 225, 231
—displaced. *See also* Access; Government; Planning; Professionals
—of task and manpower system, 301; directed by social policies, 57, 104–8, 263–65; health goals. *See* Health, goals; pursued, 89, 138–39, 225, 254, 263, 266, 268
Government: goals, 89–92, 143, 224, 254–56, 293, 351, 382. *See also* Goals; Policy; Social policy; Impacts; Planning
—activities. *See* Bureaucracy; Administration; Administrators; Civil service; funding, 150, 293, 340, 345, 352. *See also* Costs; Resource, allocation; involvement in health care, 3–6, 14, 72–88, 117–18, 138–39, 182–83, 222, 251, 259, 261–66, 316–17, 326, 343, 380; involvement in health planning, 245, 315–20, 322–25; involvement in social welfare. *See* Poverty; Voluntary organizations; Welfare state; relations with entrepreneurs, 156, 263, 274–75, 343; relations with professionals, 82, 153, 162, 221, 265, 277, 316, 351; relations with providers; 77, 345, 380. *See* Payment schemes; Manpower; Professional associations
—powers, 139, 144–45, 241, 288–90, 293, 361–68, 379, 381–82; jurisdictions, 43–44, 264–65, 326, 345, 354, 379, 381–82; responsibility for modification of human behaviour, 21, 252
Group practice: 346, 349; health centres, 153–54, 282, 292, 293, 326, 351; health maintenance organizations, 154–55, 264, 349; polyclinic, 75–83

Health: definitions, 3, 112, 115; determinants of, 7–16, 263. *See also* Sick role; Disability; Poverty; Deviance; Charter for Canadians, 262; as ends or means, 253–54; and ethnicity, 225–63
—improvements in, 7–11, 351; indicators, 7–16, 225, 246, 313. *See also* Mortality; Morbidity; Social indicators
—policies, 3–5, 98–108, 146–57, 251–67 passim; dilemmas, 138–39, 146–57, 225, 253, 263, 268, 316; rationality, in, 251, 263; regulation of, 72–88. *See also* Policy
Health insurance: history, 72–88 passim, 89–91, 218–19, 221–22, 263–64, 351–52; funding issues, 150–57 passim, 223, 351. *See also* Choice; Payment schemes; Social security
Health services organization: 18–22, 72–88, 89–97, 126–32, 219–22, 334–44. *See also* Access; Change; Choice; Hospitals; Insurance; Manpower; Payment schemes; Public health
History: 7–16 passim, 57–62 passim, 72–88 passim
Hospitals: in consortia, 355; development, 72–88, 130; goals, 341, 353–54; and social class, 160, 258–60; as symbols, 128, 353; teaching and non-teaching compared, 348; as workshops, 85, 259–60, 353
—funding, 72, 75–82, 160, 221, 265, 350–51, 353–54; control over professionals, 181–83, 340, 348; controls over standards and costs, 154, 348–49, 353–54. *See also* International comparisons, hospitals
—organization of, 150, 160, 282, 355–56. *See also* Management; Bureaucracy; Negotiation

Ideology:
—affects analysis and development of policies:

social, 48, 216–18, 243–45, 289, 291, 299, 304, 372; health, 61, 66, 72–88, 93, 105, 224–26, 254, 314, 337, 343. *See also* Values; Knowledge; International comparisons
—concerned with rights. *See* Rights; Equality; Fraternity; Liberty
—concerned with social control, 126–32. *See also* Social order; Government; Nations; Imperialism
—and goals, 29–30. *See* Goals; Maps
—of groups within a society, 219–24; of consumers, 223–24; conservative, 105; liberal, 140, 142–45, 206–9, 214, 218, 240–41, 255, 271, 274–75, 298–99; Marxist, 113, 166–68, 187, 216–17, 230, 233, 240; political parties, 278–81, 289; of professionals, 116, 183, 212, 219–22, 233, 243–45, 370; religious, 26–27, 99; socialist, 86, 121, 203–10, 215, 249, 327–30
—within ideology, 378, 380
—theories: 212–24, 230–39, 240–41, 278, 299, 374, 378; structure use of knowledge, 213, 372
Impacts: 64, 336–38; analysis of, 57, 62, 64, 205, 313, 330–35, 380; unintended consequences, 94, 235, 382
—communication failures, 303, 314; of ideas from other countries, 62, 266
—interest in: governments', 205; planners', 323–24, 341–42
Imperialism: 114, 144, 217–19, 256, 262, 301
Incrementalism: 64, 99–103, 104, 209, 281. *See also* Change
—planning in relation to 104–5, 244, 322–23, 379
Individual: goals and responsibilities, 5, 143–44, 190, 205, 245; adjustment to social norms, 262. *See also* Deviance; Poverty
—individualism, 136, 139–40, 144, 215; vs. collectivity, 156–57, 225, 251–68
—initiatives: in social change, 5, 29, 119; in health care, 4, 26, 225–26, 253. *See also* Consumers; Behaviour
Inference: frames of, 66, 89–97, 323–24, 326, 378, 381
Inputs: into policy making processes, 62–65, 103, 333–34, 380, 382; into the political system, 271, 325
Inquiry, Committees of: 315–79; Australian, 62, 170, 200, 225, 283, 328; British, 80–81, 101–5, 259, 261–62, 265, 274, 282, 290, 345, 381; Canadian, 200, 257–58, 262, 265, 277, 282, 324, 328, 349, 350, 379; U.S., 262, 342
Integration: of health services, 20, 25, 78, 223, 261–63, 343, 350, 354. *See* Solidarity
—of policy analysis and decision making, 29–30
International comparisons (specific): borrowing of concepts, 62–63, 104; of colonialization, 114, 144, 217, 219, 256, 262; of government activities, 224; of legislating behaviour, 273–74; of political ideologies, 67, 114, 214–16, 265; political structures, 135–56, 317–18; of support for legislation, 282. *See also* Inquiry, committees of; revolutions, 190; of task and manpower systems, 164
—of health care systems, 58, 72–88, 221, 349; hospitals, 73–75, 259–60, 348–49, 356–57; medical payment schemes, 73–86, 352–53; provision of medical care, 74, 117, 346, 350
—of interest groups: doctors, 219–22, 273–74, 351; consumers, 379; trade unions (health), 222
—of social policy, 98–105, 217–18, 255, 262; by British and American analysts, 57, 224, 381; of health policy, 3, 71–88, 256, 264–65; of science policy, 299–306 passim
—of social security, 79–82, 89–97, 151–53, 217–19, 221, 261–64, 351; of welfare states, 126–32, 144, 209, 215–18, 261–63, 273, 290–91, 492
—of voluntary organizations, 354–55
Issues: definition, 292
—in health policy, 106, 211–26, 274–75, 304
—movement into/through the political system, 115, 246–47, 271–72, 280–81, 287–97, 319, 321, 380–81. *See also* Legitimacy; Feasibility; Support

Jurisdictions: 3–5, 20, 28, 99, 128, 263, 265, 322–26, 345, 354, 379, 382–83
Justice: for individuals. *See* Laws; Rights
—and equality, 192–93, 204; effect of 'welfare state' policies, 118. *See also* Equality, implementation; Liberty
—in health care, 220, 223, 277
—in mass societies, 190–93, 256, 266; group vs. individual, 225; relative deprivation of, 195; social, 67, 192

Knowledge: 41–42, 180, 183, 213, 281, 291, 331, 352–53, 356, 372, 373–75, 376–80

Labour: division of, 47, 178, 183, 340; exploitation of, 144, 180, 214, 233. *See also* Protestant ethic; Stratification
Legitimation: defined, 112; levels of, 289
—of pluralist politics, 343; conferred by doctors' authority, 47; of privilege, 112; of policy issues, 66, 89, 115, 271–75, 287–97 passim, 345; of science 303. *See also* Feasibility; Support
—of values, 129, 216, 255
Liberalism: 140, 142–45, 206–9, 214, 218, 240–41, 255, 271, 274–75
Liberty: 190–93, 204–9, 214–15, 241, 266, 314
Life: chances, 216; at any price, 254; prolonged, 263, 337; as right, 190, 263
Litigation: between clients and professionals, 149, 277, 347

Maintenance policies: 5, 30, 100–1, 111, 159, 322, 326. *See also* Change
Management: of health services, 86, 105, 154, 282–83, 346–54 passim, 355–57. *See also* Administrators; Hospitals
Manpower: allocation of statuses by tasks, 5, 46, 48, 51, 159–62, 214; health care providers, 84–87, 103–5, 130, 147–48, 151–52, 183, 220–21, 224, 251, 264–66, 305–6, 322, 352; impact on health costs, 322. *See also* Education; Entrepreneurs; Labour; Medical Education; Professionals; Stratification; patterns of migration, 222, 226, 266, 299, 305; scientists, 300–3; and task system, 5, 51–52, 112–13, 171–77, 180–83, 301
Maps: 19, 212–14, 236, 369
Marxism: 113, 116–18, 187, 216, 230, 233, 240. *See also* Radicals; Socialism
Mechanisms: cooptation, 126–32, 181, 276, 380; of social regulation/control, 5, 49, 50–54, 61, 115–18, 126–32, 159, 181, 276, 380; vocationalism, 219, 222. *See* Patronage; Peer groups; Professional associations; Professionals; Mediation
—change. *See* Change
—for evaluation. *See* Research; Social audits
—market, 52, 181, 244
—for maintaining professional dominance, 117, 126–32. *See also* Sick role
—for planning, 244, 361–62
Mediation: 85–87, 92–93, 150, 182–83, 221, 261, 348, 350
Medibank: 221, 264, 351
Medicaid: 152–53, 221
Medical care:
—continuity of, 82–83; attitudes about affect organization, 85–87; in health field context, 15
—evaluation of, 336–38. *See also* Doctors; Professionals
—goals of, 14–16, 268; contribution to health and well-being, 3–4, 146–57 passim; history of, 7–16, 72–88; inputs into, 154–55; and uncertainty, 149
—and the poor, 72–88, 256–57, 352. *See also* Medibank; Medicaid; Medicare; socialized vs. private, 153. *See* Choice; Collectivism; Payment schemes
Medical education: 15, 103–5, 117, 151, 258–59, 340, 350, 546–47
Medicare: 89–97, 152, 221, 351. *See also* Elderly; Poverty
Mental health (and mental illness): 73, 99, 129, 147, 222, 257–58
Morbidity: 4, 7–22, 62, 130–31, 136, 146–50, 225, 252–54, 259
Mortality: 7–22, 62, 225, 254, 263
Mutual aid: 76–77. *See* Consumers; Equality, of condition; Peer groups; Pressure groups; Social security; Solidarity

National Health Service (NHS): 81–82, 85–86, 98–108, 223, 225, 265
Nations: goals, 90; ideologies, 29–30, 140, 214–19
Needs: definition, 181; emergent, 152–53, 182; local, 154, 345; unmet, 128
—policies to meet, 25, 217, 251, 302; control of 73–74, 156, 181, 264; medical judgment, 74, 128, 220–21
Negotiation: and ideologies, 212–14; theory, 184–88
—of benefits, 84–85, 151, 161, 222, 224–25, 353. *See also* Bargaining; Trade unions
—procedures: in planning, 89–97, 315. *See also* Buffer groups; Mediation; in policy making, 224; political, 28, 112, 381; trade-offs, 28, 94, 254, 283, 325
—of social order, 112, 164, 184–88, 195, 203–10, 255–56, 382. *See also* Justice
Norms: social organization normative, 49, 111, 189, 252, 261, 305; individuals adjust to,

51, 261; deviate from, 111. *See also* Deviance; social well-being normative, 252, 255
—social science research normative, 66–67
—in women's roles, 131; in family life, 172; in medical practice, 347–48
Nurses: 102–3, 219–22, 346, 356

Outcomes: 7–16, 94, 151, 271, 337–38. *See also* Impacts
Outpatient care: 265, 349. *See also* Community health services; Doctors; Group practice; Health maintenance organizations; Public health

Paradigms: 56–71, 271, 369–82. *See also* Frameworks
—of government activities, 224, 255–56, 382
—of knowledge, 372
—of negotiated social order, 164, 184–88; of change. *See* Change
—of political system, 271, 278; of interest groups in planning, 123, 219, 264, 339–44, 379; of policy development, 278, 287–97
—of power and the professions, 160–62, 316, 382; Ehrenreich's, 126–33; the sick role, 115–16
Patronage: 160, 179–82, 220, 260–61, 316–20
Payment schemes (for health services): affect organization of services, 83; development of, 76–87, 221, 350–52
—categorized, 352
—contracts and doctors, 83–84, 221, 349–50; doctors' negative attitudes to government prepayment schemes, 82, 154, 162, 221, 265, 277, 316, 351
—public subsidies for health services, 75–87, 340, 352; reimbursement schemes, 79, 84. *See also* Choice; Health Insurance
—rewards, 52–53, 74–75, 171–77, 219, 247, 352
—third party schemes, 74–87, 220, 222, 223–25, 348, 349, 350–52 passim, 356. *See also* Mediation; government as a third party, 247, 277, 350–52 passim
Peer groups: in hospitals, 160, 348; in medical education, 117; in science policy-making, 316
—collegial control, 160, 180–83, 260, 302, 316. *See also* Professional associations
Philosophy: 111, 113, 203, 373–77
Planning: goals, 242–45, 339–44. *See* Categories; Mechanisms
—by academics, 62, 315, 320; by advocates, 315, 325–26, 341, 365; by bureaucrats, 242, 313–14, 322–26, 339–40, 361–68; interdisciplinary, 58; by interest gorups, 264, 317, 339–44; by technocrats/experts, 320–21, 379
—communication, 323–24, 325, 341, 364
—conflicts, 219, 264–65, 339–44, 379; ethics, 315–16
—and policy making, 19, 268, 312, 318–19; in Canada, 325; of economy, 321; by government, 245, 262, 268, 315, 317–18, 322–25; for NHS, 82, 86, 265; by non-governmental health agencies, 82, 345–59. *See also* Manpower
—standing plans, 104, 121, 244, 254, 322–23, 376–79
Pluralism: 98–103, 114, 123, 156–57, 264, 273, 326, 339, 343
Policy: defined, 4, 33, 45–55 passim, 56, 66, 111, 369; categorized, 287–97
—analysed, 36, 47–48, 89–108, 321, 330–35, 371, 382; analysts, 3–4, 62, 380
—economic: science, 298–302, 316. *See also* Economic analysis; Costs; Disability policy; Health policy; International comparisons; Science; Social policy
—goals: maintenance or change, 29–30. *See* Goals: Ideologies; Dilemmas; choices, 57, 83, 99–108, 139, 247–50
—making, 100, 102; bounded, 4, 89–108; knowledge in, 373, 376–80; rational evidence in, 89–92, 313–15; science in, 4–5, 298–307, 356, 373; structures, 266
—processes, 5, 98–108, 266, 281, 355–57, 361–68, 380; impacts of, 98–94. *See also* Paradigms; Research; Resources, allocation; pressure groups in, 102–3, 265, 287–97, 365
Political parties: attitudes to economic growth, 191, change over time, 278–81, 288, 325, 366; platforms, 251, 365–66; power, 191, 195, 288. *See also* Ideologies; Paradigm
Politicians: 156, 211, 247; as policy makers, 268; and professionals, 306, 309. *See also* Policy making
Polyclinics: 75, 83
Population: modern rise in, 8–16, 103–4, 266; ageing. *See* Elderly

Poverty: cultural attitudes to, 126–32, passim, 314, 381; "the dangerous classes," 61, 117, 126–32, 159; the deserving and undeserving, 37, 166; doctors' attitudes to, 129, 220–22, 340; "have nots," 301; liberal attitudes to, 165, 256; less eligibility, 129, 166–67; middle class attitudes to, 262; poor relief, 40, 101–3; the poor as a social responsibility, 36–37, 73, 126–27, 165–67, 241, 249; regulation of charities, 260. *See also* Voluntary organizations; war on, 33; residual welfare, 46–47, 128–29. *See also* Welfare state
—and health policy, 256; and community health, 75–76; and hospitals, 81, 160, 258; Medicaid, 151–52, 221; and public health, 257. *See also* Medicare; Medibank; Medical care; Equality
—no longer inevitable, 136, 195, 225; difficulties in redistributing wealth, 207
Power: knowledge as, 179, 375, 379; theories of. *See* Theories; Categories
—to control emergence of issues, 115, 123, 372, 382
—of government, 241, 287, 289–91, 293, 343, 379, 382; in government, 315–16, 320; inequality between doctors and patients, 150, 180–81, 220, 341. *See also* Capitalism; Stratification; Privileges; in health services; in hospitals, 353; of institutions, 339, 342; of private sector, 343; of professionals, 93, 127–28, 155, 160, 162, 178–83, 316, 340, 382; of providers, 84–85, 87, 100; of trade unions, 93, 222
—social, 99, 179; affected by distribution of tasks, 24, 112, 154, 380; allocation of, 100, 112, 171, 255–56; and change, 111, 211; of elites. *See* Elite; mechanisms of social control, 114–16, 294–96, 379; of middle classes, 193–94, 320, 343; and pressure groups, 123
Pressure groups: *See* Categories: Theories
—and power, 93, 123, 254, 273, 295; and planning, 314–15, 317, 325, 330–44; and policy making, 102–3, 265–66, 287–97, 365; and privileges, 164
—of providers and consumers, 219; for the aged, 92; for the disabled, 310; medical profession as, 78, 93, 99–100, 276; trade unions as, 162
Privileges: 131, 159–60, 220, 305, 306; allocation of, 47, 112–13, 159, 211–26; economic institutions, 143. *See also* Stratification; Power; to middle class, 194; negotiation of, 382; preservation of, 196
Professionals. *See* Bureaucracy; Doctors; Civil service; Government; Nurses; Pharmacists; semi-professionals, 103, 155, 161, 195, 220
—associations, 25, 100, 260–61, 346–48
—and government, 86, 93, 101, 182, 221, 260–61, 348. *See also* Peer group; as negotiators, 93, 161, 224
—knowledge of, 373, 375; attitudes to change, 100–3, 222, 273–74, 348; ethics, 265, 315–16, 347; ideologies of, 212, 219–24, 273, 277, 380
—power. *See* Categories; Providers; accountability, 348; ambiguity, 161; authority, 24, 375; control, 180–81, 346–53 passim, 374; discretion, 316. *See also* Litigation; Consumers; Doctors
—privileges, 131, 154, 160–61, 211, 220
—roles. *See* Categories; as social controllers, 115, 117, 126–32, 161, 223, 276; providers of service, 222, 265, 305, 316, 345; as rationers, 154, 223, 251, 277, 347; as decision makers, 127, 309–10
Protestant ethic: 61, 126–31, 135–36, 158–59, 193–94, 217, 225–26, 255, 379
Providers of service: 117–18, 149; ideologies of, 212, 219–22; tension among, 345
—distribution of, 352–53; reaction to demand, 225, 251, 265. *See also* Manpower
—power of, 85, 87, 100, 178–83, 219
—prerogatives and rights of, 219, 251; awareness of roles, 19; community control over, 340, 342; relationships with consumers, 76, 150, 180–82, 220–21, 342; relationships with government, 77–78, 345–46, 380. *See also* Professionals; Payment schemes; Relationships; Teamwork
Public health: historical development, 166, 257, 261
—entitlements to, 52, 257
—programs, 3, 153, 221, 263, 309; infection control, 3, 9–11, 73, 252, 257, 263; prevention, 3, 22, 83, 154–55. *See also* Community health services

Quality: of life, 25, 46, 49–50, 51, 254, 362
—of medical care, 87, 101, 147, 155, 336–38, 340, 342

Radicals: 27, 116–18, 128, 154
Rationality: 62, 65; bounded, 27–28, 304, 314, 378. *See also* Science; in decision making, 302–3, 372; multiple levels, 100, 299
—corporate, 219, 264, 340–44, 379
—of health system, 103, 151, 260, 264
— in social change, 27; rational actor model, 89–92
Redistribution: by governments, 25, 28, 207, 217, 218, 251, 263, 273, 291, 316, 382. *See also* Equality; Manpower distribution; Resources
Regulation: government's part in, 143, 224, 246, 273, 316, 320, 345; of social relationships, 45–55 passim, 112, 181, 236, 291
—in health policy, 72–87 passim, 251. *See also* Frameworks; Government
Research: and values, 66–67, 302, 374
—applications, 30, 54, 57, 301, 330–35; evaluation, 34, 57, 98–105 passim, 203, 314, 334; historical, 57; impact, 57, 62, 64–65, 205; on policy, 312–36 passim, 376
—biomedical, 15–16, 301–2, 341
—communication of results, 302, 303, 308–11, 315. *See also* Theories
—funding, 87, 302, 303
—importance of data base, 313; variables, 4, 20, 22, 30, 331, 369
—on programs, 57, 103–5, 312, 318, 320, 321; in health field framework, 4, 17–22; quality of care, 64–65, 155, 336, 338, 340, 342
Resources: 36, 45, 46, 47, 52, 58, 193, 217, 247, 249, 255, 256, 293, 320, 333, 381; availability affects rights, 51, 136; development of, 46, 158, 218, 246–49, 266, 302; distribution of, 5, 47, 138–39, 263; excluded from social policy, 25; exploitation of, 5, 26, 61, 214, 299, 301; health, 100, 121, 154, 164, 254, 265, 277, 309, 314, 317, 324, 325, 347; Hirsch's paradox, 136, 138; professionals as rationers, 154, 251, 277, 347. *See* Government funding; Hospital funding; Manpower; rationing of, 148, 156, 223, 265
Revolution: change through, 111, 121, 379; and evolution, 271; fear of, 165
—commercial or mercantilist, 135–38, 144, 165–67, 206, 374
—political: French and American, 73, 144, 190; liberalism, 206; in Quebec, 121, 274
—in social policy, 42
Rights: 51–52, 131, 190, 211–29 passim, 381; definition of, 190, 191–93; human expectations extended, 136, 221
—civil, 34; distribution, 5, 46, 47–48, 113, 381; of economic institutions, 143; and equality, 192, 263; legal and moral, 190–91; political, 194, 205, 215; and resources, 51–54
—to health services, 75, 81, 251; of disabled, 200; to life and death, 263
—and prerogatives in health system, 220, 222, 251, 274. *See also* Stratification; Justice

Science: 370–71, 372. *See also* Research
—science policies, 299–302, 316; biomedical science, 17, 30, 149, 252, 258, 301; communication problems, 303; contribution to health and social problems, 252, 253, 256, 300, 301, 303, 321, 372; on politics, 304; paradigms, 371, 375–76; science, 300–1; science and politics, 298–307, 356. *See also* Economists; Economic analysis; Epidemiology; Political science; Sociology
—as subculture, 38–39, 298–307 passim, 302–3, 306, 372
Scientists
—as contributors to policy researchers and policy making, 257, 266, 316
—as communicators, 303, 315
—as experts, 375; in bureaucracies, 220; in relation to elite, 114
—privileges, 159, 211. *See also* Science; Research
Sick role: 115–16, 126, 380
Social audits: 330–35
Social indicators: 25, 49, 51, 266, 313, 362, 381. *See also* Health, indicators
Social movements: 76, 120–23 passim, 372, 375, 379
Social order: 111–32, 378. *See also* Deviance; Norms; causes of disorganization, 123, 194, 216, 255, 313; change, 39, 46, 118–23, 196, 211, 313, 380. *See also* Revolution, industrial; and social mobility, 163, 193–96 passim; and the "dangerous classes," 61, 117, 159; Ehrenreich's views, 130–31; Hobbesian view, 111, 158; lack of solidarity, 38, 117, 231–32. *See also* Solidarity; maintenance, 159; in mass societies, 61, 144, 158, 181, 256; McBeath's view, 46; Parsonian view, 111; and power alignments, 113; Protestant ethic, 193–94;

Rousseau's view, 189; in solidarity societies, 61, 158–59, 255, 256
—negotiated, 112, 164, 184–88, 255, 256; mechanisms of control, 28, 49, 114–15, 117, 126–32, 276, 379–80
—reciprocities, 61, 122, 158–59, 167, 189, 215, 219, 251, 255–56. *See also* Society; Stratification
Social policy: definitions of, 35–44 passim, 45–54
—goals, 45–54, 159, 163–67, 258, 260, 290, 352
—and ideologies, 216–18
—movement, 20–23, 25–26, 32–44, 45, 49, 56–67, 244, 281–82, 301, 380–82 passim
Social problems: 92, 181, 281, 301–2, 313, 375. *See* Deviance; Dilemmas; Needs
Social security: 166–67, 196. *See also* Elderly; Equality of condition; Insurance; International comparisons; Redistribution
Social welfare:
—ideologies, 217. *See also* Protestant ethic
—interventions, 46, 190, 283
—social well being, 25, 241, 254–55
Social workers: 64, 261, 277–78, 301
Socialism: 86, 121, 203–10, 215, 249, 327–30. *See also* Ideologies; International comparisons; Marxism
Society:
—health issues, 252, 253–54, 262–63, 266. *See* Poverty; Social order; Solidarity
—national goals, 45–55, 143, 209, 241
—social organization, 47, 51–52, 61, 111–12, 135–36, 142–45, 159, 171–77, 184, 216
Sociology:
—functionalism, 143, 180, 234, 303–4. *See* Conflict; Social order; Marxism; Radicals; Stratification; Research; Theories
—and knowledge, 300–1, 373–75, 376–78
Solidarity:
—definition, 38–39, 61, 112–13, 117, 136, 158–59, 216, 232, 255–56, 266
—and social policies, 195, 302. *See also* Revolution; Social order; Society
—wars and, 118, 195, 253
Standards: control of medical, 76, 87, 155, 221, 224, 336–38, 346–49
Stigmatization: 63, 166, 262
Strain: 153, 209, 211–12, 218, 231–39, 378. *See also* Social order; Solidarity
Strategies: 89–97, 231, 240, 288
Stratification: 47, 112, 163, 171–77, 194, 208, 216, 266, 381
—differential distribution of privileges, 163, 173, 211, 231; of health services, 151–52, 155–56, 221–23, 256–58; of social services, 240–41, 261, 265, 351
—different norms by strata, 211, 262
—division of labour, 47, 103, 178, 181
—health services controlled by upper middle classes, 325, 343
—Hirsch's paradox, 135–40, 211–12
Structures:
—for goal attainment, 62–65, 105, 224, 349; of policy making, 266, 282, 314, 317–18
—political, 271, 381; adaptability of, 64, 139–40; administrative, 209, 263, 334, 338; planners' interest in, 323–25; social workers' attitudes to, 64. *See also* Civil Service; Frameworks; Knowledge; Ideologies; Laws; Regulations; Theories
—of thought, 369; as context of negotiation, 185–86; and values, 118, 255, 315
Support: for issues, 156, 271, 273–74, 281, 283, 287–88, 294–96, 363–68
Surveillance: of professionals, 339–54; of women, 130–31

Technology:
—contribution to policy making, 291, 298–307
—defined, 135; and change, 263, 345–47, 378; and political invention, 140
—and development, 263–65, 293–94, 301, 352; intermediate, 137
—and distribution of privileges, 159–60, 166–67
—and division of labour, 340
—and health care, 138, 179, 220, 223–25, 252–54, 256, 259, 261, 268, 301–2
—and planning, 104, 320–21, 347
Theories:
—of cognitive dissonance, 101–2
—of health systems, 26. *See* Knowledge; Frameworks; Science
—of ideology, 212–13, 230–39; of pressure groups, 103, 122–23, 219
—of organization, 58, 375; middle range, 27, 99, 187, 304, 376; of social analysis, 291, 304
—of social order, 94–96, 99, 111–18, 123, 167–70, 178–83, 215, 230, 372–73
Timing: 29, 104, 146, 282, 292, 294, 314, 325, 361–68, 381

Trade unions: 87, 94, 122–23, 162–63, 219, 222, 273, 351
Trends: 22, 57, 104, 118–19

Utilitarian: 144, 204–6, 214–15, 225, 231

Values:
—and policy making, 101, 103, 105, 180, 240, 255, 310
—of professional planners, 315–16
—in science, 66, 302, 374
—as sorting mechanism for knowledge, 372. *See also* Ideologies; Goals
—transmission of, 115; and change, 273–74
Voluntary organizations: 44, 72–88 passim, 260, 345, 354–55

War: 119, 139, 195, 214, 217, 225, 249, 253, 289, 299, 301, 306, 375, 381
Welfare state: 27, 217–19, 263, 290

About the Author

Anne Crichton emigrated to Canada in 1969 in order to develop a Master's Degree program in Health Services Planning at the University of British Columbia in Vancouver in the Department of Health Care and Epidemiology. It was envisioned that this programme, which puts strong emphasis on policy development, would attract students from the Canadian health care industry who were in senior government or hospital appointments. Before coming to Canada, the author taught social administration students at University College Cardiff, Wales. It is out of her experience in these two programmes that she has developed this book.